JUDICIAL REVIEW OF LEGISLATION IN CANADA

Judicial Review of

Legislation in Canada

B. L. Strayer

UNIVERSITY OF TORONTO PRESS

© University of Toronto Press 1968
Printed in Canada
Reprinted in 2018
ISBN 978-1-4875-7357-7 (paper)
SBN 8020 1532 8

To Eleanor

Foreword

Judicial review of legislation, the power of the courts to declare any statute valid or invalid, is an inherent part of Canadian federalism, though the justification for it, as Professor Strayer makes clear, is by no means so evident as has usually been assumed. The BNA Act makes no mention of it, and the framers of the Act, in so far as they spoke about the subject at all, showed surprisingly little knowledge of its meaning or implications. It stemmed from the constitution of the Empire as it stood in 1867 rather than from any text of law. Yet the whole course of our constitutional development has depended on it.

That evolution has been shaped, and in some respects I venture to suggest deformed, by the opinions as to the purpose and meaning of the BNA Acts delivered by courts which treated constitutional disputes very much as they would dispose of rights conflicts between private litigants, in which context they generally arose. Perhaps for the judges sitting on the Judicial Committee of the Privy Council in England, trained in the common law of a unitary state, no other course seemed possible. Canadian courts which might have played a more imaginative rôle were not free to do so for until the abolition of appeals to the Privy Council in 1949 they did not have the final word. Yet even today, when our Supreme Court is at last supreme, very little change of approach has become apparent. Stare decisis is forever raising its warning finger. Moreover this legal traditionalism has hitherto lacked any systematic study of the nature of the problems to be faced in the delicate process of dividing legislative authority into its legal parts. Here, as in so many other areas, the pace of constitutional development has proceeded faster than its analysis by scholars. Professor Strayer is to be congratulated, not only for giving us the first thorough study of judicial review in Canadian legal literature, but for having done it with a masterful capacity to steer through "the vast confusion of the case law" that cannot but command the respect of theorists and practitioners alike.

He has set himself, indeed, a formidable task, no less than an attempt to separate out and assess those rules which apply, or should apply, specifically to constitutional litigation. In the light of discussions now launched on the status of the Supreme Court of Canada as final arbiter of constitutional disputes such a book comes at an appropriate time. His historical review shows that concern among French Canadians over the rôle of the Court is as old as Confederation itself. But the present controversy centres more around the composition and appointment of the Court, and over its jurisdiction, than upon its procedures and techniques of adjudication. While not indifferent to these questions, Professor Strayer is primarily concerned with the judicial process itself – the process by which a body of men with a highly specialized training in legal interpretation apply their skills to the distribution of legislative powers in an increasingly industrialized and technological society. Even a reformed Supreme Court, if bound by the conceptualism and rigidity of the past, might still be unable to fulfil its creative function: indeed, it might be even less able if it ceased to be a court and became a representative body.

It is a thesis of this book that constitutional amendment is not likely to be an effective means for keeping the Canadian constitution abreast of developments, and that the rôle of the courts becomes therefore increasingly important. To a large extent the results arrived at in the constitutional cases depend on the techniques used to raise the questions before the courts, in the introduction or exclusion of evidence, and in the analytical processes employed in the judgment itself. On all these matters there is a wealth of information to be derived from decided cases, even where "they largely defy explanation." The confused behaviour patterns of the past, seen in historical perspective, look wholly inadequate as guides to the judicial activism required of the future. Why cannot the federal Parliament regulate "particular trades," if they are national in scope? Why should the "regulation" of trade and commerce exclude the prohibition of trade? Why was the economic depression of the 1930s not a sufficient national emergency to justify the use of federal powers under the "peace, order, and good government" clause? Why does insurance, which plays so important a part in shaping the investment policy of the country, largely escape federal jurisdiction? Judicial answers to these questions are of course in the books, but how were they arrived at, and on what evidence were they based? The conditions preceding and surrounding the making of the decision, the procedures adopted and the factors admitted, are part also of the legal process, often more conclusive than any system of logic.

Professor Strayer does not rest on analysis only; where his research discloses contradictions and deficiencies in the law he does not hesitate to suggest change or clarification. He urges a wider permission for the citizen to bring constitutional issues before the courts when he perceives a serious matter is raised on which it is desirable to give judgment. He urges a liberalization of rules of evidence in constitutional cases so that the courts may be adequately informed as to the social and economic context of legislation over which they have the power of life and death. He wants a critical reassessment of earlier decisions rather than a strict adherence to precedent in all cases. Only thus, he believes, will the judiciary be able to accommodate most effectively "the vital forces of parliamentary sovereignty to the restraints of federalism." I believe few readers of this book will disagree with him, for these proposals are not, like so many contemporary proposals for change, spun out of thin air but are based on a thorough knowledge of the "black-letter-law" of the constitution.

F. R. Scott

North Hatley, P.Q.
July 16, 1968

Preface

As in most other federal states, the courts in Canada perform important functions both in delineating the limits of federal and provincial legislative power and in adjusting those limits occasionally to meet changing social needs. Since we have so far been unable to devise very satisfactory machinery for formal change in the text of the constitution, we must rely on judicial reinterpretation as one of the principal means of constitutional development. This reinterpretation is generally carried out, in an *ad hoc* fashion, in the process of judicial review of the validity of any legislation which happens to be challenged in the courts.

Because of the great functional importance of judicial review in the operation of our constitution, I have attempted to examine the problems peculiar to this aspect of judicial work. It was my hope that this study, by giving an organized and sustained attention to such problems, would not only provide an analysis of existing law but also would suggest the need for improvements in rules and procedures to meet the particular needs of constitutional litigation.

I wish to acknowledge my obligation to many people and institutions who have furthered the completion of the book. The manuscript was originally prepared as a S.J.D. thesis for the Harvard Law School where I was enabled to study by a Ford Foundation Fellowship in Law Teaching. My thesis examiners there, Professors Cavers, Freund, Jaffe, and Cox, made many helpful comments from which I have profited in the work of revision. The University of Saskatchewan has greatly assisted me with research grants and the provision of various services. Dean O. E. Lang of the College of Law, University of Saskatchewan, has given constant encouragement and support. Valuable suggestions on the content have come from Professor F. R. Scott of McGill and from one of the manuscript readers of the University of Toronto Press. I have also greatly gained from the editorial work of Miss Prudence Tracy and Miss Jean Houston of that Press.

My research assistants on this project have included Mr. Kenneth E. Norman, Mr. Henry Kloppenburg, and Miss Susan Steer. While a number of typists have shared in the work over the course of several years, I should make particular mention of Mrs. Vera Cyr for her typing of the final version of the thesis manuscript.

I wish to acknowledge the permission of the Queen's Printer of Canada, and the Queen's Printer of Saskatchewan, for the inclusion of the respective statutory material in the appendices. I also wish to acknowledge the kind consent of Mr. E. A. Driedger, Q.C., and of the Queen's Printer of Canada with respect to the inclusion as Appendix A of Mr. Driedger's annotated version of the British North America Acts, 1867–1965. The University of Toronto Press has permitted me to include, in chapter four, material which appeared in substantially the same form in my essay in Lang (ed.), *Contemporary Problems of Public Law in Canada: Essays in Honour of Dean F. C. Cronkite* (University of Toronto Press, 1968).

While expressing my gratitude to all these persons who have assisted me in the completion of the book, I hasten to add that any errors which may remain must be attributed to me. Finally, I wish to pay tribute to my wife, Eleanor, and my children, Alison, Jonathan, and Colin, who patiently endured the prolonged writing process.

                                                              B.L.S.

Contents

JUDICIAL REVIEW OF LEGISLATION IN CANADA

CHAPTER ONE

Introduction

JUDICIAL REVIEW AND THE COMMON LAW

The concept of judicial review of legislation in Canada is not an inheritance from the common law. We have come to accept it as a fundamental, authorized by that unwritten law which is the source of so much of the judicial power. But it must be acknowledged that English common law as received by Canada had rejected the claim of some judges to the right to review acts of Parliament for validity. The practice which came to be so widely accepted within the Imperial system with respect to colonial legislation was an outgrowth of that particular system, implicit in the royal instructions, charters, or Imperial statutes creating the colonial legislatures.

It is true that English courts had more than once asserted a power to pass judgment on the validity of parliamentary legislation. The most outstanding example of this was found in Lord Coke's pronouncement in *Dr. Bonham*'s case: "And it appears in our books, that in many cases, the common law will controul Acts of Parliament, and sometimes adjudge them to be utterly void: for when an Act of Parliament is against common right and reason, or repugnant, or impossible to be performed, the common law will controul it, and adjudge such Act to be void. . . ."[1] This appeal to a fundamental law was obviously expedient for one apprehensive of the power struggle between Parliament and the Crown which was developing in the early seventeenth century. While some other English judges accepted and applied Coke's dictum, and the principle received some support from contemporary digests and treatises, its star was in descent by the start of the eighteenth century and fallen into oblivion by the middle of the nineteenth.[2] In the end, the supremacy of Parliament was

1. (1610), 8 Co. Rep. 113b, at 118a; 77 E.R. 646, at 652 (K.B.).
2. Plucknett, "Bonham's Case and Judicial Review" (1926), 40 *Harv. L. Rev.* 30, *passim*.

accepted in England in preference to the supremacy of the courts. At the end of the last century Maitland was able to dismiss in a few words the concept of judicial review: "Just now and then in the last of the Middle Ages and thence onwards into the eighteenth century, we hear the judges claiming some vague right of disregarding statutes which are directly at variance with the common law, or the law of God, or the royal prerogative. Had much come of this claim, our constitution must have taken a very different shape from that which we see at the present day. Little came of it. . . . [T]he theory is but a speculative dogma. . . ."[3]

It is not surprising, however, that the concept of a higher law (imposed by the judges) controlling Parliament commended itself to the North American colonies which subseqently formed the United States of America. The views of Coke and his seventeenth-century supporters were well known in the colonies settled in that period.[4] In the following century these colonies developed a strong antipathy to Parliament and to the principles of parliamentary supremacy. This antipathy, combined with the philosophy of natural rights popularized in revolutionary America, gave fertile ground for the seeds sown by Coke. Some courts in the thirteen colonies were able to pass judgment on colonial legislation, invoking a higher principle such as "natural law" or the "common law."[5] This set the stage for judicial review based on the limitations of written constitutions, a development which culminated in the celebrated *Marbury* v. *Madison*.[6]

In the colonies which were later to become part of the Dominion of Canada, there is little evidence that Coke's dictum ever had any serious effect. No doubt many factors would contribute to this situation. For example, settlement in the English-speaking areas was insignificant until the eighteenth century – after the English civil wars of the preceding century had established the supremacy of Parliament to the general satisfaction of the populace. During and after the American Revolution loyal supporters of the Crown in the northern colonies were also inclined to reject the natural rights theories which had contributed to the open breach between England and their neighbours.

Among the French settlers there was even more antipathy toward the republicanism and what they regarded as the excesses of democracy to the south. The Imperial Parliament was not to them the inevitable oppressor: the Quebec Act, 1774,[7] which to the thirteen colonies was one of the "Intolerable Acts," was to them a guarantee of their law and religion.

3. 2 Maitland, *Collected Papers* (1911), 481.
4. Plucknett, *supra* note 2, at 61–62; McGovney, "The British Origin of Judicial Review of Legislation" (1944), 93 *U.Pa. L. Rev.* 1, at 7–8.
5. Plucknett, *supra* note 2, at 61–68.
6. (1803), 1 Cranch 137 (U.S.).   7. 14 Geo. III, c.83.

Apart from these factors, when the Dominion of Canada finally emerged as an entity in 1867 positivism was in the ascendancy in England. The whole letter and spirit of the British North America Act[8] bears witness to this fact. The Act is as prosaic as any municipal charter. Absent are the ringing declarations of the United States Constitution and its amendments – declarations involving eternal principles such as "justice," "liberty," "freedom," or "due process." The Canadian constitution assumes the supremacy of the legislative branch: Parliament and the provincial legislatures are given powers which, according to the Privy Council "cover the whole area of self-government within the whole area of Canada."[9] While this oversimplifies the situation, there are only a few sections of the BNA Act which prevent legislative action at both the federal and provincial levels. These include the guarantees with respect to the use of English and French (s. 133), denominational schools (s. 93), an annual session of Parliament (s. 20), and duty-free movements of goods among the provinces (s. 121). It is arguable that there are some other guarantees expressed or implied in the Act.[10] But these guarantees are limited and in the main inherently related to the federal and bicultural nature of the Canadian state. They do not reflect any general belief that the people of Canada required protection against omnipotent legislatures.

As a result, judicial review of legislation in Canada has been concerned almost exclusively with the division of powers between the provinces and the Dominion. The courts have refused to concern themselves with the wisdom or fairness of legislation,[11] or even the possibility of abuse of a legislative power,[12] so long as the impugned legislation is not being used as a means of invading a forbidden area under the guise of exercising a power given to the enacting legislature.[13] That is, provided that the Dominion does not infringe on provincial powers, nor the provinces on the Dominion power, the courts will not interfere.

In short, it may be said that the limitations on legislative power which the courts enforce in Canada are mainly quantitative, not qualitative. A

8. 30–31 Vict., c.3. See Appendix A.
9. *A.G. for Ont.* v. *A.G. for Canada*, [1912] A.C. 571, at 581 (P.C.).
10. See e.g. Laskin, "An Inquiry into the Diefenbaker Bill of Rights" (1959), 37 *Can. B. Rev.* 77, at 99–100.
11. See e.g. *A.G. for Ont.* v. *A.G. for Can.*, *supra* note 9, at 583; *Royal Bank* v. *the King*, [1913] A.C. 283, at 296 (P.C.); *Co-operative Committee on Japanese Canadians* v. *A.G. for Can.*, [1947] A.C. 87, at 102 (P.C.).
12. *Bank of Toronto* v. *Lambe* (1887), 12 App. Cas. 575, at 587 (P.C.); *A.G. for Can.* v. *A.G. for Ont. et al.*, [1898] A.C. 700, at 712–13 (P.C.).
13. See e.g. *A.G. for Ont.* v. *Reciprocal Insurers*, [1924] A.C. 328 (P.C.); *A.G. for Alberta* v. *A.G. for Can.*, [1939] A.C. 117 (P.C. 1938); *Canadian Federation of Agriculture* v. *A.G. for Que.*, [1951] A.C. 179 (P.C. 1950).

Canadian judge would be alarmed if he were asked to exercise the jurisdiction which Coke claimed. Judicial review in Canada is a product of the
Imperial system, based on a jurisdiction implicit in the Imperial statutes
which distributed legislative power with respect to Canadian affairs. It is
not based on a jurisdiction inherent in Anglo-Canadian courts by virtue
of the common law.

PRE-CONFEDERATION PRACTICE

Throughout the Empire, colonial legislatures were legislatures of limited
power. Apart from their territorial limitations (they could not pass extra-
territorial legislation), they were enjoined from enacting laws conflicting
with those of the mother land. The extent of this latter restriction was for
many years in doubt. As early as 1696 an Imperial statute entitled "An
act for preventing frauds, and regulating abuses in the plantation trade"
had provided:

IX. And it is further enacted and declared by the authority aforesaid, That
all laws, by-laws, usages or customs, at this time, or which hereafter shall be
in practice, or endeavoured or pretended to be in force or practice, in any of
the said plantations, which are in any way repugnant to the before mentioned
laws, or any of them, so far as they do relate to the said plantations, or any of
them, or which are any way repugnant to this present act, *or to any other law
hereafter to be made in this kingdom, so far as such law shall relate to and
mention the said plantations*, are illegal, null and void, to all intents and purposes whatsoever.[14]

This statute clearly indicates that a colonial law would not be void unless
it conflicted with an English *statute* either existing or future ("law hereafter to be *made* in this kingdom"), which specifically applied to the
colony or colonies.

The colonial charters, granted in the exercise of the royal prerogative
and usually in the form of instructions to the governor with respect to the
establishment of a colonial legislative body, were not always as specific.
While they generally restricted the legislative power, the extent of the
limitation was not clear. Typical of such instructions were those issued
to Governor Edward Cornwallis by letters patent in 1749 with respect to
establishment of the first representative assembly in the colonies now forming part of Canada. The commission provided that the Governor, with the
advice and consent of this assembly, ". . . shall have full power and
authority to make, constitute and ordain Laws, Statutes and Ordinances
for the Publick peace, welfare and good government of our said province
. . . which said Laws, Statutes and Ordinances are not to be repugnant

14. 7 & 8 Will. III, c.22, s.9: emphasis added.

but as near as may be agreeable to the Laws and Statutes of this our Kingdom of Great Britain."[15]

The commission to Governor Murray of Quebec in 1763 authorizing an assembly (which was never elected or summoned) had an identical wording[16] and the pre-Confederation prerogative constitutions of other colonies now part of Canada had similar or identical provisions.[17]

What did this clause mean? To what "Laws and Statutes of this our Kingdom of Great Britain" did it refer? Did it include all the law, including the common law, and all the statutes including those which did not specifically apply to the colonies? It is clear that some colonial courts took a narrow view of this royal injunction. In testing the validity of colonial statutes they took into account only those Imperial statutes clearly extending to the colony.[18] In other parts of the Empire this restriction on the legislative power was given a much wider meaning.[19] Largely as a result of the enthusiasm of Mr. Justice Boothby in South Australia for striking down colonial laws on the basis of repugnancy,[20] the rule was clarified and narrowed by the Colonial Laws Validity Act, 1865. This Act provided that colonial laws would be void only for repugnancy to "any Act of Parliament extending to the Colony to which such Law may relate, or . . . to any Order or Regulation made under Authority of such Act of Parliament, or having in the Colony the Force or Effect of such Act. . . ."[21] In the meantime, the united province of Canada had already achieved this position by Imperial statute.[22]

This background is important now only to the extent that it helped to set the stage for judicial review throughout the Empire. The Colonial Laws Validity Act, 1865, is still in force today with respect to one Imperial statute extending to Canada, that is, the BNA Act. While the Statute of Westminster, 1931, released both Parliament and the provincial legislatures from the general prohibition of the Colonial Laws Validity Act against passing laws repugnant to Imperial statutes, the BNA Act was

15. Akins, *Selections from the Public Documents of the Province of Nova Scotia* (1869), 497, at 500.
16. Shortt and Doughty, *Documents Relating to the Constitutional History of Canada, 1759–1791* (1918), 173, at 175.
17. See Read, "The Early Provincial Constitutions" (1948), 26 *Can. B. Rev.* 620, *Passim.*
18. See *Uniacke* v. *Dickson* (1848), 2 N.S.R. 287 (N.S. Ch.).
19. See e.g. *Winthrop* v. *Lechmere* (1727), 3 *Acts of the Privy Council (Colonial Series)* (1910), at 139–50.
20. For the consequences to Mr. Justice Boothby of his actions, see Todd, *Parliamentary Government in the British Colonies* (2nd. ed., 1894), at 846–54; 1 Keith, *Responsible Government in the Dominions* (1912), at 402ff.
21. 28–29 Vict., c.63, s.2. See also s.3.
22. Union Act (1840), 3 & 4 Vict., c.35, s.3.

kept under the protection of the 1865 Act.[23] When a Canadian court strikes down a statute for constitutional invalidity, it is inarticulately applying the Colonial Laws Validity Act, holding void the Canadian statute for repugnancy to the provisions of the BNA Act distributing power between Parliament and legislatures.[24] It may be noted in passing that neither of these Imperial statutes specifically empowered the courts to exercise this power. The judiciary has simply continued a practice which was implicitly permitted by earlier charters and statutes of the Imperial system.

In the northern colonies, which now form part of Canada, there had been courts in operation from the early days of British rule. The first such court was established in 1721 at Annapolis Royal, by order in council of Governor Phillips, which court was to have the same powers and procedures as did the General Court in Virginia.[25] Less than two months after the fall of Quebec Governor Murray established a court, and there has been an unbroken succession of judicial institutions in British North America since that time.[26]

There is, however, no clear evidence that prior to Confederation any of these courts actually struck down a colonial statute for invalidity. They apparently were prepared to hold invalid other exercises of legislative power where such power had been delegated to the executive branch. The Supreme Court of Prince Edward Island in 1856 held invalid an order of the lieutenant governor in council on the grounds that it was not authorized by the statute under which it was passed.[27] A Lower Canadian court held void letters patent of the local governor which purported to give precedence to a judge newly appointed to its bench. The decision was reversed by the Privy Council,[28] but on substantive grounds not connected with the right of review of the colonial court. Also, in New Brunswick the Supreme Court, while rejecting the argument that it could hold a colonial statute invalid simply because it interfered with property rights, clearly recognized in *obiter* that it could hold invalid a statute which was repugnant to Imperial law extending to the colony.[29]

These reported decisions all indicate an awareness in the courts of the

---

23. 22 Geo. V, c.4, s.7; the BNA acts 1867–1930 were all so protected therein.
24. In earlier times the courts sometimes expressly applied the Colonial Laws Validity Act, 1865. See e.g. *The Queen* v. *Chandler* (1869), 12 N.B.R. 556 (N.B. Sup. Ct. 1869).
25. 3 *Nova Scotia Archives*, at 28–29, quoted in Chisholm, "An Approaching Bicentenary" (1918), 38 *Can. L. T.* 727, at 728.
26. Riddell, "The First British Courts in Canada" (1924), 33 *Yale L.J.* 571.
27. *Bourke* v. *Murphy* (1856), 1 P.E.I. L.R. 126 (P.E.I. Sup. Ct.).
28. *In re Bedard* (1849), 1 Can. Rep. 328 (P.C.).
29. *R.* v. *John Kerr* (1838), 2 N.B.R. 553, Ber. 367 (N.B. Sup. Ct.).

northern colonies that they could supervise the exercise of limited powers granted under charters or statutes. Whether the courts in what is now Canada ever invalidated ultra vires legislation is not clear, but it may be assumed fairly confidently that at the time of Confederation they would have been prepared to do so in a proper case. If the legislative instrument of a colonial lieutenant governor in council could be set aside for want of authority, the same could be done to a colonial statute which exceeded the legislative powers conferred on the colonial assembly.

The practice in other parts of the Empire would have reassured British North American courts in this regard. There is evidence that in the eighteenth century the courts in the colonies to the south had reviewed the validity of colonial statutes[30] and had even attempted to review orders of the Privy Council.[31] The Judicial Committee of the Privy Council itself had implicitly approved the practice of judicial review in colonial courts. In the case of *Cameron* v. *Kyte*[32] in 1835 the Judicial Committee upheld a decision of the Supreme Court of Civil Justice of the West Indian colony of Bernice, in which that court had treated a regulation passed by the governor as being of no effect. The regulation was a legislative instrument purporting to reduce the commission payable to the vendue master, a public official who conducted all public auctions. The local court had given judgment for the vendue master for the full amount of his commission, thus refusing to apply the governor's regulation. With respect to this decision the Privy Council judgment stated: "But if the Governor be an officer, merely with a *limited authority* from the Crown, his assumption of an act of sovereign power, out of the limits of the authority so given to him, would be purely void, and the Courts of the colony over which he presided could not give it any legal effect."[33] This points up the essential element of judicial review in the Empire: a "limited authority," the purported exercise of which could always be examined for validity by the courts.

English courts did not hesitate to test the validity of colonial legislative instruments, even those issued by the Imperial authorities. In the well-known case of *Campbell* v. *Hall*[34] Lord Mansfield held invalid letters patent issued in London fixing a duty of four and one-half per cent on all sugar exported from Grenada. Here again limited authority was being

---

30. McGovney, *supra* note 4, *passim*.
31. Davis, "The Case of Frost v. Leighton" (1896–7), 2 *Am. Hist. Rev.* 229; Smith, *Appeals to the Privy Council from the American Plantations* (1965), at 328–33.
32. (1835) 3 Knapp's P.C. 332; 12 E.R. 678 (P.C.).
33. 3 Knapp's P.C., at 344; 12 E.R., at 683: emphasis added.
34. (1774), 1 Cowp. 204; 98 E.R. 1045 (K.B.).

exercised: the royal prerogative with respect to the colony was subject to restrictions imposed by Parliament and to restrictions resulting from previous prerogative acts done with respect to the colony. The latter type of restriction was decisive here, because previous letters patent in April 1764 had authorized the summoning of a legislative assembly (which was in fact summoned in 1765). The letters patent with respect to the export duty were issued in July 1764. In an action brought in England against Hall, the collector of the export duty, for a return of sums paid pursuant to the latter letters patent, Lord Mansfield held them to be invalid because the king had precluded himself from further legislative action with respect to the colony once he authorized the summoning of a local legislature.

Legislative or quasi-legislative action of colonial assemblies also came before domestic English courts. In *Watson*'s case[35] an application was made in the English King's Bench for habeas corpus on behalf of Watson who was being detained at Liverpool awaiting transportation to Van Diemen's Land. Conditionally pardoned for offences against the state in Upper Canada, he had been ordered transported and was in transit when this application was made. The validity of Upper Canadian legislation authorizing this procedure was challenged, and the King's Bench, after thorough consideration, upheld it as being authorized by the Constitutional Act, 1791.

This practice in other colonial courts and in the domestic English courts must have been known to the pre-Confederation courts in British North America, and they must have accepted it as a proper exercise of judicial power. More important even than these precedents, however, would be the practice of the Privy Council as the supreme appellate tribunal of the Empire. The history and functions of that body deserve special examination.

THE PRIVY COUNCIL AND JUDICIAL REVIEW

The king as the fountain-head of justice is an ancient concept in English law.[36] With the creation of the ordinary courts for handling domestic judicial business, the judicial power of the king's prerogative courts became more and more reduced. The Star Chamber continued to exercise powers with respect to domestic matters until its activities were finally stopped by act of Parliament in 1641.[37] This statute not only abolished

---

35. (1839), 9 Ad. & El. 731; 112 E.R. 1389 (K.B.).
36. See e.g. Bracton, *Treatise on the Laws and Customs of England* (Twiss ed., 1878–83), fol. 107.
37. 16 Car. I, c.10 (1641).

the Star Chamber and similar tribunals, but also forbade the king and his Privy Council from exercising judicial power in matters which the ordinary courts of law were already empowered to hear.

This prohibition did not apparently extend to matters arising within the king's domains beyond England: such matters were not necessarily within the jurisdiction of English courts.[38] It was not surprising then that questions arising within the colonies might be considered to fall within that residual royal prerogative of justice. As early as the fifteenth century, appeals to the Privy Council from the Channel Islands had been regulated, and in an order of 1674 the trade and plantations committee of the Council was assigned the duty of dealing with such matters.[39] In the eighteenth century further orders in council provided generally for appeals from the colonies.[40] It was said in *obiter* by Lord Macclesfield in a 1724 Chancery case[41] that English domestic courts could not deal with appeals from colonial courts, that such appeals must go to the king in council.

The modern era of the Privy Council's judicial work begins in 1833 when the Judicial Committee was first created by statute.[42] Until this time the composition of the committee which heard appeals was often unsatisfactory, with many lay members. The 1833 Act created the "Judicial Committee of the Privy Council" to be composed of the president of the Privy Council, the Lord Chancellor, the Lord Chief Justice, and various judges. The Act gave the Committee jurisdiction over Admiralty appeals from the colonies, and conferred on it power to hear all appeals which the king or the king in council had previously been authorized to hear. A further statute of 1844 extended the Committee's jurisdiction by authorizing appeals from the lower colonial courts, even with respect to those jurisdictions where local law only permitted appeals to the Judicial Committee from the final court of appeal in the colony.[43] The basic jurisdiction of the Committee did not change significantly thereafter until after the Statute of Westminster, 1931, though a number of statutes altered its composition by making eligible for membership various other English and colonial judges.[44]

After the middle of the seventeenth century the colonial charters

38. See Smith, *supra* note 31, at 3–5.
39. *Ibid.*, at 70.
40. Finlason, *The History, Constitution and Character of the Judicial Committee of the Privy Council* (1878), 37–39; Pierson, *Canada and the Privy Council* (1960), 6–7.
41. *Fryer v. Bernard* (1724), 2 P. Wms. 261, at 262; 24 E.R. 722, at 723 (Ch.).
42. 3 & 4 Wm. IV, c.41 (1833).
43. 7 & 8 Vict., c.69, s.l. (1844).
44. See e.g. 44 & 45 Vict., c.3 (1881); 58 & 59 Vict., c.44 (1895); 8 Edw. VII, c.51 (1908); 3 & 4 Geo. V, c.21 (1913).

generally specified a right of appeal from colonial courts to the Privy Council.[45] There was usually a limitation to the effect that decisions of the local courts would be final unless there was more than a specified minimum amount involved. Where so authorized by its charter the local legislature could further limit, abolish, or extend the appeal as of right.[46] The 1844 Act which extended the jurisdiction of the Judicial Committee apparently empowered the Queen in council to circumvent local limitations on appeals as of right from the lower courts.[47] While colonial law might restrict or abolish appeals as of right from the highest court in the colony, there remained the power of the Judicial Committee to grant special leave to appeal from any colonial court. This was a continuation of the old prerogative power of the Crown as the fountain-head of justice. The challenge to this power by the Parliament of Canada, and the failure of that challenge, will be discussed later.

Within this framework of appellate jurisdiction, the Privy Council was able and willing to review the validity of colonial legislation from time to time. There is evidence of this power being used at least four times with respect to legislation in the American colonies prior to 1776 and the Revolution, the first instance being the case of *Winthrop* v. *Lechmere* in 1726.[48] After the American Revolution the Privy Council apparently did not have the occasion to use the power for some time.

We have already seen that in 1835 in the case of *Cameron* v. *Kyte*[49] the Judicial Committee affirmed the judgment of the Supreme Court of Civil Justice of Bernice, striking down the order of the governor which had reduced the vendue master's commission. In *Kielley* v. *Carson*,[50] in 1842, the Committee heard an appeal from the Supreme Court of Judicature of Newfoundland which turned on the validity of a resolution of the legislature of that colony. The plaintiff had, pursuant to the resolution, been imprisoned for contempt of the legislature with respect to certain remarks he had made outside that assembly. He sued the speaker and others for assault, battery, and false imprisonment, contending that the legislature had no power to commit for contempt. The local court had dismissed the action, but the Judicial Committee allowed the appeal. It found that the legislature had no authority to punish for contempt not committed in the face of the legislature. Such action was outside the grant of powers in

45. See Read, *supra* note 17.
46. *Cuvillier* v. *Aylwin* (1832), 2 Knapp's P.C. 72; 12 E.R. 406 (P.C.); *disapproved* in *Cushing* v. *Dupuy* (1880), 5 App. Cas. 409, at 417 (P.C.).
47. 7 & 8 Vict., c.69, s.1 (1844).
48. McGovney, *supra* note 4, at 13–34.
49. *Supra* note 32 and accompanying text.
50. (1842), 4 Moo. P.C. 63; 13 E.R. 225 (P.C.).

the Commission which, in 1832, had conferred on the inhabitants the right to have a legislative assembly. It was said that such a power could not be implied in the mere authority to have an assembly.

In *Re Cape Breton*[51] the Judicial Committee was asked to consider the validity of royal instructions issued in London in 1820 to the governor of Nova Scotia. The commission indicated that Cape Breton Island was to be annexed to Nova Scotia. A petition was presented to the Queen opposing this action, it being contended *inter alia* that the prerogative power to annex Cape Breton to another colony had been irrevocably divested by the Crown when it had granted letters patent in 1784 authorizing a separate government and assembly for the island. The Queen's advisors referred the petition to the Judicial Committee for a determination of the legal, as opposed to the policy, questions[52] and that body rejected the petition. The decision was in the form of a report simply expressing the opinion that the inhabitants of the island were not entitled as of right to a constitution of their own.

There is nothing to indicate that the Judicial Committee or its predecessor, the committee on trade and plantations, ever suffered from any doubts about the propriety of reviewing the exercise of subordinate legislative authority with respect to the colonies. Its practice would undoubtedly have been well known throughout the Empire, providing strong precedents for the exercise of a similar power by colonial courts.

It could be argued, of course, that the Privy Council in reviewing colonial legislation was performing a political function. The royal power of disallowance of colonial legislation was well recognized. Since 1631, when the laws of the newly constituted royal province of Virginia were first sent to England for royal assent, the Crown had played a vital political role in the colonial legislative process.[53] In the royal province of Massachusetts, for example, in the period 1691–1775 some fifty-nine statutes were disallowed.[54] Of these, some thirteen were disallowed because they were "repugnant to the Laws of England" or otherwise exceeded the powers granted under the colonial charter.[55] At first blush it might seem difficult to distinguish this procedure – where the King's advisors would recommend disallowance of a colonial act for excess of jurisdiction – and that

---

51. (1846), 5 Moo. P.C. 259; 13 E.R. 489 (P.C.).
52. By 3 & 4 Will. IV, c.41, s.4 (1833) the sovereign was given power to refer to the Judicial Committee "any such other matters whatsoever as His Majesty shall think fit. . . . "
53. Dorland, *The Royal Disallowance in Massachusetts*, Bulletin No. 22, Departments of History and Political and Economic Science, Queen's University, Kingston (1917), at 1–5.
54. *Ibid.*, at 5.   55. *Ibid.*, at 6, 23.

procedure by which his Privy Council would advise that a colonial law was invalid because of a similar excess. Could it be argued that the Committee was really performing a political function in reviewing colonial legislation, a function to which colonial courts themselves could not aspire? It has been pointed out that in the modern constitution the Privy Council would be subject to the control of Parliament,[56] and therefore it could be considered purely a political body. It has also been noted that in one aspect of its work the Judicial Committee acts more like a political than a judicial agency: it does not publish dissenting opinions but instead reveals only one conclusion, advice for the sovereign unqualified by the dissents of those members of the committee who have been overruled by the majority.[57] One would expect the members of a purely judicial tribunal to be free to express the views to which they are led by their reason and conscience, not forced to conceal their honestly held opinions for the sake of unanimity.

In spite of the foregoing, it must surely be conceded that, in review of legislation on appeal from the colonies, the Committee was exercising a judicial function. Firstly, the power of disallowance and the power of judicial review are distinguishable. The effect of disallowance is to nullify the statute as of the date it is disallowed. A judicial determination of invalidity means that it was void *ab initio*. Disallowance was used for a variety of reasons unassociated with validity.[58] As we have seen, the Judicial Committee or its forerunner dealt with the validity of royal instruments other than those to which the power of disallowance would apply. Secondly, the Committee on Trade and Plantations or the Judicial Committee did in substance act in a judicial manner in dealing with appeals. As early as the *Winthrop* case in 1727 lawyers were engaged in presenting argument and the proceedings were apparently conducted like those in court. Thirdly, when the new Committee was established by statute in 1833, it was composed predominantly of judicial, not political, officers. The adjective "Judicial" used in the title clearly indicates the intention of Parliament. Since 1833 the changes made in its composition have been directed to strengthening the Committee's judicial character.

We can thus see that, as Confederation approached, the judges and lawyers in the colonies of British North America must have been familiar to some degree with the British doctrine of judicial review of colonial legislation. Courts in other colonies had exercised this function, some British

56. Haines, "Judicial Review of Legislation in Canada" (1915), 28 *Harv. L. Rev.* 565, at 587–88.
57. Finlason, *supra* note 40, at iii–xi.
58. Dorland, *supra* note 53, at 6.

North American courts had at least exercised an analogous function, and the English courts had not hesitated to deal with colonial legislative validity where it was relevant to their proceedings. The Judicial Committee, as the supreme judicial body of the colonial system, had provided ample precedents for judicial review. Its practice would have led the colonial courts to consider the question of validity where necessary, in anticipation of that issue being dealt with in London on appeal.

The constitutional law of the Empire in 1867 apparently embraced the convention that where legislative powers were granted subject to limitations the courts would enforce those limitations. The BNA Act was drafted and enacted in this context.

CONFEDERATION AND AFTER

It is surprising that the question of judicial review and the position of the courts in relation to the new Parliament and legislatures of Canada was not given more express consideration at the time of Confederation. The records of the Quebec Conference of 1864 do not suggest that this matter was discussed directly, though there was some interest in the possible creation of a general court of appeal. In the Confederation Debates in the Parliament of the province of Canada in 1865 little mention is made of it and the comments which do appear are not very helpful.

Sir John A. Macdonald, Attorney General West, minimized the problem, through either shrewdness or naïveté. In the Confederation Debates he explained the virtues of the proposed constitution as outlined in the Quebec Resolutions of the previous year:

We have given the General Legislature all the great subjects of legislation. We have conferred on them, not only specifically and in detail, all the powers which are incident to sovereignty, but we have expressly declared that all subjects of general interest not distinctly and exclusively conferred upon the local governments and local legislatures, shall be conferred upon the General Government and Legislature. We have thus avoided that great source of weakness which has been the cause of the disruption of the United States. *We have avoided all conflict of jurisdiction and authority.* . . .[59]

Besides all the powers that are specifically given in the 37th and last item of this portion of the Constitution, confers [sic] on the General Legislature the general mass of sovereign legislation, the power to legislate on "all matters of a general character, not specifically and exclusively reserved for the local governments and legislatures." This is precisely the provision which is wanting in the Constitution of the United States. It is here that we find the weakness

---

59. *Parliamentary Debates on the Subject of Confederation*, 3rd Sess., 8th Parliament of Canada at 33 (1865): emphasis added.

of the American system—the point where the American Constitution breaks down.[60]

There are numerous subjects which belong, of right, both to the Local and the General Parliaments. In all these cases it is provided, in order to prevent a conflict of authority, that where there is concurrent jurisdiction in the General and Local Parliaments, the same rule should apply as now applies in cases where there is concurrent jurisdiction in the Imperial and in the Provincial Parliaments, and that when the legislation of the one is adverse to or contradictory to the legislation of the other, in all such cases the action of the General Parliament must overrule, ex necessitate, the action of the Local Legislature.[61]

Though Macdonald did not deal directly with the question of judicial review, these excerpts suggest he did not consider that any serious "conflict of jurisdiction or authority" would arise. If both Parliament and legislature had authority, the act of Parliament would prevail. Perhaps one may assume that he expected the courts to determine who did have legislative authority in such cases. One might suspect, however, that Sir John may have foreseen a role for the Canadian Parliament similar to that of the Imperial Parliament. That is, the Canadian Parliament would be a sovereign body subject to no external restraints, whose legislation would not be subject to review by the courts. The Quebec Resolutions and, later, the BNA Act did put the federal cabinet in the position that the Imperial cabinet had formerly occupied with respect to the power of disallowance of provincial legislation.[62] If the federal executive clearly was to assume certain powers of the Imperial executive, it would not be difficult to conclude that the federal Parliament was to be put in the same position as the Imperial Parliament. Its legislation would be supreme over legislation of the inferior provincial assemblies, subject only to the exercise in London of the power of disallowance retained there with respect to federal enactments.

There is other evidence that immediately after Confederation Macdonald assumed that the proper and perhaps the only control on invalid provincial legislation would be the power of disallowance resting with the governor general. He explained to the provinces the use of the power on this basis in 1868, and he privately expressed fears that federal cabinets

---

60. *Ibid.*, at 41. The "37th item" referred to is head 37 of section 29 of the Quebec Resolutions of 1864. Section 29 was the original draft of what is now section 91 of the BNA Act, dealing with federal powers.

61. *Ibid.*, at 42. Macdonald is here summarizing the effect of section 45 of the Quebec Resolutions. There is no counterpart of this section in the present BNA Act, although the courts have reached essentially the same result by the "paramountcy" rule.

62. 30–31 Vict., c.3, ss.55–57, 90, based on sections 50 and 51 of the Quebec Resolutions.

full of "states rightists" might in the future refuse to exercise the power.[63] If it was assumed that the protection against invalid provincial legislation was the governor general's power of disallowance it should further have been assumed that the protection against invalid federal legislation was the Queen's power of disallowance. In such a system, the courts would have no important role.

The information available concerning Macdonald's views on the subject of judicial review is inconclusive. He may have assumed that the courts would exercise this power. His apparent familiarity with the constitution of the United States should have suggested this to him. Or he may have assumed that other arrangements – a general supremacy of the federal Parliament and the powers of disallowance – would serve the same purpose in the new Dominion.

Other members speaking in the Confederation Debates reveal the confusion prevailing on this subject. The following exchange occurred between A. A. Dorion (Hochelaga), an opponent of Confederation, and the Hon. George E. Cartier (Montreal East), Attorney General East:

HON. MR. DORION: . . . In case of difference between the Federal Power and the local governments, what authority will intervene for its settlement?

HON. ATTY. GEN. CARTIER: It will be the Imperial Government.

HON. MR. DORION: In effect there will be no other authority than that of the Imperial Government, and we know too well the value assigned to the complaints of Lower Canadians by the Imperial Government.

HON. ATTY. GEN. CARTIER: The delegates understood the matter better than that. Neither the Imperial Government nor the General Government will interfere, but the courts of justice will decide all questions in relation to which there may be differences between the two powers.

A VOICE: The Commissioners' courts (Hear, Hear).

HON. MR. DORION: Undoubtedly. One magistrate will decide that a law passed by the Federal Legislature is not law, whilst another will decide that it is law, and thus the differences instead of being between the legislatures will be between the several courts of justice.

HON. ATTY. GEN. CARTIER: Should the General Legislature pass a law beyond the limits of its functions, it will be null and void *pleno jure*.

HON. MR. DORION: Yes, I understand that, and it is doubtless to decide questions of this kind that it is proposed to establish Federal courts.

HON. ATTY. GEN. CARTIER: No, No! They will be established only to apply and adjudicate upon the Federal laws.

HON. MR. DORION: . . . If the differences between the Federal and the Local Parliaments are not to be submitted to the decision of a Supreme Federal Court, I do not see who can possibly decide them (Hear, Hear).[64]

63. Farr, *The Colonial Office and Canada, 1867–1887* (1955), at 110.
64. *Supra* note 59, at 690.

Mr. Dorion proceeded to state his fears that a federal court of appeal would have at best only one Lower Canadian ("who may be selected out of the English population") and that Lower Canadian interests would inevitably suffer before such a court.

Cartier's remarks as quoted are remarkably unedifying. He first casually explains that the Imperial government will decide disputes over jurisdiction. When this proves objectionable to his compatriot, he suggests that the courts will decide "differences." He then is forced to say that it will not be the federal courts, the creatures of Parliament, which will decide.

One might have expected the two principal law officers of the government, Attorneys General Macdonald and Cartier, to have been more precise and lucid on this not insignificant subject. At least it may be said that Cartier was consistent in his ambiguity.[65] It may be concluded, perhaps, that the government was trying to avoid stirring up the issue on which Dorion touched. If there was to be judicial review, which courts should exercise it? Would it be a Canadian court, appointed by the federal government and composed predominantly of English-speaking Protestant Canadians? To avoid this issue, the problem was glossed over. The jurisdiction of the Privy Council was in no way affected, and the proposed constitution did not in fact create a "General Court of Appeal." As enacted, it only empowered the federal Parliament to create such a court if it saw fit.[66]

If the members of the government found it necessary to skirt the issue, it was still possible for a backbencher to express what must have been obvious to many. Joseph Cauchon (Montmorency) subsequently commented on the remarks of A. A. Dorion, some of which were quoted above. Cauchon noted the practice in the United States. "If any conflict arises between the Federal Legislature and that of the states, it is decided by the judicial tribunals. . . . Why then should the case be otherwise so far as we are concerned?"[67]

The discussion of the BNA Act in committee in the House of Commons at Westminster indicates an awareness of the problem, but two possible cures for invalid legislation were again suggested. In answer to the question how conflicts of jurisdiction would be settled, Mr. C. B. Adderley, parliamentary under-secretary of the Colonial Office, said "he did not think that any serious conflict of the kind anticipated by the honourable member could take place so long as a supreme power was vested in the

65. See his answer to a question asked by Joseph Cauchon (Montmorency) concerning the jurisdiction of the proposed Supreme Court, *ibid.*, at 576.
66. 30–31 Vict., c.3, s.101, based on section 31 of the Quebec Resolutions.
67. *Supra* note 59, at 698.

Governor General to veto Acts." Another member complained that there was no Supreme Court, such as existed in the United States, to decide as to the validity of *federal* laws. The former colonial secretary, Edward Cardwell, in reply to this criticism:

said he was afraid that the defect pointed out by the honourable and learned Member was not one which, in the present state of feeling in the North American Provinces, it was possible to remedy. As matters now stood if the Legislature of Canada acted *ultra vires*, the question would first be raised in the Colonial Law Courts; and would ultimately be settled by the Privy Council at home. No doubt it was a defect, but this point had undergone consideration by the delegates, who thought it would be better to leave things in this state.[68]

Here again we see both disallowance and judicial review suggested as devices for curing excesses of legislative authority. Again we hear the overtone of the internal struggle between the two major races in Canada, making impolitic any further clarification of the situation.

Whatever the views of statesmen, whatever the political difficulties inherent in judicial review, the Canadian courts after Confederation showed themselves ready to pass judgment on the validity of legislation. In 1868 the Supreme Court of New Brunswick in *The Queen* v. *Chandler*,[69] held invalid a statute of that province on the grounds that it related to bankruptcy, a federal matter. The court distinguished its decision thirty years earlier in *R.* v. *John Kerr*[70] wherein the court had refused to hold an act of the local legislature invalid on the ground that it was unjust or interfered with private property. In the *Chandler* case it was pointed out that, whatever the merits of *Kerr*, there had been a substantial change brought about by the enactment of the BNA Act. The powers of the local legislature were now considerably curtailed. Moreover, there was no repugnancy to an Imperial statute involved in the *Kerr* decision, whereas in *Chandler* the provincial statute was repugnant to the BNA Act. In the case of *L'Union St. Jacques de Montréal* v. *Bélisle*[71] the Quebec Circuit Court in 1870 held invalid a provincial statute on the grounds that it related to the federal matter of insolvency. This decision was upheld two years later by the Quebec Court of Queen's Bench.[72] Also in 1872, the Quebec Court

68. (1867), 185 House of Commons, *Debates*, 3rd ser., at 1319–20. Perhaps the Colonial Office officials did not share Cardwell's belief that the lack of a supreme court was a "defect." Sir Frederic Rogers, Permanent Under-Secretary, in 1869 could see nothing "inadequate or unsatisfactory" in questions of validity of laws being decided by local courts subject to an appeal to the Judicial Committee. See Farr, *supra* note 63, at 111–12.
69. (1868), 12 N.B.R. 556 (N.B. Sup. Ct.).
70. *Supra* note 29.
71. (1870), 15 L.C.J. 212 (Que. Circ. Ct.).
72. (1872) 20 L.C.J. 29 (Que. Q.B.) *Rev'd* (1874), L.R. 6 P.C. 31 (P.C.).

of Queen's Bench held invalid a provincial statute establishing the court of the Fire Commissioners, and the appeal from this decision apparently gave the Judicial Committee its first opportunity to construe the BNA Act.[73] In 1871 in Ontario the Court of Chancery had to consider the validity of a private act of the provincial legislature which in effect altered the disposition made by the will of a deceased. The court upheld the statute, and the Court of Appeal affirmed this decision after further examination of the validity of the law.[74] The Nova Scotia Supreme Court took up constitutional review in *Keefe* v. *McLennan*[75] in 1876. The court upheld a local statute establishing a system of issuing licenses for retail liquor outlets. It rejected the argument that this related to "trade and commerce," a federal matter.

The newly created Supreme Court of Canada officially acquired its judicial functions on January 11, 1876.[76] The first reported decision in which it considered the constitutional validity of any statute was *Severn* v. *the Queen*[77] in 1878. The court, without showing any hesitation concerning its right to do so, reviewed the validity of an Ontario statute and reversed a decision of the Court of Queen's Bench for that province which had held the statute to be valid. The Supreme Court took the view that the Ontario license on brewers was invalid as a restraint on "trade and commerce." A year later the court had occasion to review the validity of a federal statute, the Dominion Controverted Elections Act, 1874, in the case of *Valin* v. *Langlois*.[78] It was argued there that Parliament could not validly impose a duty on provincial courts to try controverted federal election cases. The Supreme Court upheld the Act. Chief Justice Ritchie took this opportunity to state his views on the role of the Court in the federal structure. Referring to the question before them, he said:

This, if not the most important, is one of the most important questions that can come before this court, inasmuch as it involves, in an eminent degree, the respective legislative rights and powers of the Dominion Parliament and the Local Legislatures, and its logical conclusion and effect must extend far beyond the question now at issue. In view of the great diversity of judicial opinion that has characterized the decisions of the provincial tribunals in some provinces, and the judges in all, while it would seem to justify the wisdom of the Dominion Parliament, in providing for the establishment of a Court of Appeal such as this, where such diversity shall be considered and an authoritative declaration of the law be enunciated, so it enhances the responsibility of those called on in

---

73. *The Queen* v. *Coote* (1873), L.R. 4 P.C. 599 (P.C.).
74. *Re Goodhue* (1873), 19 Grant 366 (Ont. C.A.).
75. (1876), 2 Russell & Chesley 5 (N.S. Sup. Ct.).
76. See *Taylor* v. *the Queen* (1876), 1 S.C.R. 65.
77. (1878), 2 S.C.R. 70.
78. (1879), 3 S.C.R. 1, *aff'd.* (1879), 5 App. Cas. 115 (P.C.).

the midst of such conflict of opinion to declare authoritatively the principles by which both federal and local legislation are governed.[79]

And so the Canadian courts were launched on a course from which they have never swerved. The ease with which they could take up judicial review of legislation after Confederation must have been the result of the situation existing prior to 1867. There was a continuity of judicial practice because the Imperial structure had not changed basically. Colonial laws, and the Dominion of Canada was really only a colony, still were subject to overriding Imperial laws. The Colonial Laws Validity Act, 1865, could be relied on by a court in order to strike down a provincial or federal statute, just as the courts before 1865 could strike down any colonial statute for being "repugnant to the laws of England." Colonial legislatures, whether Dominion or provincial, were limited legislatures, and the courts could enforce the limitations.

The expectation of some that problems of invalidity would be dealt with through the power of disallowance was never realized. In the first place, the power of disallowance did not inherently exclude other forms of review of legislation. While the exercise, or threatened exercise, of the power did prevent considerable invalid legislation taking effect, the use of the power for this purpose was gradually discontinued. By agreement, London's power of disallowance over federal legislation had been eliminated by 1930.[80] By 1935, the federal government had asserted that its power of disallowance over provincial legislation ought not to be used solely on the grounds of legislative invalidity. It was conceded that the courts were the proper agencies to determine whether a statute was ultra vires of a provincial legislature.[81]

It is fortunate that disallowance did not become the principal means for enforcing the BNA Act's restrictions on legislative power. Disallowance had to be exercised on the advice of political officers of a senior government. Many issues quite irrelevant to constitutionality could bear on the decision about its use. Disallowance could be exercised only within one year after enactment in the case of provincial legislation and two years in the case of federal legislation.[82] Constitutional problems not apparent at first might subsequently arise after the limitation period had expired.

79. (1879) 3 S.C.R., at 9–10.
80. *Report of the Conference on the Operation of Dominion Legislation and Merchant Shipping, 1929* (1929), at 20.
81. See La Forest, *Disallowance and Reservation of Provincial Legislation* (1955), at 76–77. While invalid provincial legislation has been occasionally disallowed since, the federal government has claimed some other ground in addition to invalidity: *ibid.*, at 77–82, 99–101.
82. 30–31 Vict., c.3, ss.56, 90.

Regulations made pursuant to a statute and going beyond the constitutional authority of the government passing them could not be nullified because disallowance only extended to statutes. Also, if disallowance were relied on solely, rights could be affected by an invalid statute which would be effective upon enactment and continue to operate until disallowed. In a system which embraces judicial review, the citizen is enabled to treat an invalid statute as void *ab initio* and to assert this position in court if the need arises.

THE FRAMEWORK OF JUDICIAL REVIEW

The most significant development in the judicial structure since 1867 has been the rise of the Supreme Court of Canada and the fall of the Judicial Committee of the Privy Council as the final court of constitutional adjudication. The BNA Act did not establish the Supreme Court. Section 101 merely provided that "The Parliament of Canada, may, notwithstanding anything in this Act, from time to time, provide for the Constitution, Maintenance, and Organization of a General Court of Appeal for Canada, and for the Establishment of any additional Courts for the better Administration of the Laws of Canada." There were probably sound political reasons for not expressly creating this court at the time of Confederation. Macdonald but touched on the problem when he remarked during the Confederation Debates that "There are many arguments for and against the establishment of such a court."[83] In fact, the Supreme Court issue was bound up with the sensitive subject of judicial review. The problems involved and the attitude of French-speaking Canada to a new Canadian tribunal have been adverted to previously.[84] French Canadians feared that a final court of appeal for the whole of the Dominion would be composed predominantly of English-speaking protestant common lawyers who would neither understand the civil law nor be impartial where racial or religious issues were involved. Henri A. Taschereau (Beauce), speaking in the Confederation Debates, asserted that his compatriots would "assuredly be less satisfied with the decisions of a Federal Court of Appeal than with those of Her Majesty's Privy Council."[85] Cartier, in response to a question concerning the possible court of appeal reassured the House in these words: "but I do hold, and the spirit of the conference at Quebec indicated, that the appeal to the judicial committee of Her Majesty's Privy Council must always exist, even if the Court in question is established."[86] On this basis the Lower Canadians permitted section 101 of the BNA Act to become law.

83. *Supra* note 59, at 41.
84. See notes 64 to 67 *supra*, and accompanying text.
85. *Supra* note 59, at 897. 86. *Ibid.*, at 576.

So delicate was the situation that no serious attempt was made for several years to establish a final court of appeal for the new Dominion. Appeals continued to go directly from the provincial courts to the Judicial Committee. In 1875, during the Mackenzie government, the legislation was enacted establishing the Supreme Court and the Exchequer Court.[87] Generally speaking, the court was given jurisdiction to hear appeals from the final judgments of the court of final resort in each of the provinces.[88] Provisions of this Act with respect to appeals to the Privy Council will be considered later.

As we have seen, there were two types of appeal to the Judicial Committee, those as of right and those with leave. The Judicial Committee Act of 1833 simply provided that Committee hear appeals "which, either by virtue of this Act, or of any Law, Statute, or Custom, may be brought before His Majesty or His Majesty in Council. . . ."[89] As the Act did not, except with respect to certain specialized matters, create any new right of appeal, it seemed to leave it to the particular law relating to the colonies and the law with respect to the royal prerogative of justice to fix the scope of appeals. The Judicial Committee Act of 1844 went further in specifically authorizing Her Majesty "to provide for the admission of any appeal of appeals. The Judicial Committee Act of 1844 went further in specifi-crees or Orders of any Court of Justice within any British Colony or Possession abroad. . . ."[90] Although the main purpose of this statute seems to have been to overcome colonial restrictions which prevented appeals from courts other than final appellate courts, it was broad enough to authorize an order in council permitting any appeal in any case from any colonial court. In this way the royal prerogative of justice was formalized by statute.

From the foregoing it may be seen that the appeal as of right was fixed by colonial law, the appeal by leave of the Judicial Committee being provided for by Imperial statute. The appeal as of right was usually defined monetarily, the decision of the local court being "final" except where the amount involved was, for example, over £300. In the earlier colonial period the right of appeal was set out in the charter or the commission to the governor,[91] and the colonies were not permitted to alter it.[92] The Constitutional Act of 1791 creating Upper Canada and Lower Canada

---

87. 38 Vict., c.11 (1875) (Can.).   88. *Ibid.*, s.17.
89. 3 & 4 Wm. IV, c.41, s.3.   90. 7 & 8 Vict., c.69, s.l.
91. See e.g. Read, "The Early Provincial Constitutions" (1948), 26 *Can. B. Rev.* 620 *passim.* Shortt and Doughty, *Documents Relating to the Constitutional History of Canada, 1759–1791* (1918), at 676–83.
92. The legislature of the Massachusetts Bay Colony in 1691 attempted to impose a limitation on appeals to the Privy Council. The statute was disallowed by London because it was said the legislature had no authority to alter the right of appeal. Dorland, *supra* note 53, at 24.

authorized the legislatures of those colonies to legislate with respect to appeals from colonial courts.[93] Both colonies were quick to exercise the power, restricting appeals to matters involving more than £500.[94] It was apparently thought at one time that the colonial legislatures had been empowered by the 1791 Act to restrict the appeal with leave – the so-called prerogative appeal – as well as the appeal as of right.[95] Later Privy Council decisions made it clear, however, that whether or not this power had been conferred, a colonial legislature would have to legislate specifically in this regard to restrict the prerogative appeal.[96] This finding was simply an application of the general rule that the court will not imply that a Crown prerogative has been taken away by statute. Prior to Confederation there is no indication that any of the British North American colonies did succeed in limiting the "prerogative" appeal with leave.

The BNA Act did not deal with Privy Council appeals expressly, but it may implicitly have granted some legislative power on the subject. The provinces were given jurisdiction over "the Administration of Justice in the Province, including the Constitution, Maintenance, and Organization of Provincial Courts, both of Civil and of Criminal Jurisdiction, and including Procedure in Civil Matters in those Courts."[97] As we have seen, Parliament was empowered by section 101 to legislate with respect to a "General Court of Appeal for Canada." It was unclear whether the power to create local courts involved some power to regulate appeals from their judgments subject, at least, to Imperial statutes or orders in council. Ontario and Quebec, as successors to Upper and Lower Canada, continued to legislate in relation to appeals as of right from provincial courts to the Privy Council.[98] Imperial orders in council were passed under the Judicial Committee act of 1844 with respect to the other provinces, regu-

---

93. (1791), 31 Geo. III, c.31, s.34. Some doubt has been expressed that this section really authorized colonial limitations on the appeal as of right: see Duff C.J. in *Reference re: An Act to Amend the Supreme Court Act*, [1940] S.C.R. 49, at 65; Jowitt L.C. in *A.G. for Ont.* v. *A.G. for Canada*, [1947] A.C. 127, at 145 (P.C.). But the terms of the section seem reasonably clear and the Privy Council has assumed the validity of limitations enacted under it: see *Re Louis Marois* (1862), 15 Moo. P.C. 189, 15 E.R. 465; *Nadan* v. *The King*, [1926] A.C. 482, at 493.
94. 34 Geo. III, c.6, s.30 (1794) (L.C.); 34 Geo. III, c.2, s.36 (1794) (U.C.).
95. *Cuvillier* v. *Aylwin* (1832), 2 Knapp's P.C. 72, 12 E.R. 406 (P.C.).
96. *Re Louis Marois, supra* note 93; *Cushing* v. *Dupuy* (1880), 5 App. Cas. 409 (P.C.).
97. 30–31 Vict., c.3, s.92 (14).
98. After Confederation Ontario and Quebec would have to justify their legislation under section 92 (14), "The Administration of Justice in the Province. . . . " In *Reference re: An Act to Amend the Supreme Court Act, supra* note 93, three of the judges (Duff C.J., at 57, Rinfret J., at 72, and Judson J., at 128) held that section 92 (14) did not authorize provincial limitations on appeals from provincial courts to the Privy Council. On appeal to the Privy Council in this case, *sub. nom. A.G. for Ont.* v. *A.G. for Can., supra* note 93, at 152, Lord Jowitt L.C. expressed doubts as to the

lating appeals as of right where the provinces themselves had not done so.[99] Appeals from the provincial courts by leave of the Judicial Committee were not affected. All in all, the system of appeals from provincial courts as of right or by leave gave rise to few controversies.

It was otherwise with respect to the Supreme Court of Canada. The very creation of the court was jeopardized by a controversy over the appealability of its decisions. The Act establishing the Supreme Court did not purport to interfere with appeals from provincial courts to the Judicial Committee. But with respect to appeals from the new federal tribunal, section 47 provided that "[t]he judgment of the Supreme Court shall in all cases be final and conclusive. . . . Saving any right which Her Majesty may be graciously pleased to exercise by virtue of Her Royal Prerogative."[100] The Imperial authorities threatened disallowance of the whole Act on the ground that it purported to bar appeals from the Supreme Court to the Privy Council. It was only after the Canadian government conceded that the Act did not extend to appeals by leave – the "prerogative" appeals – that London agreed to allow the Act to take effect.[101] The net result was that there were no appeals as of right from the Supreme Court of Canada to the Judicial Committee, but appeals by leave were permitted. The Committee was circumspect in granting leave to appeal from the Supreme Court. Summing up the Committee's policy in 1926, Viscount Haldane said:

In Canada there are a number of cases in which leave to appeal is granted because Canada is not a unitary state, and because it is the desire of Canada itself that the Sovereign should retain the power of exercising his prerogative; but that does not apply to internal disputes not concerned with constitutional questions, but relating to matters of fact. There the rule against giving leave to appeal from the Supreme Court of Canada is strictly observed where no great constitutional question, or questions of law, emerges.[102]

provincial power but declined to decide the question. It is submitted that, on principle, the provinces did have the power to regulate appeals from provincial courts subject to both overriding federal legislation under section 101 and, until the Statute of Westminster, overriding Imperial laws. The provincial aspect of this subject is in relation to "Administration of Justice in the Province including the Constitution, Maintenance and Organization of Provincial Courts. . . . " It does not cease to be "in the Province" merely because the appeals may be heard elsewhere. See *infra* note 108.

99. The statutes and orders in council are reproduced in Cameron, *The Canadian Constitution* (1915), at 30, 32, 145–165.
100. 38 Vict., c.11, s.47 (1875) (Can.).
101. A detailed account of the struggle may be found in Farr, *supra* note 63, chap. 5. See also Underhill, "Edward Blake, The Supreme Court Act, and the Appeal to the Privy Council, 1875–6" (1938), 19 *Can. Hist. Rev.* 245, and "Edward Blake's Interview with Lord Cairns on the Supreme Court Act, July 5, 1876," *ibid.* 292; MacKinnon, "The Establishment of the Supreme Court of Canada" (1946), 27 *Can. Hist. Rev.* 258.
102. *Hull* v. *M'Kenna*, [1926] I.R. 402, at 405.

Despite Haldane's complacent assumption concerning the "desire of Canada itself," the Parliament of that country, during the seventy-five years after the creation of the Supreme Court, passed a number of measures with the purpose of making its judgments final. In 1887 a statute was enacted purporting to abolish all appeals in criminal matters from any court in Canada to any tribunal in the United Kingdom.[103] Sir John Thompson, minister of justice, in introducing the measure indicated that he thought the bill only expressed what was already understood to be the law. It is difficult to take this suggestion seriously, but the Act appears to have passed without serious opposition.[104] This provision was carried forward as section 1025 of the Criminal Code in the Statutes of 1906,[105] and was not effectively challenged until the decision in *Nadan* v. *The King*[106] in 1926. The Judicial Committee, though it refused leave to appeal in that case, held that section 1025 was invalid and that there still existed a "prerogative" appeal in criminal cases. It was held that the Criminal Code provision was repugnant to Imperial statutes, namely, the Judicial Committee acts of 1833 and 1844 which had authorized the Crown to permit appeals in any cases from any colonial courts. By virtue of the Colonial Laws Validity Act, 1865,[107] this repugnancy made the Canadian statute void. In addition, it was held to be void on the rather questionable ground that it would have extra-territorial effect.[108]

The final chapter in the abolition of Privy Council appeals began with the passing of the Statute of Westminster, 1931.[109] This Act, as we have seen, permitted Canadian legislatures to legislate in a manner inconsistent

103. 50–51 Vict., c.50 (1887) (Can.), amended by 51 Vict., c.43 (1888) (Can.).
104. [1887] 2 Can. H.C. *Debates*, at 644–46. It is probable that this bill was introduced as a result of the appeal taken in the case of *Riel* v. *R.* (1885), 10 App. Cas. 675. Riel, the leader of the Northwest Rebellion, had been convicted of treason and his conviction was upheld by the Queen's Bench of Manitoba on appeal from the territorial court in Regina. His application for leave to appeal to the Judicial Committee was refused. This may be the "recent case" to which Sir John Thompson referred, in which Crown counsel were instructed to argue against the right of appeal but in which the appeal was dismissed on other grounds. See Can. H.C. *Debates*, *supra*, at 644. There was some impatience felt over delays in administration of criminal justice because of such appeals being taken.
105. R.S.C. 1906, c.146, s.1025.
106. [1926] A.C. 482 (P.C.).
107. 28–29 Vict., c.63, s.2. See note 17 *supra*, and accompanying text.
108. The conclusion that this was an extra-territorial measure because the Judicial Committee sat in London seems specious. Had it not been for the Imperial connection, no one would ever have suggested that the regulation of appeals and the creation of a court of final resort was not a purely local matter. The Privy Council later recognized this in *British Coal Corporation* v. *The King*, [1935] A.C. 500, at 521. The operative obstacle to termination of appeals before the Statute of Westminster was surely the problem of repugnance to the Judicial Committee Acts.
109. 22 Geo. V, c.4: See note 23 *supra*, and accompanying text.

with existing Imperial statutes. By section 3, Parliament was also empowered to legislate extra-territorially. Taking its cue, Parliament in 1933 added a section to the Criminal Code similar to the old section 1035.[110] This time, the provision cutting off appeals in all criminal cases from all courts was upheld,[111] the Judicial Committee relying on the changes effected by the Statute of Westminster, 1931. After the second world war, and after a further reference to the Judicial Committee[112] which established that Parliament had the right to terminate all appeals both civil and criminal, the last step was taken. In 1949 the Supreme Court Act was amended to prohibit appeals from any judgment of any court in Canada to the Judicial Committee. The Judicial Committee acts of 1833 and 1844 were repealed by the Canadian Parliament insofar as they applied to Canada.[113] This bond of Empire was not cut without considerable controversy[114] but there are now few who would advocate a reversion to the previous system of appeals.[115]

As a result, the Supreme Court of Canada was made what its name implied: a final court for Canadians. Henceforth, the constitution would be authoritatively interpreted on Canadian soil by those familiar with the context in which it was to operate. But would the abolition of appeals bring real independence to the Supreme Court? Would the Court be free to take bold initiatives in developing the law, or would it be bound as before by its own past decisions and those of the Imperial tribunal? These questions cannot yet be answered with assurance.

Prior to the abolition of appeals to the Privy Council, it appeared that the Supreme Court was bound by its own previous decisions, and by decisions of the Privy Council in appeals from Canada.[116] With its new status as a final appellate court, the Supreme Court should have been at liberty to reassess its attitude to stare decisis. Torn between models such as the House of Lords with its rigid adherence to precedent, and the United States Supreme Court with its candid revisionism, it might at least have been expected to abandon stare decisis in constitutional matters.[117] The

110. 23 and 24 Geo. V, c.53, s.17 (1933) (Can.).
111. *British Coal Corporation* v. *The King, supra* note 108.
112. *A.G. for Ont.* v. *A.G. for Can.*, [1947] A.C. 127 (P.C.).
113. 13 Geo. VI, c.37, s.3 (1949) (2nd sess.) (Can.).
114. See Pierson, *Canada and the Privy Council* (1960), at 69–94.
115. But see the remarks of Lord Justice Diplock, (1963), 46 *Proc. Can. Bar Assoc.* 150, at 156–57. He suggested a final court of appeal for the Commonwealth, a court which would travel on circuit.
116. For a discussion on the authorities see Joanes, "Stare Decisis in the Supreme Court of Canada" (1958), 36 *Can. B. Rev.* 175.
117. See *ibid.*, at 193–200; Laskin, "The Supreme Court of Canada: A Final Court of and for Canadians" (1951), 29 *Can. B. Rev.* 1038, at 1073.

formal rigidity of a federal constitution requires some flexibility of interpretation. This is in contrast to other areas of law where the courts can be
extricated from bad precedents by statutory change. Secondly, the constitution is not otherwise susceptible to modification in the light of changing
social and economic conditions. Judicial review provides a means of constitutional development if the courts will seize the opportunity. The Privy
Council declined to accept this positive role. One of the expectations of
those who advocated finality for Supreme Court decisions was that the
Canadian tribunal would be more capable of and disposed to perform
such a role.

While the Supreme Court, since 1949, has not openly declared itself in
favour of abandoning stare decisis, at least it has not rejected the possibility. More importantly, it has shown that it is sometimes prepared to
avoid the implications of earlier decisions, both its own and those of the
Privy Council. For example, in the 1963 decision in *Barfried Enterprises
Ltd.* v. *Attorney General for Ontario*[118] the court reached a conclusion
about the scope of the federal power over "interest" which was logically
irreconcilable with an earlier Privy Council decision.[119] In the 1966 decision of *Munro* v. *National Capital Commission*[120] it declined to ascribe
federal legislation dealing with community planning and development in
the Ottawa area to any provincial head of jurisdiction. In upholding the
legislation as a matter of "peace, order, and good government" it gave
a breadth to the clause which had long been denied it by the Privy
Council.[121] From this one may hope that the Supreme Court will fulfil the
aspirations of many; that it will display where necessary a healthy irre-
verence for the past. If the grant of final appellate authority to a
Canadian court is to be more than a mere matter of form, it should release
indigenous judicial initiatives, especially in the area of constitutional
development.

118. [1963] S.C.R. 570, 42 D.L.R. (2d) 137.
119. *A.G. for Sask.* v. *A.G. for Can.*, [1949] A.C. 110 (P.C. 1948).
120. [1966] S.C.R. 663, 57 D.L.R. (2d) 753.
121. See e.g. *In re Board of Commerce Act, 1919*, [1922] 1 A.C. 191 (P.C. 1921);
Toronto Electric Commissioners v. *Snider*, [1925] A.C. 396 (P.C.); *A.G. for Can.*
v. *A.G. for Ont.* (Labour Conventions case), [1937] A.C. 326 (P.C.).

CHAPTER TWO

Nature of the Power of Judicial Review: The Conflicting Principles

In *British Columbia Power Corporation* v. *British Columbia Electric Company et al.* the late Chief Justice Kerwin stated:

In a federal system, where legislative authority is divided, as are also the prerogatives of the Crown, as between the Dominion and the Provinces, it is my view that it is not open to the Crown, either in right of Canada or of a Province, to claim a Crown immunity based upon an interest in certain property, where its very interest in that property depends completely and solely on the validity of the legislation which it has itself passed, if there is a reasonable doubt as to whether such legislation is constitutionally valid. To permit it to do so would be to enable it, by the assertion of rights claimed under legislation which is beyond its powers, *to achieve the same results as if the legislation were valid.* In a federal system it appears to me that, in such circumstances, the Court has the same jurisdiction to preserve assets whose title is dependent on the validity of the legislation as it has to determine the validity of the legislation itself.[1]

This statement once again raises certain basic questions concerning the rights of the courts to review the validity of legislation. These questions arise out of a conflict in two frequently asserted principles: the supremacy of Parliament, on the one hand, and the "inherent right and duty" of the courts to enforce constitutional limitations on the other hand. In the *B.C. Power* case, the Supreme Court of Canada, in the passage quoted, came down in favour of the latter principle. The provincial Crown could not, they said, by asserting an immunity from judicial review of impugned legislation *"achieve the same results as if the legislation were valid."*

The claims of parliamentary sovereignty in Canada are nevertheless

1. [1962] S.C.R. 642, at 644–45; 34 D.L.R. (2d) 196, at 275–76: Emphasis added. For a further discussion of this case see *infra* chapter four.

strong. The preamble of the British North America Act, 1867, states the intention to create a union "with a constitution similar in Principle to that of the United Kingdom. . . ." In the constitution of the United Kingdom, Parliament has been supreme in law since it became supreme in fact, in the seventeenth century. It declared its supremacy as early as 1642,[2] and the Bill of Rights, 1688, was certainly predicated on that supremacy when it stated that "the freedom of Speech, and debates or proceedings in parliament ought not to be impeached or questioned in any court or place out of parliament."[3] Here Parliament firmly limited the jurisdiction of the courts in one important aspect.

In Dicey's classical formulation of the supremacy of Parliament, the jurisdiction of the courts was always subject to limitation by Parliament and certainly did not include the power to determine the validity of legislation. "English judges do not claim or exercise any power to repeal a Statute, whilst Acts of Parliament may override and constantly do override the law of the judges. Judicial legislation is, in short, subordinate legislation, carried on with the assent and subject to the supervision of Parliament."[4] According to Dicey, one of the "traits of Parliamentary sovereignty as it exists in England" was "the non-existence of any judicial or other authority having the right to nullify an Act of Parliament, or to treat it as void or unconstitutional."[5]

It has more recently been thought that Dicey went too far in his assertion that parliamentary power was without limit, at least where matters affecting the Treaty of Union with Scotland[6] might be involved. That Treaty may have placed some limitations on the Parliament of the United Kingdom, creating a "fundamental law" which could prevent Parliament from enacting certain types of legislation.[7] But even the Scottish Court of Session was unwilling to assert in 1953 that it had jurisdiction to determine whether official action conflicted with this "fundamental law." At issue in the case of *MacCormick* v. *Lord Advocate* was the right of Her Majesty to use the numeral II in her title of "Queen Elizabeth II." The petitioners sought to interdict the publication pursuant to Act of Parliament of a proclamation entitling the sovereign in this fashion. It was alleged, *inter alia*,

2. See McIlwain, *The High Court of Parliament and its Supremacy* (1910), at 336–46, 389–90.
3. 1 Wm. III and Mary, 2nd sess., c.2, preamble, *The Subjects' Rights*, no. 9.
4. Dicey, *Introduction to the Study of the Law of the Constitution* (10th ed., 1959), at 60–61.
5. *Ibid.*, at 91.
6. See Union with Scotland Act, 1706, 5 Anne c.8 (Eng.).
7. See e.g., Mitchell, "Sovereignty of Parliament: Yet Again" (1963), 79 *L.Q. Rev.* 196, at 202–06. But see Gough, *Fundamental Law in English Constitutional History* (1955), at 179–80.

NATURE OF THE POWER

that the use of the numeral II would be a violation of the Treaty of Union. The Lord President (Lords Carmont and Russell concurring) expressed the view that neither a Scottish nor an English court could entertain proceedings to determine whether there had been a breach of the fundamental law. To the question whether such an issue "is determinable as a justiciable issue in the Courts of either Scotland or England, in the same fashion as an issue of constitutional *vires* would be cognisable by the Supreme Courts of the United States, or of South Africa or Australia"[8] a negative answer was given.

It is therefore necessary to question the assumption, as exemplified in Chief Justice Kerwin's statement previously quoted, that because there may be some limits placed on Parliament's power the courts are empowered to enforce those limitations. This conclusion does not necessarily follow.[9] Apart from the position under the constitution of the United Kingdom where the courts apparently have no such jurisdiction, one can find examples in federal states where the courts have no jurisdiction to declare void a statute overstepping the division of powers between national and local government.[10]

What then are the arguments in support of the judicial review of legislation in Canada? In the former colonial system, it seems to have been assumed that Her Majesty's colonial courts had a duty to enforce the restrictions imposed by Imperial statute. The Imperial law officers in 1861 stated the proposition in this manner. "The powers of the Colonial Legislature being conferred by Act of the Imperial Parliament, and limited by the same enactment, and so, valid or invalid, as they keep within or transgress the prescribed limits, the Supreme Court of South Australia is, in our opinion, bound (and certainly at liberty) to satisfy itself of the legal validity of any Act of the Colonial Legislature, the provisions of which it is called upon to administer."[11] (In that situation there was no suggestion that the local legislature had attempted to limit the power of the court in this regard.) A similar view was propounded in *obiter* by Lord Selborne in an 1878 Privy Council decision.

The Indian Legislature has powers expressly limited by the Act of the Imperial Parliament which created it, and it can, of course, do nothing beyond the limits which circumscribe these powers. . . . The established courts of Justice, when a question arises whether the prescribed limits have been exceeded, must of

---

8. [1953] Sess. Case 396, at 412–13.
9. See Mitchell, *supra* note 7, at 197.
10. See e.g. Wheare, *Federal Government* (4th ed., 1963), at 17, 64–65.
11. Quoted in Keith, *Responsible Government in the Dominions* (1912), Vol. I, at 405. See also Todd, *Parliamentary Government in the British Colonies*, (2nd ed., 1894), at 301–02.

necessity determine that question; and the only way in which they can properly do so, is by looking to the terms of the instrument by which, affirmatively, the legislative powers were created, and by which, negatively, they were restricted.[12]

This statement was approved by the Supreme Court of Canada in the following year.[13]

This view of the power of colonial courts in relation to colonial legislation needed to be reconciled with the theories of parliamentary sovereignty previously mentioned. Dicey, the great expounder of parliamentary sovereignty, argued that in a federal state the various legislatures were essentially the same as joint stock companies, limited in their power by the Charter which created them. Speaking of the situation in the United States and Canada he said "Congress and the London, Chatham, and Dover Railway are in truth each of them nothing more than subordinate law making bodies. Their power differs not in degree, but in kind, from the authority of the sovereign Parliament of the United Kingdom."[14] From this it followed, according to Dicey, that just as a court could quash a company bylaw if ultra vires, so it could set aside an invalid statute in a federal state. Dicey was not alone in comparing legislatures of limited powers to corporations. Baron Parke, in *Kielley* v. *Carson*[15] in 1842, had stated that it was no more possible to imply a power of the Newfoundland legislature to commit for a contempt perpetrated outside the legislature than it would be to imply a power in a company to commit for contempt.[16] Lord Watson, in the famous *Local Prohibition* case in 1896, held, *inter alia*, that the power of the Parliament of Canada to "regulate" trade did not include the power to prohibit trade.[17] In coming to this conclusion he relied solely on the authority of *City of Toronto* v. *Virgo*,[18] a Privy Council decision of the previous year, which dealt solely with the powers of a municipal corporation to pass bylaws pursuant to its statutory authority to regulate a trade. Lord Watson imposed the same restrictive interpretation on the legislative power of the Parliament of Canada as had been

12. *R.* v. *Burah* (1878), 3 App. Cas. 889, at 904–05 (P.C.). Approved in *James* v. *Commonwealth*, [1936] A.C. 578, at 613 (P.C.). See also *Harris* v. *Minister of Interior*, [1952] 2 So. Afr. L.R. 428 (Sup. Ct.); *Minister of Interior* v. *Harris*, [1952] 4 So. Afr. L.R. 769, at 779 (Sup. Ct.).
13. *Valin* v. *Langlois* (1880), 3 S.C.R. 1, at 17–18 (1879).
14. Dicey, "Federal Government" (1885), 1 *L.Q. Rev.* 80, at 85. See also Dicey, *supra*, note 4, at 150–51.
15. (1842), 4 Moo. P.C. 63; 13 E.R. 225 (P.C.).
16. 4 Moo. P.C., at 89; 13 E.R., at 235.
17. [1896] A.C. 348, at 363 (P.C.).
18. [1896] A.C. 88 (P.C. 1895).

imposed on the bylaw making power of the city of Toronto. Over a generation later Street, in his authoritative work *The Doctrine of Ultra Vires*, similarly compared such legislatures to corporations and concluded that "whenever powers have been exceeded, it is the business of the Courts to restrict them."[19]

Essential to this analogy with ordinary corporate action is the assumption that the courts must necessarily recognize and enforce any limitations on the exercise of legislative power. Another way of expressing this is to say that the courts must apply not only part of the law, but the whole of the law relevant to any case coming before them. If there are relevant constitutional limitations, these are part of the law which must be taken into account. Dicey, drawing on American practice and experience, said that "the American judge must in giving judgment obey the terms of the constitution, just as his English brother must in giving judgment obey every Act of Parliament bearing on the case."[20] He then proceeded to generalize from the situation in the United States and to conclude that this is a feature essential to all federal states. At least one Canadian judge expressly followed American decisions in coming to a similar conclusion. Chief Justice Meredith of the Quebec Superior Court in *Langlois* v. *Valin*[21] in 1879, was faced with an argument that the courts must give effect to any statute coming before them if its unconstitutionality was not pleaded. After referring with approval to Chief Justice Marshall's judgment in *Marbury* v. *Madison*,[22] he dismissed this argument in the following terms: "To me it seems plain that a statute, emanating from a legislature not having power to pass it, is not law; and that it is as much the duty of a judge to disregard the provisions of such a statute, as it is his duty to obey the law of the land."[23]

While one may accept this kind of reasoning up to a point, there are reasons for limiting in some measure these general statements on the right and obligation of judicial review of legislation. The governments created by the BNA Act were something more than municipal corporations or joint stock companies. This was made clear by the Privy Council with respect to provincial legislatures (and at least as much can be said for the Parliament of Canada) in *Hodge* v. *The Queen* in 1883. It was argued in that case, *inter alia*, that a provincial legislature had no power to delegate

19. Street, *The Doctrine of Ultra Vires* (1930), at 416–17.
20. Dicey, *supra* note 4, at 159.
21. (1879), 5 Que. L.R. 1; *Aff'd* (1880), 3 S.C.R. 1 (1879); *Leave to appeal refused* (1879), 5 App. Cas. 115 (P.C.).
22. (1803), 1 Cranch 137; 5 U.S. 87.
23. 5 Que. L.R., at 17.

the law-making authority to a municipal agency. The maxim *delagatus non potest delegare* was relied on. In refuting this, Sir Barnes Peacock, in his judgment, said of the provincial legislatures that

they are in no sense delegates of or acting under any mandate from the Imperial Parliament. When the British North America Act enacted that there should be a legislature for Ontario, and that its legislative assembly should have exclusive authority to make laws for the Province and for provincial purposes in relation to the matters enumerated in sect. 92, it conferred powers not in any sense to be exercised by delegation from or as agents of the Imperial Parliament, but authority as plenary and as ample within the limits prescribed by sec. 92 as the Imperial Parliament in the plenitude of its power possessed and could bestow.[24]

From this it may be seen that the Canadian legislatures were given a genuinely sovereign legislative power, and that certain restrictive rules suitable for the interpretation of municipal or corporate bylaws were not readily applicable.

A more fundamental limitation on the "inherent right" of judicial review may be seen in the express words of the BNA Act. Section 92 of the Act provides in part as follows:

92. In each Province the Legislature may exclusively make Laws in relation to Matters coming within the Classes of Subjects next hereinafter enumerated. . . .

    14. The Administration of Justice in the Province, including the Constitution, Maintenance, and Organization of Provincial Courts, both of Civil and of Criminal Jurisdiction, and including Procedure in Civil Matters in those Courts.

Section 101 provides that

101. The Parliament of Canada may, notwithstanding anything in this Act, from time to time, provide for the Constitution, Maintenance, and Organization of a General Court of Appeal for Canada, and for the Establishment of any additional Courts for the better Administration of the Laws of Canada.

These sections seemingly put the very existence of the courts, and their jurisdiction, at the mercy of the legislative branch of both levels of government. Parliament and the provincial legislatures are surely distinguishable in this manner from joint stock companies or municipal corporations. These latter bodies have no power to regulate the courts which might be called on to review their bylaws. Parliament and the legislatures, it would seem, might preclude or limit judicial review of their own legislation. If, for example, Parliament gave exclusive jurisdiction in constitutional matters to a new "Constitutional Court," could it not validly prevent the

24. (1883), 9 App. Cas. 117, at 132 (P.C.). See also *Liquidators of the Maritime Bank* v. *Receiver General of New Brunswick*, [1892] A.C. 437, at 441–43 (P.C.).

Supreme Court or the Exchequer Court from hearing cases involving the constitutional validity of statutes?

As previously noted, Dicey and others have supported their case for the inherent right of judicial review in Canada by reference to principles and practices of judicial review in the United States. The analogy is far from perfect. The constitution of the United States specifically guarantees the existence of, and confers certain jurisdiction on, the federal judiciary. Article III states:

1. The judicial Power of the United States shall be vested in one supreme court, and in such inferior Courts as the Congress may from time to time ordain and establish. . . .
2. The judicial powers shall extend to all Cases, in Law and Equity, arising under this Constitution. . . .

Thus the creation of the Supreme Court was in effect required by the constitution, and wherever federal courts were created they were to exercise the "judicial power" which would extend to all cases "arising under this Constitution." In the seminal case of *Marbury* v. *Madison* Chief Justice Marshall, while stressing the logical necessity of courts enforcing constitutional limitations wherever a written constitution may be found, also relied on these specific provisions of the American constitution.

The judicial power of the United States is extended to all cases arising under the constitution. Could it be the intention of those who gave this power, to say, that in using it, the constitution should not be looked into? That a case arising under the constitution should be decided, without examining the instrument under which it arises? This is too extravagant to be maintained. In some cases, then, the constitution must be looked into by the judges. And if they can open it at all what part of it are they forbidden to read or to obey?[25]

Similarly, Article VI imposes like obligations on the state judiciary where it provides that:

this Constitution . . . shall be the supreme Law of the Land; and the Judges in every State shall be bound thereby, any Thing in the Constitution or Laws of any State to the Contrary notwithstanding.

Here again, the state judges are bound to apply constitutional limitations and no legislature can interfere with their power to do so.

These specific guarantees of judicial review are reinforced by the concept of separation of powers which pervades American constitutional law at both the federal and the state level. By this concept, the judicial branch is considered to be co-ordinate with the legislative and executive branches of government. The courts are not superior to the other branches but on

25. 1 Cranch at 178–79; 5 U.S., at 112.

occasion they must, in a case properly before them, refuse to give effect to actions of the other branches of government when these conflict with the constitution. This is a function which cannot be denied the courts by the legislature or executive. This situation is in contrast to that under the constitution of the United Kingdom where Parliament is considered to be supreme, where the executive holds office only so long as it has the confidence of the House of Commons, and where the courts have only such jurisdiction as Parliament confers on them.

It is submitted that the Canadian constitution embodies these principles of the United Kingdom constitution except where they have been modified expressly or implicitly by the BNA Act. It is further submitted that the latter statute does not guarantee the judicial power of review to the extent that the American constitution does. Sections 92(14) and 101 give to the provincial legislatures and Parliament, respectively, complete power to legislate for the "Constitution, Maintenance, and Organization" of provincial and federal courts. These provisions must surely permit a fairly extensive regulation of the jurisdiction of such courts in all matters.

It has been suggested by some that the BNA Act does guarantee a judicial power not unlike that referred to in Article III of the United States constitution. In *Ottawa Valley Power Company et al.* v. *Hydro-Electric Power Commission et al.*[26] the Ontario Court of Appeal was considering the validity of a statutory provision which prohibited any action being taken against the defendant Commission with respect to certain contracts. The contracts in question had been declared invalid by the provincial legislature. It was held that this declaration was ultra vires as involving civil rights outside the province. In addition, Fisher J. A. stated in *obiter* that the effect of the prohibition against these contractual actions, involving, as they might, certain constitutional issues was

to take away from the Supreme Court one at least of the essential characteristics of a Superior Court. The British North America Act does not, it is true, guarantee the continued existence of the Superior Court in each of the Provinces. But it is quite clear that both secs. 96 and 127 [*sic*] are founded upon an unwritten guarantee of the continuance of the Superior Courts in the Provinces. To alter the essential character of the Supreme Court as a Superior Court in any vital particular, is contrary to the spirit of the British North America Act, and tantamount to an unauthorized repeal of that Statute in that respect.[27]

---

26. [1937] O.R. 297, [1936] 4 D.L.R. 594 (Ont. C.A.) *reversing* [1937] O.R. 265, [1936] 3 D.L.R. 468 (Ont. H.C.).
27. [1937] O.R. 333, [1936] 4 D.L.R. 594. See also *Independent Order of Foresters* v. *Lethbridge Northern Irrigation District*, [1938] 2 W.W.R. 194, at 211, [1938] 3 D.L.R. 89, at 102–03 (Alta. Sup. Ct. App. Div.), *affirming* [1937] 3 W.W.R. 424, [1937] 4 D.L.R. 398 (Alta. Sup. Ct. Trial Div.).

Dean Lederman has taken up this argument and elaborated it. He asserts that sections 96 to 101 of the BNA Act disclose an intention to reproduce provincial and federal superior courts "in the image of the English central royal courts."[28] From this assumption he proceeds to the conclusion that, just as the central royal courts had the jurisdiction to supervise the exercise of powers by other public officers and agencies, so it must be presumed that Canadian superior courts were guaranteed a similar jurisdiction including the supervision of the various legislatures.[29]

This argument is questionable. It ignores the basic fact that the jurisdiction of the "central royal courts" was subject to limitation by Parliament. Parliament could and still can prevent judicial review of the actions of public officers or agencies.[30] Moreover, the "central royal courts" never had the power to review acts of Parliament for validity, in spite of the pretensions of Coke and others.[31] It is therefore impossible to imply an inviolable right of judicial review in Canadian superior courts on the basis that this is an inherent characteristic of "superior courts."

From the foregoing it is apparent that there is no simple explanation for the phenomenon of judicial review of legislation. It should first be conceded that constitutional limitations on legislative power imply, in the absence of some conflicting principle, a judicial power to enforce these limitations. The BNA Act was obviously intended to create a federal form of government, with necessary limitations on legislative power at each level. The Act must be interpreted to give effect to this intention except where a contrary intention appears. As judicial review was well known in the Imperial system at the time of Confederation it is fair to assume that this was looked upon as at least a possible means of enforcing the divisions of legislative power. Thus the courts should normally be allowed to determine constitutional validity of legislation lest, as Chief Justice Kerwin said, the legislature be allowed "to achieve the same results as if the legislation were valid."[32] Judicial review is to be preferred as a practical matter as well because experience has shown that it represents one of the most effective means of making a federal constitution work.[33]

It is submitted, however, that the right of judicial review is not in all respects absolute, that there are occasionally conflicting principles which

28. Lederman, "The Independence of the Judiciary" (1956), 34 *Can. B. Rev.* 769 (Part I), 1139 (Part II), at 1160, 1175.
29. *Ibid.*, at 1174–75, 1176–77.
30. See e.g. *Smith* v. *East Elloe R.D.C.*, [1956] A.C. 736 (H. of L.).
31. See *Dr. Bonham's Case* (1610), 8 Co. Rep. 113, at 118a; 77 E.R. 646, at 652 (K.B.). See also *supra* at 3–4.
32. *Supra* note 1.
33. See McWhinney, *Judicial Review in the English Speaking World* (3rd. ed., 1965), at 14–15.

may support some limitation on the jurisdiction of the courts to test legislative validity. The BNA Act in no place specifically provides for judicial review nor does it specifically guarantee the jurisdiction of the courts in this regard. There may be an implication in favour of judicial review, but that implication can be taken no farther than the needs of the BNA Act demand, and it must be subject to limitations both expressed and implied in the Act. For example, express limitations arise out of the grants of power to Parliament and the legislatures, in sections 101 and 92(14) respectively, to regulate the "Constitution, Maintenance, and Organization" of the courts, while implied limitations may be found in the fact that the BNA Act created quasi-sovereign legislative bodies and executives which were to exercise the Crown prerogatives.[34]

We must as a result avoid easy generalizations and ascertain to what extent the BNA Act requires and protects judicial review. In order to do this it is necessary to examine various legislative and non-legislative attempts to limit judicial review, and the judicial reaction to these attempts. This will be undertaken in chapters three and four.

34. See case cited *supra* note 24.

CHAPTER THREE

Legislative Limitations
on the Power of Review

It has been shown in the preceding chapter that there are competing principles involved wherever Canadian legislative bodies seek to limit the power of judicial review. On the one hand, there is clearly power in Parliament and the legislatures to govern the constitution and jurisdiction of the courts, to deny rights to citizens, or to impose restrictions on access to the courts. On the other hand, these powers cannot be exercised in such a way as to prevent all judicial review and thus facilitate the violation of the constitution.

In other words, legislative bodies may not, in the guise of legislating with respect to matters otherwise within their jurisdiction, in essence legislate so as to exceed their jurisdiction and prevent the courts from reviewing their actions. This is only a particular application of the general rule against colourability: legislation which on its face appears valid may be found invalid if its essential object and effect is to deal with some matter beyond the jurisdiction of the enacting legislature.[1]

The colourability rule, though easily formulated, is difficult to apply. This chapter will deal in detail with the principal types of limitations on judicial review imposed by the legislatures. With respect to each it will be necessary to examine how far the legislative body may go in imposing limitations before it runs afoul of the rule against colourable legislation.

PROCEDURAL REQUIREMENTS

The most common procedural prerequisite to judicial review is the service of notice on the appropriate attorney general advising him of an impending attack on the validity of a particular piece of legislation.

1. See e.g. *Madden* v. *Nelson and Fort Sheppard Ry.*, [1899] A.C. 626 (P.C.); *A.G. for Ont.* v. *Reciprocal Insurers*, [1924] A.C. 328 (P.C.); *Canadian Federation of Agriculture* v. *A.G. for Que.*, [1951] A.C. 179 (P.C. 1950); Laskin, *Canadian Constitutional Law* (3rd. ed., 1966), at 190–91.

The importance of government participation in constitutional litigation became apparent almost as soon as judicial review began in the Anglo-American legal world. In 1727 in *Winthrop* v. *Lechmere*, the first recorded appeal from the American colonies involving validity of a colonial statute, the Privy Council held a Connecticut intestacy law to be invalid. The soundness of this decision was seriously questioned as it held, in effect, that a colonial legislature had no power to alter in the colony the rule of primogeniture which applied, under English law, in England. *Winthrop* v. *Lechmere* was a purely private piece of litigation, but the effects of it in Connecticut were far-reaching. When twenty years later the validity of a similar law was about to be considered by the Privy Council in the case of *Clark* v. *Tousey*, the Connecticut legislature voted to lend Tousey £500 to assist him in employing good counsel to present the case for the statute. Consequently an opposite result from that in *Winthrop* v. *Lechmere* was obtained and the statute was upheld.[2]

In Canada, *Russell* v. *The Queen*[3] is a leading example of an early decision which upheld Dominion legislation without participation of any provincial attorney general in the proceedings. The appellant had been convicted at Fredericton, New Brunswick, under the Canada Temperance Act, 1878. He sought certiorari to quash the conviction, contending that the Act was ultra vires of Parliament on the grounds that it was legislation in relation to property and civil rights in the province, matters of a local or private nature, or licensing (all of these matters being within provincial jurisdiction under section 92 of the British North America Act). The Privy Council upheld the validity of the Canada Temperance Act, and the decision was subsequently[4] understood to mean that this law was within the federal power to legislate for the "peace, order, and good government of Canada" as provided by the opening words of section 91. This was one of the most important and controversial decisions ever rendered in the interpretation of the BNA Act, and it was rendered in a proceeding between a private prosecutor and an accused person. Neither the Attorney General of Canada nor the attorney general of any province was represented. There was some subsequent feeling that the decision might have been otherwise had one or more of the provinces been heard,[5] though in

2. See McGovney, "The British Origin of Judicial Review of Legislation" (1944–45), 93 *U.Pa. L.Rev.* 1.
3. (1882), 7 App. Cas. 829 (P.C.).
4. In the case of *A.G. for Ont.* v. *A.G. for Can.* (local prohibition), [1896] A.C. 348, at 362 (P.C.).
5. This seems to be the implication of Lord Watson's comments in *A.G. for Ont.* v. *A.G. for Can.*, [1896] A.C. 348, at 362 (P.C.). See also *In re Board of Commerce* (1920), 60 S.C.R. 456, at 507–08, 54 D.L.R. 354, at 391; *Re Natural Products Marketing Act*, [1936] S.C.R. 398, at 420, [1936] 3 D.L.R., at 638–39.

fairness it must be noted that the counsel leading the attack on the federal legislation was no less a personage than J. P. Benjamin, Q.C., former attorney general of the Confederate States.

It is probably no coincidence that machinery was introduced in Canada soon thereafter to ensure that the appropriate attorneys general would be notified of, and permitted to appear in, constitutional litigation. Legislation to this end was passed in Quebec in 1882,[6] Ontario in 1883,[7] and subsequently in all other provinces except Newfoundland, Prince Edward Island, and Nova Scotia.

One of the broadest[8] of the current statutory provisions in this regard is section 8 of The Constitutional Questions Act[9] of Saskatchewan.

8. (1) Where in any court in Saskatchewan the constitutional validity of any Act or enactment of the Parliament of Canada or of the Legislature or the validity of any order in council is brought in question, the same shall not be adjudged to be invalid until after notice has been given to the Attorney General of Canada, or the Attorney General of Saskatchewan, as the case may be.

(2) The notice shall state what Act or part of an Act or what order in council or part thereof is in question, and the day on which the question is to be argued, and shall give such other particulars as are necessary to show the constitutional point proposed to be argued.

(3) The notice shall be served six days before the day named for the argument.

(4) The Attorney General of Canada and the Attorney General of Saskatchewan shall be entitled, as of right, to be heard, either in person or by counsel, notwithstanding that the Crown is not a party to the action or proceeding in which the question arises.

Three aspects are of particular interest at this point. First, it will be noted that this procedure is to apply with respect to a challenge to the validity of any legislation, whether federal or provincial. Secondly, it applies to proceedings in any court in the province, no matter what the nature of the proceedings before the court. Thirdly, it purports to prevent any adjudication of invalidity unless the requirement of notice has been complied with, no matter what the views of the court may be on the validity of a statute before it.

Four other common law provinces – Alberta, British Columbia, Manitoba, and Ontario[10] – have basically similar statutes though they do not

6. 45 Vict., c.4, s.1 (Que.).
7. 46 Vict., c.6, s.6 (Ont.).
8. Similar statutes in the other common law provinces do not require notice where orders in council are attacked.
9. R.S.S. 1965, c.86. See Appendix C.
10. R.S.A. 1955, c.164, s.31; R.S.B.C. 1960, c. 72, s.10; R.S.M. 1954, c.52, s.72; R.S.O. 1960, c.197, s.33.

require notice where only an order in council is attacked.[11] The New Brunswick statute[12] applies only to proceedings where the validity of a provincial statute is in question. It makes no reference to attacks on federal legislation nor does it provide for any notice to the attorney general of Canada. It requires the court to make the provincial attorney general a party where provincial legislation is impugned, but no sanction, such as a prohibition against an adjudication of invalidity in the absence of compliance with the section, is imposed.

In Quebec, article 95 of the Code of Civil Procedure as revised in 1965[13] applies to attacks on federal or provincial legislation and federal or provincial orders in council, in any provincial court, though it does not specifically prohibit an adjudication where notice to the attorney general has not been given. Article 95 merely provides that "the constitutionality of any statute of the province or of Canada . . . cannot be put in question before the courts of this province . . . " unless the notice has been given. But it also provides that the party giving notice must set out the grounds on which he relies "which will be the only grounds upon which the court can adjudicate." What would the position of the court be where invalidity was patent but had not been pleaded because the notice requirement was not met or the notice did not raise the particular grounds which would justify a finding of invalidity? It is possible that the court might still feel able, or even bound, to adjudicate upon the validity of the statute.[14]

While there is no comparable federal statute, the rules of the Supreme Court of Canada have, since 1905, provided for notice to the attorney general where the validity of a statute is challenged. Formerly the rules required such notice only to the attorney general of Canada where a federal statute was involved, and only to that attorney general and the attorney general of the particular province where a provincial statute was questioned.[15] The rule is now somewhat broader:

Rule 18: Where the validity of a Statute of the Parliament of Canada or a Statute of a Legislature of a Province of Canada is brought in question in an appeal, a notice of such appeal, stating the matter of jurisdiction raised, shall be served on the Attorney General of Canada and the Attorney General of all the Provinces within twenty days of the service of the notice of appeal required

---

11. Notice in such cases may nevertheless be desirable. See *Charter Airways Ltd.* v. *A.G. for Canada* (1955), 17 W.W.R. (n.s.) 129 (Alta. Sup. Ct., App. Div.).
12. R.S.N.B. 1952, c.120, s.24.
13. Stats. Que. 1965, c.80.
14. See *Langlois* v. *Valin* (1879), 5 Que. L.R. 1 (Sup. Ct.); Scott, Note (1966), 12 *McGill L.J.* 136. But cf. *Street* v. *Ottawa Valley Power Co.* (1938), 65 Que. K.B. 504, at 509, aff'd. [1940] S.C.R. 40, [1939] 4 D.L.R. 574.
15. *Supreme Court Rules*, 1945, rules 18 and 19 as originally promulgated.

by the the Act. Such notice shall further provide that if an Attorney General desires to intervene application for such purpose shall be made at a time stated in the notice and such time so stated shall be a time fixed by the Chief Justice or a judge upon a previous *ex parte* application for such purpose.[16]

It will be noted that the rule does not purport to deny the court jurisdiction on the constitutional issue where such notice is not given, though presumably the court would refuse to proceed with the hearing until notice was effected.

The relevant legislation in Alberta, British Columbia, Manitoba, and Saskatchewan apparently does not make the attorney general who appears in response to the notice a party to the action in which the constitutional issue is raised. Nor does rule 18 of the Rules of the Supreme Court of Canada do this; it merely permits the attorney general to apply to intervene. It has been held that in this type of procedure notice does not make the attorney general or the Crown a party to the action,[17] and the court is not thereby entitled to award any substantive relief against the Crown which it could not otherwise have granted in the absence of notice and appearance.[18] Thus such immunity from suit as the Crown may enjoy as part of the Crown prerogative is not destroyed by a statutory provision for notice and appearance. Also, when the attorney general appears in this way as intervener or even as a party to argue the constitutional question alone, it is not customary to award costs against him. The New Brunswick statute specifically requires that the attorney general be made a party, but it also prohibits the awarding of costs for or against the Crown and appears to limit the Crown's participation to the constitutional question alone. The Ontario statute, amended in 1959, now provides that where the attorney general (federal or provincial) appears in such proceedings, he "shall be deemed to be a party to the action or proceeding for the purpose of an appeal from any adjudication as to the constitutional validity of any Act or enactment in question in the action or proceeding and each has the same rights with respect to an appeal as any other party to the action or proceeding."[19] The effect of this is not entirely clear, but it would appear that the attorney general would be a party for a very limited purpose only. He would be entitled as a party to initiate an appeal whereas as

---

16. *Supreme Court Rules*, 1945, rule 18 as amended, effective January 2, 1961.
17. *Florence Mining Co. Ltd.* v. *Cobalt Lake Mining Co. Ltd.* (1909), 18 O.L.R. 275, at 284 (Ont. C.A.); *Aff'd* on other grounds (1918), 43 O.L.R. 474 (P.C.) (1910). *Beauharnois Light, Heat & Power et al.* v. *Hydro-Electric Power Commission*, [1937] O.R. 796, at 823, [1937] 3 D.L.R. 458, at 463 (Ont. C.A.).
18. *Florence Mining* case, *ibid*.
19. R.S.O. 1960, c.197, s.33 (5), including the amendment made by Stats. Ont. 1959, c.47, s.1.

a mere intervener he could not.[20] No remedy could be given against the Crown which would not otherwise be available apart from this section, however. Although the Ontario section says nothing about costs, one would assume that the courts would refrain from awarding costs for or against the attorney general in such proceedings in accordance with the general practice prior to the amendment of the section.

The former Quebec provision, article 114 of the Code of Civil Procedure which was replaced in 1965, did not expressly make the attorney General a party but the effect seemed to be the same as that of the Ontario statute. Article 114 provided that, where the attorney general intervened, "the judgment of the Court must mention such intervention and such conclusions on which it renders judgment *as if the Attorney General were a party to the suit*."[21] It was held in *Attorney General for Quebec* v. *Bérubé and the Attorney General for Canada*[22] that an attorney general who intervened pursuant to this article was in a position analogous to an ordinary party and could maintain the proceedings by himself even if the original parties of like interest withdrew. The Supreme Court of Canada in fact held that such an intervention by an attorney general in Quebec created a *lis* between himself and the party attacking the legislation. In *Switzman* v. *Elbling*[23] the provincial attorney general intervened pursuant to article 114 because the validity of the so-called "Padlock Act"[24] was in question. The plaintiff landlord had commenced action against the defendant tenant to have his lease set aside and to claim damages, on the grounds that the leased premises had been used for purposes prohibited by the statute. The defendant as part of his defence challenged the validity of the Act and served notice on the attorney general. The plaintiff succeeded in the trial and appellate courts in Quebec. When the defendant appellant reached the Supreme Court of Canada with his appeal it was argued that there was no *lis inter partes* before the court because the term of the original lease had, in the meantime, expired. It was said that the appellant therefore had no interest to assert before the Supreme Court. The plaintiff-respondent in fact took no part in the appeal. Chief Justice Kerwin disposed of this objection by holding that the intervention of the attorney general of Quebec raised an issue between him and the appellant as to the constitutionality

20. *A.G. for Alta.* v. *Kazakewich*, [1937] S.C.R. 427, [1937] 3 D.L.R. 574.
21. Emphasis added.
22. [1945] Que. K.B. 77, [1945] 4 D.L.R. 306, *aff'd* without reference to the point in [1945] S.C.R. 600, [1945] 4 D.L.R. 326.
23. [1957] S.C.R. 285.
24. An Act to Protect the Province against Communistic Propaganda, R.S.Q. 1941, c.52.

of the statute. This issue was enough to permit the court to hear the appeal.[25]

The new Code of Civil Procedure appears to achieve the same result by simpler means. Article 492 provides that "the Attorney-General may, *ex officio*, appeal from a final judgment rendered in an action raising a ground of public order, as if he were a party to the action." It apparently does not matter whether the attorney general has received notice or has intervened below, so far as his right of appeal is concerned.

Statutory requirements of notice have been strictly applied in several cases, and courts have refused to consider or decide the question of constitutionality where notice has not been given.[26] The decision in *Mohr* v. *North American Life Assurance* is particularly significant, because the proceedings therein arose under a federal statute and the impugned legislation was an amendment to that statute. The Saskatchewan Court of Appeal concluded, however, that because no notice had been served on the attorney general as required by provincial law "this Court is therefore precluded from holding that the amendment is invalid under the provisions of this [Constitutional Questions] Act."[27] In other words, provincial law prevented a superior court, in a proceeding under a federal statute, from examining that federal statute for constitutional validity.

For the notice requirements to be applicable, there must be a genuine and relevant constitutional question raised. Thus, where the court can find that the impugned statute is inapplicable to the subject matter before the court, notice is not required, as the constitutional question can be avoided.[28] Similarly, where a plaintiff can make out his case otherwise without reliance on an impugned statute, notice and a constitutional determination are unnecessary.[29] It must also be noted that these requirements only apply where the constitutionality of a statute or (in Saskatchewan

---

25. *Supra* note 23, at 286–87.
26. E.g. *McLeod* v. *Security Trust Co.*, [1940] 1 W.W.R. 423, [1940] 2 D.L.R. 697 (Alta. Sup. Ct., Trial Div.); *Mohr* v. *North American Life Assurance*, [1941] 1 W.W.R. 15, [1941] 1 D.L.R. 427 (Sask. C.A.); *Pelletier* v. *Imperial Oil Limited*, [1941] 2 W.W.R. 75 (Sask. D.C.).
27. *Ibid.*, [1941] 1 W.W.R. at 19, [1941] 1 D.L.R. at 431.
28. *Goring* v. *London Mutual Fire Insurance Company* (1886), 11 O.R. 82 (Ont. High Ct.). This particular decision is questionable because, in the circumstances, the determination as to the inapplicability of the impugned federal statute was based on certain constitutional principles, hence it could be argued that a constitutional question was involved. See also *Saumure* v. *Building Materials Joint Committee*, [1943] Que. K.B. 426, at 434–35; *McKay* v. *The Queen*, [1965] S.C.R. 798, 53 D.L.R. (2d) 532.
29. *Placatka* v. *Thompson*, [1941] 1 W.W.R. 528, [1941] 2 D.L.R. 320 (Alta. Sup. Ct., App. Div.).

and Quebec) of an order in council is in question. Other constitutional issues, such as the validity of a municipal bylaw, are not affected.[30]

From the foregoing it may be seen that judicial review of legislation by provincial courts has been restricted to some extent by provincial legislation. To the extent that the Supreme Court rules accomplish the same purpose – that is, facilitating government participation in constitutional litigation – they are self-imposed by the Court and do not raise an absolute bar to adjudication. But in the face of assertions, previously referred to, of the inherent right of judicial review in a federal state, how can one justify the provincial statutes which prevent provincial courts from considering constitutional validity where notice to the attorney general is not given? This question seems to have gone unanswered by the courts so far.

The constitutional basis for provincial notice requirements must be found in section 92 (14) of the BNA Act giving the provinces jurisdiction, it will be recalled, over "the Administration of Justice in the Province, including the Constitution, Maintenance, and Organization of Provincial Courts, both of Civil and of Criminal Jurisdiction, and including Procedure in Civil Matters in those Courts." If one looks at the notice requirement as a limitation on the jurisdiction of the courts, this probably can be justified as a matter of "constitution" or "organization." If one looks upon it as a procedural matter only (and perhaps this is all it is under the New Brunswick legislation, at least where there is no express prohibition against constitutional adjudication in the absence of notice) it could be justified, in civil actions, as "procedure in civil matters."

These justifications are probably adequate where the proceeding before the provincial court is itself one over which the province has jurisdiction. This would include most civil actions (being matters of "property and civil rights in the province") or prosecutions for violations of provincial statutes ("the imposition of punishment . . . for enforcing any law of the province . . . " under section 92 (15)). Serious doubts might be raised, however, about the validity of the provincial notice requirement where the provincial court is involved in a proceeding essentially within federal jurisdiction. Parliament can confer jurisdiction on provincial courts with respect to matters within federal legislative competence,[31] and can also regulate procedure in relation to these matters. In such proceedings can the provincial legislature still limit the jurisdiction of its courts? For example, in the case of *Mohr* v. *North American Life Assurance* the Sas-

---

30. *Poole* v. *Tomlinson* (1957), 21 W.W.R. (n.s.) 511, 118 C.C.C. 384 (Sask. Q.B.).
31. *Valin* v. *Langlois* (1879), 5 App. Cas. 115 (P.C.); *In re Vancini* (1904), 34 S.C.R. 621.

katchewan Court of Appeal was entertaining an appeal from an application made under the Farmers' Creditors Arrangement Act, 1934,[32] a federal statute previously held to be within Parliament's jurisdiction over "bankruptcy and insolvency."[33] As previously noted, the Court refused to consider the constitutional attack on a certain relevant section of the Act, because no notice had been served on the attorney general as required by provincial law. It is submitted that where a court is exercising a jurisdiction conferred on it expressly or impliedly by a federal statute, provincial limitations on its jurisdiction are irrelevant. This is particularly obvious in the field of criminal law, where the courts are created by the province but have their jurisdiction in criminal matters very closely defined by the federal Criminal Code. Parliament is apparently able to effect this definition through its jurisdiction over "procedure in criminal matters" pursuant to section 91 (27) of the BNA Act. Parliament also has a paramount authority over the jurisdiction of provincial courts dealing with other federal matters.[34] If Parliament assigns to a provincial court the duty of applying certain federal laws, must not the court apply the "whole law" taken in the context of constitutional limitations? If so, when provincial statutes, of which The Constitutional Questions Act of Saskatchewan is typical, provide that: "where *in any court in Saskatchewan* the constitutional validity of any Act . . . of the Parliament of Canada or of the Legislature . . . is brought in question, the same shall not be adjudged to be invalid until after notice has been given . . ."[35] they may cut too wide a swath. To the extent that they purport to limit the jurisdiction of a court in a proceeding under a federal statute, they may be invalid.

A question remains whether these requirements of notice to the attorney general can ever be reconciled with general principles of judicial review. When properly applied, notice requirements can act as a bar to an adjudication by a court on the constitutional validity of a statute involved in proceedings before it. If one takes an absolute approach to judicial review, and argues that the courts must always be entitled to review because they are "superior courts" or because they must apply the "whole law," or because they are operating in a federal system, such limitations on adjudication should be held invalid. It is submitted, however, that such an approach is unjustified. These procedural limitations are a legitimate exercise of the grant of power to the provinces to create and regulate the jurisdiction of their courts, at least in proceedings involving substantive

32. 24–25 Geo. V, c.53, (1934) (Can.).
33. *A.G. for B.C.* v. *A.G. for Canada*, [1937] A.C. 391 (P.C.).
34. See Laskin, *Canadian Constitutional Law* (3rd ed., 1966), at 831–33.
35. *Supra* note 9. Emphasis added.

questions within the provincial sphere. This is the power which justifies the provincial requirements of notice to the attorney general as a condition precedent to constitutional adjudication. Similarly, Parliament in the exercise of its jurisdiction over federal courts and the criminal law, and incidentally to the regulation of other federal matters, could introduce similar restrictions in any proceedings in federal courts or brought under federal law.

Notice requirements are not colourable devices essentially directed to the prevention of judicial review. The practical effect of these requirements must surely be to facilitate rather than to hamper the functioning of a federal system. They do not operate as an absolute bar to adjudication, but merely create conditions precedent with which it is not difficult to comply. They ensure that the appropriate governments have an opportunity to be represented so that the constitutional issues may be thoroughly canvassed by those having a continuing concern and interest with respect to the validity of legislation. The desirability of notice to the attorney general has been judicially recognized even where not strictly required by statute.[36] The notice procedure has advantages over a system where constitutional decisions with far-reaching consequence may be made in litigation between private parties, sometimes in share-holders' or other similar actions where the conflict between the parties is more apparent than real.[37] Although the notice requirements may on occasion limit the right of judicial review, they thereby achieve the fundamental objective of making the courts effective agents in the operation and supervision of the federal structure.

"PRIVATIVE CLAUSES" EXCLUDING JUDICIAL REVIEW

Another type of statutory limitation on judicial review has appeared in legislation establishing various administrative tribunals or agencies. It is not uncommon for these statutes to contain a "privative clause" which purports to limit or prohibit review by the courts of administrative decisions. The significance and effect of these clauses in administrative law have been extensively discussed by others,[38] and need not be explained

36. *Charter Airways Ltd.* v. *A.G. for Can.* (1955), 17 W.W.R. (n.s.) 129, 1 D.L.R. (2d) 110 (Alta. Sup. Ct., App. Div.).
37. See e.g. Grant, "Judicial Review in Canada: Procedural Aspects" (1964), 42 *Can.B.Rev.* 195, at 214–21. And see *Union Colliery Co.* v. *Bryden*, [1899] A.C. 580, at 584 (P.C.).
38. E.g. Laskin, "Certiorari to Labour Boards: The Apparent Futility of Privative Clauses" (1952), 30 *Can.B.Rev.* 986; Millward, "Judicial Review of Administrative Authorities in Canada" (1961), 39 *Can.B.Rev.* 351.

further at this point. But their special implication for judicial review of legislation should be noted.

A typical privative clause may provide that: "there shall be no appeal from an order or decision of the board under this Act, and its proceedings, orders and decisions shall not be reviewable by any court of law or by any *certiorari, mandamus*, prohibition, injunction or other proceeding whatever."[39] While privative clauses may contain one or more of a variety of elements,[40] the two elements relevant for present purposes may be seen here. The section quoted purports to prevent any appeal from a labour relations board and also prohibits the use of *certiorari* or any other remedy to bring the correctness of a board decision into question before a court. What then if the decision of the board involved a determination as to the constitutional scope of the board's jurisdiction? If a provincial labour relations board held, for example, that its statute authorized it to regulate employees of interprovincial bus companies, could this decision be protected from judicial review so that the validity of the statute, as applied to these proceedings, could not be challenged?

The refusal of the courts to give effect to privative clauses is notorious.[41] The courts have in general held that privative clauses are no bar to judicial review where the board has exceeded, or refused properly to exercise, its jurisdiction. The rationale of this principle is far from clear, with at least two possibilities being suggested at various times.

Some judges appear to take the view that the right of judicial review of administrative action is to be presumed unless the legislature has clearly excluded it.[42] The difficulty with this approach is that the legislature has usually expressed itself quite emphatically in favour of excluding judicial review but the courts have nevertheless persisted in exercising jurisdiction. If the review of decisions in such circumstances were really dependent on the presumption in favour of this judicial power or the presumption in favour of the right of access of the citizen to the courts, then the courts should decline to act in the face of a clear privative clause. The proper and traditional application of these presumptions may be seen in *Smith* v. *East Elloe R.D.C.*[43] where the House of Lords, in 1956, gave effect to a privative clause. The East Elloe Rural District Council had made a

39. The Trade Union Act, R.S.S. 1965, c.287, s.20, as amended by Stats. Sask. 1966, c.83, s.12.
40. Comment (1952), 30 *Can.B.Rev.* 69.
41. See articles cited *supra* note 38. And see Strayer, "The Concept of Jurisdiction in Review of Labour Relations Board Decisions" (1963), 28 *Sask.B.Rev.* 157.
42. E.g. *Toronto Newspaper Guild* v. *Globe Printing Company*, [1953] 2 S.C.R. 18 at 38, [1953] 3 D.L.R. 561 at 581.
43. [1956] A.C. 736 (H. of L.).

compulsory purchase order with respect to certain of Smith's land, pursuant to the Acquisition of Land (Authorization Procedure) Act, 1946.[44] Paragraph 16 of part IV of schedule I to the Act provided that, except for review by procedures specified in the schedule, "a compulsory purchase order . . . shall not . . . be questioned in any legal proceedings whatsoever. . . ." Smith did not attack the order by the means and within the time specified by the schedule, but instead later commenced an action for damages, for an injunction, and for a declaration that the order was invalid on the grounds that it was allegedly made in bad faith. It was argued that paragraph 16 could not be deemed to apply where an order was made in bad faith. In support of this it was argued that it cannot be assumed that the legislature intended to oust the jurisdiction of the Courts, except where clear words are employed. Various cases were cited to support this proposition. Viscount Simonds, after referring to these contentions said:

I do not refer in detail to these authorities only because it appears to me that they do not override the first of all principles of construction, *that plain words must be given their plain meaning*. There is nothing ambiguous about paragraph 16; there is no alternative construction that can be given to it; there is in fact no justification for the introduction of limiting words such as 'if made in good faith', and there is the less reason for doing so when those words would have the effect of depriving the express words 'in any legal proceedings whatsoever' of their full meaning and content.[45]

Lord Morton of Henryton and Lord Radcliffe gave similar judgments.

The effectiveness of privative clauses in England has since been statutorily diminished,[46] but it is submitted that the *East Elloe* case represents the correct use of the relevant canons of statutory interpretation. The presumption in favour of judicial review can be applied only in the absence of clear words to the contrary. Upon re-examination of the privative clause earlier quoted[47] one is struck by the seemingly plain meaning of phrases such as " . . . its . . . orders . . . shall not be reviewable by any court of law or by any *certiorari, mandamus*, prohibition, injunction or other proceeding whatever." Yet the courts have managed to find such words inapplicable where defects of jurisdiction are alleged against an administrative tribunal.[48] This judicial ignoring of express legislative directions cannot be defended on the basis of any canon of statutory interpretation.

The courts may be implicitly applying some real or imagined constitutional guarantee of judicial review in ignoring the attempts of the legislatures to make final the decisions of tribunals. This would be a very

44. 9 & 10 Geo. VI, c.49.
45. *Supra* note 43, at 751: emphasis added.
46. Tribunals and Inquiries Act, 1958, 6 & 7 Eliz. II, c.66, s.11(1).
47. *Supra* note 39, and accompanying text.
48. *Supra* note 38.

different basis for review – that the courts need not confine themselves to seeking the intention of the legislature but may override the wishes of the legislature and review administrative acts by virtue of a constitutional grant of power for that purpose. If this is the premise on which some courts ignore privative clauses, they should so state and explain the basis of their power. This they have not done in any clear and emphatic way.

Yet they have sometimes referred to an (ill-defined) constitutional right of the citizen to access to the courts, at least to challenge the jurisdictional decisions of administrative tribunals. Mr. Justice Rand hinted at it in *Toronto Newspaper Guild* v. *Globe Printing Company* when he said that the court could review such decisions in spite of a privative clause. "Any other view would mean that the legislature intended to authorize the tribunal to act as it pleased, subject only to legislative supervision: but that is within neither our theory of legislation *nor the provisions of our constitution.*"[49] What the precise "provisions" were, he did not specify. Other judicial decisions are inexplicable, however, unless one assumes the existence of a constitutional principle authorizing judicial review in spite of privative clauses. For example, in *Town of Dauphin* v. *Director of Public Welfare*[50] the Manitoba Court of Appeal upheld the right to grant certiorari where there was an express statutory provision excluding this remedy. Section 682 of the Criminal Code of Canada had been made applicable to appeals from the decision of a juvenile court judge acting under a provincial statute. Section 682 provided in effect that no order of such a judge should be "removed by *certiorari* . . . where the defendant appeared and pleaded and an appeal might have been taken, but the defendant did not appeal." In this case the Town, against which an order had been made, failed to commence an appeal within the required time. It then sought certiorari. The Court of Appeal apparently adopted the reasoning of the trial judge that certiorari would always issue "notwithstanding any statutory provisions to the contrary. . . ." There could be no justification here for applying the canon of interpretation in favour of judicial review, because the statute in express terms prohibited the use of certiorari. In fact, this canon of interpretation, if it is based on the presumption that there is to be recourse to the courts except where clearly excluded, is not even relevant. Here the Town was given a right of access to the courts, through an appeal procedure which it did not use. Thus the Manitoba Court of Appeal could not have been applying rules of statutory interpretation, but instead must have been relying on some inarticulate constitutional principle.

Dean Lederman has provided one possible basis for a constitutional

49. [1953] 2 S.C.R., at 28, [1953] 3 D.L.R., at 522: emphasis added.
50. (1956), 19 W.W.R. (n.s.) 97, 5 D.L.R. (2d) 275.

guarantee of judicial review in spite of privative clauses. In his view,[51] both federal and provincial superior courts have a constitutionally protected jurisdiction similar to that of the "English central royal courts" which enjoyed the power of supervision over public officials by means of the prerogative writs. According to him, when the Act referred to "superior courts" it implicitly guaranteed to such courts the jurisdiction of the English superior courts. As mentioned in chapter two, this theory may be questioned on the grounds that, in the context of the BNA Act, Parliament and the legislatures were empowered to legislate with respect to the "Constitution, Maintenance, and Organization . . ." of the superior courts. This legislative power could well include the right to limit the jurisdiction of the courts in the same way that the United Kingdom Parliament may on occasion exclude the jurisdiction of the English courts in certain matters.[52]

This lingering conflict over the suggested constitutional guarantee of judicial review has recently been brought to a head in the British Columbia case of *Farrell* v. *Workmen's Compensation Board*. Farrell had died suddenly while at work, and his widow subsequently applied to the Board for compensation. The Board refused to pay compensation on the grounds that death did not occur as the result of an "accident arising out of and in the course of . . . employment" as required by the Workmen's Compensation Act.[53] Mrs. Farrell then applied for mandamus and certiorari against the Board, alleging *inter alia* that it had erred in law in its interpretation of this requirement. Section 76 of the Act provided that board decisions should be final, that there should be no review in any court by any proceeding whatsoever:

and without restricting the generality of the foregoing the Board shall have exclusive jurisdiction to inquire into, hear, and determine:

(a) The question whether an injury has arisen out of or in the course of an employment within the scope of this Part.

The applicant contended that section 76 was ultra vires of the provincial legislature (and would be ultra vires of the Parliament of Canada) because it deprived claimants of an inherent constitutional right under the BNA Act to have recourse to the courts for the determination of questions of law. She also contended that section 76 was invalid because it represented an attempt by a provincial legislature to establish a tribunal with a jurisdiction analogous to that of a court provided for by section 96 of the BNA Act, a court whose judges must be appointed by the governor general.

---

51. Lederman, "The Independence of the Judiciary" (1956), 34 *Can.B.Rev.* 769 (Part I), 1139 (Part II), at 1160, 1175.
52. See e.g. *Smith* v. *East Elloe R.D.C., supra* note 43.
53. R.S.B.C. 1948, c.370, s.7.

In the Supreme Court of British Columbia Mr. Justice Manson accepted these arguments with approval. In the main he appears to have found a clear constitutional right of access to the courts. This may be seen in the following passages from his judgment:

Sec. 76 in so far as it purports to deprive a claimant of a right to resort to the courts on points of law violates a principle which has run through our law from time immemorial. It is part of the spirit of *Magna Carta* that subjects of the sovereign shall have the opportunity of having their rights, both criminal and civil, determined by the courts. . . .[54]

Acts of Parliament and of legislatures are not sacrosanct – not even in our democratic system. The right of the subject to have his rights determined by a court of law is, in my view, more sacred than an Act of a legislature. It is said that Parliament is supreme. That is too wide a statement. Both Parliament and legislatures can only legislate within the limits prescribed by our constitution.[55]

The learned justice also suggested that, even assuming the validity of section 76, it was not specific enough to override the presumption in favour of the subject's right of access to the courts.[56] He then proceeded to hold the section invalid on other grounds as well: for conflict with section 96 of the BNA Act, because it made the Workmen's Compensation Board "a judicial tribunal analogous to a Superior Court. . . ."[57]

In the Court of Appeal, the constitutional validity of section 76 was upheld. The argument based on section 96 of the BNA Act was generally dismissed on the basis that the type of jurisdiction exercised by the Board was not analogous to that of a superior court. The Board dealt only with issues between a claimant and itself: the compensation it awarded came out of its own funds.[58] Davey J.A. alone appears to have dealt specifically with the argument based on an alleged inherent constitutional right of judicial review. He could find no such right:

In my opinion, generally people ought to be permitted to have recourse ultimately to the traditional courts of law to determine substantial questions of law upon which their rights rest, and there seem to be some plausible arguments supported by occasional dicta to support that view. However, so far as policy is concerned that is for the legislature, not judges, to decide, and so far as law is concerned the current of authority upholding legislation such as sec. 76 is so strong that only the Supreme Court of Canada can reverse it.[59]

The Supreme Court of Canada, however, declined to reverse this "current of authority." On appeal to that body Mrs. Farrell abandoned the

54. (1960), 31 W.W.R. (n.s.) 577, at 581, 24 D.L.R. (2d) 272, at 276 (B.C. Sup. Ct.)
55. 31 W.W.R. (n.s.), at 582, 24 D.L.R. (2d), at 277.
56. 31 W.W.R. (n.s.), at 583–86, 24 D.L.R. (2d), at 278–80.
57. 31 W.W.R. (n.s.), at 589, D.L.R. (2d), at 283.
58. (1960), 33 W.W.R. (n.s.), 433, at 440–42, 449, 453, 26 D.L.R. (2d) 185, at 192–94, 200–01, 203–04 (B.C.C.A.).
59. 33 W.W.R. (n.s.), at 440, 26 D.L.R. (2d), at 192.

constitutional argument based on section 96 of the BNA Act, but maintained the other argument based on the right of access to the courts.[60] In elaborating this argument the appellant referred to the preamble of the Act which expresses the desire of Canada to have "a Constitution similar in principle to that of the United Kingdom." Various dicta of Duff and Cannon JJ. in the *Reference re: Alberta Legislation*[61] were quoted with respect to the alleged guarantee of free speech implicit in these words. From this it was argued that the preamble also implied the guarantee of the rule of law in Canada, safe from any legislative (or at least provincial) interference. For a definition of the rule of law Dicey was relied on, in particular his assertion that under that rule "every man, whatever be his rank or condition, is subject to the ordinary law of the realm and amenable to the jurisdiction of the ordinary tribunals."[62] On this basis the appellant drew the following conclusion:

Thus in 1867, by virtue of the B.N.A. Act, Canadians acquired a Bill of Rights, rights which can not now be infringed by Parliament or the Provinces. We in Canada do possess a written constitution. We *do* possess inalienable rights. Legislation which trenches upon those rights is unconstitutional, and it is unconstitutional because it warps the whole fabric of the constitution itself. Section 76 (1), trenching as it does upon the Rule of Law, and infringing as it does the right of the subject to enforce the Rule of Law, violates our constitution and is ultra vires Parliament and the Provinces.[63]

The Supreme Court of Canada, in a brief judgment written by Mr. Justice Judson, rejected this argument. After noting that the argument based on section 96 of the BNA Act had been abandoned and that "it is very questionable whether there could be any profitable argument on this point . . ." Mr. Justice Judson concluded as follows:

If an argument based upon s. 96 of the *British North America Act* is untenable, the other argument based upon right of access to the courts falls with it. Its rejection as far as this Board is concerned is implicit in the judgments in the *Dominion Canners* case and in the *Alcyon* case. The restrictions on the legislative power of the province to confer jurisdiction on boards must be derived by implication from the provisions of s. 96 of the *British North America Act*. Short of an infringement of this section, if the legislation is otherwise within the provincial power, there is no constitutional rule against the enactment of s. 76(1).[64]

From this decision, particularly in the context of the argument placed before the court, it would appear that the Supreme Court is not prepared

60. Appellant's factum, at 29–39.
61. [1938] S.C.R. 100, [1938] 2 D.L.R. 81.
62. Appellant's factum, at 36.
63. *Ibid.*, at 38.
64. [1962] S.C.R. 48, at 52, 31 D.L.R. (2nd) 177, at 181.

to recognize any general constitutional right of access to the courts. As a general rule, then, it may be said that neither Parliament nor the provincial legislatures are constitutionally precluded from preventing judicial review of the decisions of other public agencies.

One qualification of this general rule may be found in the limitation on provincial legislative power arising out of section 96 of the BNA Act. The authorities on the extent of this limitation are numerous and need not be explored further here.[65] Generally speaking it may be said that for a provincial tribunal to be invalidated because it has been given a jurisdiction intended by section 96 for federally appointed judges, it must exercise a judicial function and its jurisdiction must broadly conform to that exercised by superior, district, or county courts.[66] To come within the latter condition, the tribunal would have to be dealing with something in the nature of a suit between parties, where the interests of these particular parties were the sole concern of the tribunal.[67] Thus most provincial administrative tribunals escape the limitations implied in section 96 because they either are not required to act judicially or they are not truly dealing with a *lis inter partes*.[68] While they may have to decide questions of law from time to time, they may be given an exclusive jurisdiction to do this within the context of what are generally functions not contemplated by section 96.[69] The qualifications on provincial powers arising out of section 96 should therefore not pose any serious threat to privative clauses.

There may, however, be another more important principle which does in some cases guarantee the right of access to the courts for the review of administrative action. Implicit in the constitution is the principle that neither Parliament nor the legislatures can exercise their jurisdiction with respect to the "constitution, maintenance, and organization" of the courts in a colourable way so as to defeat the other limitations placed on their

65. E.g. *Reference re The Adoption Act*, [1938] S.C.R. 398, [1938] 3 D.L.R. 497. *Labour Relations Board for Sask.* v. *John East Iron Works Ltd.*, [1949] A.C. 134, [1948] 4 D.L.R. 673; *Dupont* v. *Inglis*, [1958] S.C.R. 535, 14 D.L.R. (2nd) 417; *A.G. for Ont.* v. *Victoria Medical Building Limited*, [1960] S.C.R. 32, 21 D.L.R. (2nd) 97; *Brooks* v. *Pavlick*, [1964] S.C.R. 108, 42 D.L.R. (2nd) 572, also Willis, "Section 96 of the British North America Act" (1940), 18 *Can.B.Rev.* 517; Laskin, "Municipal Tax Assessment and Section 96 of the British North America Act" (1955), 33 *Can.B.Rev.* 993.
66. *Labour Relations Board* case, *ibid.*
67. *Ibid.*; and see *Dupont* v. *Inglis*, *supra* note 65.
68. *Labour Relations Board* case and *Dupont* case, *supra* note 65; *Farrell* case, *supra*, note 64; Comment (1963), 41 *Can. B. Rev.* 446.
69. *Farrell* v. *Workman's Compensation Board*, [1962] S.C.R. 48, at 51, 31 D.L.R. (2nd) 177, at 179; *Quebec Labour Relations Board* v. *Burlington Mills Hosiery*, [1964] S.C.R. 342, at 347, 45 D.L.R. (2d) 730, at 737–38. *Contra R.* v. *Ontario Labour Relations Board, ex parte Ontario Food Terminal Board* (1963), 38 D.L.R. 530 (Ont. C.A.).

authority by the BNA Act. Where this would be the effect of the privative clause, it can be ignored to the extent required to give effect to this principle.

It was this principle, in another context, to which the late Chief Justice Kerwin was probably referring in the *B.C. Power* case where he said that the legislature could not, by trying to prevent judicial review of legislation, "achieve the same results as if the legislation were valid."[70] In the end the court must be able to intervene to prevent the actual exercise of power under a statute which it was beyond the jurisdiction of the legislature to enact.

In the context of administrative tribunals and privative clauses, the principle would mean that in some circumstances the privative clause would have to be ignored in order, for example, to prevent a provincial tribunal from exercising jurisdiction in a federal field. To take a common situation: provincial labour relations boards occasionally have to determine whether certain persons are in the employ of an industry within provincial or within federal jurisdiction.[71] Where there is no dispute over the identity of the employer or the contract of employment the decision whether the enterprise is within provincial or federal jurisdiction would almost certainly be one of constitutional law. If the board makes a wrong decision in favour of its own jurisdiction and then attempts to exercise that jurisdiction, it would seem that the courts should be able to intervene at some stage. Otherwise, the province would be allowed to exercise an authority which it was never given.

There will remain certain lingering problems in this formulation, however. Where does one draw the line between purely constitutional decisions, subject to judicial review, and other non-reviewable decisions, which may nevertheless have consequences of constitutional significance? For example, suppose the hypothetical labour relations board must decide whether certain persons who seek certification are employed by a parent company admittedly engaged in interprovincial transport or a subsidiary company which is admittedly engaged in intraprovincial transport. The Supreme Court of Canada has said that the power to decide who is the employer may be conferred exclusively on a provincial board, because "employment is a question of fact and depends upon contract."[72] If the

70. [1962] S.C.R. 642, at 645, 34 D.L.R. (2nd) 274, at 276. See *supra* at 29.
71. See e.g., *Pronto Uranium Mines Ltd.* v. *Ontario Labour Relations Board*, [1956] O.R. 862, 5 D.L.R. (2nd) 342 (Ont. H.C.); *R.* v. *Ontario Labour Relations Board, ex parte Dunn* (1963), 39 D.L.R. 346 (Ont. H.C.). *Re Armstrong Transport and Ontario Labour Relations Board* (1963), 42 D.L.R. 217 (Ont. H.C.).
72. *Labour Relations Board* v. *Traders Service Ltd.*, [1958] S.C.R. 672, at 678, (1959), 15 D.L.R. (2nd) 305, at 321.

board decides that the applicants are employed by the subsidiary company, it will proceed to apply the provincial statute to them. Suppose also that the parent company asserts that the employees are actually in its employ, and that the provincial statute cannot validly apply to it or to its employees. Suppose further that the statute purports to protect the board's decisions from review on any grounds, including jurisdictional grounds. How far should a court go in these circumstances in overriding the privative clause in order to preserve the constitutional limitations on the power of the province and its tribunals?

One could say, as did the Supreme Court of the United States in *Crowell v. Benson*, that where constitutional rights are involved there must be an opportunity for a judicial, as opposed to an administrative, determination of all facts upon which the existence of the right may depend.[73] Chief Justice Hughes, in delivering the opinion of the court, held that the federal court must have a right to ascertain for itself whether a claimant under the Longshoreman's and Harbor Workers' Compensation Act had in fact suffered accidental injury in employment upon navigable waters of the United States. If the injury was not suffered in such employment the federal statute could not validly require compensation for him. The finding of the employer-employee relationship by the deputy commissioner of the United States Employees' Compensation Commission could not be regarded as final as this would deprive the federal courts of part of the judicial function entrusted to them by the Constitution. Mr. Justice Brandeis, in his dissenting opinion, took issue with this assumption that there must be a judicial determination of so-called "constitutional facts" in order to decide whether the administrative tribunal has acted within a constitutionally limited jurisdiction. With reference to the finding of the deputy commissioner, he said that "the existence of a relation of employment is a question going to the applicability of the substantive law, not to the jurisdiction of the tribunal. Jurisdiction is the power to adjudicate between the parties concerning the subject-matter."[74]

Professor Jaffe has more recently criticized the view that a finding of "jurisdictional fact" must inevitably be open to judicial review *de novo*:

[A] finding is an assertion that a phenomenon has existed, does exist, or will exist. The finding stands for the fact. It is not the fact itself. Its function is to provide an acceptable basis for the exercise of power. It is based upon a reasoned inference from evidence. A court cannot any more than any other human agency break down the barrier between appearance and reality. In short, the

---

73. (1932), 285 U.S. 22, at 54–61.
74. *Ibid.*, at 85.

court can be wrong. If the validity of an exercise of power is to depend on the absolute existence of a fact there can be no exercise of power.[75]

He points out, however, that in many cases a judicial determination may provide a better means of deciding certain matters. He favours considerations such as these instead of the more abstract concept of "jurisdictional fact" in any delineation of the proper scope of judicial review.

Canadian courts might well consider the points of view expressed by Mr. Justice Brandeis and Professor Jaffe. They should not automatically assume, when a tribunal's decision is attacked on constitutional grounds, that the court must independently make all findings upon which the constitutional right must depend. They should recognize that certain matters pertain only to application of the law, based on findings of fact which are best left to the tribunal. In the hypothetical problem referred to above, the decision of the board as to who is the employer should be respected, because this is a matter of industrial relations best suited for the board. On the other hand, any decision by the board that any particular employer is carrying on a business within federal jurisdiction is a matter going beyond the particular expertise of the board and is one which the courts could properly decide de novo. It is at this point that the court should step in and disregard any privative clause. They must enforce the constitutional limitations to prevent, for example, a provincial tribunal from exercising authority over a business which, or a person who, is not, as a matter of constitutional law, subject to provincial jurisdiction. But beyond this they should not go. "Jurisdiction," said Mr. Justice Brandeis, "is the power to adjudicate between the parties concerning the subject matter." Our courts should look to see if the person against whom the provincial board's order is made can be subject to provincial control. If so, the court should not go further to see if the board has properly applied provincial law in this particular case.

In summary, it may be said that Parliament and the legislatures may exclude judicial review of administrative decisions except where review is necessary to prevent a colourable overstepping of constitutional limitations. To avoid judicial review the legislature must be very explicit, more explicit in fact than the courts have found most Canadian statutes to be. But, assuming a completely explicit statute barring judicial review, it is now clear that there is no constitutional right of review save the one mentioned. It is only where the refusal to review would enable a government or legislature to exercise a jurisdiction denied it by the constitution that the courts should override such a privative clause.

75. Jaffe, "Judicial Review: Constitutional and Jurisdictional Fact" (1957), 70 *Harv. L. Rev.* 953, at 966.

EXCLUSION OF JUDICIAL REVIEW THROUGH STATUTORY DENIAL OF A RIGHT OF ACTION

Other attempts have been made occasionally to prevent judicial review of legislation, through limiting or abolishing the right of action in which the constitutional point might have been raised. Such attempts involve the same issues as privative clauses, and, where challenged, have universally failed. Examples of this device are almost all to be found in provincial legislation. The provinces, through purported exercise of their jurisdiction over "administration of justice in the province, including the constitution, maintenance, and organization of provincial courts . . . including procedure in civil matters," and over "property and civil rights in the province" have interfered with substantive rights not within their jurisdiction and then have proceeded to bar the enforcement of those rights in provincial courts. If such legislation had been given full effect, the courts might have been prevented from determining whether these substantive rights had been validly abrogated by the provincial legislation. The courts have refused to give such scope to provincial power under these heads of jurisdiction.

The most wide-sweeping formulation of the judicial position may be seen in *Ottawa Valley Power Company* v. *The Hydro-Electric Power Commission*.[76] The Ontario Power Commission Act[77] of 1927 provided, in sub-section 4 of section 6, that: "(4) Without the consent of the Attorney General, no action shall be brought against the Commission or against any member thereof for anything done or omitted in the exercise of his office." By the Power Commission Act, 1935, section 2, it was declared that certain contracts between the defendant Commission and the plaintiff Company were illegal, void, and unenforceable against the Commission.[78] This statute went on to state: "3. No action or other proceeding shall be brought, maintained or proceeded with against the said Commission founded upon any contract by this Act declared to be void and unenforceable, or arising out of the performance or non-performance of any of the terms of the said contracts." The Company brought action against the Commission and other defendants asking *inter alia* for a declaration that the 1935 Act was ultra vires as interfering with civil rights outside the province, for a declaration that the contracts were valid and binding, and for the payment of money by the Commission under one of the contracts.

76. [1937] O.R. 297, [1936] 4 D.L.R. 594 (Ont. C.A.) *reversing* [1937] O.R. 265, [1936] 3 D.L.R. 468 (Ont. High Ct.).
77. R.S.O. 1927, c.57.
78. Stats. Ont. 1935, c.53.

The Commission relied on section 6(4) of the 1927 Act because no consent had been given by the attorney general thereunder, and on section 3 of the 1935 Act. At trial the action was dismissed by Rose C.J.H.C. on the basis of section 6(4) of the 1927 Act.

The Court of Appeal split three to two in favour of allowing the appeal. The majority judges, by reasoning which is far from satisfying, held section 6(4) to be inapplicable. They then proceeded to hold this section and sections 2 and 3 of the 1935 Act to be ultra vires. It was at this point that Mr. Justice Masten, speaking for himself and Mr. Justice Middleton, made the classic statement which has since found favour elsewhere.

The conclusion at which I have arrived is as follows:—(1) The general rule is clear that the administration of justice being by The British North America Act committed to the Provinces, the jurisdiction of the several Courts set up by the Legislature to administer justice is that which is prescribed by the Legislature. Generally speaking any statute passed by a Provincial Legislature limiting the jurisdiction of the Provincial Court is binding on it. (2) But to that general rule I think there is this exception, namely, that the Legislature cannot destroy, usurp, or derogate from substantive rights over which it has by the Canadian constitution no jurisdiction and then protect its action in that regard by enacting that no action can be brought in the Courts of the Province to inquire into the validity of its legislation, thus indirectly destroying the division of powers set forth in the British North America Act. In other words, it cannot by such indirect means destroy the constitution under which it was created and now exists.[79]

The other majority judge held section 2 of the 1935 Act to be invalid because it interfered, *inter alia*, with civil rights outside the province and thus could not be justified under section 92(13) of the BNA Act. It then followed that the provisions designed to prevent these rights from being enforced were also invalid.

The authority of the *Ottawa Valley* decision is weakened by the two strong dissents of Latchford and Riddell JJ. A. Both judges thought that section 6(4) of the 1927 Act clearly applied, and was valid. Mr. Justice Riddell took the view that " 'the right to bring an action is a civil right'; and, of course, the right to bring an action in an Ontario Court is a 'Civil Right in the Province'."[80]

The principles stated by Masten and Middleton JJ. A. in the *Ottawa Valley* decision have nevertheless been confirmed in several other cases. At about the same time as the *Ottawa Valley* case there was a dispute in Alberta over the validity of legislative attempts to reduce the amount of interest payable on certain provincially guaranteed securities. The first

79. [1937] O.R., at 309, [1936] 4 D.L.R., at 603.
80. [1937] O.R., at 340, [1936] 4 D.L.R., at 598.

statute[81] for this purpose reduced the interest rate thereon from six per cent to three per cent and then denied a right of action for the recovery of any higher rate in any provincial court. In *Independent Order of Foresters v. Lethbridge Northern Irrigation District*[82] this legislation was struck down as interfering with "interest," a federal matter, and with property and civil rights outside the province. New legislation was then passed, similarly reducing interest,[83] accompanied by another statute which provided that "no action . . . shall be commenced . . . in respect of any guaranteed security . . . without the consent of the Lieutenant Governor in Council."[84] This legislation was held invalid for similar reasons. With respect to the various attempts to deny the right of action, Ives J., at the first trial, said that a province could not prevent access to the courts to challenge the validity of a provincial statute, because to permit this result "is most repugnant to one's instinctive sense of justice."[85] At the second trial Ewing J. cited the *Ottawa Valley* decision with approval, and said that if the province could prevent its courts from declaring provincial laws ultra vires "then the division of powers as contained in the B.N.A. Act, 1867 is a futility."[86] On appeal[87] from the second trial, three concurring judges (Harvey C.J.A., Lunney and Shephard JJ. A.) confined their decision to holding that the restriction on access to the courts was in this case an attempt to accomplish indirectly what could not be done directly, that is, to reduce enforceable rates of interest. Only McGillivray J. A. sought broader grounds for holding invalid the denial of right of action. He relied on the *Ottawa Valley* decision and declared that if a province could avoid judicial review of its legislation in this way "then the whole scheme of Confederation may be set at naught at the will of any provincial legislature."[88] When the case reached the Privy Council that body declined to go beyond a finding that the whole scheme was an indirect attempt to invade the federal field of "interest" and thus invalid.[89]

In one further case members of the Alberta Appellate Division had the opportunity to state the broader principle of the inherent right of judicial review. In *Reference re the Validity of The Legal Proceedings Suspension Act, 1942*[90] the court held invalid a statute which purported to stay all

81. The Provincial Securities Interest Act, 1936, Stats. Alta. 1936, 2nd sess., c.11.
82. [1937] 1 W.W.R. 414, [1937] 2 D.L.R. 109 (Alta. Sup. Ct., Trial Div.).
83. Stats. Alta. 1937, c.12.
84. Stats. Alta. 1937, c.11, s.3.
85. [1937] 1 W.W.R., at 416, [1937] 2 D.L.R., at 110.
86. [1937] 3 W.W.R. 424, [1937] 4 D.L.R. 398 (Alta. Sup. Ct., Trial Div.).
87. [1938] 2 W.W.R. 194, [1938] 3 D.L.R. 89 (Alta. Sup. Ct., App. Div.).
88. [1938] 2 W.W.R., at 211, [1938] 3 D.L.R., at 102.
89. [1940] A.C. 513 (P.C.).
90. [1942] 2 W.W.R. 536, [1942] 3 D.L.R. 318 (Alta. Sup. Ct., App. Div.).

actions involving the validity of The Debt Adjustment Act, 1937, until the Privy Council had disposed of an appeal then pending from the Supreme Court of Canada on this issue. In a 3-to-2 split decision, a majority of the court said that the legislature might not "determine . . . its own legislative authority . . ." even for a short time. They found that "it is of the essence of our constitution which assigns definite and limited powers of legislation to the Legislatures that the Courts should determine whether the Legislature has exceeded these limits. . . ."[91] They also held that the effect of the legislation, if valid, would be to ignore the *Winstanley* case,[92] a previous Supreme Court of Canada decision wherein certain aspects of The Debt Adjustment Act, 1937, had already been held invalid.

From the foregoing it may be seen that two possible principles emerge for the setting aside of provincial legislation of this nature. The broader principle is based on some inherent right of the provincial courts to pass on the validity of provincial legislation. The narrower principle is that a province cannot indirectly deny rights arising under federal law or within federal jurisdiction where it could not accomplish this purpose directly. It is significant that the broader principle has been stated only by two provincial appellate courts. In only one of these cases, the *Legal Proceedings Suspension Act* decision, did a majority of the court adopt it. Not only in the *I.O.F.* case already referred to but in other cases of a similar nature, the Supreme Court of Canada and the Privy Council[93] have declined to state their grounds so broadly. The latter tribunals have consistently struck down such legislation on the simple basis that it purported to prevent the enforcement of rights granted under federal law. ·

These two possible principles arise out of two conflicting views of the scope of provincial power over the "Administration of justice . . ." and over "property and civil rights in the province" granted under heads 14 and 13 respectively of section 92 of the BNA Act. The broad principle would require that provincially created courts must be allowed to hear every case where the constitutional validity of a provincial statute might be put in issue. It is submitted that it is impossible to imply so great an exception to the express powers of regulating courts conferred on the provincial legislatures. It may well be argued that such an exception would be desirable, but there is nothing in the BNA Act or in the history of its interpretation to justify such an implication at present. The narrower principle can, on the other hand, be justified as a necessary corollary of

91. [1942] 2 W.W.R., at 540, [1942] 3 D.L.R., at 321.
92. *Atlas Lumber Company* v. *Winstanley*, [1941] S.C.R. 87, [1941] 1 D.L.R. 625.
93. *Winstanley* case, *ibid.*; *A.G. for Alberta* v. *A.G. for Can.* (*Debt Adjustment Act* case), [1943] A.C. 356, [1943] 2 D.L.R. 1 (P.C.).

the federal system and the division of legislative powers between dominion and provinces. Parliament is given jurisdiction to create certain rights, for example, with respect to "interest." If Parliament can create such rights, it can provide directly or indirectly for their enforcement. It has long been held that where a right existed under federal law and no other means of enforcement was provided, a provincial superior court was deemed to have jurisdiction to enforce it.[94] It has also long been recognized that Parliament could confer judicial duties and powers on provincial courts.[95] It would not necessarily follow that provincial courts would have an obligation to hear such cases where they were expressly prohibited from doing so by provincial law and where there was no express federal law requiring them to do so.[96] But where federal law expressly so required, it should prevail over provincial law. Here, as elsewhere, the "trenching" doctrine would permit federal law to prevail so that Parliament, in conferring certain rights pursuant to section 91 of the BNA Act, could incidentally make provision for their enforcement. To the extent necessary to accomplish this purpose Parliament "trenches" on the jurisdiction otherwise conferred on the provinces by section 92(14). If the provincial legislature were permitted to prevent this, the federal system might[97] be upset because the province would be barring the effective exercise of federal jurisdiction. This would be a colourable use of provincial power over the administration of justice.

Again we come back to the fundamental rule stated by Chief Justice Kerwin in the *B.C. Power* case that the province may not, by barring access to the courts, "achieve the same results as if the legislation were valid." In a federal system this must mean that a province must not be permitted by such means to interfere with or exercise authority over persons, businesses, or things not otherwise within the jurisdiction permitted to them under the BNA Act. It must be admitted at once that this rule will invalidate most legislative attempts under section 92(13) or (14) to bar actions involving constitutional questions. But some jurisdiction in this regard must surely remain. A legislature should be able to prevent certain provincial courts from deciding constitutional questions, as long as some (e.g. appellate) courts may do so. It may surely impose procedural limitations and other conditions precedent, at least so long as compliance with these is not impossible. It might, for example, prevent

94. *Board* v. *Board*, [1919] A.C. 956, 48 D.L.R. 13 (P.C.).
95. *Valin* v. *Langlois* (1879), 5 App. Cas. 115 (P.C.).
96. Comment (1940), 18 *Can.B.Rev.* 725.
97. *Quaere*, could Parliament not confer the necessary jurisdiction on the Exchequer Court of Canada pursuant to s.101?

provincial courts from deciding on the validity of *federal* laws as this would not in any way permit the province to exceed its own jurisdiction.

A more difficult problem arises where rights normally within a legislature's power are interfered with by legislation which is invalid for other reasons. For example, suppose property is confiscated under a provincial anti-gambling law which is subsequently held to be ultra vires because it is characterized as criminal law legislation. Could the province subsequently retain the property pursuant to a new statute which simply provided that any such property in the hands of the Crown would be considered Crown property? If there is no extra-provincial element involved, the question of title seems on its face to be a matter of "property and civil rights in the province." It is arguable that legislation giving title to the Crown in such a case would be in essence an exercise of the property and civil rights power, and not a continuation of the wrongful exercise of the criminal law power which is denied to the provinces.

Support for this approach may be found in *Vancouver Growers Limited* v. *McLenan et al*,[98] a decision of the British Columbia Court of Appeal. While the case involved an invalid federal, rather than provincial, statute, the same principle would apply. Under the federal Natural Products Marketing Act, 1934,[99] boards were appointed to regulate the marketing of certain natural products. The defendants in the *Vancouver Growers* case were members of such a board responsible for the marketing of vegetables grown in a certain area of British Columbia. The board had required the plaintiff to market its vegetables through the board, the vegetables being then sold interprovincially by the board. The plaintiff sued for money had and received by the board for the use of the plaintiff. It was contended that the board had no valid existence and that it held the money (or such portion as it had retained) illegally. In 1936, while the *Vancouver Growers* case was pending, the British Columbia legislature enacted that

no action shall be brought against any person who . . . has acted or purported to act . . . as a member of any board appointed under or pursuant to the provisions of "The Natural Products Marketing Act, 1934" of the Dominion . . . for anything done by him in good faith in the performance of his duties under either of the said Acts, and every action now pending which if it were brought hereafter would be within the scope of this section is hereby stayed.[100]

---

98. [1937] 3 W.W.R. 119, 52 B.C.R. 42 (B.C.C.A.). See also *Royal Trust Co.* v. *A.G. for Alberta*, [1936] 2 W.W.R. 337, [1936] 4 D.L.R. 98 (Alta. Sup. Ct. Trial Div.); *Re Bergethaler Waisenamt*, [1949] 1 W.W.R. 323, at 328, [1949] 1 D.L.R. 769, at 773 (Man. C.A.).
99. Stats. Can. 1934, c.57.
100. Stats. B.C. 1936, 2nd sess., c.30, s.5.

Before judgment was entered the Privy Council held, in an appeal from a reference to the Supreme Court of Canada, that the Natural Products Marketing Act, 1934, was ultra vires the Dominion.[101] The British Columbia courts followed this decision and treated the federal Act as invalid. The Court of Appeal nevertheless upheld the 1936 provincial statute as a valid defence to the plaintiff's action. The court apparently distinguished between two issues: the validity of the statute on the one hand, and the right of redress for things done under the invalid statute on the other hand.

This approach may have validity in some situations but as a general proposition it creates difficulties. If the legislature seeks by subsequent legislation to prevent redress for action taken under a law which was constitutionally invalid, this appears to be a colourable attempt, as Chief Justice Kerwin said in the *B.C. Power* case, to "achieve the same results as if the legislation were valid" originally. When the occasion arises, the *Vancouver Growers* case should be reviewed in the light of the 1956 Privy Council decision in *Commissioner for Motor Transport* v. *Antill Ranger & Co. Pty. Ltd.*,[102] on appeal from Australia. Pursuant to a motor-vehicle licensing system, the State of New South Wales had collected certain mileage charges from persons operating motor vehicles engaged in interstate trade. In 1954 the Privy Council had held the licensing system to be invalid as contravening the guarantee of freedom of interstate trade in section 92 of the Australian constitution. The New South Wales legislature passed a statute purporting to prevent any action for recovery of the sums so collected under the invalid licensing system. In the *Antill Ranger* case, this legislation was also held by the Privy Council to be invalid because it was simply another means of imposing a forbidden burden on interstate trade. It was considered to be, not a law pertaining to property or the right of action, but a law with respect to trade. This was because its only object was to validate an enactment which had itself been imposed as a trade measure.

This approach is also not without difficulty, but is preferable to that taken in the *Vancouver Growers* case. As long as the main effect of the protective legislation is indirectly to validate action which is otherwise invalid, it is a colourable overreaching of constitutional barriers.

There may nevertheless be a legitimate place for some kinds of legislation preventing redress for acts done under invalid statutes. For example, there are some federal and provincial laws which would protect a public

101. [1937] A.C. 377, [1937] 1 D.L.R. 691 (P.C.).
102. [1956] A.C. 527, [1956] 3 A11 E.R. 106 (P.C.). See also *Barton* v. *Commissioner for Motor Transport* (1957), 97 C.L.R. 633 (H.C.).

officer from personal liability with respect to acts done by him pursuant to a statute that subsequently is found to be invalid.[103] Such laws can be characterized as related to the efficient functioning of the public service and of the courts. They are not primarily designed to further projects which are constitutionally invalid or to retain ill-gotten gains for the government. They simply represent a legislative judgment that it is more important for the morale and proper functioning of public officers that they should be prepared to act under statutes they believe to be valid, without fear of personal liability should the statute subsequently prove to be invalid. It is interesting to note that the United States Supreme Court, by an extension of common law principles, has made the same judgment without the aid of a statute. It has recently held [104] that officers who arrest under a statute they reasonably believe to be valid are not civilly liable for false arrest should the statute prove to be invalid.

In considering the validity of such protective legislation in particular cases, it will be necessary to make distinctions. Legislation which protects public officers in a general way (without reference to a particular scheme the validity of which may be obviously in doubt) should normally be valid as a law in relation to the public service. However, such laws should give protection only where the public officer has acted in good faith: that is, in an honest belief in the validity of his authority. They should not be allowed to protect officers who knowingly exceed their constitutional authority. Protective laws which make governments generally immune from suit are far less justifiable. The government should be able to bear the financial risk of the invalidity of its legislation, and laws prohibiting the recovery of damages or money wrongfully collected do not seem in the normal case to be justifiable. Such legislation, if worded generally, might have more chance of success than the kind of legislation in the *Antill Ranger* case, for example, which pertained to particular sums collected on criteria related to interstate trade and thus appeared to be an extension of the legislation previously held invalid. The problem of governmental immunities in constitutional litigation will be discussed more fully in the next chapter.

It is submitted, therefore, that provincial power over the jurisdiction of, or rights of action in, provincial courts is not entirely excluded where constitutional issues are involved. The provincial legislature cannot restrict jurisdiction in such a way as to permit it colourably to accomplish

103. See e.g., The Criminal Code, Stats. Can. 1953–54, c.51, s.689; Public Authorities Protection Act, *R.S.O.* 1960, c.318, s.13; The Proceedings Against the Crown Act, R.S.S. 1965, c.87, s.5(7); Magistrate's Privileges Act, R.S.Q. 1964, c. 25, ss.6,7.
104. *Pierson* v. *Ray* (1967), 386 U.S. 547, at 555.

ends otherwise denied it by the constitution. Short of this, there is no other necessary exception to be implied in the express grants of power to the provinces in heads 13 and 14 of section 92.

As mentioned previously, all of the decisions in this field have arisen out of provincial legislation. Any future federal measures of this type are potentially limited because Parliament's power in section 101 of the BNA Act is restricted to "the Constitution, Maintenance, and Organization of a general Court of Appeal for Canada, and for the Establishment of any additional Courts for the better Administration of the Laws of Canada." Parliament could attempt to restrict judicial review in the Supreme Court of Canada, perhaps, and could also attempt to deprive the Exchequer Court or any other federally created court of the power to consider constitutional issues. The results might not be as serious as the results of some of the provincial measures already discussed. In a case appealed to the Supreme Court, for example, the constitutional issues would already have been canvassed in the provincial courts. In the Exchequer Court only rights arising under federal law are enforceable, unlike the situation in provincial courts which normally deal with cases under both federal and provincial law. Thus the possibility of Parliament invalidly barring provincially created rights of action by means of the Exchequer Court Act could not arise. If, however, in proceedings under the Income Tax Act in the Exchequer Court, for example, the taxpayer was precluded from attacking the Act's validity, this might violate the principles heretofore advanced. That is, Parliament, like the legislatures, is precluded from limiting the jurisdiction of its courts to the extent that it is thereby enabled to evade effectively the constitutional limitations on its own jurisdiction. This exception to its power under section 101 is necessarily implied in the existence of a federal division of legislative power.

LEGISLATIVE PRE-DETERMINATION OF JUDICIAL FINDINGS

Where the courts are permitted to embark on judicial review of legislation, it is clear that the legislature cannot dictate the conclusion which they must reach on the constitutional question. The highest courts have apparently not yet had occasion to deal with such legislative attempts. When they do, they can hardly escape the conclusion that the legislature could not be permitted to exceed its jurisdiction merely by requiring a court to make findings of fact or law in its favour.

Perhaps the strongest decision to this effect in the provincial courts is *Home Oil Distributors Limited* v. *Attorney General for British Columbia*.

A provincial royal commission had investigated the fuel industry, apparently in part because of the competition being given local coal producers by the sale of imported fuel oil at less than cost price. The report and recommendations were submitted to the legislature. Later the Coal and Petroleum Products Control Board Act, 1937[105] was passed. The plaintiff sued for a declaration and an injunction contending that the Act interfered with interprovincial or international trade, matters within federal jurisdiction with respect to "the regulation of trade and commerce." It was also contended that the Royal Commission report should be admitted as evidence and that the report indicated that a purpose was to be achieved which was ultra vires the legislature. On an appeal from an order granting an interlocutory injunction, the British Columbia Court of Appeal held the report to be admissible "in so far only as it finds facts which are relevant to the ascertainment of the said alleged purpose and the effect of the enactment."[106]

Four days later, while further proceedings were pending, the legislature amended the impugned statute as follows: "This Act is not intended to implement or carry into effect the recommendations or findings of any report made or to be made by the Commission appointed by the Lieutenant-Governor in Council under the 'Public Inquiries Act' ... ; and in construing this Act and ascertaining its purpose, intention, scope and effect no reference shall be made to any such reports. ..."[107] Nevertheless, at the trial Mr. Justice Manson proceeded to look at the report. He noted that the report indicated that the petroleum industry had an international aspect, and that the legislature had apparently thought that by its declaration it could prevent the court from looking at the report or finding the true purpose of the statute. "It need scarcely be said that if the legislation encroaches upon the legislative jurisdiction of the Dominion with respect to trade and commerce the declaration will not save the situation. As I have already said, mere assertion does not change facts."[108]

On appeal, the Court of Appeal reversed the decision and held the statute to be intra vires. While the judges did not consider the international aspects of the petroleum industry as revealed by the report to be decisive, they did not hesitate to look at the report itself. Speaking for the Court, Chief Justice Martin said that "we have not given effect to the amending

105. Stats. B.C. 1937, c.8.
106. [1939] 1 W.W.R. 49, at 51, [1939] 1 D.L.R. 573, at 574 (B.C.C.A.). This decision as to admissibility was apparently disapproved by Cartwright J. in *A.G. for Canada* v. *Reader's Digest Assoc. (Canada) Ltd.,* [1961] S.C.R. 775, at 791, 30 D.L.R. (2nd) 296, at 311.
107. Stats. B.C. 1938, c.5.
108. [1939] 1 W.W.R. 666, at 681 (B.C. Sup. Ct.).

statute . . . because we regard that interlocutory enactment as ineffective to curtail the unassailable jurisdiction of the Courts of Canada to adjudicate upon constitutional questions under the *British North America Act.* . . ."[109] On appeal to the Supreme Court of Canada[110] only Kerwin J. (Rinfret J. concurring) held the report to be admissible. The other judges either ignored the report or declined to make a decision as to its admissibility.

While the validity of the *Home Oil* decision with respect to the admissibility of a royal commission report as evidence of statutory effect might now be questionable,[111] the principle stated by the Court of Appeal is probably unassailable. That is, the legislature cannot preclude the court, where the constitutional issue is properly before it, from reaching certain conclusions as to the effect of the legislation.

At least one judge of the Supreme Court of Canada has expressed this view. In the *Reference re: Validity of Section (5) of the Dairy Industry Act*[112] (the margarine case) the court was asked to answer certain questions concerning a section of a federal statute which prohibited the manufacture, sale, etc. of margarine in Canada. Those seeking to uphold the validity of the Act argued, *inter alia*, that it was valid "criminal law" enacted under section 91, head 27 of the BNA Act. To support the argument that Parliament had thereby intended to prohibit a public evil, they quoted the preamble to the original Act which began: "Whereas the use of certain substitutes for butter, heretofore manufactured and exposed for sale in Canada is injurious to health, and it is expedient to prohibit the manufacture and sale thereof; . . . ."[113] In subsequent general revisions the preamble had been deleted, in accordance with legislative practice. Mr. Justice Rand commented that

ordinarily a preamble indicates the purpose of the statute and it may be a guide to the meaning and scope of the language where that is doubtful or ambiguous. But when the question is the real character of the legislation for the purposes of jurisdiction between two legislatures under a federal constitution, different considerations arise. A legislation [*sic*] cannot conclude the question by a declaration in a preamble: at most it is a fact to be taken into account, the weight to be given to it depending on all the circumstances. . . .[114]

It is important to note here that Rand J. distinguishes between normal interpretation of a statute and interpretation for the purpose of determining constitutional validity. Ordinary statutory interpretation is carried

---

109. [1939] 2 W.W.R. 418, at 419–20, [1939] 3 D.L.R. 397, at 398–99 (B.C.C.A.).
110. [1940] S.C.R. 444, [1940] 2 D.L.R. 609.
111. See *Reader's Digest* case, *supra* note 106.
112. [1949] S.C.R. 1, [1949] 1 D.L.R. 433 (1948).
113. Stats. Can. 1886, c.42.
114. *Supra* note 112, at 47–48.

out to ascertain the real intention of the legislature. Any clear assertion by the legislature as to its intention is therefore the best evidence and in most cases will be conclusive. Where a constitutional issue is involved, however, it is necessary to ascertain whether the effect of the legislation is within the jurisdiction of the enacting legislature. A legislature cannot be allowed to legislate colourably and thereby achieve an effect not within its powers merely by asserting that it intends to achieve some effect within its powers.

This distinction may have been lost sight of in the case of *Beauharnois Light, Heat & Power Co. Ltd.* v. *Hydro-Electric Power Commission.*[115] Just as in the *Ottawa Valley*[116] case, the Power Commission relied on section 6(4) of the Power Commission Act of 1927 as a defence to *Beauharnois'* action. Section 6(4), it will be recalled, seemed to require the consent of the attorney general before action could be commenced against the Commission. In the *Ottawa Valley* case the section had been held inapplicable to that type of action and this decision was followed at trial in the *Beauharnois* case. After trial the Ontario legislature enacted a declaration[117] as to what "the meaning and effect . . ." of the subsection "is and always has been. . . ." This declaration very specifically set out the meaning so that the subsection would clearly be a bar to the *Beauharnois* type of action.

The Court of Appeal nevertheless held the declaration to be inapplicable. Speaking for the court, Mr. Justice Middleton stated that

the Legislature, in matters within its competence, is unquestionably supreme, but it falls to the Courts to determine the meaning of the language used. If the Courts do not determine in accordance with the true intention of the Legislature, the Legislature cannot arrogate to itself the jurisdiction of a further appellate court and enact that the language used in its earlier enactment means something other than the Court has determined. It can, if it so pleases, use other language expressing its meaning more clearly. It transcends its true function when it undertakes to say that the language used has a different meaning and effect to that given it by the Courts, and that it always has meant something other than the Courts have declared it to mean.[118]

With respect, it is submitted that this states the power of the legislature too narrowly. The legislature can, when a statute is first passed, expressly state how it is to be construed (in the absence of any constitutional problem). Similarly it may surely make such a declaration later and make it retroactively, as there is nothing in the Canadian constitution to prevent the

---

115. [1937] O.R. 796, [1937] 3 D.L.R. 458 (Ont. C.A.).
116. *Supra* note 76 and accompanying text.
117. Stats. Ont. 1937, c.58.
118. [1937] O.R., at 822–23, [1937] 3 D.L.R., at 462–63.

enactment of laws *ex post facto*. Even though a trial court has pronounced on rights under a statute, that statute may subsequently be altered retroactively to remove the basis for the earlier judgment, and an appellate court should take cognizance of this alteration. Thus, the statement by Mr. Justice Middleton in the *Beauharnois* case must be confined to situations where the legislative declaration could preclude a judicial finding of constitutional invalidity. Otherwise the statement would be too broad in its implications.[119] Again, provincial power is limited only as required to prevent the legislature achieving a constitutionally invalid result.

CONCLUSION

The discussion in chapter two indicated that the right of judicial review is not absolute, that it must be considered qualified by other factors. One of these is the express legislative power conferred on Parliament and the legislatures by the BNA Act. By section 92(14) the provincial legislatures, and by section 101 Parliament, were given jurisdiction to regulate the "constitution, maintenance, and organization" of the courts. They were also given jurisdiction to create, alter, or abolish substantive rights in their respective spheres.

In the legislative attempts to limit judicial review, as herein examined, we have seen the complexities involved in balancing the forces of judicial review and legislative power. Legislatures have been permitted to impose procedural requirements as long as they do not thereby create an absolute bar to judicial review. They have been permitted to delegate to non-curial bodies the power to determine certain issues relevant to the application of constitutional norms, provided that the courts can ultimately define the constitutional limits of jurisdiction of such bodies. Legislatures may not use their control over the courts to prevent the enforcement of rights not within their legislative jurisdiction. But they can confirm rights vested under invalid legislation provided that those rights would normally lie within their own sphere. They may also dictate to the courts the meaning of legislation, but not its constitutional effect.

These examples are sufficient to demonstrate the impossibility of thinking in absolute terms when considering legislative restrictions on judicial review. Lawyers and judges who assert an absolute parliamentary sovereignty or an absolute right of judicial review will fail to cope with the more important issues. Instead we should start with the premise that legislatures

119. See comments on this case by Cartwright J. in *Western Minerals Ltd.* v. *Gaumont*, [1953] 1 S.C.R. 345, at 372, [1953] 3 D.L.R. 245, at 269. But cf. *Liyanage* v. *R.*, [1967] A.C. 259, [1966] 1 All E.R. 650 (P.C. 1965).

can normally regulate the work of the courts, and then concentrate on determining in each case whether the legislative attempt at regulation has gone as far as to threaten the maintenance of the federal structure. Will it really effect an alteration in the division of powers by allowing the legislature to prevent an adjudication as to validity, or will it merely impose a special procedure, alter the available remedies, or change the available judicial forum? These are the kinds of questions the courts should ask in examining the substance, not merely the form, of legislative limitations on judicial review. For their part, the legislatures should eschew any exercise of their jurisdiction over the courts and over substantive rights which might amount to a colourable invasion of the ultimate power of judicial review required for the maintenance of the federal structure.

CHAPTER FOUR

Crown Prerogative
and the Power of Judicial Review

GENERAL PRINCIPLES OF CROWN IMMUNITY

At common law the citizen had no right to sue the Crown. In spite of a steady development away from this position in favour of Crown liability, problems still arise when an action is brought against the Crown or its representatives. In a federal state such as Canada, with a written constitution limiting legislative and executive powers, these problems take on a special significance where the complaint against the Crown is that it acts or has acted pursuant to an invalid statute. In such circumstances the question arises of the extent to which traditional Crown immunity can prevent the courts from entertaining an action to determine the validity of legislation.

In England the Crown was immune from suit because the central courts were the king's courts, and like any feudal lord he was not subject to the jurisdiction of his own courts. From about 1300 onwards, the petition of right procedure was available to permit many actions. By this procedure a claim was submitted to the king and if he in his unfettered discretion saw fit he could by his fiat refer it to the courts for adjudication in the normal way. This procedure was regularized and simplified by statute in 1860.[1] However, it was never available for actions in tort: at least those which were not real actions. Tort actions were denied because the Crown was not considered capable of committing a tort: "the king can do no wrong." Petition of right was thus used mainly in actions for the recovery of money or property in the hands of the Crown or for the enforcement of contracts. Where no such relief was sought it was not available.[2]

1. Petition of Right Act (1860), 23 & 24 Vict., c.34.
2. See Holdsworth, "The History of Remedies Against the Crown" (1922), 38 L. Q. Rev. 141; Morgan, Introductory Chapter, in Robinson, *Public Authorities and Legal Liability* (1925), at xviii–liii; Street, *Governmental Liability* (1953), at 1–6; Halsbury, 9 *Laws of England* (2nd ed., 1933), at 691.

In Canada the same rules applied to proceedings against the Crown, both federal and provincial. The Dominion and some provinces had their own legislation pertaining to petition of right, while other provinces apparently left unaltered the uncertainties of the common law which had obtained in England prior to 1860.[3] The Dominion did, at an early stage, extend the scope of petition of right by permitting actions for tort in some cases.[4] But it was clear in Canada that the Crown's representative – either the governor general or the lieutenant governor – had an unlimited discretion in this matter. A refusal to grant a fiat could not be questioned in the courts, even where the proceedings were to be used to test the validity of legislation.[5] If an action could be framed so that the Crown was not a necessary party, the problem of Crown immunity did not arise. But wherever Crown title or interests in property would be affected, the Crown had to be made a party.[6] Petition of right was the proper procedure where such rights could be directly affected by a request for relief which would deprive the Crown of its property or money.[7]

Even in its most extended application the principle of Crown immunity was only a limited obstacle to constitutional litigation. If the action were so framed as to constitute a claim for damages against a person or company acting under an invalid statute, this was permissible without petition of right so long as Crown property interests were not directly attacked. One could always maintain an action against a fellow subject of the Crown under such circumstances.[8] A public officer could be sued for damages for unauthorized acts committed by him,[9] or could be restrained by injunction from committing such acts.[10] In none of these cases was petition of right

3. For a survey of Canadian law prior to recent statutory modifications see "The Crown as Litigant: Report of Committee on Comparative Provincial Legislation and Law Reform, 1936" (1936), 14 *Can.B.Rev.* 606.
4. See Exchequer Court Act, R.S.C. 1952, c.98, s.18 and its predecessors. See also *infra* note 35, and accompanying text.
5. *Orpen v. A.G. for Ont.*, [1925] 2 D.L.R. 355 (Ont. High Ct.), *aff'd.*, [1925] 3 D.L.R. 301 (Ont. Sup. Ct., App. Div.); *Lovibond v. Gov. Gen. of Canada*, [1930] A.C. 717 (P.C.).
6. *Esquimalt & Nanaimo Ry. v. Wilson*, [1920] A.C. 358, at 369 (P.C.).
7. *A.G. for Ont. v. McLean Gold Mines Ltd.*, [1927] A.C. 185 (P.C.); *Lovibond v. Grand Trunk Ry.*, [1936] 2 W.W.R. 298, [1936] 3 D.L.R. 449 (P.C.); *Contact Mining & Development Co. Ltd. v. Craigmont Mines Ltd.* (1961), 35 W.W.R. 480, 29. D.L.R. (2nd) 592 (Sup. Ct. of Can.), *affiming* without written reasons (1960), 35 W.W.R. 214, 26 D.L.R. (2nd) 35 (B.C. C.A.).
8. *Lovibond* case, *supra* note 7, [1936] 2 W.W.R., at 311–12, [1936] 3 D.L.R., at 460–61.
9. *Musgrave v. Pulido* (1879), 5 App. Cas. 102 (P.C.); *Roncarelli v. Duplessis*, [1959] S.C.R. 121, 16 D.L.R. (2nd) 689.
10. See Strayer, "Injunctions Against Crown Officers" (1964), 42 *Can.B.Rev.* 1.

required to question the validity of the authority under which the person, officer, or agency had acted or intended to act.

The Crown itself could apparently be sued without petition of right by means of an action for a declaratory judgment where the citizen sought a clarification of his rights, and Crown property or money interests were not directly at stake. The leading modern English case on this point is *Dyson v. Attorney General*[11] decided in 1911. The plaintiff had received a notice (some eight million such notices had been sent out) from the Commissioners of Inland Revenue requiring him to make certain returns with respect to his property. Failure to deliver the returns would make him liable to a penalty recoverable at the suit of the attorney general. The plaintiff commenced action for a declaration that the notice and other requirement were not in accordance with the statute and were ultra vires of the Commissioners. The attorney general moved to strike out this pleading on the grounds that such action could be maintained only by petition of right because the rights of the Crown would be directly affected. The Court of Appeal held that the action would lie and that a petition of right was not necessary.

The *Dyson* decision is far from clear on the question whether petition of right would be required where the Crown's rights were directly affected. Cozens-Hardy M. R. seems to treat it as a case directly affecting Crown rights but cites authority from the Court of Exchequer to show that a declaration could be made in such circumstances.[12] Farwell L. J. appears to hold that Crown rights were only indirectly affected, and for that reason the action would be maintainable.[13] Fletcher Moulton L. J. objected to the point being dealt with on a motion to strike out pleadings and simply held that it should be left for decision at the trial. It would appear, however, that Crown rights would be affected very indirectly if at all in this action. No existing property of the Crown was involved. At most the decision could only affect possible future revenues. The issue of the ultimate liability of the plaintiff to pay taxes was not raised, although the decision could have an adverse effect on the right of the Crown to enforce the penalty. One of the counsel in the case, later elevated to the bench, interpreted the *Dyson* action as one which affected Crown rights only

11. [1911] 1 K.B. 410. See also Edwards, *The Law Officers of the Crown* (1964), at 293–95.
12. *Ibid.*, at 415–17. For a criticism of this reliance on Exchequer decisions see Street, *supra* note 2, at 132–34. The arguments there stated are probably not relevant in many Canadian jurisdictions where the superior courts were given the same jurisdiction as all of the royal courts in England had enjoyed.
13. *Ibid.*, at 421–22.

indirectly.[14] The Privy Council similarly regarded the decision,[15] and it refused to allow declaratory actions which would directly affect Crown rights in the absence of petition of right.[16] The Supreme Court of Canada distinguished between the petition of right, properly used only where some relief was sought against the Crown involving its interest in property, and a declaration against the attorney general which did not deal with such rights.[17] This is consistent with the traditional principles of Crown immunity which would prohibit a court from depriving the Crown of its property. The modern constitutional justification for this is more clearly attributable to parliamentary supremacy. If the court could, without consent of the legislature (granted only under petition of right legislation), order the payment of public funds or the transfer of Crown property, then the legislature's primary jurisdiction over these matters would be denied. But where the court order in the form of a declaratory judgment would not involve interference with public property, the court may proceed without infringing on Crown or legislature.

The declaratory action without petition of right had particular significance in a federal system such as Canada's. It provided a means for raising constitutional issues in situations where it was not necessary to attack Crown title to property or seek recovery of money from the Crown. As in England, legislation in most Canadian jurisdictions permits the grant of a declaration though no other relief is sought.[18] The constitutional validity of governmental action could thus be attacked without government consent. It has in fact been held that the declaration is the proper method of attacking legislative validity where Crown rights are not directly involved,[19] and that petition of right is not an appropriate procedure in such cases.[20]

14. Rowlatt J. in *Bombay & Persia Steam Navigation Co.* v. *MacLay,* [1920] 3 K.B. 402, at 408.
15. *A.G. for Ont.* v. *McLean Gold Mines Ltd., supra* note 7, at 191. See also *Esquimalt & Nanaimo Ry.* v. *Wilson, supra* note 6.
16. *McLean* case, *ibid.; Lovibond* v. *Grand Trunk Ry., supra* note 7.
17. *The King* v. *Bradley,* [1941] S.C.R. 270, at 276.
18. See e.g., R.S.M. 1954, c.52, s.62(8); R.S.O. 1960, c.197, s.15(2); R.S.S. 1965, c.73, s.45(17). The situation in Quebec is still unclear: see *Saumur* v. *A.G. for Que.,* [1964] S.C.R. 252, 45 D.L.R. (2d) 627, discussed *infra* at 100–2. For a history of this aspect of the declaratory action see Zamir, *The Declaratory Judgment* (1962), at 7–17.
19. *Esquimalt & Nanaimo Ry.* v. *Wilson, supra* note 6, at 364.
20. *Canadian Pacific Ry.* v. *A.G. for Sask.* (1951), 1 W.W.R. 193, [1951] 3 D.L.R. 362 (Sask. K.B.); appealed (1951), 2 W.W.R. 424, [1951] 4 D.L.R. 21 (Sask. C.A.), [1952] 2 S.C.R. 231, [1952] 4 D.L.R. 11, without reference to this point. See also *Tiny Separate School Trustees* v. *The King,* [1927] S.C.R. 637, at 706–07, 713, [1927] 4 D.L.R. 857, at 906, 911.

STATUTORY MODIFICATION

The foregoing common law rules with respect to Crown immunity from suit have now undergone changes through both legislative and judicial action. Important legislative reform came in England with the passage of the Crown Proceedings Act, 1947.[21] Section 1 of that Act provided that, in all cases where a person had a claim against the Crown which previously would have been enforceable only by petition of right, the claim could now be enforced as of right and without fiat. Section 21 provided that the court could make such orders against the Crown as it could against a subject, except that instead of making an order for delivery of property by the Crown the court was confined to making a declaratory order.[22]

In Canada the use of declaratory judgments against a representative of the Crown was facilitated by statute in some jurisdictions many years ago. Typical of these statutory provisions is section 32 of The Judicature Act of Alberta[23] which confers jurisdiction on the Supreme Court of the province as follows:

(1) the Court has jurisdiction to entertain an action at the instance of either
    (i) the Attorney General for Canada, or
    (ii) the Attorney General of the Province
for a declaration as to the validity of a statute or a provision in a statute of the Legislature of the Province though no further relief is prayed or sought;

(m) an action under clause (1) for a declaration as to the validity of a statute or a provision thereof shall be deemed sufficiently constituted if the two Attorney Generals [sic] are parties thereto, and a judgment in such action may be appealed against as other judgments of the Court. . . .

This procedure was provided in Ontario as early as 1886 and is now also found in Manitoba, British Columbia, and New Brunswick.[24] The Ontario provision,[25] though cast somewhat differently, seems to be similar in effect, except that it provides in addition that the validity of federal legislation may also be questioned in this manner. Where such provisions are in force it would seem that no problem of Crown immunity would arise in the grant of a declaratory judgment against the attorney general of the province. Whereas by the common law no such judgment could be given

21. 10 & 11 Geo. VI, c.44.
22. For details of practice with respect to declaratory actions under the Act see Zamir, *supra* note 18, at 289–97.
23. R.S.A. 1955, c.164, s.32(1).
24. R.S.M. 1954, c.52, ss.61, 62(8); R.S.B.C. 1960, c.72, s.11; R.S.N.B. 1952, c.120, s.24.
25. R.S.O. 1960, c.197, s.20.

without petition of right if the Crown's rights were directly affected, by this statutory innovation the attorney general is made subject to suit regardless of the effect on Crown rights. The effect of such procedure, while no doubt beneficial in situations where it applies,[26] is nonetheless very limited. It is of no use to private litigants because the action must be instituted by an attorney general – almost certainly the attorney general of Canada who would probably be most reluctant to institute such proceedings. It is useful only as against provincial legislation, except in Ontario. It is not available in many provinces, and not at all in the federal courts except through appeal to the Supreme Court of Canada.

More significant in Canada have been the general statutory modifications of Crown immunity which have facilitated private actions – including those challenging legislative validity – against the Crown. There had been discussion in Canada for years as to the need for reform of the Crown prerogative of immunity from suit.[27] Passage of the Crown Proceedings Act, 1947, in England gave the necessary impetus to action, and in 1948 the Conference of Commissioners on Uniformity of Legislation in Canada undertook a study of the problem. In 1950 a model act[28] was adopted, patterned very closely after the English Act. This statute has been adopted in almost identical terms in Alberta, Manitoba, New Brunswick, Nova Scotia, Ontario, and Saskatchewan.[29] Section 4 of the Uniform Act, which is similar to section 1 of the English Act, provides that: "Subject to this Act, a claim against the Crown, that, if this Act had not been passed, might be enforced by petition of right, subject to the grant of a fiat by the Lieutenant Governor, may be enforced as of right by proceedings against the Crown in accordance with this Act, without the grant of a fiat by the Lieutenant Governor." Section 5(1) abolishes the rule that "the King can do no wrong" by making the Crown liable as an ordinary person would be in tort, including vicarious liability for torts of Crown servants, liability of

26. See Grant, "Judicial Review in Canada: Procedural Aspects" (1964), 42 *Can.B. Rev.* 195, at 202–03.
27. See e.g. Kennedy, "Suits by and Against the Crown" (1928), 6 *Can.B.Rev.* 329; "Report" *supra* note 3. Some progress had been made in establishing the liability to suit of some Crown agencies incorporated with capacity to sue and be sued. See Smith, "Liability to Suit of an Agent of the Crown" (1950), 8 *U. Toronto L.J.* 218; *Yeats* v. *Central Mortgage & Housing Corp.*, [1950] S.C.R. 513; The Government Companies Operation Act, Stats. Can. 1946, c.24, as amended by Stats. Can. 1950, c.51, s.13.
28. [1950] *Proceedings of Conference of Commissioners on Uniformity of Legislation in Canada* (hereinafter cited as Uniform Act), at 76.
29. Stats. Alta. 1959, c.63; R.S.M. 1954, c.207; R.S.N.B. 1952, c.176; R.S.N.S. 1954, c.225; Stats. Ont. 1962–63, c.109, replacing Stats. Ont. 1952, c.78 which was never proclaimed; R.S.S. 1965, c.87.

a master to his servants, liability "in respect of any breach of the duties attaching to the ownership, occupation, possession or control of property . . ." and liability imposed by or under any statute. Section 5(3) makes clear that the Crown will be liable even if the Crown servant has acted in an unauthorized fashion while carrying out the duties assigned to him. "Where a function is conferred or imposed upon an officer of the Crown, as such, either by any rule of the common law or by statute, and that officer commits a tort in the course of performing or purporting to perform that function, the liability of the Crown in respect of the tort is such as it would have been if that function had been conferred or imposed solely by virtue of instructions lawfully given by the Crown." Subject to certain limitations stated therein, sections 4 and 5 of the Uniform Act eliminate Crown immunity from suit. Where action could previously be initiated only by petition of right – that is, where Crown property was directly involved – no petition is now required. Where the Crown could not be sued at all – that is, for liability in tort – it can now be sued in an ordinary action.

These changes effected by the Uniform Act are of considerable importance for constitutional litigation. A citizen wishing to sue the Crown in right of a province for recovery of property or for damages in tort may well allege that Crown title is defective because it is based on an ultra vires statute, or that acts by Crown officers causing damage to him were committed under invalid legislation. Courts have sometimes been precluded in such cases from dealing with the constitutional point because of the immunity of the Crown from the action itself. No such situation need now arise in the provinces which have adopted the Uniform Act. The Act does in certain cases limit particular remedies against the provincial Crown. No injunction may be given against the Crown[30] or an officer of the Crown,[31] nor may an order for the recovery of land or the delivery of property be made against the Crown or its officers.[32] In each case, however, the court is permitted in lieu of such orders to make a declaratory order as to respective rights. Rights, including constitutional rights, may thus be adjudicated though certain remedies are precluded.

30. Section 16(2).
31. Section 16(4). But even where the Act has been adopted, this does not prevent a provincial court from granting an injunction against a federal Crown agency. See *Baton Broadcasting Ltd.* v. *C.B.C.*, [1966] 2 O.R. 169, at 175 (Ont. H.C.). The "Crown" referred to in the provincial statutes is the Crown in right of the respective province.
32. Section 16(3) and (4). See section 21 of the Crown Proceedings Act, 1947, *supra* note 21, for comparable provisions in England.

Quebec has recently achieved a similar result by an amendment[33] to the Code of Civil Procedure. Article 94, as amended, provides that "any person having a claim to exercise against the Crown, whether it be a revendication of moveable or immoveable property, or a claim for the payment of moneys on an alleged contract, or for damages, or otherwise, may exercise it in the same manner as if it were a claim against a person of full age and capacity, subject only to the provisions of this chapter." Article 94b provides that "no extraordinary recourse or provisional remedy lies against the Crown" and article 94j makes execution procedures inapplicable to the Crown.

At the federal level the immunity of the Crown in right of Canada has been similarly reduced. The first Petition of Right Act[34] of the Dominion, passed in 1875, in effect adopted the same rules as those obtaining in England under the Petition of Right Act of 1860 and the common law.[35] Twelve years later a modification of those rules began in Canada with the passage of an amendment to the Supreme and Exchequer Courts Act giving the Exchequer Court jurisdiction in certain tort actions against the Crown. While the jurisdiction was at first quite limited, applying only in cases of claims arising out of "death or injury to the person or to property on any public work . . ." resulting from the negligence of a Crown officer or servant acting within the scope of his employment, it did represent one of the earliest exceptions in the Empire to the rule that "the king can do no wrong." This jurisdiction was gradually widened so that after 1938 the court had jurisdiction over claims arising out of such death or injury through negligence whether or not it occurred in connection with a "public work."[36]

It had been necessary, of course, to use petition of right procedure for such tort actions as well as for most other actions against the Crown and to obtain the fiat of the governor general consenting to the action. The governor general had an unfettered discretion to refuse his fiat.[37] This obstacle was eliminated in 1951 by an amendment[38] to the Petition of Right Act abolishing the requirement of the governor general's fiat, with

33. Stats. Que. 1966, c.21, s.5.
34. Stats. Can. 1875, c.12.
35. See *Queen* v. *McFarlane* (1882), 7 S.C.R. 216; *Queen* v. *McLeod* (1882), 8 S.C.R. 1.
36. See Stats. Can. 1917, c.23, s.2; Stats. Can. 1938 c.28, s.1; R.S.C. 1952, c.98, s.18(1)(c). Another important extension of liability was effected by Stats. Can. 1943–44, c.25 making members of the armed forces "servants of the Crown" for the purpose of imposing vicarious liability on the Crown in actions under the Exchequer Court Act.
37. *Lovibond* case, *supra* note 5.
38. Stats. Can. 1951, c.33, s.1.

respect either to a claim or counter claim against the Crown.[39] While the action is still initiated by a petition of right, the petition need not be submitted to the governor general for approval.

Shortly after the elimination of the procedural need for consent, the substantive liability of the Crown federal was enlarged by the enactment of the Crown Liability Act[40] in 1953. The most important provision therein is section 3 which provides in part:

3.(1) The Crown is liable in tort for the damages for which, if it were a private person of full age and capacity, it would be liable
(a) in respect of a tort committed by a servant of the Crown, or
(b) in respect of a breach of duty attaching to the ownership, occupation, possession or control of property.

Clause (b) of sub-section (1) extended the scope of Crown liability by making the Crown liable as an owner and occupier of property instead of merely vicariously liable for the negligence of its servants, although the practical results of this change may not have been significant.[41] Clause (a), however, substantially extended Crown liability in tort. The latter had previously been confined by the Exchequer Court Act[42] to a "claim against the Crown arising out of any death or injury to the person or to property resulting from the negligence of any officer or servant of the Crown while acting within the scope of his duties or employment." The 1953 Act for the first time made the Crown in right of Canada generally liable in tort.[43] It also enabled a claimant to sue in the provincial courts in tort where small amounts are involved.[44]

The net effect of these developments is that the Crown in right of Canada now enjoys practically no immunity from suit. It would therefore not be possible for the government of Canada to avoid, as it has on at least one occasion[45] in the past, the judicial review of Parliament's legislation through a refusal to grant a fiat. The citizen now can, without obstruction, sue the Crown in tort, contract, or for the enforcement of property rights and in the process challenge the validity of legislation under which the Crown acts or intends to act.

39. *Queen* v. *Pfinder*, [1959] Ex. C.R. 31.
40. Stats. Can. 1952–53, c.30.
41. Through its liability for the negligence of Crown servants the Crown had been made answerable for the condition of its property. See e.g. *R.* v. *Canada Steamship Lines Ltd.*, [1927] S.C.R. 68; *Johnson* v. *R.*, [1931] Ex. C.R. 163; *Farthing* v. *R.*, [1948] Ex. C.R. 134; *Grossman* v. *R.*, [1952] 1 S.C.R. 571.
42. R.S.C. 1952, c.98, s.18(1)(c).
43. For the significance of this change see *Magda* v. *The Queen*, [1964] S.C.R. 72, at 76–78, 42 D.L.R. (2nd) 330, at 334–35.
44. *Supra* note 40, ss. 8–14.
45. See *Lovibond* cases, *supra* note 5 and note 7.

JUDICIAL MODIFICATION

While Crown immunity has thus been denied by statute within the federal jurisdiction and seven provincial jurisdictions, the common law position remains relevant for three of the provinces.[46] It is possible that the law has been developed sufficiently by the courts, however, so that Crown immunity is no longer a substantial obstacle to judicial review of legislation in these jurisdictions even in the absence of legislative reform. A comparison of two leading Canadian authorities will indicate the extent of this judicial development.

In the first of these cases, *Lovibond* v. *Grand Trunk Ry.*,[47] the Judicial Committee of the Privy Council in 1936 held Crown immunity to be an obstacle to claims based on the alleged invalidity of federal statutes. By means of various federal statutes and orders in council passed thereunder the minister of finance had become owner in trust for the Crown of certain stock in the Grand Trunk Railway. This stock had been taken compulsorily from its former holders in 1923 and the Grand Trunk had been merged with another line to form the new Canadian National Railway. In 1929 the plaintiff, Lovibond, who as a stockholder had been deprived of his stock in this manner, presented a petition of right to seek a declaration that the stock was still legally vested in the previous holders on the grounds that the various acts of Parliament and orders in council were ultra vires. The governor general's fiat was refused and the Privy Council refused to review the governor general's decision.[48] Lovibond then obtained transfers of certain Grand Trunk shares from some of the previous stockholders and sought to be registered as the new holder. The Grand Trunk and Canadian National officers refused to so register him. He then commenced action against the Grand Trunk, the Canadian National, and the attorney general of Canada seeking three types of relief. First, he sought declarations that the various statutes, together with the orders in council and agreements made thereunder, were ultra vires the Parliament and government of Canada. Secondly, he sought other declarations that his old stock had not been validly transferred to the minister and an order against the railways requiring them to rectify the stock register of the Grand Trunk so as to show him as owner of this stock and of the new stock recently transferred to him. He also sought damages against the railways, as an alternative remedy, for failure to restore his name as stockholder or to register him as owner of the stock newly transferred to him.

46. British Columbia, Newfoundland, and Prince Edward Island.
47. *Supra* note 7.
48. *Lovibond* v. *Gov. Gen. of Canada, supra* note 5.

The Privy Council held that the second type of relief could not be had without petition of right.[49] The effect of such declarations and orders would be to take stock away from the minister of finance, who was trustee for the Crown. The Crown would thus be deprived of its beneficial interest in property and this could only be done by petition of right. With respect to the declarations sought, it was held that these were "sought as foundations upon which to base the claims to have the names of the old holders of the junior stocks restored as such to the register of the Grand Trunk: in other words they are ancillary to the claims which can only be the subject of a petition of right. The action cannot be allowed to proceed in regard to them."[50] As the attorney general was sued only with respect to these declarations, it was held that he was no longer a party. The Privy Council did find, however, that the action for damages could proceed without petition of right. This claim was against the railway companies, not the Crown. Lord Russell of Killowen said that it could proceed because the relief sought would not involve the Crown as a party nor would the Crown be deprived of its interest in property by an award of damages against the railway companies. It was immaterial that the basis for claiming damages might be the alleged invalidity of various statutes and orders in council.[51]

This decision made Crown immunity from suit a formidable obstacle to judicial supervision of constitutional limitations. From his earlier experience it was clear to the plaintiff here that a fiat would probably not be granted to him in petition of right procedure. He was thus effectively barred from asserting against the Crown, the new beneficial owner of his property, a claim to that property based on the unconstitutionality of the Crown's title. In this case he might have obtained some relief through the recovery of damages from the railway companies, but one can imagine situations where there might not be any such convenient defendants against whom the constitutional claim could be urged. If, for example, the Crown had, under similar legislation, seized real property from him directly without intervention or assistance of other agencies, he might well be barred from all action. Even in the circumstances of the *Lovibond* case, of course, the plaintiff could never recover his property no matter how invalid the Crown title. He would have to settle for damages instead.

The *Lovibond* case was criticized at the time by Mr. F. A. Brewin,

49. [1936] 2 W.W.R. 298, at 310–11, [1936] 3 D.L.R. 449, at 459–60.
50. [1936] 2 W.W.R., at 312, [1936] 3 D.L.R., at 461.
51. [1936] 2 W.W.R., at 311–12, [1936] 3 D.L.R., at 460–61. The damage action subsequently failed on substantive grounds, *sub. nom., Lovibond* v. *Grand Trunk Railway Co.* [1939] O.R. 305, [1939] 2 D.L.R. 562 (Ont. C.A.).

writing in the *Canadian Bar Review*.[52] He suggested that the principles of Crown immunity should be modified in a federal state where both legislative and executive powers are limited by the constitution. In his view, the Crown prerogative to refuse to permit actions involving Crown title to property ought not to extend to cases where that title was being attacked on constitutional grounds. The decision has, however, been followed in Canada in a constitutional dispute[53] and has never been expressly repudiated by any Canadian court.

Before leaving the *Lovibond* case it is interesting to note that the trial judge whose decision[54] the Privy Council affirmed in part was Mr. Justice Kerwin of the Ontario High Court. He had held that no part of the action, not even the claims for damages against the railways, could proceed without petition of right. The Privy Council agreed in part but felt that he had defined Crown immunity too broadly. Mr. Justice Kerwin was appointed in 1935 to the Supreme Court of Canada and was an important figure in the other leading case on this subject now to be discussed.

In *British Columbia Power Corporation* v. *British Columbia Electric Company*[55] the Supreme Court of Canada was faced with a similar problem with respect to the effect of Crown immunity on actions challenging constitutional validity of legislation. B.C. Electric was a provincially incorporated company the shares of which were wholly owned by B.C. Power, a federally incorporated company. The British Columbia legislature passed the Power Development Act, 1961,[56] which purported to vest all of the shares of B.C. Electric in the Crown in right of the province. The company was also declared to be an agent of the Crown. Compensation was fixed in a manner unsatisfactory to B.C. Power. The latter attempted to commence action against the Crown in September 1961 by petition of right to claim additional compensation. A fiat was refused.

In November 1961, B.C. Power commenced an action without petition of right against B.C. Electric, the attorney general of British Columbia, and others. As later amended, the claim of the plaintiff sought, *inter alia*, various declarations as to the invalidity of the Power Development Act. The legislation was attacked on the grounds that it "sterilized" a federally incorporated company, that B.C. Electric was an undertaking connecting the province with other provinces and with the United States and thus beyond provincial jurisdiction, that there was a denial of "due process of

52. "Comment" (1936), 14 *Can.B.Rev.* 621.
53. *Royal Trust Co.* v. *A.G. for Alta.*, [1936] 2 W.W.R. 337, [1936] 4 D.L.R. 98 (Alta. S.C.).
54. [1933] O.R. 741, [1933] 1 D.L.R. 798 (Ont. H.C.).
55. [1962] S.C.R. 642, 34 D.L.R. (2nd) 196.
56. Stats. B.C. 1961, 2nd sess., c.4.

law," and that it would frustrate the Columbia River Treaty, a matter of federal concern.

At the end of March 1962 the legislature passed two further acts with respect to the B.C. Electric takeover. The Power Development Act, 1961, was amended[57] to increase the compensation for B.C. Electric shares, which compensation was not to be open to question in any court. Section 5 of the amending Act provided that the meaning or effect of the Act as amended should not be reviewable by a court except through petition of right proceedings. The other statute enacted at this time was the British Columbia Hydro and Power Authority Act, 1962.[58] It created the Authority by merger of B.C. Electric and the British Columbia Power Commission. The new Authority was made the owner of all the assets of B.C. Electric and was declared to be an agent of the Crown in right of the province.

Meanwhile, in interlocutory proceedings in its action, the plaintiff B.C. Power Corporation applied for and obtained an order appointing a receiver and manager of the undertaking, property, and interests of the B.C. Electric Company pending the trial of the action. This order was appealed and was set aside by the Court of Appeal. B.C. Power appealed the latter decision and in this manner brought the case before the Supreme Court of Canada.

While the attorney general of British Columbia did not contend that a court could not review the validity of these Acts in some proceeding, he took the position that a receivership order could not be made pending determination of the constitutional issue. It was argued that such an order would directly affect the estate of the Crown. If the Court appointed a receiver of the assets, the Crown would be barred from exercising its rights as sole shareholder to bring about a merger of these assets into the new Hydro Authority. The Power Development Act had also made B.C. Electric an agent of the Crown, and it was contended that B.C. Electric's assets were those of the Crown held by its agent. Thus no such order could be made except through petition of right procedure.[59] The respondent Hydro and Power Authority took much the same position, citing *inter alia* the *Dyson* and *Lovibond* cases.[60]

The appellant B.C. Power put forward four main arguments on this aspect of the jurisdiction of the Court to make the order appointing a receiver. First, it was asserted that whatever the position of the Crown

57. Stats. B.C. 1962, c.50.
58. Stats. B.C. 1962, c.8.
59. Factum of the Attorney General of B.C., at 3–5.
60. Factum of the B.C. Hydro & Power Authority, at 6–7.

prerogative of immunity from suit might be in England, the prerogative was necessarily limited in Canada. The Privy Council decision of *Bonanza Creek Gold Mining Company* v. *The King*[61] was cited, wherein it was held that the Crown prerogative had by implication been divided among the Dominion and provincial executives in a manner correlative to the distribution of legislative powers.[62] Secondly, on the assumption that the court had jurisdiction to decide as to the constitutional validity of the statutes in question, the order appointing a receiver was said to be necessarily incidental to that jurisdiction. It was suggested that otherwise a declaration of invalidity could "be meaningless if in the meantime the Legislature has been able to achieve by indirect means its illegal object."[63] An analogy was drawn with cases where an interim injunction had been granted against Crown officers pending trial of a constitutional dispute. Thirdly, it was argued that the order would not directly affect the rights of the Crown and therefore, on an analogy with the *Dyson* case, the court could make such an order without petition of right. It was contended that the only right of the Crown here was the right to appoint directors of B.C. Electric, which right was not interfered with even though effective power of the directors might be curtailed by the apppointment of a receiver.[64] Fourthly, and in the alternative, it was urged that even if the order would directly affect the rights of the crown, these were rights arising under a statute the validity of which was under attack. Further reference was made to the limited nature of the Crown prerogative in a federal state as interpreted by the *Bonanza* case, and to cases where interim injunctions had been issued against Crown officers pending the trial of actions involving constitutional issues.[65]

Chief Justice Kerwin, on behalf of the majority, disposed of these detailed and substantial arguments in summary fashion. After referring very briefly to the contentions of the attorney general, he made this pronouncement.

In a federal system, where legislative authority is divided, as are also the prerogatives of the Crown, as between the Dominion and Provinces, it is my view that it is not open to the Crown, either in right of Canada or of a Province, to claim a Crown immunity based upon an interest in certain property, where its very interest in that property depends completely and solely on the validity of the legislation which it has itself passed, if there is a reasonable doubt as to whether such legislation is constitutionally valid. To permit it to do so would

---

61. [1916] 1 A.C. 566, at 579–80, 586–87 (P.C.).
62. Appellant's factum, at 10.
63. *Ibid.*, at 11.
64. *Ibid.*, at 13–14.
65. *Ibid.*, at 14–16.

be to enable it, by the assertion of rights claimed under legislation which is beyond its powers, to achieve the same results as if the legislation were valid. In a federal system it appears to me that, in such circumstances, the court has the same jurisdiction to preserve assets whose title is dependent on the validity of the legislation as it has to determine the validity of the legislation itself.[66]

No other reference was made to the arguments or to the cases cited. Five judges concurred with the Chief Justice, and Mr. Justice Abbott alone dissented.

This decision is remarkable more for what it omits than for what it says. How did the Court avoid the inhibiting influence of the Privy Council's *Lovibond* decision, or the whole line of authority starting with *Dyson* which distinguished between orders directly and indirectly affecting the Crown? Were these decisions repudiated or were they distinguished on the grounds that the receiver order would not directly affect Crown property? Unless the latter represents the true decision it is hard to see how the *Lovibond* case could be other than a binding precedent against the grant of such relief. It is clear from the factums that *Lovibond* and associated cases were brought to the attention of the Court. And one must assume that Chief Justice Kerwin, who had been the trial judge in the *Lovibond* case, must have been fully aware of its implications with respect to the order sought by B.C. Power.

It might be argued that the Supreme Court's decision herein is of limited scope and not an abandonment of common law principles of Crown immunity. While the Court does not say so, the order appointing a receiver need not necessarily have been construed as an interference with Crown property in the sense that the Crown would be permanently divested of its interest or title. An order made *pendente lite* for the preservation of the status quo would be much less serious in its effects than a declaration as sought in the *Lovibond* case that the Crown never had, and should no longer assert, an interest as *cestui que trust* in the shares of a railway company.

It is submitted, however, that the implications of the B.C. *Power* case are much wider than this. It should first be noted that Chief Justice Kerwin states his opinion more broadly when he says that "it is not open to the Crown, either in right of Canada or of a Province, to claim a Crown immunity based upon an interest in certain property . . . " where the existence of that interest depends on the validity of impugned legislation. This is the clearest and broadest possible denial of Crown immunity from property actions. From this it would appear that in such circumstances even a direct attack on Crown title could be entertained by a court without

66. *Supra* note 55, [1962] S.C.R., at 644-45, 34 D.L.R. (2nd), at 275-76.

petition of right. Apart from this, while the order in question in the *B.C. Power* case was of limited effect it was still a direct interference with Crown property interests. It is hard to accept the argument of the appellant that the only Crown right involved was that of appointing directors, which right remained untouched. By the Power Development Act, B.C. Electric had been made an agent of the Crown and by the Hydro and Power Authority Act its assets were transferred to the Authority which was in turn declared to be an agent of the Crown. As a result, the assets of B.C. Electric, itself an agent of the Crown, transferred to another agent of the Crown, were surely Crown assets being held for the Crown by its agent. The interference with Crown property interests is at least as clear here as in the *Lovibond* case where shares were by statute vested in the name of the minister of finance as trustee for the Crown. While the Crown would not be permanently deprived of title to its property by an order appointing a receiver of that property, it would certainly be deprived of many of the incidents of title – such as the exclusive right of use, possession, and disposition – for a substantial period of time.[67]

CONCLUSION

It must be concluded, therefore, that the Supreme Court has intentionally repudiated the English rule of immunity as applied in *Lovibond*. It has rejected Crown immunity as a limitation on judicial review in Canada where constitutional issues are involved, even in those jurisdictions which have not removed that immunity by statute. After ninety-five years of fairly consistent Canadian adherence to the rule as developed in the legislative union of the United Kingdom, this judicial innovation should be greeted with enthusiasm. It is hard to deny the logic of the argument suggested in Mr. Brewin's comment in 1936,[68] advanced by the appellant in the *B.C. Power* case, and apparently accepted by the Supreme Court. That is, the prerogative in Canada as enjoyed by the Crown in right of Canada or of any particular province is a limited prerogative. It has long been settled that the division of prerogative powers in Canada corresponds to the division of legislative powers.[69] Moreover, the property rights of the Crown, which are protected from challenge by the Crown prerogative to refuse a fiat, arise out of legislation the validity of which may be under

67. The order appointing a receiver was made on March 22, 1962. The decision of the trial judge in the action was not handed down until July 29, 1963, reported in (1963), 44 W.W.R. 65 (B.C. S.C.).
68. *Supra* note 52.
69. *Bonanza* case, *supra* note 61. See also *A.G. for Can.* v. *A.G. for Ont.*, [1898] A.C. 247 (P.C.).

attack. It is therefore begging the question for the Crown to claim immunity on the grounds that its title is being threatened, because the existence of that title is the very point in issue. This practice in a federal state such as Canada could well upset the division of legislative powers prescribed by the British North America Act. As Chief Justice Kerwin said, it would allow the Crown "by the assertion of rights claimed under legislation which is beyond its powers, to achieve the same result as if the legislation were valid."

It may be noted in passing that the immunity rule was an anomaly even in England. It had been accepted there for over three centuries that the courts were in other cases entitled to review the legality of the exercise of the prerogative, though not the manner in which it was exercised. That is, the courts could ascertain whether the Crown was acting within the legal limits of prerogative power.[70] Unlike the legislative power of Parliament, the prerogative power was limited by statute and by judicial decision so that there were grounds for the exercise of judicial review in the maintenance of these limitations. But immunity from suit where the Crown's claim to property was directly attacked precluded review of the exercise of the prerogative in such cases. It is little wonder that the rule was abolished in England by the Crown Proceedings Act, 1947. The decision of the Supreme Court of Canada to modify the rule in a country of divided legislative powers was long overdue.

Where Crown immunity was formerly a bar to suit, it could constitute an obstacle to effective judicial review of the validity of legislation. That obstacle has now been eliminated, by statute in most jurisdictions and by an authoritative judicial decision binding on the remainder. Thus neither government nor legislature can prevent the judicial review of legislation by raising the shield of Crown immunity. In the struggle between judicial review and the prerogative, judicial review has emerged supreme.

70. See Heuston, *Essays in Constitutional Law* (2nd ed. 1964), at 58–81.

CHAPTER FIVE

The Elements
of a Constitutional Case

GENERAL CONSIDERATIONS

In considering the propriety or the legality of Canadian courts giving decisions on questions of constitutional validity, it is essential to keep in mind that they are not restricted by any concept of separation of powers. Canadian courts have not been confined to a purely "judicial" role in such a manner as to prevent them from exercising, with legislative sanction, a non-judicial function in the rendering of constitutional opinions. In this respect their position differs from that of the courts in the United States and Australia.

It has been held that there is no constitutional separation of powers at either the provincial or the federal level in Canada. Thus the delegation by legislatures[1] or Parliament[2] of part of their law-making power to executive or other agencies has been upheld.[3] It is also apparent that the executive branch of government can exercise judicial functions on occasion, subject to the requirement that the members of any agency exercising functions analogous to a superior, district, or county court must, by virtue of section 96 of the British North America Act, be appointed by the governor general.[4]

It has also been held that the courts may perform non-judicial as well

---

1. *Hodge* v. *The Queen* (1883), 9 App. Cas. 117 (P.C.).
2. *Re Gray* (1918), 57 S.C.R. 150, 42 D.L.R. 1; *Reference re Chemicals Regulations*, [1943] S.C.R. 1, [1943] 1 D.L.R. 248.
3. The opposite has been held in the United States on occasion. See e.g. *Panama Refining Co.* v. *Ryan* (1935), 293 U.S. 388; *Schechter Poultry Corp.* v. *U.S.* (1935), 295 U.S. 495.
4. *Labour Relations Board of Sask.* v. *John East Iron Works Ltd.*, [1949] A.C. 134 (P.C.); *Farrell* v. *Workmen's Compensation Board*, [1962] S.C.R. 48, at 52, 31 D.L.R. (2d) 177, at 180–81; *Brooks* v. *Pavlick*, [1964] S.C.R. 108, 42 D.L.R. (2d) 572. See also *supra*, at 53–55.

as judicial functions. The leading decisions in this field arose out of disputes over the use of the power given to the governor in council or the lieutenant governor in council to refer constitutional questions to federal and provincial courts respectively. In *Attorney General for Ontario* v. *Attorney General for Canada*[5] the governor general, acting pursuant to the Supreme Court Act,[6] had referred to the Supreme Court of Canada some questions of law involving the extent of the provincial power with respect to the incorporation of companies. Several provinces intervened to object to such a reference, asserting that the provision for references in the Supreme Court Act was ultra vires. The Supreme Court, in a split decision, rejected this contention. When the matter came on appeal to the Privy Council the provinces argued *inter alia* that Parliament had no power to require the Supreme Court to perform non-judicial functions. It was said that section 101 of the British North America Act, in empowering Parliament to create a "Court of Appeal," required the court so established to be a truly judicial body. The giving of opinions on questions of law was characterized as an executive function not suitable for a genuine court.

Earl Loreburn L.C., in his judgment for the Judicial Committee, started with the premise that collectively the powers given to the dominion and the provinces "cover the whole area of self-government within the whole area of Canada."[7] The implication was clear that, except for the limitations imposed by the division of powers between dominion and province, and except for any other clear limitations in the BNA Act on legislative power, it was open to Parliament or the legislatures to distribute governmental power within their own spheres in such manner as they chose. The question then remaining was, did section 101 with its reference to a "Court of Appeal," constitute such a clear limitation as to preclude the creation of a body which might be obliged to perform an advisory function? Lord Loreburn felt that it did not. He seems to have been particularly impressed by the fact that other courts more familiar to him had been required to perform the same function. The Judicial Committee of the Privy Council was itself given this duty in its original Act.[8] It was also noted that the

---

5. [1912] A.C. 571 (P.C.).
6. R.S.C. 1906, c.139, s.60 which provided in part: "60. Important questions of law or fact touching (a) the interpretation of the British North America Acts, 1867 to 1886; or (b) the constitutionality or interpretation of any Dominion or provincial legislation; . . . may be referred by the Governor in Council to the Supreme Court for hearing and consideration. . . ."
7. [1912] A.C., at 581.
8. 3 & 4 Wm. IV, c.41, s.4. For an example of the use of the power see *Re Cape Breton* (1846), 5 Moo. P.C. 259, 13 E. R. 489 (P.C.); *Re Parliamentary Privilege Act, 1770*, [1958] A.C. 331 (P.C.). The provision in the Supreme Court Act seems

judges of the superior courts in England had in some cases answered questions referred to them by the House of Lords,[9] though Lord Loreburn felt that practice to be somewhat distinguishable in that there the questions would arise out of pending litigation. But he thought it significant that the Privy Council had in numerous appeals from Canada dealt with reference cases, and this without any suggestion that such a procedure was subversive of the judicial function. Even many of the provinces which now argued against the validity of references by the federal government had themselves provided for such references to be made by the provincial government to a provincial superior court. This also reinforced the view that such a function was not generally considered to make the tribunal exercising it something other than a court.

While the Privy Council thus held that a "court" could be required by statute to answer questions referred to it, the decision indicated that this was definitely not a judicial function. According to Lord Loreburn, "the answers are only advisory and will have no more effect than the opinions of the law officers." The distinction between the adjudicatory function and the advisory function, and the constitutional validity of the latter, were both affirmed again by the Privy Council two years later. Viscount Haldane made some general comments on the reference procedure.

It is at times attended with inconveniences, and it is not surprising that the Supreme Court of the United States should have steadily refused to adopt a similar procedure, and should have confined itself to adjudication on the legal rights of litigants in actual controversies. But this refusal is based on the position of that Court in the Constitution of the United States, a position which is different from that of any Canadian Court, or of the Judicial Committee under the statute of William IV. The business of the Supreme Court of Canada is to do what is laid down as its duty by the Dominion Parliament, and the duty of the Judicial Committee, although not bound by any Canadian statute, is to give to it as a Court of review such assistance as is within its power.[10]

With respect to similar powers of reference by provincial governments to provincial courts, Canadian decisions have been the same. The Supreme Court of Canada originally refused to entertain appeals from provincial courts where the original decision took the form of an opinion on a reference. It was held that the relevant provincial statute itself, by stating that such a decision "shall be deemed a judgment" was an admission that it

---

originally to have been based on this section: *A.G. for Ont.* v. *A.G. for Can., supra* note 7, at 577, 585.

9. See e.g. *In re Westminster Bank* (1834), 2 Cl. & F. 191, 6 E. R. 1127; *M'Naghten's Case* (1843), 10 Cl. & F. 200, 8 E. R. 718.

10. *A.G. for B.C.* v. *A.G. for Can.*, [1914] A.C. 153, at 162 (P.C. 1913).

was not a judgment. In the view of the Supreme Court "There is no judgment to be appealed from. . . . There is no action, no parties, no controversy perhaps. . . . " The Supreme Court had jurisdiction only to entertain appeals from "judgments."[11] It required an amendment[12] to the Supreme Court Act before the court would hear appeals from decisions in reference cases. In spite of this clear recognition that the reference procedure was not judicial in nature, the provincial courts nevertheless accepted the obligation to render advisory opinions when asked to do so by the lieutenant governor in council.[13]

It is apparent, therefore, that in the matter of giving advisory opinions the provincial courts and the Supreme Court of Canada do not perform strictly judicial functions. It is equally apparent that there is no constitutional bar to their making decisions on issues not arising out of litigation. They may be required by statute to make such decisions. It is also arguable that, even in the absence of clear statutory direction, they have more discretionary power to accept or reject disputes for decision than have the courts of countries where the separation of powers prevails.

The contrast is quite sharp between the Canadian situation and the situation prevailing in countries such as the United States or Australia. In the United States the constitutional limitation on the federal judicial role is illustrated in *Muskrat* v. *United States*.[14] Congress, in 1904 and 1906, by statute increased the size of the class entitled to share in the final distribution of lands and funds of the Cherokees. As there were complaints about such legislation from those who had been previously entitled, Congress passed a statute in 1907 permitting certain named persons to bring a class action in the Court of Claims to determine the validity of the 1904 and 1906 legislation. It was specified that the United States should be the defendant, that the attorney general should defend the suits, and that there should be a right of appeal to the Supreme Court. An action was brought pursuant to the statute and was dismissed in the Court of Claims on the basis that the 1904 and 1906 legislation was valid. On appeal to the Supreme Court, that body held the 1907 statute and the proceedings taken thereunder to be invalid. The court referred to article III of the constitution, which in section 1 confers the "judicial power" on the federal courts established by Congress and in section 2 defines the "judicial power" as

11. *Union Colliery Co.* v. *A.G. for B.C.* (1897), 27 S.C.R. 637, at 639 (1897).
12. Stats. Can. 1922, c.48, s.1.
13. *In re Order in Council: In re Crop Payments Act*, [1926] 2 W.W.R. 844, [1927] 2 D.L.R. 50 (Man. C.A.).
14. (1911), 219 U.S. 346.

extending to the "cases" and "controversies" specified therein. Relying on various precedents[15] the Supreme Court held that the duty which the 1907 statute purported to cast on the federal courts was not a judicial duty because it did not involve a case or controversy. "That judicial power, as we have seen, is the right to determine actual controversies arising between adverse litigants, duly instituted in courts of proper jurisdiction."[16] But, under the 1907 statute the purpose of the action "is not to assert a property right as against the Government, or to demand compensation for alleged wrongs. . . . The whole purpose of the law is to determine the constitutional validity of this class of legislation. . . . "[17] In other words, the United States had no interest adverse to the plaintiffs, and was a party only to facilitate the determination of the Act's validity. Hence there was no case or controversy. Congress, it was held, could not validly confer on the Court of Claims or the Supreme Court the duty to entertain this type of proceeding.

It is therefore apparent that in the United States the federal courts which are established under article III of the constitution must confine themselves to deciding matters which they are prepared to regard as involving a "case" or "controversy."[18] Nor can Congress require them to deal with other matters such as the giving of opinions, because to do so would be to force them into non-judicial functions.

In Australia the situation is similar. The Commonwealth of Australia Constitution Act,[19] section 71, vests the "judicial power" of the Commonwealth in the High Court and other federal courts created by Parliament. Section 73 sets out the High Court's appellate power, and sections 75 and 76 confer on it original jurisdiction with respect to certain "matters" therein specified. Parliament in the early part of this century attempted in

15. *Hayburn's Case* (1792), 2 Dall. 408 (Cir. Ct.); *U.S.* v. *Ferreira* (1851), 13 How. 39 (Sup. Ct.); *Gordon* v. *U.S.* (1864), 117 U.S. 697. Reference was also made to Chief Justice Jay's celebrated answer to President Washington in 1793 in which he stated that it would not be proper for the judges of the Supreme Court to advise the executive branch on legal questions.
16. 219 U.S., at 361.
17. *Ibid.*
18. This is not true in the state courts of those states where the state constitution permits advisory opinions to be given. For the classic criticism of the advisory opinion system, see Frankfurter, "A Note on Advisory Opinions" (1924), 37 *Harv. L. Rev.* 1002. It is arguable that where the state courts are prepared to entertain an action involving the federal law or constitution, the U.S. Supreme Court should be able to treat an appeal from that decision as a "case or controversy" even though a similar action, if commenced in a federal court, would not be regarded as a "case or controversy." See e.g. Scharpf, "Judicial Review and the Political Question: A Functional Analysis" (1966), 75 *Yale L.J.* 517, at 521.
19. 63 & 64 Vict., c.12 (1900).

section 88 of the Judiciary Act[20] to give to the High Court "jurisdiction to hear and determine . . . any question of law as to the validity of any Act or enactment of the Parliament" which the governor general might refer to it. In *In re the Judiciary Act*[21] the High Court rejected this jurisdiction in a case referred to it under the Judiciary Act with respect to the validity of the Navigation Act, a federal statute. The majority of the court took the view that Parliament was seeking, through this device, to obtain authoritative declarations of the law. They believed that the making of such declarations would be a judicial function. While thus coming to a different conclusion than that of the Canadian and United States courts about the judicial nature of advisory opinions, they nevertheless held that the giving of such opinions would be unconstitutional.[22] The scope of the judicial power of the federal courts was that spelled out in the constitution. As this was an original jurisdiction which the Judiciary Act purported to confer, it would have to be brought under section 75 or 76 of the constitution. Section 75 being inapplicable, they considered and rejected section 76 as a possible source of power. "[W]e do not think that the word "matter" in Section 76 means a legal proceeding, but rather the subject matter for determination in a legal proceeding. In our opinion there can be no matter within the meaning of the section unless there is some immediate right, duty or liability to be established by the determination of the Court."[23] They were unable to find anything in the constitution which would authorize Parliament to confer power on the High Court "to determine abstract questions of law without the right or duty of any body or person being involved."[24]

The contrasting situation in the United States and Australia points up the comparative freedom of the judiciary in Canada. Where it is so provided by the legislature, Canadian courts have both a right and a duty to exercise the function of deciding issues, even those not raised in the course of a real dispute between two or more adverse parties. In the light of this freedom from constitutional restraint, it may be open to Canadian courts to entertain proceedings of various kinds (even in the absence of express legislative sanction) in situations where the United States federal courts would not find a "case or controversy" or the Australian federal courts would not be able to identify a "matter" suitable for litigation.

20. Stats. Austl. 1903 c.6, 1920 c.38.
21. (1921), 29 C.L.R. 257.
22. The assumption that this was a judicial power has since been criticized. It is also now clear that judicial and non-judicial functions may not be given to the same tribunal: *R. v. Kirby, ex parte Boilermaker's Society*, 94 C.L.R. 254. See also Wynes, *Legislative, Executive and Judicial Powers in Australia* (3rd ed. 1962), at 545–82.
23. 29 C.L.R., at 265.   24. *Ibid.*, at 267.

THE PROPER PARTIES

STANDING TO RAISE THE CONSTITUTIONAL ISSUE

Where the validity of legislation is attacked in ordinary litigation between citizens or between the citizen and the state, the parties clearly have standing to raise a constitutional issue. In such cases the individual is seeking to assert some right for himself. In the process of establishing this right he contends that legislation which would interfere with it is invalid. This is an incidental and collateral attack on legislation in the process of claiming a right peculiar to the claimant. For present purposes this type of action may be referred to as a "private" action because the constitutional issue is raised solely to assert one's own interests. It might embrace a diversity of proceedings such as an action for damages,[25] for recovery of money,[26] for enforcement of a contract,[27] a prosecution,[28] an action for enforcement of taxes,[29] or an application for certiorari to quash an order of an inferior tribunal.[30] The challenge to the validity of a statute might be raised as a ground for the claim or as a defence. The feature which these "private" actions have in common is that they involve a matter of particular concern to the party raising the constitutional issue, a right which is peculiar to him and which he can establish only by showing the statute to be of no effect. "Private" actions of this nature create no particular problem for the court because they involve real disputes over rights pertaining to the actual parties.

At the other pole are those situations in which an individual challenges legislation or official action on behalf of the public at large. In such cases he does not claim a right peculiar to himself. At best his position is that of a member of the public seeking to have the court enforce the requirements of the constitution. Such proceedings may perhaps best be described as "public actions."[31]

---

25. E.g. *Murphy* v. *C.P.R.*, [1958] S.C.R. 626, 15 D.L.R. (2d) 145; *Transport Oil Co.* v. *Imperial Oil Co.*, [1935] O.R. 215, [1935] 2 D.L.R. 500 (Ont. C.A.).
26. E.g. *Cairns Construction Ltd.* v. *Government of Saskatchewan*, [1960] S.C.R. 619, 24 D.L.R. (2d) 1; *Fort Frances Pulp and Power* v. *Manitoba Free Press*, [1923] A.C. 695 (P.C.).
27. E.g. *John Deere Plow Co.* v. *Wharton*, [1915] A.C. 330 (P.C.); *Beauharnois Light, Heat & Power Co.* v. *Hydro-Electric Power Commission*, [1937] O.R. 796, [1937] 3 D.L.R. 458 (Ont. C.A.).
28. E.g. *R.* v. *Pee-Kay Smallwares Ltd.* [1947] O.R. 1019, [1948] 1 D.L.R. 235 (Ont. C.A.); *R.* v. *Campbell*, [1964] 2 O.R. 487, 46 D.L.R. (2d) 83 (Ont. C.A.).
29. E.g. *King* v. *Caledonian Collieries Ltd.*, [1928] A.C. 358 (P.C.).
30. E.g. *Labour Relations Board of Sask.* v. *John East Iron Works Ltd.*, [1949] A.C. 134 (P.C.).
31. See Jaffe, "Standing to Secure Judicial Review: Public Actions" (1961), 74 *Harv. L. Rev.* 1265.

Between the two polar situations represented by purely "private" actions and purely "public" actions there are a variety of possibilities. There may be situations, for example, in which the person seeking to raise a constitutional point may assert the interest of a class constituting only a portion of the public. Or he may assert some interest which the courts do not recognize as a matter of "right" or "duty": the type of matters with which they normally deal. In such cases the problem of standing to sue arises just as in the purely "public" action. Attention must therefore be given to all situations involving proceedings other than "private" actions. This is the real problem area with respect to standing in constitutional disputes.

In the United States the federal courts have shown a particular reluctance to entertain attacks on the validity of legislation where the plaintiff's status does not create a "case or controversy." They have insisted that, to have standing to raise a constitutional issue, a party must be asserting a legal right (as opposed to some interest no matter how real)[32] which right must be asserted as his own [33] and not on behalf of the public at large.[34] This strictness of approach seems to be interwoven with the constitutional limitations on the federal judiciary imposed by article III of the constitution, and is therefore not necessarily relevant to Canadian practice. To a certain extent, however, the American rules reflect a natural judicial reluctance to decide constitutional questions except where such decisions cannot be avoided.[35] In this they may have some significance for Canadian courts.

In Canada no general doctrines have ever been developed by the courts with respect to standing to raise constitutional issues. The cases in which the problem has been raised are surprisingly few. Such rules as do exist are not peculiar to constitutional issues but arise instead out of the requirements for the granting of particular remedies. One must then look to the remedies or proceedings most likely to be used in actions of a public or quasi-public nature involving constitutional issues.

(a) Requirements for Particular Remedies
(i) *Declarations*: Where a litigant seeks to enforce his own private rights a declaration can be issued even though a number of other persons could bring actions for similar invasions of their private rights. In the famous case of *Dyson* v. *Attorney General*[36] the plaintiff was the recipient of one

32. E.g. *Tennessee Electric Power Co.* v. *T.V.A.* (1939), 306 U.S. 118.
33. E.g. *Tileston* v. *Ullman* (1943), 318 U.S. 44.
34. E.g. *Frothingham* v. *Mellon* (1923), 262 U.S. 447.
35. See Lewis, "Constitutional Rights and the Misuse of Standing" (1962), 14 *Stan. L. Rev.* 433, at 448.
36. [1911] 1 K.B. 410. See *supra*, at 75–76.

of some eight million similar notices sent out by the Commissioners of Inland Revenue requiring the making of certain tax returns. Failure to make the returns would subject the recipient to penalties. Dyson, while occupying a position similar to that of millions of others, nevertheless could show that he would suffer injury to specific private rights of his own, and he was therefore allowed to seek a declaration that the notice was ultra vires of the Commissioners.

While the *Dyson* case involved an attack on public officers for exceeding their powers,[37] no doubt the same principle would apply if one attacked the constitutional validity of the statute under which such officers acted. If a provincial statute purported to expropriate the land of all aliens, for example, it would be open to any individual landowning alien to seek a declaration that his ownership remained unimpaired because the statute was ultra vires. The fact that similar property rights of hundreds or thousands of other aliens might be similarly affected would be no bar to his action.[38]

There appear to be no special criteria for the "interest" which will be sufficient to provide standing to seek a declaration on a constitutional matter. The problem has apparently been considered in just two cases in the Supreme Court of Canada. In both cases the action for a declaration was refused, though refusal was seemingly based on general principles applicable to constitutional and non-constitutional cases alike.

In *Smith* v. *Attorney General for Ontario*[39] the plaintiff was a resident of Ontario who wished to attack the validity of the Canada Temperance Act as applied in his province. Part IV of the Act prohibited interprovincial movement of liquor into provinces which had adopted suitable local prohibition legislation and had passed a legislative resolution making the federal Act apply. In 1920 the Ontario legislature passed such a resolution and the federal cabinet passed an order in council declaring part IV to be in force in the province. Smith subsequently ordered from a dealer in Montreal some whiskey, ale, and beer. The dealer declined to accept the order because the Canada Temperance Act prohibited such importation into Ontario. No attention was ever paid to this exchange by any government official.

Smith then sued the attorney general of Ontario for a declaration that the Canada Temperance Act did not validly apply in Ontario. He contended that existing provincial legislation was not of the type required to

37. See also *Gruen Watch Company* v. *A.G. for Can.* [1950] O.R. 429, [1950] 4 D.L.R. 156 (Ont. High Ct.).
38. See generally Zamir, *The Declaratory Judgment* (1962), at 250–54.
39. [1924] S.C.R. 331, [1924] 3 D.L.R. 189.

make the Canada Temperance Act validly applicable. On the question of standing, he argued that he was illegally prevented from exercising his right to import liquor into the province, except under intolerable conditions, that is, the subjection of himself and his employees to possible criminal proceedings. He relied on the *Dyson* case to justify the form in which the action was brought.

The court,[40] in a series of separate judgments, held that Smith had no standing to bring an action for a declaration under these circumstances. Idington J. distinguished the *Dyson* case on the grounds that there the Crown had actually made a claim against Dyson. By sending him the tax return, they had put him in the position where, if he did not act by completing the return, the attorney general could proceed against him for penalties. In the *Smith* case, however, there was no similar foundation laid for such proceedings by the Crown against Smith. The possibility of such action was purely speculative. It could not arise until Smith had actually imported some liquor. Idington J. took the view that the plaintiff was merely trying to elicit an opinion from the court and that such an attempt should be rejected "unless we are quite prepared to assent to such like requests on any point of law puzzling any private citizen on any question. . . . "[41]

Duff J. (Maclean J. concurring) took a similar view. The *Smith* case was unlike *Dyson* because it involved only a hypothetical state of facts. "[O]nly if the liquor ordered were actually shipped, that is to say, only in a contingency which has not happened, could the appellant be put in jeopardy."[42] Smith had argued that the existence of the Canada Temperance Act, the resolution of the Ontario legislature, and the order in council constituted an implied threat to many people including himself, a threat that if they carried on their lawful business they would be prosecuted. Mr. Justice Duff had some sympathy for the point of view that one ought not to have to subject himself to prosecution in order to raise the constitutional point.

We think, however, that to accede to appellant's contention upon this point would involve the consequence that virtually every resident of Ontario could maintain a similar action; and we can discover no firm ground on which the appellant's claim can be supported which would not be equally available to sustain the right of any citizen of a province to initiate proceedings impeaching the constitutional validity of any legislation directly affecting him, along with other citizens, in a similar way in his business or in his professional life.

40. Davies C. J., Idington, Duff, Mignault, and Maclean JJ.; Sir Louis Davies died before judgment was delivered. Maclean J. was sitting only *ad hoc.*
41. [1924] S.C.R., at 333–34, [1924] 3 D.L.R., at 190.
42. [1924] S.C.R., at 336, [1924] 3 D.L.R., at 192.

We think the recognition of such a principle would lead to grave inconvenience and analogy is against it. An individual for example, has no status to maintain an action restraining a wrongful violation of a public right unless he is exceptionally prejudiced by the wrongful act.[43]

Mignault J. in agreeing with Duff J. stated that the position of this plaintiff did not differ materially from that of hundreds of other citizens who might be opposed to prohibition. Smith was not in jeopardy at the time he commenced the action. It would be a great inconvenience to allow actions to be brought by those not showing any special interest.

All of the judges thus held that Smith had no right to a declaration. As long as he had not received any liquor from outside the province he was not in any danger of prosecution. In their view he was not being required by the impugned law to take any action or to give up his property. Thus he had no private right to assert or protect. He was in the same position as any other person who might like to import liquor but who would not be prepared to do so as long as there was a prohibitory law on the statute books.

Curiously, three of the judges, after coming to the conclusion that Smith had no standing to raise the issue as to the validity of the Canada Temperance Act in Ontario, proceeded to decide against him on the substantive issue as well. Duff J. (Maclean J. concurring) had indicated that to decide such an issue at the suit of such a party would lead to "grave inconvenience." Having established this principle he indicated that the judges were "loath to give a judgment against the appellant solely based upon a fairly disputable point of procedure. . . . " He then analyzed the means by which the Act had been applied to Ontario and held them to be adequate. Mignault J. similarly found the procedural objection sufficient to dispose of the matter but in addition held the Act to be validly in force. One cannot fail to note the contrast here with the practice of United States federal courts. It is most improbable that one of those courts would find that a plaintiff had no standing to bring the action in question and then proceed to decide a constitutional or quasi-constitutional issue such as this. The difference in treatment must reflect to some extent the comparative lack of constitutional restraint imposed on Canadian courts. As they are not strictly limited to the exercise of "judicial" functions alone, Canadian courts are free to render a decision with respect to an issue raised by a person not properly a party before the court. In this case it seems to have been a matter of discretion for the Supreme Court of Canada whether they dealt with the substantive issue. Though all the judges had decided that to entertain actions of this type would, as a general rule, lead to "incon-

43. [1924] S.C.R., at 337, [1924] 3 D.L.R., at 193–94.

venience," three of them could not bring themselves to dismiss this particular action. They were "loath" to do so on a "disputable point of procedure." Apparently they considered that the power was in their hands to deal with the substantive question of validity if they chose to do so.

The 1964 decision of *Saumur and Jehovah's Witnesses* v. *Attorney General for Quebec* saw another attempt to obtain a declaration of invalidity thwarted by the Supreme Court. Earlier efforts by the city of Quebec to regulate by bylaw the distribution of religious pamphlets on city streets had been successfully attacked in 1953 by Saumur, a minister and missionary of the Jehovah's Witnesses.[44] On January 28, 1954, there came into effect an amendment to the provincial Freedom of Worship Act. This amendment[45] prohibited the distribution of any pamphlets containing abusive attacks on the religion of any portion of the population. Speeches and broadcasts containing attacks of this nature were also prohibited. On the next day, January 29, 1954, the plaintiffs commenced this action for a declaration that the amendment was ultra vires of the Quebec legislature. They also asked for injunctions against the police and the attorney general to prevent enforcement of the new law. The plaintiffs alleged that they carried on their proselytizing by distribution of pamphlets, preaching, etc. They asserted that their actions did not violate the prohibitions of the amendment, but that they believed that it was the immediate intention of the city of Quebec and its officers to use the provincial law to stop the activities of the Jehovah's Witnesses. They attempted to introduce evidence at the trial to the effect that the premier and attorney general had made statements in the legislature indicating that the Act was to be used against the Witnesses. This evidence was held to be inadmissible and the action was dismissed.

The attorney general had contended, *inter alia*, that in Quebec there was no action for a declaration such as that used in the *Dyson* case. It was also contended that the plaintiffs did not have the "interest" which is required to bring an action in Quebec.[46] On appeal[47] to the Court of Queen's Bench, Appeal Side, two of the judges (Rinfret and Choquette JJ.) held that Quebec law did not recognize the action for a declaration of invalidity of a statute. Owen J. (Taschereau J. concurring) was content

44. *Saumur* v. *Quebec*, [1953] 2 S.C.R. 299, [1953] 4 D.L.R. 641. Here the plaintiff in seeking a declaration could show that he had already been prosecuted under the impugned bylaw.
45. Stats. Que. 1953–54, c.15, amending R.S.Q. 1941, c.307.
46. Code of Civil Procedure, 1897, article 77: "No person can bring an action at law unless he has an interest therein. Such interest, except where it is otherwise provided, may be merely eventual." See now Code of Civil Procedure, Stats. Que. 1965, c.80, article 55 to a similar effect.
47. [1963] Que. Q.B. 116, 37 D.L.R. 703.

to hold that the plaintiffs had no "interest" as required by article 77 of the Code of Civil Procedure because there had been no attempt to apply the impugned statute to them. He declined to decide whether the declaration was permitted in Quebec law. Casey J. held that a declaration of invalidity was not available to one who has not yet been attacked or prosecuted or whose property has not yet been affected pursuant to the impugned statute. He did not expressly exclude the possibility of a declaratory action where the plaintiff had been affected, but considered that the plaintiffs in this case had not yet suffered under the statute. Nevertheless he did hold that the plaintiffs probably had a sufficient "interest" here to meet the requirements of article 77.

The uncertainty as to the effect of this decision was partially removed on the appeal to the Supreme Court of Canada.[48] The judgment of the court was given by Chief Justice Taschereau whose authority on the subject of Quebec law few would question. He stated that "[d]ans la province de Québec l'action déclaratoire n'existe pas."[49] At first blush this would suggest to the common lawyer that Quebec courts could never give a declaration as to rights. It seems, however, that the Chief Justice may merely have intended to say that Quebec courts will never make a declaration unless there is a real dispute between parties, for he proceeded thereafter as follows. "Ses tribunaux ne donnent pas des consultations légales; ils jugent les litiges. Les questions académiques et théoriques où aucun lis n'existe leur ont toujours été étrangères. La seule crainte que peut avoir un citoyen qu'un jour une action possible peut être instituée contre lui ne justifie pas *per se* un recours en justice."[50] The judgment appears to hold that the "interest" which was required in article 77 was the sort of interest which would in any event be required before a Quebec court could entertain any proceeding to hold a statute invalid. It was found that the plaintiffs here had no such interest because they had not been injured in any way since the Act came into effect. Their statement of claim itself alleged that the type of activities carried on by the Jehovah's Witnesses would not violate the statute and if this were so the statute could not be applied to them.

By asserting that their own practices were not a violation of the statute the plaintiffs made their claim to *locus standi* tenuous. It is probably safe to assume that no Canadian court, inside or outside Quebec, would entertain an attack on a statute by a private citizen who asserts that the statute could not apply to him. A different line of attack, and one which the Supreme Court might have considered, could have been that the amendments to the

48. [1964] S.C.R. 252, 45 D.L.R. (2d) 627.
49. [1964] S.C.R. at 257, 45 D.L.R. (2d) at 630.
50. *Ibid.*

Freedom of Worship Act were so imprecise in their intended application that they constituted a threat to the plaintiff's freedom of speech and religion. While perhaps untried in Canada, this approach has been used in the United States to invalidate various laws which have not adequately defined the prohibited acts and have thus created an undue hazard for persons wishing to exercise their constitutional freedoms.[51] On this basis it might well have been held that the amendments did interfere with the plaintiffs' rights, and thus they would have the required "interest." But in the face of the contention that the amendments could not apply to the plaintiffs' activities, the 1964 *Saumur* decision applies a principle which is not exclusive to Quebec.

It is doubtful that Chief Justice Taschereau's broad assertion should be taken to mean that there could be no action for a declaration in Quebec. Perhaps all that was intended was that there could be no action for a declaration unless the plaintiff had some interest in having the question determined. If this was the intended meaning, the position in Quebec was essentially the same as in the common law provinces.[52] The situation in Quebec has been clarified subsequently by the new Code of Civil Procedure,[53] which provides as follows: "453. Any person who has an interest in having determined immediately, for the solution of a genuine problem, either his status or any right, power or obligation which he may have under a contract, will or any other written instrument, statute, order in council, or resolution or by-law of a municipal corporation, may, by motion to the court, ask for a declaratory judgment in that regard." This makes clear that the position of the declaratory action in Quebec law is essentially the same as it is in the common law provinces, and the same in cases involving attacks on legislative validity as in other cases.

Can one reconcile the *Smith* case and the *Saumur* case? In both cases the Supreme Court found that the plaintiff had no special interest different from that of the public at large. Yet in the *Smith* case the Court did

51. See e.g. *Cantwell* v. *Connecticut* (1940), 310 U.S. 296; *Ashton* v. *Kentucky* (1966), 384 U.S. 195; *Keyishian* v. *Board of Regents* (1967), 385 U.S. 589.

52. The point is obscured because he speaks of declaratory proceedings as "consultations légales." This is seemingly based on the assumption that declaratory proceedings in other provinces can be taken by parties having no legal interest at stake; that declaratory judgments answer "les questions académiques. . . . " If this is what he means by "l'action déclaratoire" then it may be said that as a general rule such actions do not exist in other provinces either. However, other Quebec actions for declarations in constitutional cases had proceeded without difficulty: e.g. *Saumur* v. *Quebec, supra* note 44; *A.G. for Canada* v. *Reader's Digest*, [1961] S.C.R. 775, 30 D.L.R. (2d) 296. See Scott, "Comment" (1965), 11 *McGill L.J.* 88. For a recent statement of the common law position see *Cowan* v. *Canadian Broadcasting Corporation*, [1966] 2 O.R. 309, 56 D.L.R. (2d) 578; Strayer, "Comment" (1967), 45 *Can. B. Rev.* 154.

53. *Supra*, note 46.

proceed to make a decision as to the validity of the application of the Act in question. The *Saumur* case seems to set up an absolute bar against the grant of a declaration in such cases, whereas the *Smith* case seems to leave a certain discretion in the Court. The distinction between the two cases may be attributable simply to the fact that one involved Ontario law, the other Quebec law. But one might also argue that there were stronger reasons for the Court considering the substantive question in the *Smith* case. There the plaintiff had actually been prevented from obtaining liquor. He had made an attempt to do so and had been thwarted because of the Montreal liquor dealer's refusal to risk a violation of the Canada Temperance Act. Smith was asserting that the Act would apply to him if he carried on his normal activities. The plaintiffs in the *Saumur* case, on the other hand, asserted that the statute could not be applied to them because their activities did not come within its ambit. Also, by commencing action the day after the Act came into effect they made it difficult to show any real injury to themselves as a result of its passage. So even if one were to assume that Ontario law and Quebec law are identical with respect to declaratory actions, a much stronger case could be made for the Court entertaining the action in the *Smith* case.

Thus, as long as a plaintiff is in some measure seeking to assert his own private rights, he may be able to maintain an action for a declaration as to the validity of a statute. If he seeks to vindicate purely public rights, however, he cannot by himself bring an action for a declaration. It is the attorney general who has the right to bring actions to protect public interests. Only the attorney general may sue for a declaration that a public body is exceeding its powers.[54] Presumably this could include situations where it is alleged that the public body acts without jurisdiction because the statute under which it purports to act is itself ultra vires. While the attorney general has a right of action only if the public as a whole is affected,[55] it would seem that the question of whether a statute of the legislature is valid or not would be of concern to the public as a whole.

The application of these common law principles within a federal system might well cause considerable difficulty. Could a provincial attorney general commence action in this way to challenge the authority of a federal agency on the grounds that its act of Parliament was ultra vires? Could the attorney general of Canada challenge a provincial statute in a

54. *Robertson* v. *Montreal* (1915), 52 S.C.R. 30, 26 D.L.R. 228; *Loggie* v. *Town of Chatham* (1927), 54 N.B. 230, [1928] 2 D.L.R. 583 (Sup. Ct. N.B. App. Div.); *Jenkins* v. *Winnipeg*, [1941] 1 W.W.R. 37, [1941] 1 D.L.R. 477 (Man. K.B.) and see Zamir, *supra* note 38, at 254–70.
55. *Livingstone* v. *Edmonton* (1915), 8 W.W.R. 976, 24 D.L.R. 191 (Alta. Sup. Ct.).

similar manner? These questions have never been answered in Canada. In Australia the High Court has held that a state attorney general had a sufficient title to challenge the validity of the federal Pharmaceutical Benefits Act as it operated within his state.[56] The soundness of this view seems open to question. It is submitted that each attorney general would on principle be entitled to an action only with respect to the laws of the jurisdiction to which he belongs. The right of the attorney general in these cases probably stems from the Crown's prerogative rights as *parens patriae*. It has been held in other situations that the extent of the prerogative in right of the Dominion or of a province corresponds to the distribution of legislative power under the BNA Act.[57]

If this constitutional distribution does apply to declaratory actions by attorneys general, it is unlikely that they will ever be a means of bringing a public action to challenge directly the validity of legislation. This action has the virtue of simplicity in that the attorney general need prove no interest in the matter to commence action. But in bringing action he must challenge the validity of acts of his own legislature. He is a member of the cabinet responsible to that legislature and if he has formed the opinion that the legislation is invalid he should advise that it be repealed. If the government rejects his advice he must either accept the majority decision or resign. If he merely has doubts about the validity of the law or if outright repeal is impolitic, then the easier course is for him to advise the cabinet to refer the matter to the courts for an opinion.

It is possible for a private citizen to initiate such proceedings by way of a relator action. In such cases he must obtain the consent of the attorney general to commence the action in the latter's name.[58] Presumably the same principles which would inhibit the attorney general from suing by himself would deter him from granting his consent to a private citizen to bring this unique public action.

The attorney general's action against public bodies to prevent an excess of jurisdiction might be used in a quasi-constitutional manner. This could arise where the allegation was that the public body was wrongly exercising valid statutory powers, in a manner which would apply the statute unconstitutionally. Thus a provincial attorney general might seek a declaration that a municipality had exercised its power to make bylaws for the preservation of order on municipal streets in a way which conflicted with the

---

56. *A.G. for Vict. (Ex. rel. Dale)* v. *Commonwealth* (1945), 71 C.L.R. 237 (H.C.). But see *South Carolina* v. *Katzenbach* (1966), 383 U.S. 301, at 324.
57. *Bonanza Creek Gold Mining Company* v. *The King*, [1916] A.C. 566 (P.C.); *A.G. for Can.* v. *A.G. for Ont.*, [1898] A.C. 247 (P.C.) (1897).
58. See Zamir, *supra* note 38, at 262–66.

Criminal Code.[59] This would not involve an attack on the provincial statute under which the municipality purported to make its bylaw, but only an attack on the bylaw itself as being outside the contemplation of that statute.

In strictly constitutional disputes it would appear therefore that the declaratory action will not be commonly employed except by individuals bent on protecting their own interests. The question will always remain as to what interest a plaintiff must show to achieve standing. Normally for a court to entertain such an action, there must be a definite disagreement between the parties, with respect to specific facts which have occurred and are not hypothetical only. As well there must be some practical advantages in the making of a declaration.[60] In exceptional cases, however, it is apparently open to the court to make a declaration with respect to even a theoretical problem.[61] It is submitted that when the matter in issue involves the validity of a statute there are often exceptional circumstances which should induce the court to permit a declaratory proceeding.

Apart from the apparent discretion which courts have in recognizing *locus standi* in declaratory actions (as noted in the *Smith* case) it is also clear that they have a discretion to refuse the declaration even where the action is properly instituted. Even if the plaintiff has standing, considerations of utility may deter the court from granting the declaration. The importance of the issue to the parties, the usefulness of a declaration in the dispute, the existence of sufficient facts on which to base a decision, the question of whether matters of public importance may also be conveniently settled at the same time, the balance of convenience to the parties, and similar criteria will influence the court in the exercise of its discretion.[62]

It is clear then that discretion plays a major part in a court's decision, first, to entertain a declaratory action, and, secondly, to grant or refuse a declaration. It is submitted that in constitutional cases there are special factors which should be of importance in the exercise of that discretion. What those factors are will be discussed subsequently.[63]

(ii) *Injunctions*: To seek an injunction the plaintiff must be able to show an "interest."[64] A purely public right unconnected to any personal interest cannot be asserted by an individual by means of an injunction.[65]

59. See *Kent District Corporation* v. *Storgoff and A.G. for B.C.* (1962), 40 W.W.R. (n.s.) 278 (Sup. Ct. of B.C.).
60. See Zamir, *supra* note 38, at 51–67.   61. *Ibid.*, at 67–68.
62. *Ibid.*, at 191–201.   63. See *infra*, pp. 123–25.
64. 21 *Halsbury's Laws of England* (3rd ed., 1957), at 407.
65. See *MacCormick* v. *Lord Advocate*, [1953] Sess. Cas. 396 (Scottish Court of

Normally the injunction is sought as incidental relief in association with some other remedy. Where the claim for the principal remedy is barred the incidental relief by injunction falls with it.[66] There are some additional requirements peculiar to injunctions which would probably prevent their use except in the clearest case of imminent violation of the plaintiff's property or personal interest. A court would refuse to issue an injunction where damages would be an adequate remedy, or where the plaintiff did not have "clean hands," for example. The grant is normally also subject to an equitable discretion.[67] Thus the injunction is not likely to become a common device for challenging legislative validity but will be employed incidentally in actions for damages or declarations.

An injunction may be sought by the attorney general in a purely "public" action to enforce the law. In such cases the injunction may be granted even though other sanctions or remedies are provided by statute and even though there is no invasion of property rights actual or apprehended.[68] However, the probability of an attorney general seeking such a remedy to restrain the enforcement of an ultra vires statute of his own legislature is not very great.

(iii) *Certiorari*: There appears to be no requirement of "interest" on the part of an applicant for certiorari. The general rule in England is that even a "stranger" may apply for certiorari though the court would have a discretion to refuse the application. A "person aggrieved" (who may be anyone affected, however slightly) is entitled to the issue of the writ, but even he may be barred by his own conduct from obtaining certiorari if the court so decides.[69] This probably means that in each case the court has a discretion to permit anyone to seek certiorari.[70]

The few Canadian cases which consider the question at all are consistent with the English position. In *Re Corporation of District of Surrey*[71]

Session). *Grant* v. *St. Lawrence Seaway Authority*, [1960] O.R. 298 (Ont. C.A.), 23 D.L.R. (2d) 252 (leave to appeal refused by Supreme Court of Canada, June 6, 1960).
66. See e.g. *Loggie* v. *Town of Chatham*, and *Jenkins* v. *Winnipeg, supra* note 54.
67. See Snell, *Principles of Equity* (26th ed., 1966), at 698–705.
68. *A.G. for B.C.* v. *Cowen* [1938] 2 W.W.R. 497, [1938] 4 D.L.R. 17 (B.C.C.A.); *aff'd* [1939] S.C.R. 20, [1939] 1 D.L.R. 288 without reference to this point. See also *S.M.T.* v. *Winner*, [1951] S.C.R. 887, [1951] 4 D.L.R. 529 where it was noted that the Attorney General of New Brunswick, originally an intervenant in a private action for an injunction, had been made a party in a newly constituted relator action.
69. De Smith, *Judicial Review of Administrative Action* (1959), at 310–16; Jaffe, *supra* note 31, at 1274–75.
70. Yardley, "Certiorari and the Problem of Locus Standi" (1955), 71 *L.Q.Rev.* 388, *passim*.
71. (1956), 6 D.L.R. (2d) 768 (B.C. Supreme Ct.).

the court found the applicant to be a "person aggrieved" though he had no direct personal "interest" affected by the municipal order he sought to attack. He was allowed as a resident of a town to apply for certiorari to quash a decision of the municipal planning board which had permitted a club to reconstruct its building, allegedly without adequate parking space. Mr. Justice Wilson held "that under modern conditions of congestion that any person who lives and carries on business in an urban area . . . may be a person aggrieved . . . " by such an order.[72] This clearly appears to be a case of a public action, because it is hard to see here that the applicant had substantially any more reason to complain than any other member of the community.

The decision in *Young* v. *Attorney General for Manitoba*[73] is somewhat less clear. In this case a medical doctor applied for certiorari to quash an inquest verdict with respect to the death of a child. The applicant had been the attending physician at the time of the child's death but his name was not mentioned in the verdict. His application was refused in a two-to-one decision of the Manitoba Court of Appeal. Schultz J. A. exercised his discretion and dismissed the application because of delay, without reference to the question of standing. The other majority judge, Miller J. A., rejected the application on the simple ground that the applicant had no standing. He believed that an applicant had to be an "aggrieved party" and that while this term might be given a broad interpretation in quasi-judicial matters the same should not be done in criminal matters. In his view the coroner's proceeding was a criminal proceeding. The coroner's verdict had not convicted the applicant and had not even mentioned his name. Thus he had no standing. The opposite view was taken by the dissenting judge, Freedman J. A. He felt that the doctor was an aggrieved party because the evidence at the inquest combined with common public knowledge would identify him as the attending physician. It should have been open to him to introduce extrinsic evidence to show his relationship to the proceedings.

The *Young* case is inconclusive because of the division of judicial opinion. It is submitted that the dissenting judgment is preferable. The judgment of Miller J. A., the only one who found a lack of *locus standi*, is too formalistic. To say that a doctor is not "aggrieved" by such a verdict simply because it does not name him is to put form before reality. Such a conclusion is anomalous and not likely to be accepted elsewhere.

Certiorari should thus be available, at the discretion of the court, to all or a large portion of the public. As a result, it can be used to attack validity

72. 6 D.L.R. (2d), at 769–70.
73. (1960) 33 W.W.R. (n.s.) 3, 25 D.L.R. (2d) 352 (Man.C.A.).

of legislation where the applicant can show that a judicial or quasi-judicial proceeding has been carried out pursuant to an invalid statute. The court will have a discretion to refuse applications where it feels the applicant has no good reason for asserting this public right. Some proper considerations in the exercise of this discretion will be referred to later.[74] But it is clear that within the rather narrow field where certiorari is an appropriate remedy, standing will create few problems.

(iv) *Prohibition*: While the rules for standing in prohibition proceedings are basically similar to those for certiorari, there is one situation where a "stranger" has a clear right to prohibition. Where he alleges a defect of jurisdiction which is patent on the face of the proceedings in question the court must grant his application for prohibition.[75] Otherwise the court has a discretion to grant or refuse the application of a stranger.[76]

How do these rules apply where the excess of jurisdiction alleged is of a constitutional nature? When could it be said that the constitutional invalidity of a statute would be patent, rendering the attempted proceedings thereunder invalid so as to require the issue of a writ of prohibition? In almost every case where a statute is impugned there is serious doubt as to how the statute ought to be characterized in order to decide whether it genuinely comes within the jurisdiction of the enacting legislature. In other cases there will be doubt whether the statute can be validly applied to the facts in question.

Thus, in *R. v. Ontario Labour Relations Board, Ex parte Dunn*[77] prohibition was sought by a stranger to proceedings before the Board, in order to stop the Board from taking a vote among employees of a certain company. The applicant asserted that the company and its employees came under federal jurisdiction because it was a subsidiary of a company operating an undertaking which was within federal jurisdiction. Various factual issues concerning the nature of the relationship between the two companies were involved. Because of this complex legal and factual question the invalidity of the Board's proceedings was far from "patent." The judge, as a result, admitted to having some doubt as to the standing of the applicants but proceeded to deal with the application on its merits. In this he appeared to be exercising his discretion in favour of allowing standing to a stranger.

It is suggested that most prohibition applications raising questions of

74. See *infra*, pp. 123–25.
75. Re *Lott* v. *Cameron* (1897), 29 O.R. 70 (Ont. Div. Ct.); *Re Holman and Rea* (1912), 27 O.L.R. 432 (Ont. Div. Ct.); see also De Smith, *supra* note 69, at 308–10.
76. *In re Board of Manhood Suffrage Registrars* (1901), 13 Man. 345 (Man. K.B.); see also De Smith, *ibid.*
77. [1963] 2 O.R. 301, 39 D.L.R. (2d) 346 (Ont. H.C.).

statutory validity will involve similarly difficult questions. As a result, it will be rare indeed that the constitutional defect will be so patent that the court will be bound to issue the writ. Instead it will have to exercise its discretion.[78]

(v) *Mandamus*: The requirements for standing in mandamus applications appear to be somewhat more stringent than those applying to certiorari and prohibition.[79] It has been suggested that here an applicant has no *locus standi* unless he has a specific legal right to performance of the official act with respect to which he seeks mandamus.[80] While a legal right will give an applicant the required standing, so apparently will some other special interest which the applicant has which is greater than the interest of the public generally.[81] Or he may sue on behalf of a class where that class has a special interest, even though it is not a legal interest. For example, a municipal taxpayer can apply for mandamus to require proper tax enforcement if he sues on behalf of all taxpayers, though he cannot apply on his own behalf alone because he has no interest greater than the taxpayers generally in the proper administration of municipal finances.[82] Nor, apparently, can a provincial voter require the issue of an election writ because he has no extraordinary interest in the holding of an election.[83]

    Whereas the court may exercise a discretion in favour of granting standing to any applicant for certiorari or prohibition, the same is not true of mandamus. But the court may take a generous view of what constitutes a "special interest" sufficient to set the applicant apart from the general public. He need not show that in the absence of mandamus he would be entitled to sue for damages for the failure to perform the duty in question.[84]

    How useful could mandamus be in judicial review of legislation? To use this remedy an applicant would have to show that a public officer had a constitutional duty to perform and that he was prevented from acting by an invalid statute. The possibility of finding a constitutional duty of this

78. See *infra*, pp. 123–25.
79. See generally Jaffe, *supra* note 31, at 1269–73.
80. E.g. *Hughes et al.* v. *Henderson* (1963), 46 W.W.R. (n.s.) 202 (Man. Q.B.).
81. *The King* v. *Publicover* (1940), 15 M.P.R. 187, at 193, [1940] 4 D.L.R. 43, at 45 (N.S. Sup. Ct.); De Smith, *supra* note 69, at 441–44.
82. *Re Leahy and Garvey*, [1935] O.W.N. 41 (Ont. C.A.).
83. According to the Ontario Court of Appeal, in *Temple* v. *Bulmer*, whose decision is reported in [1943] S.C.R. 265, at 267, [1943] 3 D.L.R. 649, at 651. *Aff'd* on other grounds by the Supreme Court of Canada, *ibid*. But see *The Saskatchewan Bill of Rights*, R.S.S. 1965, c.378, s.7 which recognizes the right of the voter to require that a legislative assembly shall not continue for more than five years.
84. De Smith, *supra* note 69, at 441–44.

sort cast on a particular official would be rather small. Also, mandamus would not be an appropriate remedy where the official is primarily responsible to the Crown[85] or to the legislature[86] for the way in which he exercises his functions. As a result, mandamus is not likely to be used very extensively for the purpose of raising constitutional issues.

(vi) *References*: By legislation in each of the provinces the lieutenant governor in council is empowered to refer constitutional questions to a provincial superior court (usually the court of last resort) for an opinion. Similarly the Supreme Court Act permits the governor in council to refer "important questions of law or fact" touching, *inter alia*, the constitutionality of legislation.[87]

The requirements of standing appear to be largely irrelevant where a constitutional issue is referred to the courts. In the first place, the court is obliged to consider such questions and to answer them if possible, even if there is no actual controversy between interested parties.[88] The court would seemingly have to perform this function even if no one appeared to argue for or against the validity of legislation.

Statutes authorizing references do make provision for the presentation of argument by interested persons, however. A typical provincial statute states: "The court may direct that any person interested, or where there is a class of persons interested, any one or more persons as representatives of such class, shall be notified of the hearing, and such persons shall be entitled to be heard."[89] Similar provisions can be found in all of the provinces and in the Supreme Court Act.[90] While there appears to be a requirement that a person to be heard must be "interested," this is interpreted very loosely in practice. In examining reports of decisions in constitutional references one may sometimes wonder what recognizable "interest" some of the "parties" would have had. It was clearly not a legal "interest" of the type required to bring an action for damages. For example, in *Reference re Validity of Wartime Leasehold Regulations*[91] concerning the validity of certain federal rent controls, the following

85. *The Queen* v. *Lords Commissioners of the Treasury* (1872), 7 L.R.Q.B. 387.
86. *Temple* v. *Bulmer, supra* note 83.
87. See chapter seven, *infra*.
88. *A.G. for Ont.* v. *A.G. for Can., supra* note 5; *A.G. for B.C.* v. *A.G. for Can., supra* note 10; *In re Order in Council: In re Crop Payments Act, supra* note 13.
89. R.S.S. 1965, c.86, s.5. See Appendix C.
90. R.S.A. 1955, c.55, s.6; R.S.B.C. 1960, c.72, s.7; R.S.M. 1954, c.44, s.4; R.S.N.B. 1952, c.120, s.24(4); Stats. Nfld. 1953, c.3, s.2; R.S.N.S. 1954, c.50, s.4; R.S.O. 1960, c.64, s.4; R.S.P.E.I. 1951, c.79, s.39(4); R.S.Q. 1964, c.10, s.4; R.S.C. 1952, c.259, s.55(4).
91. [1950] S.C.R. 124, [1950] 2 D.L.R. 1.

organizations were heard by the Supreme Court: "Tenants within Canada," the Canadian Legion of the British Empire Service League, the Canadian Federation of Property Owners Association, and the Canadian Congress of Labour.

If persons concerned with the legislation do not come forward to participate, provision is made in most jurisdictions for presentation of argument on behalf of unrepresented interests. The Saskatchewan Constitutional Questions Act states: "Where any interest affected is not represented by counsel, the court may request counsel to argue the case in such interest, and reasonable expenses thereof shall be paid out of the consolidated fund."[92] Comparable provisions may be found in six other provinces[93] and in the Supreme Court Act.[94] This clearly indicates that a "dispute" may be manufactured by the court where no genuine conflict of interest between individuals has emerged.

The foregoing rules all relate to the hearing at first instance in the court to which a question is initially referred. What of provincial references which are appealed from the court of last resort in the province to the Supreme Court? The Supreme Court Act now specifically permits appeals in such cases[95] and it would appear that any one permitted to be heard in the provincial court could obtain leave to participate in the hearing before the Supreme Court. That Court could also give leave for additional persons to intervene at this stage even if they had not been heard in the provincial court.[96]

The reference system does provide a means whereby constitutional issues may be fought in the courts by persons with no legal interest at stake. This has the advantage of permitting judicial review in some situations where it would not otherwise be available because no one would have standing to raise the issue. For example, in the absence of a clear denial of his established right to vote in a given election, it is uncertain that a citizen has sufficient standing to go to court over the way in which the election machinery is operated.[97] He probably could not prevent a reapportionment of constituencies which would wrongly reduce the number of members which his province was entitled to in the House of Commons. Yet, in the reference *Attorney General for Prince Edward Island* v. *Attorney General for Canada*,[98] the Supreme Court and Judicial Committee of the

92. R.S.S. 1965, c.86, s.6.
93. R.S.A. 1955, c.55, s.7; R.S.M. 1954, c.44, s.5; Stats. Nfld. 1953, c.3, s.2; R.S.N.S. 1954, c.50, s.5; R.S.O. 1960, c.64, s.5; R.S.P.E.I. 1951, c.79, s.39(5).
94. R.S.C. 1952, c.259, s.55(5).
95. *Ibid.*, s.37.
96. Rules of the Supreme Court of Canada, 1945, rules 50, 60.
97. See *infra*, pp. 114–17.   98. [1905] A.C. 37 (P.C. 1904).

Privy Council were enabled to consider the validity of such a reapportionment. A judicial interpretation was given to the provisions of the BNA
Act, upholding the reduction in the number of members of Parliament
from Prince Edward Island and New Brunswick. Here there was an issue
suitable for judicial action – that is, the interpretation of the meaning of a
formula laid down by statute. It was an issue which might well have gone
without judicial solution had it not been for the reference system.

(vii) *Appeals by an attorney general as intervenant*: In most provinces
and in the Supreme Court of Canada the provincial or federal attorney
general must be given notice and allowed to appear in cases where someone has attacked the validity of legislation.[99] Normally, of course, the
attorney general would appear in a position analogous to defendant and
the standing problem would not arise. Suppose, however, that the lower
court fails to uphold his argument in favour of validity. Suppose further
that other parties of like interest wish to drop the matter at this stage but
the attorney general wishes to appeal the constitutional point. Can he
maintain an appeal in his own right where he would have to appear as
appellant and not merely as intervenant?

In those provinces where the attorney general is given the status of an
intervenant only, he cannot maintain an appeal in the absence of another
party of like interest. In those provinces where by statute he is made a
party or put in the same position as a party he can apparently maintain the
appeal by himself.[100] The same should be true where he has been added
as a party in the original court.

The latter situation provides another example of a person being allowed
to bring a constitutional issue before the courts where he has no legal
interest at stake.

(viii) *Statutory rights of action*: At least two obvious examples may be
noted of actions specially authorized by law where a legal interest may be
lacking in the person instituting the action.

Provincial statutes governing municipalities usually permit action to
be brought to quash municipal bylaws. Often the action is allowed to
persons not having a legal interest in the narrow sense.[101] The grounds of
attack might be that the provincial legislature had no jurisdiction to confer
power on the municipality to pass such a bylaw.[102]

99. See *supra*, pp. 39–43.
100. See *supra*, pp. 43–45. This could be particularly useful where the original
action was collusive. Cf. *U.S.* v. *Johnson* (1943), 319 U.S. 302.
101. See Rogers, *The Law of Canadian Municipal Corporations* (1959), at 888.
102. *Ibid.*, at 912. And see e.g. *City of Winnipeg* v. *Barrett*, [1892] A.C. 445.

Another special action is that permitted to attorneys general in some of the provinces for a declaration as to the validity or invalidity of statutes. Four of the provinces, Alberta, British Columbia, Manitoba, and New Brunswick, permit such actions, at the instance of either the attorney general of Canada or the attorney general of the province, with respect to the validity of provincial legislation. Ontario legislation goes farther in allowing a similar action with respect to federal legislation.[103] It has been held that such provisions authorize an action to be brought by an attorney general even where no rights of his government are at stake.[104]

(b) Interests Recognized in Particular Classes of Persons

(i) *Voters*: The common law since *Ashby* v. *White* has recognized that a qualified voter has a right to his vote in the nature of a property interest. In the absence of some valid statute denying that right, he will have an action for damages against those who prevent him from exercising it.[105] It would therefore appear that if legislation purported to deny the franchise to a person otherwise entitled by law to vote he would have sufficient standing, in attacking the constitutional validity of that legislation, to employ any remedy for which an "interest" is required.[106] As well, some electoral laws permit an appeal to the courts from the decision of election officials with respect to the right of a person to vote. In such cases there appears to be no difficulty in the appellant challenging the validity of legislation which has deprived him of his vote.[107]

Short of an absolute loss of his vote, of what other abuses of the electoral system can a voter complain? In Canada such authority as can be found seems to indicate that the voter has few if any other rights in relation to the way in which the electoral machinery is operated. He cannot require that an election be held because the election officials are responsible only to the legislature; the voter has no right to have an election held unless

---

103. For particulars of these actions see *supra*, pp. 77–78.
104. *A.G. for Ont.* v. *A.G. for Can.*, [1931] O.R. 5, [1931] 2 D.L.R. 297 (Ont. High Ct.).
105. *Ashby* v. *White* (1704), 2 Ld. Raym. 938, 92 E.R. 126 (H.L.); *Crawford* v. *St. John* (1898), 34 N.B. 560 (N.B. C.A.). In some jurisdictions the right to damages as against election officials is limited or abolished by legislation. Even where the right to damages is abolished, there would presumably still be a right of action against other persons interfering with the franchise, and there should still be a recognition that the citizen has a legal "interest" in his franchise. The civil law in Quebec has apparently also recognized such an interest see, e.g. Mignault, 5 *Droit civil canadien* (1901), at 363.
106. See *Collins* v. *Minister of Interior*, [1957] 1 So. Afr. L.R. 552 (So. Afr. Sup. Ct. App. Div.).
107. *Cunningham* v. *Tomey Homma*, [1903] A.C. 151 (P.C.).

some statute specifically confers that right upon him.[108] Thus it would seem that a voter would have no special interest to enforce section 50 of the BNA Act which requires in effect that an election for the House of Commons be held at least once every five years. Yet a federal statute which purported to delay the election beyond this period would, under ordinary circumstances, be invalid. The life of the House of Commons can only be extended "in time of real or apprehended war, invasion or insurrection" and then only if less than one-third of the members of the House object.[109] No voter would have standing to challenge the validity of a wrongful extension, at least if he employed a remedy which required him to have an "interest."

The position of the voter with respect to redistribution or reapportionment of constituencies is less certain. While there seems to be no decision on the precise point, he appears to have no interest in any election matter not actually constituting a deprivation of his vote. He has no standing to complain about how the voter's list is prepared, as long as he cannot show that his name will be wrongfully left off the list.[110] Apart from special statutory provisions, he has no right to insist on a recount of votes being held, even if he is both a voter and a defeated candidate.[111] In neither case can he complain that he has been denied a vote, and thus the principles of *Ashby* v. *White*[112] do not apply. It is therefore doubtful that a Canadian court would recognize an interest vested in any voter to cast his vote in one constituency as opposed to another, or to cast his vote in a constituency of any particular size. Thus, for example, no voter would have an interest to enable him to enforce the constitutional formula for periodic redistribution of seats in the House of Commons. Section 51 of the BNA Act requires a redistribution after each decennial census, to be effected (with a few exceptions) on the basis of representation by population. If Parliament should fail to effect a redistribution after the decennial census,[113] no voter could attack the validity of the existing distribution. Nor, if a redistribution is carried out, would he have a sufficient interest to challenge the legislation effecting it. He would have to employ some remedy for which he would not have to show an interest. Alternatively the courts

108. *Temple* v. *Bulmer, supra* note 83. But see the Saskatchewan Bill of Rights, *supra* note 83.
109. BNA Act, ss.50, 91(1).
110. *In re Board of Manhood Suffrage Registrars* (1901), 13 Man. R. 345 (Man. K.B.).
111. *McLeod* v. *Noble* (1897), 38 O.R. 528 (Ont. Div. Ct.).
112. *Supra* note 105.
113. Three federal elections were held after the 1961 census without any redistribution.

could be called on for an opinion by means of a governmental reference.[114]

It must nevertheless be recognized that in other common law jurisdictions voters have been allowed status in court to attack redistribution schemes. In the State of Victoria, Australia, such an issue was involved in the case of *McDonald* v. *Cain*.[115] The state legislature had passed a statute establishing a commission to redistribute the electoral districts. The plaintiffs were members, and also voters, in constituencies which would probably disappear if the scheme of the Act were applied. They sought a declaration that the Act was invalid because it had not received the special majority of the vote in each house of the legislature which they claimed the constitution required. With respect to the question of their status to seek such a declaration, the court held that the plaintiffs as voters had a sufficient interest. They appear to have treated the abolition of a constituency as tantamount to a denial of the right to vote. Reliance was placed on the decision in *Ashby* v. *White* by Gavan Duffy J., and the other judgments seemed to proceed on a similar basis. The case does appear to be unique in recognizing a right in the voter to continue to vote in the same constituency, going beyond the recognition of a simple right to vote in *some* constituency. It may be noted that the declaration was in fact refused on substantive grounds.

In the United States it has been clear since the decision in *Baker* v. *Carr*[116] that a state voter has standing to bring an action to challenge the apportionment of electoral districts in a state legislature. Standing in such cases appears to turn on the existence of constitutional standards such as the guarantee of the "equal protection of the laws" in the fourteenth amendment to the federal Constitution. A voter is thereby deemed to have an interest in being able to vote in a district containing approximately the same number of voters as other districts in the state. In Canada it is difficult to find any comparable interest recognized by the constitution. Distribution of constituencies for provincial legislatures is a matter left entirely in the hands of the legislatures.[117] With respect to the distribution of federal constituencies the BNA Act confines itself to requiring proportional distribution among the various provinces. It does not require that within a given province the constituencies have to be divided on the basis of representation by population.[118] Could the voter of province X assert an interest in his province having more members of Parliament because of

114. As was done, e.g. in *A.G. for P.E.I.* v. *A.G. for Can.*, *supra* note 98.
115. [1953] Vict. L.R. 411 (Vict. Sup. Ct.).
116. (1962), 369 U.S. 186.
117. BNA Act, s.92(1).
118. BNA Act, ss. 51, 52.

a relative increase in its population? The interest here seems very remote, as a re-apportionment between provinces would not necessarily make his vote in his particular constituency any more potent.

(ii) *Taxpayers*: Apart from their special statutory rights of action previously discussed,[119] municipal ratepayers are allowed standing by the common law to challenge the validity of bylaws in certain other cases. These actions appear to be "public" actions because the ratepayer is permitted to sue even though he can show no special injury to himself or no special interest different from that of the ratepayers generally.

This right of action arises where the municipal government has made or is about to make an expenditure which is alleged by a ratepayer to be ultra vires.[120] The rationale of this action is that all municipal ratepayers are threatened with financial loss if an illegal expenditure is made, because the treasury will have to be replenished from additional or unnecessary taxes imposed on them. Thus if there is no threatened financial loss of this nature the ratepayer has no standing to challenge the validity of the municipal government's decisions. The attorney general is the only one who can commence an action to restrain ultra vires activity in such cases.[121] If the financial aspect affects not only the municipality but the province generally, then the ratepayer does not have standing.[122] The object of the action is to require the municipality to take appropriate measures to correct its error, not to raise abstract issues. Where the municipality has performed its duty and repudiated ultra vires measures, the ratepayer loses his standing.[123]

In these ratepayers' actions of a public nature, the ratepayer must sue on behalf of himself and all other ratepayers in a class action. The theory of the class action is that where there is a common interest and a common grievance, all persons sharing that interest and grievance can be represented in such a suit if the relief sought would be appropriate for all those represented.[124] Thus the relief most commonly available in ratepayers'

119. See *supra* notes 101–102, and accompanying text.
120. *MacIlreith* v. *Hart* (1908), 39 S.C.R. 657. Foll'd. *Affleck* v. *City of Nelson* (1957), 23 W.W.R. (n.s.) 386, 10 D.L.R. (2d) 442 (B.C. Sup. Ct.). For the earlier English authority see *Boyce* v. *Paddington B.C.*, [1903] 1 Ch. 109. But see *Trustees of the R.C. Separate Schools of Ottawa* v. *Mackell*, [1917] A.C. 62 (P.C.).
121. *Robertson* v. *Monteral* (1915), 52 S.C.R. 30, 26 D.L.R. 228; *S.M.T. (Eastern) Ltd.* v. *St. John* (1946), 18 M. P.R. 374 (N.B. C.A.).
122. *Loggie* v. *Town of Chatham* (1927), 54 N.B. 230 (N.B. C.A.).
123. *Dilworth* v. *Town of Bala*, [1955] S.C.R. 284, [1955] 2 D.L.R. 353.
124. *Bedford (Duke)* v. *Ellis*, [1901] A.C. 1 (H.L.); *R.C. Separate Schools Trustees for Tiny* v. *King* (1926), 59 O.L.R. 96, at 152–53 (Ont. H.C.).

actions is the declaration of invalidity, sometimes combined with an injunction. Damages are not available in such class actions.

It is obvious that where the ratepayer's action is available, it could be
used on occasion to challenge the validity of legislation under which the
municipality purported to act. Assume, for example, that provincial legislation authorized municipalities to spend money on defence by mounting
air-raid warning sirens. A ratepayer might sue in a class action for a
declaration that such expenditures by the municipality would be ultra vires
because defence is not a matter on which a province can legislate.[125] Or,
suppose that a provincial enactment is alleged to violate the guarantees
for denominational schools, by interfering with the right to give religious
education during school hours. Those persons assessed for taxes for such
schools might challenge the constitutional right of the local authority to
implement such a law if its implementation would throw additional financial burdens on them.[126]

How far can we extend the ratepayer's action by analogy into other
areas of government? If a municipal taxpayer can challenge the validity
of expenditures of a municipal government, should a provincial or federal
taxpayer be allowed to challenge the validity of expenditures of his provincial or federal government? In the United States the answer given to
this question by the federal courts with respect to federal taxpayers has
been in the negative.[127] While a local taxpayer is allowed a *locus standi*,
a federal taxpayer is not because his interest in the funds of the federal
treasury is too minute and indeterminate. In Canada there has been very
little attention given to the possibility of a provincial or federal taxpayer
having *locus standi* as such. One case which has dealt with the problem
has denied the existence of *locus standi*. In *Cowan* v. *Canadian Broadcasting Corporation*,[128] the plaintiff sought declarations and an injunction
to prevent the defendant publicly owned corporation from converting an
English-language broadcasting station in Toronto into a French-language
station. He claimed, *inter alia*, that if Parliament had authorized the
operation of a wholly French-language station the legislation was ultra
vires. He further contended that Parliament had never authorized the required expenditures. The action was dismissed on the grounds that the
plaintiff had no status to bring it. His counsel sought to amend the state-

---

125. See BNA Act, s.91(7).
126. For an example of the converse situation see *Trustees of the R.C. Separate
Schools of Ottawa* v. *Mackell, supra* note 120.
127. *Frothingham* v. *Mellon* (1923), 262 U.S. 447.
128. [1966] 2 O.R. 309, 56 D.L.R. (2d) 578 (Ont. C.A.); Strayer, "Comment"
(1967), 45 *Can. B. Rev.* 154.

ment of claim so that the action would be on behalf of the plaintiff "and all other English speaking tax payers of Metropolitan Toronto who habitually listened to broadcasting station CJBC in the English language and who have been deprived of this advantage. . . ." The Court of Appeal could not see that this strengthened the plaintiff's claim to standing and dismissed the appeal. The court held that to restrain unlawful acts of public bodies a plaintiff must show that he has a special interest just as in a nuisance case. The court also declined to extend *MacIlreith* v. *Hart*[129] beyond the field of municipal taxpayers.

A blanket denial of standing for provincial or federal taxpayers is illogical if standing can be granted to municipal taxpayers. *MacIlreith* v. *Hart*, the leading Canadian decision on the ratepayer's action, does not appear to place much emphasis on the amount of money involved (nor, by inference, on the real effect that such an expenditure would have on the ratepayer's taxes). Three of the judges in the Supreme Court (Idington and MacLennan JJ., and Fitzpatrick C.J. concurring) appeared to recognize the ratepayer's standing as a matter of general principle, without qualification. Davies J. (Duff J. concurring) did say that "it matters not whether the damage be great or small, *unless indeed the whole transaction was so trivial that the court would refuse to interfere on that ground.*"[130] But he also remarked that "the misappropriation here complained of is only $270. If it was $2,700, it should not make any difference in the determination of the right of the injured class to sue for their own protection."[131] Apparently the size of the possible share of injury which any ratepayer would have to bear would be irrelevant. Mr. Justice Davies' reference to "trivial" transactions must be intended to cover only the most infinitesimal expenditures, matters to which the maxim *de minimis non curat lex* would apply.[132] If the ratepayer's action is thus available regardless of the size of the potential injury to the ratepayer or the class he represents, there seems to be no logical reason why a provincial taxpayer, for example, should not have *locus standi* where the provincial government purports to spend money for objects beyond its jurisdiction. In some cases the amounts of money involved and the potential effect on the provincial taxpayer might be considerably greater. One might also note the disparities in size of various provincial and municipal populations. Would the taxpayer of Prince Edward Island have a less direct financial interest in

129. *Supra* note 120.
130. 39 S.C.R., at 664: emphasis added.
131. 39 S.C.R., at 664.
132. But see *Jenkins* v. *Winnipeg*, [1941] 1 W.W.R. 37, [1941] 1 D.L.R. 477 (Man. K.B.).

unlawful provincial expenditures than a taxpayer of Metropolitan Toronto would have with respect to unlawful municipal expenditures?[133]

Two qualifications of this argument should be noted in passing. First, the ratepayer's action as upheld by *MacIlreith* v. *Hart* has since been criticized by one eminent judge. Mr. Justice Duff treated it as an exception which "does not rest upon any clearly defined principle, and we think it ought not to be extended."[134] Secondly, to allow a provincial taxpayer or federal taxpayer standing might avail him nothing, as the dominant view is that the federal and provincial governments have a constitutionally unlimited spending power.[135] The matter is not, however, free from doubt. The Privy Council suggested in the *Employment Insurance Reference*[136] that there may be some limitations on the way that Parliament disposes of its tax revenues, though these possible limitations were not explained either then or subsequently. Provincial taxing jurisdiction in section 92, head (2) and (9), does specifically limit the use of the power to the raising of a revenue "for provincial . . . purposes." However, this limitation has never been given any effect by the courts.[137]

The concept of the spending power is ripe for reconsideration. Much of the current constitutional controversy in Canada centres on alleged misuse of the federal spending power. Recognition of the taxpayer's *locus standi* might well facilitate judicial consideration of this issue which has yet to be thoroughly studied by the courts. While the validity of the spending power would probably be upheld, taxpayers ought at least to be able to raise the question.

It is therefore suggested that provincial and federal taxpayers ought to be granted a *locus standi* in order to attack unlawful governmental expenditures. Where the remedy sought is one which is subject to judicial discretion, the courts might well refuse in some cases to grant the relief requested. But the taxpayer's suit should not be rejected at its inception merely because of an alleged want of interest.

(iii) *Shareholders*: The right of a shareholder to sue his company with respect to ultra vires acts is also in the nature of a public remedy which

133. The population of Prince Edward Island would be approximately one-twentieth of that of Toronto.
134. *Smith* v. *A.G. for Ont.*, [1924] S.C.R. 331, at 338, [1924] 3 D.L.R. 189, at 194.
135. See e.g. Laskin, *Canadian Constitutional Law* (3rd ed., 1966), at 666–67. *Angers* v. *M.N.R.*, [1957] Ex. C.R. 83; *Porter* v. *R.*, [1965] 1 Ex. C.R. 200; La Forest, *The Allocation of Taxing Power under the Canadian Constitution* (1967), at 36–41, 60–62.
136. [1937] A.C. 355, at 366–67.
137. La Forest, *supra* note 135, at 60–62.

could be used for raising a constitutional issue. Again the plaintiff may not be able to show any special interest in himself distinct from similar interests in many others.

The shareholder's action is available wherever it is alleged that the company has done or is about to do something which is ultra vires.[138] It is apparently not necessary that some illegal expenditure be involved. Nor is it necessary that the shareholder sue as a representative of a class. He may sue on his own behalf alone,[139] unless the court otherwise requires.

Shareholders' actions have been used in several cases as a means of challenging the validity of legislation before the courts. The device usually employed has been an action by a shareholder against the company to restrain it from carrying on business without complying with certain legislation. The company then defends on the basis that the legislation is itself ultra vires.[140] The converse method could be used as readily, with the plaintiff seeking to restrain the company from obeying a law which he alleged to be invalid.[141]

There seems to be little reason for giving company shareholders any special privileges with respect to standing in constitutional cases. Why should a shareholder through his membership in the company be able to raise the question of validity, regardless of financial prejudice to himself or to the company, when a provincial taxpayer as such cannot challenge the validity of a law which materially increases his taxes? There is also the possibility, in shareholders' actions of this kind, that the litigants are not always of adverse interest. Suspicions of collusion have been voiced by the courts in some cases. In *Union Colliery* v. *Bryden* Lord Watson remarked that the attorney general of British Columbia had suspected collusion and had intervened.[142] In *A. MacDonald Company* v. *Harmer* Idington J., in the Supreme Court of Canada, said "I am strongly impressed with a suspicion begotten of circumstances coming under my observation in these proceedings and the needless frame of the questions submitted that these actions are collusive and used as a means of interrogating this court in a way it should not submit to at the mere whim of any private individuals desiring to know how far their companies can

138. *Burland* v. *Earle*, [1902] A.C. 83 (P.C. 1901); *Dominion Cotton Mills Co.* v. *Amyot*, [1912] A.C. 546 (P.C.).
139. *Theatre Amusement Co.* v. *Stone* (1914), 50 S.C.R. 32, 16 D.L.R. 855; *Scott* v. *Sask. Co-operative Wheat Producers Ltd.*, [1933] 1 W.W.R. 726 (Sask. K.B.).
140. E.g. *Union Colliery* v. *Bryden*, [1899] A.C. 580 (P.C.); *John Deere Plow Co.* v. *Wharton*, [1915] A.C. 330 (P.C.); *Great West Saddlery Co.* v. *The King*, [1921] 2 A.C. 91 (P.C.).
141. See e.g. *Carter* v. *Carter Coal Co.* (1936), 298 U.S. 238.
142. *Supra* note 140, at 584.

go."[143] The possibility certainly exists in such litigation that the parties will not argue the issues fully and that the side which has the burden of defending the validity of legislation will do it less than enthusiastically. The statutory right of intervention by the attorney general in such cases is usually resorted to, no doubt wisely.

(c) The Role of Standing in Constitutional Cases

It is apparent that Canadian law has no coherent set of rules with respect to *locus standi*. This is equally true in both constitutional and non-constitutional litigation.

The rules of standing which do obtain display many anomalies. First, it is at once apparent that the right of a person to enforce a constitutional norm is unrelated to the norm in question. The Canadian constitution, unlike the American Bill of Rights, confers no rights on individuals.[144] When the citizen seeks to launch a constitutional attack on legislation in the courts, he is trying to enforce the federalist division of legislative authority. It might be argued that the division of powers between Parliament and the legislatures is of no legal concern to him. At least it can be said that there is no logical connection between the right granted him by the court to assert the constitutional norm and the norm itself. For example, the BNA Act, section 91(2), gives Parliament exclusive jurisdiction over interprovincial trade. Why should one trader be able to challenge a provincial law which purports to prevent interprovincial trade because he has violated the law, whereas another trader who has not yet violated it cannot do so? In neither case is the constitutional limitation designed for the individual's personal protection. Yet if it is assumed that this constitutional norm ought to be judicially enforceable, why should the one party be granted standing to enforce it while the other is not?

Secondly, the common law confers or denies standing in a capricious manner. Voters can protest denial of the bare right to vote, but they cannot prevent the dilution of their vote through failure to redistribute constituencies. Taxpayers can protest ultra vires expenditures by their municipal government, but not by their provincial or federal government. Shareholders who have no real conflict of interest with their company, and who may in fact benefit by losing their case, can nevertheless commence action to require the company to comply with a law which the company regards

---

143. 59 S.C.R. 19, at 33, 48 D.L.R. 386, at 396 (1919), *Affirmed sub nom. Great West Saddlery Co.* v. *The King, supra* note 140, without reference to this point.
144. The BNA Act, s.93 (denominational schools) and 133 (use of the English and French languages) do confer certain group rights.

as invalid. These are but examples of the illogical way in which the courts recognize or refuse to recognize standing.

The Canadian courts have a unique freedom to introduce rationality into the whole problem of standing. They are not bound by any a priori concept of the judicial function. As indicated at the start of this chapter, there are no constitutional barriers to Canadian courts deciding matters beyond the realm of the "case or controversy." They have long had non-judicial advisory functions thrust on them. Through reference proceedings, through statutory rights of action previously noted, through the rights of intervention generously bestowed in constitutional cases, the courts have been drawn into activities not strictly judicial. There is no constitutional reason why they should not take a generous view of their functions and entertain proceedings even where the initiating party is not asserting a legal right of his own.

The vehicle by which the courts may develop a rational concept of standing in constitutional cases is the judicial discretion which is accorded them with respect to several of the common remedies. It has been shown that in proceedings for declarations, certiorari, and prohibition the court can in its discretion allow the plaintiff or applicant *locus standi* even though he has no legal right, *stricto sensu*, to enforce. It only remains to ask whether some special principles should apply to the exercise of this discretion in constitutional cases, and if so, what those principles should be.

It is submitted that the courts should be especially willing to exercise their discretion in favour of conferring standing in constitutional cases. The importance of enforcing constitutional norms transcends the existence or non-existence of a legal right in a private individual in a particular case. If the constitution is to be effective, the courts must be able to act in situations where a failure to act would permit a legislature to achieve a result beyond its legal powers.[145] Assuming that there must be some limitations on the availability of judicial review, these should be related to the effective operation of the courts as guardians of the constitution. Some relevant considerations may be noted in this regard. It has been suggested that to allow parties without a legal interest to invoke the jurisdiction of the court to review legislative validity would result in grave "inconvenience" to the courts themselves.[146] This apparently reflects a fear that the courts may become overrun with litigants with no legal interest at stake who will

145. See generally chapters two and three, *supra*.
146. *Smith* case, [1924] S.C.R., at 337, 347, [1924] 3 D.L.R., at 193, 209; cited with approval in the *Saumur* case, [1963] Que. B.R. 116, at 138–39, 37 D.L.R. (2d) 703, at 724.

commence actions at the slightest provocation. Certain it is that the courts should not be obliged to entertain every such proceeding. The fact that a party is not adversely affected in any way by a statute may well be a factor in the exercise of judicial discretion against granting him standing. The fact that his alleged grievance is completely hypothetical and not real may not only suggest that there is no need for judicial intervention but may also indicate to the court that there is no issue which it can effectively decide.[147] But where, as in *Smith v. Attorney General for Ontario*,[148] it is clear that if the plaintiff does the act which he seeks to do (in that case, to import liquor), he will violate the statute, then there is surely no good reason for the court refusing him standing to attack the validity of the statute. There is no special "inconvenience" involved for the court in such a case.

The fear has also been expressed that the courts in entertaining proceedings not actually involving a controversy may prejudice private parties who would be bound by such a decision.[149] This fear seems unfounded. No issue of res judicata would arise where another party wished later to raise the same or a similar constitutional point in subsequent litigation. If, however, any individual can satisfy the court that a particular statute violates the constitution generally and not merely as applied to him there is no good reason why a judicial determination should not be made as soon as possible. No judicial decision can be applied to circumstances to which it does not logically relate, but if it holds a statute to be invalid as a whole there can be no objection to this decision affecting all persons who might otherwise be governed by that statute. Constitutional decisions in Canada are usually of this type, because they are based on the federal-provincial limitations of authority and not on guarantees of individual rights. They are by their inherent nature "depersonalized" and of general effect. In the exercise of their discretion the courts should, of course, avoid deciding matters where the constitutional issues are unlikely to be properly raised or argued.[150] To decide on the basis of inadequate pleading or argument might result in an unfortunate precedent which would later inhibit the court.

The courts have also expressed reluctance to entertain an individual's complaint because other means have been devised for public officials to bring such issues before the courts.[151] Again, there may be good grounds

147. See *infra* at 135–38.
148. [1924] S.C.R. 331, [1924] 3 D.L.R. 189.
149. See, e.g., the dissent of Trueman J.A. in *In re Order in Council: In re Crop Payments Act*, [1926] 2 W.W.R. 844, [1927] 2 D.L.R. 50 (Man. C.A.).
150. As, for example, in actions which appear to be collusive.
151. *A. MacDonald Company v. Harmer* (1919), 59 S.C.R. 19, at 33, 48 D.L.R.

for a discretionary denial of standing where other and perhaps better remedies are available. Where a controversial statute has been enacted and it is anticipated that the question of validity may be referred to the courts, a private litigant without a legal interest at stake might properly be barred in a proceeding to challenge validity. But all the circumstances should be considered. If it is apparent that no official steps are being taken, the court should be prepared to permit the individual to proceed, if the matter is otherwise suitable for consideration.

It is suggested that standing to raise the constitutional issue should generally be recognized subject to the discretionary refusal of the court. There will of course be some remedies: damages, for example, in which, to show entitlement to the relief requested, the plaintiff must show a legal interest in himself and a violation of that interest. But where remedies such as the declaration, certiorari, or prohibition are employed they may properly be used as vehicles for a judicial determination of constitutional validity, even in the absence of a legal right in the petitioning party. The demands of the federal system suggest a generous conferral of standing by the courts in such cases.

OTHER PARTIES

Assuming that someone is allowed to challenge the constitutional validity of a statute, who else must be joined in the proceedings? The general approach taken by the courts is that parties should be joined so that as far as possible all matters in controversy in the litigation may be finally settled and a multiplicity of proceedings may be avoided.[152] It is necessary to inquire what parties, if any, are essential to the final determination of constitutional questions.

There appears to be no basis on which any private person may be considered an essential party in constitutional litigations. He may of course be a necessary party to litigation where a constitutional issue is incidentally involved, but only if he seeks to justify his personal actions or assert personal rights by reliance on an impugned statute.[153] His relationship to the proceedings stems from his personal interests: he has no personal interest in the upholding of a statute's validity.

The only person who may have a special interest in constitutional litigation is the attorney general. It is doubtful, however, that at common law

---

386, at 396; *Smith* v. *A.G. for Ont.*, [1924] S.C.R. 331, at 336, [1924] 3 D.L.R. 189, at 193.

152. *Ottawa Separate School Trustees* v. *Quebec Bank* (1917), 39 O.L.R. 118, 35 D.L.R. 134 (Ont. H.C.).

153. See *Turner's Dairy Limited* v. *Williams*, [1940] 2 W.W.R. 193, [1940] 3 D.L.R. 214 (B.C.C.A.).

even he would be an essential party in constitutional litigation where no Crown or public interest were otherwise involved.

We have seen that most of the provinces and the Supreme Court of Canada have made specific provision for notice to be given to the relevant attorney general where the validity of a statute is being questioned. While some of the legislative provisions specifically make the intervening attorney general a party for certain purposes, it appears that in the absence of such provisions, or of a special order, he is not a party.[154] Apparently these provisions were introduced to assure that the attorney general would have an opportunity to appear in such cases. There is no evidence to indicate that prior to such enactments the attorney general was normally made a party in such cases, nor does this appear to be the situation in those provinces which have never adopted the notice requirement.

It is suggested that there are two different concepts which must be distinguished here. The joinder of parties is related to the rules of res judicata *inter partes*. If a person, including the Crown or its representative, is joined as a party then any decision about law or fact made in the proceedings will be binding on him or it in future in relation to the same parties.[155] On the other hand, the intervention of the attorney general subsequent to notice being given him in constitutional cases is related to the rules of stare decisis. It was deemed advisable to allow the attorney general to be heard in such cases so that the government would not be prejudiced by a decision against statutory validity, reached in a proceeding in which the views of the government had not been expressed.

It is submitted that in the absence of other factors which will be referred to below, the attorney general is not an essential party in constitutional cases. Where statutes or rules of court give him the opportunity to intervene, he may do so. If he declines to do so, he cannot be brought into the proceedings compulsorily. In jurisdictions with no such provisions, he need not be admitted to the proceedings nor can he be required to participate.

Other factors may of course involve the Crown or the attorney general as parties in constitutional cases. It may be alleged by a claimant that the Crown is acting or holding property under an invalid statute. Any such claim directly[156] or indirectly[157] affecting Crown interests would necessarily involve the Crown or the attorney general as a party. It would seem

154. See *supra* at 43–45.
155. Mundell, "The Crown and Res Judicata" in Corry, Cronkite, and Whitmore, *Legal Essays in Honour of Arthur Moxon* (1953), at 208, *passim*.
156. E.g. *Lovibond* v. *Grand Trunk Ry.*, [1936] 3 D.L.R. 449 (P.C.).
157. E.g. *Esquimalt & Nanaimo Ry.* v. *Wilson*, [1920] A.C. 358 (P.C.). And see generally chapter four *supra*.

also that if there were a constitutional problem involved in an action with respect to some public right, the attorney general might have to be a party on behalf of the Crown as *parens patriae*. His addition as a party would be required in order that the matter would become res judicata binding on the public as well as on others.[158] The possible conflict between the role of the attorney general in such a situation and his role as adviser to and a member of the government has been previously noted.[159]

These proceedings in which the attorney general or the Crown must be made parties result in judgments *inter partes* deemed res judicata only between the parties to the action. If the court declares a statute to be invalid and, for example, enjoins the officers of the Crown from enforcing it against the plaintiff, it would seem that such a decision would bind the Crown only with respect to future proceedings with this particular party.[160] It may be noted in passing, however, that it could be argued that a decision about the validity or invalidity of a statute is a judgment in rem, binding not only upon the parties but as against the whole world.[161] Halsbury gives a generally accepted definition of a judgment in rem as one "determining the status of a person or thing, or the disposition of a thing, as distinct from the particular interest in it of a party to the litigation."[162] Could it be said that a decision that a statute is invalid is a judgment as to the status of a "thing" binding on parties and non-parties alike? With one possible exception,[163] there would seem to be no judicial authority to this effect. It is submitted that on principle a decision as to statutory invalidity, made in ordinary litigation, should not lead to a judgment in rem. Such proceedings involve a collateral attack on the legislation, not a direct attack. That is, the issue before the court may involve for example a claim for damages, a criminal prosecution, or an application to quash the order of an inferior tribunal. The relief requested is not a declaration of invalidity of a statute per se, though it may be necessary for the court to

158. See *Tuxedo Holding Co.* v. *University of Manitoba & A.G. for Man.*, [1930] 1 W.W.R. 464, [1930] 3 D.L.R. 250 (Man. C.A.). *Williams & Wilson Ltd.* v. *Toronto and the A.G. for Ont.*, [1946] O.R. 309, [1946] 4 D.L.R. 278 (Ont. H.C.).
159. *Supra*, at 104–06.
160. Zamir, *supra* note 38, at 251.
161. See Mundell, *supra* note 155.
162. 22 *Halsbury's Laws of England* (3rd ed. 1958), at 742. See also Bower, *The Doctrine of Res Judicata* (1924), at 132–52.
163. In John Hampden's famous case in 1638 the Exchequer Court held that the ship-money levy imposed by the King without Parliament's approval was valid. Subsequently in *Lord Say's Case*, (1639) Cro. Car. 524, 79 E.R. 1053 (K.B.) the plaintiff tried to argue that the levy was invalid. The Attorney General argued that this matter could not be reopened as it was decided in *Hampden's Case*. The Court of King's Bench upheld this objection, apparently treating the earlier decision as a judgment *in rem*.

make some finding in this regard where statutory invalidity is alleged, as a ground for the granting of the relief requested. The court is entitled to deal with statutory validity only as it is material to the main issue before the court, that is, the right to the relief requested. It is submitted that this does not constitute a determination of the status of the statute, "as distinct from the particular interest in it of a party to the litigation."

Are there proceedings involving a direct attack on statutory validity, capable of producing a judgment in rem? In constitutional references the principle issue is that of validity. It has been held that a decision in a reference does not bind non-parties.[164] On principle, such a decision should be regarded as an opinion only, and not a judgment.[165] Perhaps the one procedure which may result in a judgment in rem is the statutory action for a declaration as to legislative validity. Five provinces provide such a right of action.[166] Here the action must be brought by the federal attorney general against a provincial attorney general, or vice versa. The declaration to be sought is "as to the validity of a statute." This clearly constitutes a direct attack on a statute, where validity is the sole issue involved. The judgment determines the "status" of the statute and may be considered a judgment in rem. No common law problem arises as to parties, however, because by the terms of the statutes the respective attorneys general must be parties and such actions will be considered sufficiently constituted if they and they alone are the parties. Once a declaration is made in such an action, the attorney general participating should be bound by the judgment in rem in relation to all other persons. This may present some difficulties, however. If an Ontario court, for example, decides in such a case that a section of the federal Criminal Code is invalid, should this decision bind the attorney general of Canada in all other provinces? It is suggested that it should not bind him except with respect to matters in the Ontario courts, even if confirmed by the Supreme Court of Canada. But the force of stare decisis will in most cases produce the same results outside Ontario, once the Supreme Court has made its decision.

In general it may be said that there are few requirements with respect to the persons who must be joined in an action in response to an attack on statutory validity. The usual need for adding parties in litigation stems from the concept of res judicata. In constitutional cases res judicata will play a very small part and, where it is relevant, statutes specifically require the appropriate attorney general to be added as a party. Otherwise the

164. *C.P.R.* v. *Estevan*, [1957] S.C.R. 365, at 368–69.
165. *Supra*, at 92–93.
166. *Supra*, at 77–78.

concept of stare decisis is more important in determining where the attorney general ought to participate in such litigation.

THE PROPER ISSUES

"NECESSARY" ISSUES

If proceedings are properly commenced and the opportunity arises for the court to make a decision as to the validity of a statute, should it do so if the matter can be disposed of on other grounds? In the United States the Supreme Court has generally refused to deal with constitutional issues under such circumstances.[167] If the Canadian courts and the Privy Council have failed to display consistently an equal restraint it may be because of the lack of comparable constitutional limitations on the judicial role in Canada.[168]

It is a general principle of the Anglo-Canadian judicial system that the courts in the course of ordinary litigations ought not to answer purely hypothetical questions.[169] The courts have piously asserted this principle in constitutional cases as well, refusing on occasions to decide constitutional issues if another ground for decision existed, or refusing to explore the constitutional implications more fully than necessary to decide the case in hand. A few examples of this attitude may be noted.

The leading declaration of judicial self-denial appeared in the 1881 decision of *Citizens Insurance Company* v. *Parsons*.[170] The Privy Council was faced with the problem of deciding, *inter alia*, whether the regulation of insurance contracts was a federal matter of "regulation of trade and commerce" or a provincial matter of "property and civil rights in the province." Sir Montague Smith noted that the various heads of sections 91 and 92 must be read together in order to understand the scope of each in relation to particular problems. He added that "in performing this difficult duty, it will be a wise course for those on whom it is thrown, to decide each case which arises as best they can, without entering more largely upon an interpretation of the statute than is necessary for the particular question in hand."[171] This statement was quoted with approval ten years later in

167. See e.g. *Coffman* v. *Breeze Corporation* (1945), 323 U.S. 316; *Rescue Army* v. *Municipal Court of Los Angeles* (1947), 331 U.S. 549.
168. *Supra*, at 90–95.
169. *Glasgow Navigation Company* v. *Iron Ore Company*, [1910] A.C. 293 (H. of L.).
170. (1881), 7 App. Cas. 96 (P.C.).
171. *Ibid.*, at 109. In spite of this caveat, the judgment proceeded, at 113, to lay down gratuitously a general definition of "regulation of trade and commerce" which has been followed ever since.

Hodge v. *The Queen*, where the Privy Council confined itself to holding that a province could regulate the conduct of taverns. It declined to lay down any broader definition of the respective scope of provincial and federal power over the liquor traffic.[172] The statement in *Citizens Insurance* was also approved in *John Deere Plow Company* v. *Wharton*. Viscount Haldane added some reasons of his own for judicial caution.

The wisdom of adhering to this rule appears to their Lordships to be of especial importance when putting a construction on the scope of the words "civil rights" in particular cases. An abstract logical definition of their scope is not only, having regard to the context of ss. 91 and 92 of the Act, impracticable, but is certain, if attempted, to cause embarrassment and possible injustice in future cases. It must be borne in mind in construing the two sections that matters which in a special aspect and for a particular purpose may fall within one of them may in a different aspect and for a different purpose fall within the other. In such cases the nature and scope of the legislative attempt of the Dominion or the Province, as the case may be, have to be examined with reference to the actual facts if it is to be possible to determine under which set of powers it falls in substance and in reality. This may not be difficult to determine in actual and concrete cases. But it may well be impossible to give abstract answers to general questions as to the meaning of the words, or to lay down any interpretation based on their literal scope apart from their context.[173]

Consistently with this view, Viscount Haldane refrained in his judgment from dealing with the wider issues raised in argument as to the possible scope of provincial power to legislate in a manner affecting the operations of dominion-incorporated companies. He confined himself to the specific sections of the provincial statute in issue in that case and found them to be ultra vires.

A modern decision showing similar judicial restraint is *Attorney General for Ontario* v. *Winner*. The proceedings started in the form of an action by S.M.T. (Eastern) Ltd., a New Brunswick transportation company, which sought to enjoin Winner from operating his bus line through New Brunswick in a manner inconsistent with the license issued to him by the provincial Motor Carrier Board. That license had permitted Winner to operate his buses through the province but forbade him "to embus or debus passengers" in the province. Winner continued to embus and debus passengers, apparently taking the view that the province had no constitutional power to impose such a limitation on an interprovincial or international undertaking which he alleged his to be. The trial judge referred to the provincial Supreme Court (Appellate Division) various

172. (1883), 9 App. Cas. 117, at 128 (P.C.).
173. [1915] A.C. 330, at 339 (P.C. 1914).

points of law for determination before the case proceeded. As finally settled, these questions raised several broad issues, including that of the general validity of a statute part of which was not otherwise involved in this proceeding. When the matter reached the Supreme Court of Canada, a majority of the judges pointed out that this was not a constitutional reference and thus the questions were too broad. They declined to answer the questions except to the extent necessary to decide whether as a matter of law the defendant had a good constitutional defence to the action for an injunction.[174] Issues of legislative validity not germane to the operations of the defendant were not dealt with. When the case reached the Privy Council, it too declined to deal with the broader issues raised by the questions. Lord Porter avoided defining for all purposes the limits on the power of the provinces to legislate in a manner affecting interprovincial undertakings. He confined his examination to the particular regulation and the particular undertaking in question.[175]

Other examples of judicial self-restraint may be found.[176] Nevertheless it must be recognized that the courts have been inconsistent in their practice. Various decisions have dealt with constitutional issues where there were other grounds for disposition.[177] For example, in *Provincial Secretary of Prince Edward Island* v. *Egan*[178] the respondent Egan had unsuccessfully attempted to obtain a driver's licence from the provincial secretary. He appealed the alleged refusal of the provincial secretary to a county court judge who allowed the appeal and ordered the provincial secretary to issue the licence. The latter appealed to the Supreme Court of Prince Edward Island, contending *inter alia* that there had been no right of appeal to the county court judge because the provincial secretary had not refused to issue a licence; that the applicant was simply barred by statute from eligibility for a licence during the period in question. The

174. *Sub. nom. Winner* v. *S.M.T. (Eastern) Ltd.*, [1951] S.C.R. 887, at 911, 915, 925, 931, 937, 942, 946; [1951] 4 D.L.R. 529, at 550, 555, 563, 569, 574, 579, 583.
175. [1954] A.C. 541, at e.g. 576–77, 579–80, 583 (P.C.).
176. E.g. *Reference re Alberta Statutes*, [1938] S.C.R. 100, [1938] 2 D.L.R. 81, where with reference to the Press Bill three of the six judges declined to deal with the issue of which legislative body has power to regulate freedom of the press. They merely held ultra vires the particular statute before them. In *A.G. for Alberta* v. *A.G. for Canada*, [1939] A.C. 117, at 128 (Bank Tax Reference) (P.C.) the Privy Council declined to consider the validity of statutes which could no longer be brought into effective operation because of the repeal of related legislation.
177. E.g. *Smith* v. *A.G. for Ont.*, [1924] S.C.R. 331, [1924] 3 D.L.R. 189; See also Laskin, "Tests for the Validity of Legislation: What's the Matter?" (1955), 11 *U. Toronto L.J.* 114, at 116–17 for a criticism of the judiciary for premature generalizing in constitutional cases.
178. [1941] S.C.R. 396, [1941] 3 D.L.R. 305.

provincial Supreme Court not only rejected this attack on the jurisdiction and decision of the county court judge, but also proceeded quite gratuitously to hold the provincial Highway Traffic Act ultra vires. This brought the attorneys general of Prince Edward Island and of Ontario into the controversy when an appeal was taken to the Supreme Court of Canada.

Mr. Justice Rinfret, writing for three of the six judges, held that there had been no right of appeal to the county court judge and that the Provincial Supreme Court ought to have found for the provincial secretary on that basis. It was unnecessary for the provincial Supreme Court to deal with the constitutional issue. What then should the Supreme Court of Canada do? "The reasons already stated are sufficient to dispose of the appeal; and, following a wise and well defined tradition, this Court should, no doubt, refrain from expressing an opinion upon any other point not necessary for the decision of the case." Referring to the constitutional decision of the court below, he continued

It is because of the declaration on that point that the Attorney General of Prince Edward Island has carried his appeal to this Court and that the Attorney General of Canada and the Attorney General for Ontario have been allowed to intervene. It was represented to us that this declaration has an important and wide consequence and that, while only an obiter dictum, it might affect the jurisprudence not only in Prince Edward Island but also in other provinces. It appears desirable, therefore, that this Court should express its opinion upon the matter.[179]

He then proceeded to explore fully the constitutional issue and held the provincial statute to be intra vires. Of the judges writing separate opinions, Taschereau J. recognized that a constitutional decision was unnecessary but proceeded to give one; Duff C.J. and Hudson J. both proceeded to deal with the constitutional issue without hesitation.

Can one reconcile the approach taken in the *Egan* case with those decisions previously discussed? If, as was suggested in the *Winner* case, a court in ordinary litigation ought not to make any decision not strictly required to dispose of the contest before it, then the Supreme Court seriously erred in *Egan*. It is submitted that the fundamental principle lies elsewhere: that a court cannot in many cases make a competent judgment on the validity of legislation in the absence of specific fact-situations to which the legislation might apply. It was observed at the beginning of this chapter that Canadian courts are relatively free of constitutional restraint in the matter of deciding hypothetical questions. But this does not free them from the practical necessity of having a factual context in which to test legislation for validity. Some statutes may bear on their face ample evidence of a

179. [1941] S.C.R., at 411–12, [1941] 3 D.L.R., at 318–19.

legislative intent to invade prohibited areas of jurisdiction. But other statutes, valid on their face, may when applied to a given situation render an invalid result. With respect to the latter it may be impossible for a court to render any precise opinion in advance of a specific problem arising.

Thus the *Egan* case involved a specific factual situation, arising out of specific sections of the Criminal Code and the provincial Highway Traffic Act. The court could determine whether the province had in the challenged sections sought to invade a federal field, or whether this section conflicted with the relevant section of the Criminal Code. But in cases such as *Winner* the questions about the general validity of the provincial statutes could not be answered except in relation to the way in which these statutes affected the particular interprovincial undertaking there involved. How they might affect other carriers, existing or future, could not be foreseen by the court with any degree of precision. It therefore declined to answer fully the questions referred by the trial judge.

That judicial self-restraint is based on practical rather than theoretical grounds may be seen in the field of constitutional references. Here the courts are not only free of constitutional restraint in the matter of answering hypothetical questions, but are positively required by statute to give an answer to whatever questions the government sees fit to refer.[180] Yet in the very case where the Privy Council most clearly acknowledged the judicial obligation to answer, it maintained that in some cases answers could not be given. "Nevertheless, under this procedure questions may be put of a kind which it is impossible to answer satisfactorily. Not only may the question of future litigants be prejudiced by the Court laying down principles in an abstract form without any reference or relation to actual facts, but it may turn out to be practically impossible to define a principle adequately and safely without previous ascertainment of the exact facts to which it is applied."[181] While the Privy Council did not have to refuse an answer in this particular case, it has done so in several references. For example, in *Attorney General for Ontario* v. *Hamilton Street Railway*[182] the provincial cabinet had referred to the Ontario Court of Appeal certain questions concerning the validity, and the proper interpretation, of various provisions in the provincial Profanation of the Lord's Day Act. The Privy Council held the Act to be invalid as an invasion of the criminal law power of Parliament. It refused to answer the other questions. While technically the reference procedure would require the answering of all

180. *Supra*, at 90–93. The Court may refuse to deal with questions logically related but not referred: *Reference re Act Respecting the Jurisdiction of Quebec Magistrate's Court*, [1965] S.C.R. 722, 55 D.L.R. (2d) 701.
181. *A.G. for B.C.* v. *A.G. for Can.*, [1914] A.C. 153, at 162 (P.C. 1913).
182. [1903] A.C. 524 (P.C. 1893).

questions put, the Privy Council felt that "it would be extremely unwise for any judicial tribunal to attempt beforehand to exhaust all possible cases and facts which might occur to qualify, cut down, and override the operation of particular words when the concrete case is not before it."[183] What statutory phrases such as "work of necessity" might mean would have to be determined if and when they were applied in specific situations. Again, in *Attorney General for Ontario* v. *Attorney General for Canada*[184] a number of abstract questions was raised in a federal reference concerning the powers of provinces to incorporate companies and to regulate dominion companies. The Privy Council in its decision simply referred to previous decisions, most of them involving actual specific disputes, and said that in their opinion the questions were answered as fully as possible in those cases. The questions not answered by the previous decisions referred to were considered best left because of their "highly abstract character."

Consistently with this position it has been held that a referred constitutional question ought not to be answered in its entirety if the issues raised by it have not been fully argued.[185] There are no pleadings and often no specific definition of the issues in a constitutional reference. If issues are not made specific through the course of argument, the court is again faced with abstract questions which may be impossible to answer.

The judicial objection to answering fully in constitutional references is sometimes based on an expressed concern for private rights unrepresented before the court. The possibility is suggested that if the questions are to be fully answered, private individuals would be prejudiced in future proceedings where the same issues might be raised.[186] This apprehension would appear to be misplaced. What justification can this provide for the courts refusing to do the very thing which under the reference procedure they are required by statute to do? Some references may involve questions the answers to which may be relevant in future litigation over private rights. But if this creates problems for future litigants who were not represented on the reference, it is a difficulty familiar to the common law system.[187] A decision in one motor vehicle accident case may create a

---

183. *Ibid.*, at 529.
184. [1916] 1 A.C. 598 (P.C.).
185. *Crawford and Hillside Farm Dairy Ltd.* v. *A.G. for B.C.*, [1960] S.C.R. 346, at 359, 22 D.L.R. (2d) 321, at 332.
186. See e.g. *In re Order in Council: In re Crop Payments Act*, [1926] 2 W.W.R. 844, at 854, [1927] 2 D.L.R. 50, at 60 (Man. C.A.); *A.G. for Canada* v. *A.G. for Ont.*, [1898] A.C. 700, at 717; *A.G. for Can.* v. *C.P.R. and C.N.R.*, [1958] S.C.R. 285, at 294, 12 D.L.R. (2d) 625, at 630.
187. See Grant, "Judicial Review in Canada: Procedural Aspects" (1964), 42 *Can. B. Rev.* 194, at 210–11.

precedent for a later case of a similar nature, but that is no reason for the court refusing to decide the first case. Technically the rules of stare decisis do not even apply to reference decisions, though as a practical matter such decisions are treated as binding. If the reference involves a specific question as to the rights of particular individuals, the court should if possible order that those individuals be given notice and be permitted to participate in the argument. If "private rights" are affected only in the sense that a decision on a general question may have implications for particular individuals in the future, there would appear to be no special need for consideration of their position. In any event, reference legislation requires that answers be given, and if an answer is otherwise possible the court ought not to hesitate through solicitude for private rights.

The involvement of "private rights" may legitimately preclude decision on a reference, however, where the necessary facts are not available to the court. For example, if the questions referred involved the effect of legislation on particular individuals or a class of individuals, it may be impossible for the court to express any opinion in the absence of specific facts concerning these individuals.[188] In such cases an answer may be impossible, again because the question is too indefinite or ambiguous.

A concern for avoiding impossibly abstract issues may also be seen in Canadian judicial treatment of the problem of "ripeness." Federal courts in the United States have usually insisted that they should not deal with issues not ripe for review. In effect this means that until a person (whose interests would clearly be affected if the statute were applied to him) is actually being subjected to an impugned statute, the issue of its validity is not ripe for determination at his request.[189] Similarly, if the situation or subject matter giving rise to the controversy has since ceased to exist, the court will not decide that which has become an academic question.[190] Canadian courts have seemingly not concerned themselves unduly with the need for an actual and continuing dispute. While the decisions are few and far from conclusive they seem to indicate once again a willingness to decide a speculative issue as long as it is a precise issue.

Thus, in *Attorney General for Ontario* v. *Smith*[191] the plaintiff had unsuccessfully attempted to import liquor into Ontario. Until he did import it he could not be subject to prosecution under the Canada Temperance Act. When he brought an action for a declaration that the Act

188. E.g. *A.G. for Can.* v. *C.P.R. and C.N.R., supra* note 186.
189. *Rescue Army* v. *Municipal Court of Los Angeles* (1947), 331 U.S. 549; *South Carolina* v. *Katzenbach* (1966), 383 U.S. 301, at 317.
190. *Doremus* v. *Board of Education* (1952), 342 U.S. 429.
191. [1924] S.C.R. 331, [1924] 3 D.L.R. 189. See *supra* at 98–101 for a full discussion of this case.

was not validly put into force in Ontario, the judges of the Supreme Court all agreed that the question was purely speculative because he was not yet faced with prosecution. Yet the majority proceeded to give an opinion on the validity of the Act as applied in Ontario. Here the nature of the dispute was clearly defined. It involved questions of law which the court was in a position to decide even in the absence of an actual prosecution. By contrast one may note *Saumur and Jehovah's Witnesses* v. *Attorney General for Que.*,[192] where the impugned legislation prohibited the distribution of pamphlets containing abusive attacks on the religion of any portion of the provincial populace. The day after the Act came into effect the plaintiffs sought declarations that the statute was ultra vires, and that in any event it did not apply to their activities. The Supreme Court of Canada agreed that this was not a proper case for adjudication. It said that the courts could not give a decision as to constitutional validity merely on the basis of some citizen's fear that the Act might some day be applied to him. In the circumstances, this seems quite sound. How the Act would apply to any individual would depend on what kind of activities he might be carrying on. In the absence of specific facts it would be impossible to say that the Act would abridge freedom of religion as alleged by the plaintiff. The issue here was not one purely of law but of fact or mixed fact and law.

Similarly, decisions on constitutional issues have been made after the termination of the situation giving rise to the dispute. In *Attorney General for Canada* v. *Cain*[193] the respondent had been arrested for the purposes of deportation. He was subsequently released by habeas corpus proceedings in which it was held that the statute under which he was arrested was ultra vires. By the time the appeal was heard in the Privy Council, the statutory period during which he could be re-arrested had expired. Thus the decision could have no effect on his position. While Lord Atkinson noted that "the question has in this instance become more or less an academic one" he proceeded to decide the constitutional issue, holding the Act to be ultra vires. Here the issue was sufficiently clear: would the Act as applied to the respondent have an extra-territorial effect? This was a question which the court could effectively answer because the judges had a factual context to which they could refer.

In other constitutional cases the courts have proceeded to a decision even where there was no longer a *lis* in the conventional sense. When private parties have raised constitutional issues in ordinary litigation and

192. [1964] S.C.R. 252, 45 D.L.R. (2d) 627. See *supra* at 101–03 for a full discussion of this case. For a somewhat similar decision see *A.G. for Can.* v. *A.G. for Ont.* (1894), 23 S.C.R. 458, at 470.
193. [1906] A.C. 542 (P.C.).

then subsequently dropped out of the proceedings, courts have heard appeals where the only adverse interest was that of an intervening attorney general.[194] In such cases the original subject matter of the controversy has disappeared and there is no real necessity for a decision. Yet because the issues have been clearly defined in terms of the original situation the court feels able to express an opinion on the validity of the impugned statute.

The ability and willingness of the court to consider speculative issues will of course vary, depending on the nature of the remedy being employed. For example, mandamus will not be issued unless the applicant can show that he has made a specific demand that a certain act be done and that there has been a refusal to act.[195] In equitable remedies the lack of necessity may be a good reason for the exercise of judicial discretion against deciding the issue.[196]

In summary it may be suggested that Canadian courts have developed no clearly defined objections to "unnecessary" constitutional decisions. The self-imposed limitation appears to be of a practical nature. The issue must be raised in a sufficiently precise manner. If it is, the courts will decide it, even where an actual conflict has not yet arisen or has since disappeared, or where the case may be decided on other grounds. This view is confirmed by the fact that even where, as in reference proceedings, the law requires an answer to be given, the courts decline to deal with those issues which are not defined with sufficient precision.

It may be argued that Canadian courts have been too willing to make constitutional decisions. Opposition in the United States to speculative constitutional litigation is fundamental.[197] It is submitted, however, that much of the objection to "judicial activism" in these situations stems from the fear that unwarranted conclusions will be reached because the issues have not been clearly defined. The Canadian courts must continue to show some discernment in their choice of cases for decision. If they accept only those in which the factual context is either not important, or, if important, well defined, they will avoid the stigma of officiousness. United States practice is not entirely comparable. A large portion of the constitutional decisions there involve the interpretation of the broad phrases of the Bill of Rights. Canadian courts most frequently deal with the relatively precise prose of the BNA Act. Where they do have a concept such as "freedom

194. E.g. *Switzman* v. *Elbling and A.G. for Que.*, [1957] S.C.R. 285, 7 D.L.R. (2d) 337.
195. See e.g. *Hughes* v. *Henderson* (1963), 46 W.W.R. (n.s.) 202 (Man. Q.B.).
196. See e.g. *Gruen Watch Co.* v. *A.G. for Can.*, [1950] O.R. 429, [1950] 4 D.L.R. 156 (Ont. High Ct.).
197. A strong expression of this viewpoint may be seen in Frankfurter, "A Note on Advisory Opinions" (1924), 37 *Harv. L. Rev.* 1002.

Since there would not appear to be anything in these constitutional requirements which has particular significance for the maintenance of the federal structure, we can probably assume that the courts would not try to enforce the criteria for legislators imposed by the BNA Act. In any event, if the appropriate legislative body chose to alter the qualifications for its members, this would appear to be within its powers under sections 91(1) or 92(1).

What of the requirement for periodic federal elections? Section 50 requires that no House of Commons shall continue more than five years, and section 20 requires a session of Parliament each year. Therefore there is a clear requirement that elections be held at least once every five years.[208] An interval of six or more years would contravene the BNA Act. Would the court order an election? The Supreme Court has refused to enforce comparable time restrictions in provincial constitutional provisions.[209] But the provinces under section 92(1) have a virtually unfettered power to amend the provincial constitution. Parliament's power with respect to amending the "Constitution of Canada" is restricted by section 91(1) so as to prevent the delay of elections except under very special circumstances. It is submitted that a court might, assuming that the issue were properly before it, declare invalid any federal statutory provision which purported to lengthen the life of Parliament in violation of section 91. But again, the problems of standing and remedies might frustrate judicial supervision of this clear constitutional directive.

The courts might be more effective in ensuring the observance of procedural requirements imposed by the BNA Act with respect to the enactment of legislation. For example, section 48 specifies the quorum required in the House of Commons, section 49 the nature of the majority required to decide questions, sections 53 and 54 the procedure for the introduction of money bills, and section 55 the necessity for royal assent. Section 90 makes several of these provisions equally applicable in provincial legislatures. It was at one time thought to be an element of parliamentary sovereignty that statutes could not be judicially challenged on procedural grounds. Any judicial investigation of such matters was thought to be an invasion of parliamentary privilege. The better view would now appear to be that a court can refuse to give effect to legislation enacted by an improper procedure, that is, not in accordance with predetermined procedural requirements.[210] Courts in other parts of the Commonwealth have

208. Subject to the exception in s.91(1) with respect to times of emergency.
209. *Temple* v. *Bulmer*, [1943] S.C.R. 265, [1943] 3 D.L.R. 649.
210. See e.g. Heuston, *Essays in Constitutional Law* (2nd ed., 1964), at 16–31; Tarnopolsky, *The Canadian Bill of Rights* (1966), at 66–89. See also *supra*, chapter two, *passim*.

been prepared to review legislation on such grounds,[211] and in Canada at least one court has held a provincial statute invalid for non-compliance with the requirements for royal assent in section 90.[212] There would be no exceptional problem with respect to standing or remedy if the court simply refused to give effect to a statute which had not been properly enacted.

The courts can probably supervise Parliament in at least one other "internal" aspect. Section 18 of the BNA Act provides that Parliament may not confer on itself any greater privileges than those enjoyed at the time by the Parliament of the United Kingdom. With the reception of the common law Canada acquired the guarantees of the Bill of Rights, 1688, section 9 of which provided that "proceedings in Parliament ought not to be impeached or questioned in any court or place out of Parliament."[213] Clearly the courts could not review the manner in which Parliament exercised its privileges, for example in punishing a person for contempt of Parliament. But it has long been held that the courts can ascertain whether the privilege asserted by Parliament is one recognized by the law.[214] Therefore, the courts could in a proper case test any statute pursuant to section 18 to determine whether the privilege it created was one which the Canadian Parliament was entitled to claim for itself. Such an issue might be raised by means of a reference or by proceedings such as habeas corpus, or damage actions on behalf of individuals who had suffered at the hands of Parliament in the exercise of its alleged privileges.

The foregoing matters have all pertained to judicial supervision of the internal operations of Parliament. In general it may be said that (subject to major and historical exceptions) the courts are able to review these operations to determine whether they are valid in a jurisdictional sense. This is possible because the jurisdictional standards are prescribed by law. Here the courts are faced with the familiar task of applying the law derived from the BNA Act and the common law.

There are at least two other areas where justiciability becomes a more serious problem. These include the interpretation of the power of Parliament to legislate with respect to "the peace, order, and good government

211. *Harris* v. *Minister of Interior*, [1952] 2 So. Afr. L.R. 428 (Sup. Ct.); *Minister of Interior* v. *Harris*, [1952] 4 So. Afr. L.R. 769 (Sup. Ct.); *Collins* v. *Minister of Interior*, [1957] 1 So. Afr. L.R. 552 (Sup. Ct.); *McDonald* v. *Cain*, [1953] Vict. L.R. 411 (Sup. Ct.).
212. *Gallant* v. *The King* (1948), 23 M.P.R. 48, [1949] 2 D.L.R. 425 (P.E.I. Sup. Ct.).
213. 1 Wm. III and Mary, 2nd. sess., c.2, s.9.
214. *Stockdale* v. *Hansard* (1839), 9 Ad. & El. 1, 112 E.R. 1112 (Q.B.); *Kielly* v. *Carson* (1842), 4 Moo. P.C. 63, 13 E.R. 225 (P.C.); *Landers* v. *Woodworth* (1878), 2 S.C.R. 158 (1878); *Re Parliamentary Privilege Act, 1770*, [1958] A.C. 331 (P.C.).

of Canada . . . " and the interpretation of the scope of Parliament's power to legislate with respect to "the criminal law. . . . " The problem arises because in some situations the power to legislate with respect to these matters is dependent on the pre-existence of a certain factual situation.

The federal power with respect to "peace, order, and good government" conferred by the opening words of section 91 of the BNA Act is in a large measure a residual power. Thus, where a matter falls entirely outside the scope of provincial powers under section 92, and is not otherwise protected from legislative interference,[215] it clearly falls within this residual federal power if it cannot be ascribed specifically to one of the enumerated heads of federal jurisdiction in section 91.[216] But there may be other situations in which federal legislation, purportedly enacted for the peace, order, and good government of Canada, may interfere with or affect certain matters within provincial jurisdiction. In the early judicial interpretation of sections 91 and 92 this was thought to be permissible,[217] but later decisions imposed more stringent limitations on the exercise of the federal power. It was suggested that "peace, order, and good government" would be justification for an interference with matters otherwise provincial only in those situations where a national emergency existed.[218] The better view has more recently been expressed by Viscount Simon in *Attorney General for Ontario* v. *Canada Temperance Federation*.

In their Lordships' opinion, the true test must be found in the real subject matter of the legislation: if it is such that it goes beyond local or provincial concern or interests and must from its inherent nature be the concern of the Dominion as a whole . . . then it will fall within the competence of the Dominion Parliament as a matter affecting the peace, order and good government of Canada, though it may in another aspect touch on matters specially reserved to the provincial legislatures. War and pestilence, no doubt, are instances; so too, may be the drink or drug traffic, or the carrying of arms. . . .[219]

By this interpretation it is necessary that a matter must have become of such national importance as to transcend local interests. Not only emergencies such as war or pestilence, but other less obvious problems may create the necessary pre-conditions for the exercise of Parliament's power. But who is to decide whether such conditions exist? A decision by Parlia-

215. I.e., is not the subject of a guarantee such as found in ss.121, 125, or 133.
216. *John Deere Plow Co.* v. *Wharton*, [1915] A.C. 330 (P.C. 1914); *In re Regulation and Control of Radio Communication in Canada*, [1932] A.C. 304 (P.C.).
217. *Russell* v. *The Queen* (1882), 7 App. Cas. 829 (P.C.).
218. See e.g. *Re Board of Commerce Act*, [1922] 1 A.C. 191 (P.C.); *Fort Frances Pulp & Power Co.* v. *Manitoba Free Press Co.*, [1923] A.C. 695 (P.C.).
219. [1946] A.C. 193, at 205–06. *Foll'd Munro* v. *National Capital Commission*, [1966] S.C.R. 663, 57 D.L.R. (2d) 753.

ment or the federal cabinet that an emergency exists because of wartime or immediate post-war conditions seems to enjoy a very strong presumption in its favour. The courts have not only accepted such decisions without question but have indicated that the opinion of Parliament and the government must be respected in the absence of very clear evidence that it is wrong.[220] But where Parliament has attempted to legislate in exercise of the "peace, order, and good government" power on matters not directly related to war, the courts have shown more independence in their approach. They have either examined the question with an open mind[221] or else have initially presumed the judgment of Parliament to be wrong in the absence of clear evidence to the contrary.[222]

In no case have the courts indicated that the opinion of Parliament on such an issue is beyond judicial review. But they ought not to examine too closely the correctness of value judgments which Parliament has been forced to make. For example, it could be argued that post-war inflation in the price of essential commodities might be regulated by the individual provinces. If, however, Parliament's decision to regulate them in the national interest is not obviously an unnecessary "invasion" of a provincial domain, the court should respect Parliament's judgment that national regulation is required. It is submitted that the proper approach is that enunciated by Lord Wright in the *Japanese-Canadians* case in 1946.

[T]he Parliament of the Dominion in a sufficiently great emergency, such as that arising out of war, has power to deal adequately with that emergency for the safety of the Dominion as a whole. The interests of the Dominion are to be protected and it rests with the Parliament of the Dominion to protect them. *What those interests are the Parliament of the Dominion must be left with considerable freedom to judge.* Again, if it be clear that an emergency has not arisen, or no longer exists, there can be no justification for the exercise or continued exercise of the exceptional powers. . . . *But very clear evidence that an emergency has not arisen, or that the emergency no longer exists, is required to justify the judiciary, even though the question is one of ultra vires, in overruling the decision of the Parliament of the Dominion that exceptional measures were required or were still required.*[223]

By this formulation the integrity of the courts as guardians of the constitution is maintained. The legitimate exercise of legislative discretion is also protected, provided that Parliament does not in its choice of measures invade provincial spheres in a manner which is patently unnecessary.

220. *Fort Frances* case, *supra* note 218, at 706; *Co-operative Committee on Japanese Canadians* v. *A.G. for Can.*, [1947] A.C. 87 (P.C. 1946).
221. *Pronto Uranium Mines Ltd.* v. *Ontario Labour Relations Board*, [1956] O.R. 862, 5 D.L.R. 342 (Ont. Sup. Ct.).
222. *Re Board of Commerce* case, *supra* note 218, at 197–98.
223. *Japanese Canadians* case, *supra* note 220, at 101–02: emphasis added.

There is of necessity a large policy element in any decision that a particular matter has become one of national concern. When Parliament makes such a decision, there should be a strong presumption in favour of the correctness of that decision, because policy decisions are properly matters for legislatures rather than courts. It is only when the discretionary power of Parliament is manifestly exercised colourably for a wrong purpose – the invasion of provincial jurisdiction rather than the essential protection of the nation – that the courts can intervene.

A similar situation arises in determining the scope of the federal power to legislate with respect to "the criminal law" under section 91(27). Again, there is a certain area of jurisdiction assured to Parliament. This includes legislation of a sort clearly recognized as criminal at the time when the BNA Act was passed.[224] But the scope of the criminal law power was not frozen as of 1867. Parliament is free to create new crimes by prohibiting certain forms of activity and attaching penal sanctions.[225] While the concept of "criminal law" is thus capable of growth to cope with changing conditions, there obviously must be some limitation on it. Otherwise Parliament could take over almost any provincial field by requiring certain forms of conduct and forbidding others, with penal sanctions attached for failure to comply.[226] A strong indication as to the judicial limitation which will be imposed on the expansion of "criminal law" emerged in the *Margarine Reference*. One of the questions raised in this case was whether a federal prohibition against manufacture and sale of margarine, even where confined to a single province, could be justified as a matter of "criminal law." Both the Supreme Court[227] and the Privy Council[228] held that it could not because it was not designed to protect the public as such against some evil. It was in essence economic legislation. Mr. Justice Rand in the Supreme Court succinctly described the distinction. "Is the prohibition then enacted with a view to a public purpose which can support it as being in relation to criminal law? Public peace, order, security, health, morality: these are the ordinary though not exclusive ends served by that law, but they do not appear to be the object of the parliamentary action here. That object, as I must find it, is economic and the legislative purpose, to give trade protection to the dairy industry."[229]

224. See e.g. *A.G. for Ont.* v. *Hamilton Street Ry.*, [1903] A.C. 524 (P.C. 1893); *Johnson* v. *A.G. for Alta.*, [1954] S.C.R. 127, [1954] 2 D.L.R. 625; *Switzman* v. *Elbling*, [1957] S.C.R. 285, 7 D.L.R. (2d) 337.
225. *P.A.T.A.* v. *A.G. for Can.*, [1931] A.C. 310, at 324 (P.C.).
226. *A.G. for Ont.* v. *Reciprocal Insurers*, [1924] A.C. 328 (P.C.); *Canadian Federation of Agriculture* v. *A.G. for Que.*, [1951] A.C. 179 (P.C. 1950).
227. [1949] S.C.R. 1, [1949] 1 D.L.R. 433.
228. *Canadian Federation of Agriculture* case, *supra* note 226.
229. [1949] S.C.R., at 50, [1949] 1 D.L.R., at 473.

It is obvious that a test of this nature will involve factual opinions and value judgments about whether the activity prohibited by the putative criminal law is one which threatens "public peace, order, security, health, morality." In the *Margarine Reference* itself it was necessary to decide whether margarine was a harmful substance which could endanger public health. The courts had in the past been reluctant to substitute their opinions on such matters for those of Parliament.[230] But where the evidence clearly showed the lack of any public danger, as it did in the *Margarine Reference*, the judicial opinion prevailed. That case may be a rarity in that the order in council referring the question of validity to the Supreme Court of Canada itself contained evidence sufficient to defeat the statute. In a reference order of unusual dimensions there was recited, *inter alia*, legislative history indicating that for a period during the first world war the sale of margarine had been legalized, and an article from the *Canadian Medical Association Journal* which attested to the healthful potential of margarine. With such evidence gratuitously provided to it by the government of Canada, the Supreme Court had little difficulty in concluding that margarine could not be considered as a serious threat to public health. It may be a rare event for a court to have such weighty evidence before it to contradict the alleged opinion of Parliament. But it would appear that, just as in the case of judicial definition of the "peace, order, and good government power," there is a point at which the courts will be prepared to question the wisdom of Parliament on such matters.

In these cases of "peace, order, and good government" and "criminal law" we see duties forced on the judiciary because of Canada's federal structure. In a unitary system the courts generally refuse to go behind a statute to question the validity of the factual assumption on which the legislature acted.[231] In a federal structure, while every deference must be shown to legislative conclusions on fact and policy, this deference must not be carried to the point of allowing the legislative body colourably to achieve some end otherwise forbidden.[232]

CONCLUSION

Canadian courts have yet to adopt any consistent policy with respect to standing and justiciability in constitutional cases. They are uniquely free

230. See e.g. *Standard Sausage Co.* v. *Lee*, (1934) 47 B.C. 411, [1934] 1 D.L.R. 706 (B.C.C.A.); *R.* v. *Perfection Creameries Ltd.*, [1939] 2 W.W.R. 139, [1939] 3 D.L.R. 185 (Man. C.A.).
231. *Labrador Company* v. *The Queen*, [1893] A.C. 104 (P.C.); *Tukino* v. *Aotea District Maori Land Board*, [1941] A.C. 308 (P.C.).
232. See generally chapter two, *supra*, *passim*.

in these matters because of the scope allowed them under the constitution. Thus we can find examples of parties achieving standing where they have no legal interest. We also find the courts deciding constitutional issues where it is not strictly necessary to do so, provided the problem is raised in a sufficiently precise manner.

As the courts have been left with such a large measure of discretion, the opportunity exists for development of a rational policy. It is suggested that they should, when confronted with a precise constitutional issue, lean in favour of judicial determination. If courts in a federal system are too reluctant to decide questions of legislative jurisdiction, the controversy will be carried on indefinitely in other forums. This can result in uncertainty for private citizens and the deterioration of intergovernmental relations. If, on the other hand, the courts are willing to decide such issues they may provide the creative leadership which is essential in the evolution of a federal constitution. As long as constitutional amendment is very difficult, as it is in Canada, there will be a need for other techniques of constitutional development. Judicial review is such a technique. The courts have effectively avoided most external barriers to judicial review. They should hesitate to erect unnecessary barriers of their own.

CHAPTER SIX

The Elements of a Constitutional Decision

THE NATURE OF CONSTITUTIONAL ADJUDICATION

To determine whether an impugned statute is valid, the court must try to "match it up" with some head of jurisdiction in the British North America Act.

Section 91 declares that "the exclusive legislative authority of the Parliament of Canada extends to all matters coming within the classes of subjects next hereinafter enumerated. . . . " Similarly, section 92 states that the provincial legislatures "may exclusively make laws in relation to matters coming within the classes of subjects next hereinafter enumerated. . . . " Each subject enumerated in sections 91 and 92 anticipates a legal regime related to the persons,[1] things,[2] or activities[3] referred to therein.[4] When provincial legislation is challenged, for example, it is necessary to ascertain whether the statute creates a legal regime related to certain of these phenomena in the provincial list of subjects. Only if such a relationship can be found will it be valid. An impugned federal statute will equally be valid if related to a subject listed in section 91. But, in addition,

1. E.g. "Indians . . . " in 91(24) or " . . . aliens" in 91(25).
2. E.g. "Sea Coast and inland fisheries" in 91(12), or "Local works . . . " in 92(10).
3. E.g. "the regulation of trade and commerce" in 91(2) or "the solemnization of marriage in the province" in 92(12).
4. It might be argued that some subjects such as "criminal law . . . ," 91(27), or "incorporation of companies with provincial objects," 92(11), do not refer to any persons, things, or activities external to the legal phenomena therein contained. It is submitted that there is in fact an implied reference to those external physical phenomena which the framers of the BNA Act commonly understood to be associated with the legal phenomena specifically mentioned. Thus "criminal law" was intended to refer to forms of activity commonly considered to be dangerous to the public. See Rand J. in the *Margarine Reference*, [1949] S.C.R. 1, at 50, [1949] 1 D.L.R. 433, at 473–74. That the reference to external phenomena is implied and not expressed makes interpretation more difficult, but not qualitatively different.

a federal statute, even if unrelated to any enumerated head of section 91, so long as it is also unrelated to an enumerated head of section 92, will be valid as an exercise of Parliament's power "to make laws for the peace, order, and good government of Canada" as conferred in the opening words of section 91.

This states in its simplest terms a process which is full of complexity and unpredictability. It is immediately obvious that before one can "match up" an impugned statute with a subject listed in the BNA Act, one must come to some conclusion with respect to what the scope of the "class of subject" is as enumerated in the constitution, and what the nature or content of the impugned statute is from a constitutional point of view.

Much has been written elsewhere in an effort to explain this decisional process. Efforts have been made to reduce it to a set of formulae for analysis of both the impugned statute and the constitution.[5] Some have suggested that construction of the impugned statute is the most important aspect of constitutional adjudication,[6] while others have stressed the importance of "the elaboration of the content of the heads of legislative power conferred by the British North America Act."[7] It is not within the scope of this work to attempt to resolve the conflicts among the authors or to seek a simple explanation for the process in question. Indeed, the decisions largely defy explanation. The better approach is to identify the factors which most probably will have some influence on the decision, without seeking to evaluate too precisely the relative weight likely to be accorded to each.

One factor to be considered is the effect of the impugned statute. It is sometimes suggested that the courts should be as concerned with "intent" of the legislature, or "purpose" of the legislation, as with its effect.[8] This confuses the issue unnecessarily. If we look upon the constitution as a set of rules for a game in which the eleven players (the federal and provincial legislatures) must each remain in his own area, then the function of the court as referee is to enforce these rules. A wrong motive or purpose on the part of a player, so long as it is not accompanied by overt trespass, is

5. Mundell, "Tests for Validity of Legislation under the British North America Act" (1954), 32 *Can. B. Rev.* 813; Mundell, "Tests for Validity of Legislation under the British North America Act: A Reply to Professor Laskin" (1955), 33 *Can. B. Rev.* 915.
6. See e.g. LaBrie, "Canadian Constitutional Interpretation and Legislative Review" (1950), 8 *U. Toronto L.J.* 298, at 312.
7. Laskin, "Tests for the Validity of Legislation: What's the Matter?" (1955), 11 *U. Toronto L. J.* 114, at 125.
8. E.g. *A.G. for Alta.* v. *A.G. for Can.*, [1939] A.C. 117, at 130–31 (P.C. 1938); LaBrie, *supra* note 6; Mundell, *supra* note 5.

of no concern to the referee. On the other hand, an overt trespass, even though innocent, is a violation of the rules. Usually the thought is father to the deed, but in the final analysis it is the deed to which we must pay regard. Thus, as Dean Lederman has clearly demonstrated,[9] the test of "effect" is crucial when legislation is colourable. If one still finds it necessary to look for "intent" or "purpose" of the legislature, he may merely assume that the legislature, like a sane man, is presumed to intend the ordinary consequences (or "effect") of its act.[10]

The other basic issue to be considered is whether the enacting legislature ought to be permitted to achieve the effect which the court attributes to its statute. In making this decision the court must reach some conclusion as to the scope of one or more of the heads of section 91 or 92. It will also have to make value judgments with respect to the statute in question. The statute may well have several "effects." Some of these might clearly fall within the provincial sphere, others within the federal sphere. For example, the federal Criminal Code protects magistrates and peace officers from civil liability when carrying out their duties with respect to administration of the criminal law. This has the effect of aiding the enforcement of criminal law, but it also has the effect of taking away a civil right of a person imprisoned through some excess of jurisdiction. It is impossible to analyze fully the process by which a court would uphold the validity of such a provision. It can be argued that the court simply concludes that "criminal law" ought to include the protection of magistrates and peace officers. Or it can be said that the court considers the salient effect of the law to be the furtherance of criminal justice. Sometimes the courts express their conclusions in one form, sometimes in the other, but the results probably represent an interaction of the two concepts.

In examining the elements of a constitutional decision, then, it is necessary to keep in mind the two questions which the court must ask: (1) What is the effect, or what are the effects, of the legislation in question? and (2) Are the most significant effects among those which are permitted to the enacting legislature under the BNA Act?

---

9. Lederman, "Classification of Laws and the British North America Act," in Corry, Cronkite, and Whitmore, *Legal Essays in Honour of Arthur Moxon* (1953), 183, at 196.
10. *Ibid.*, at 196–97. See also *A.G. for Man.* v. *A.G. for Can.*, [1929] A.C. 260, at 266–68 (P.C. 1928). But see *Robertson et al.* v. *The Queen*, [1963] S.C.R. 651, at 657–58, 41 D.L.R. (2d) 485, at 494 where it was suggested that a statute may have a constitutionally permissible "purpose" even though its "effect" would be inconsistent with this "purpose." This seems to ignore the long-established rules against "colourable" legislation discussed *supra* at 39.

this area, however, that a court would find it difficult to ignore these rules in reaching a final conclusion as to constitutional validity.

Precedent will be far less influential in the process of answering the first question referred to above: What is the effect of the impugned statute? The effect of a particular statute is likely to be unique, unless it is basically similar to other legislation not only in form but also in context within which it is expected to operate. Each new statute should raise a new question as to its effect. The rules of statutory interpretation or judicial experience with similar legislation may yield a satisfactory answer in some cases. A resort to factual material should be permittted elsewhere. The dead hand of precedent should not shut out factual illumination.

To a limited extent precedent has nevertheless precluded further inquiry as to statutory effect. With respect to one head of jurisdiction, at least, that of provincial power over "direct taxation within the province . . .," the courts have looked more to precedent than to practice in determining the effect of taxation measures. The Privy Council early adopted John Stuart Mill's definition of direct and indirect taxes: "A direct tax is one which is demanded from the very persons who it is intended or desired should pay it. Indirect taxes are those which are demanded from one person in the expectation and intention that he shall indemnify himself at the expense of another; such are the excise or customs."[21] Having accepted this as the basis of distinguishing a direct tax from an indirect tax, the courts have been unwilling to ascertain as a matter of fact whether the tax in question is or is not imposed in such a way as to permit a passing-on. They have declined to be guided by the opinions of economists on the actual effect of the tax.[22] Instead they have tended automatically to treat certain kinds of taxes as direct, other kinds as indirect. It appears to have been accepted as a matter of law that a tax on land is always a direct tax.[23] A tax on commodities is always an indirect tax, even if the possibilities of passing it on are slight.[24] Conversely, a consumption tax is a direct tax even though in a large area of commercial activity it is capable of being passed on.[25]

21. As approved in *Bank of Toronto* v. *Lambe* (1887), 12 App. Cas. 575, at 583 (P.C.).
22. *Ibid.*, at 581–82; *Cairns Construction Ltd.* v. *Government of Saskatchewan* (1958), 27 W.W.R. (n.s.) 297, 16 D.L.R. (2d) 465 (Sask. C.A.), appeal dismissed [1960] S.C.R. 619, 24 D.L.R. (2d) 1 without reference to this point.
23. *A.G. for B.C.* v. *Esquimalt & Nanaimo Ry.*, [1950] A.C. 87 (P.C. 1949); *C.P.R.* v. *A.G. for Sask.*, [1952] 2 S.C.R. 231, [1952] 4 D.L.R. 11.
24. *A.G. for B.C.* v. *McDonald Murphy Lumber Co.*, [1930] A.C. 357 (P.C.); *Lower Mainland Dairy Products Sales Adjustment Commmittee* v. *Crystal Dairy Ltd.*, [1933] A.C. 168 (P.C. 1932).
25. *Cairns Construction* case, *supra* note 22.

of no concern to the referee. On the other hand, an overt trespass, even though innocent, is a violation of the rules. Usually the thought is father to the deed, but in the final analysis it is the deed to which we must pay regard. Thus, as Dean Lederman has clearly demonstrated,[9] the test of "effect" is crucial when legislation is colourable. If one still finds it necessary to look for "intent" or "purpose" of the legislature, he may merely assume that the legislature, like a sane man, is presumed to intend the ordinary consequences (or "effect") of its act.[10]

The other basic issue to be considered is whether the enacting legislature ought to be permitted to achieve the effect which the court attributes to its statute. In making this decision the court must reach some conclusion as to the scope of one or more of the heads of section 91 or 92. It will also have to make value judgments with respect to the statute in question. The statute may well have several "effects." Some of these might clearly fall within the provincial sphere, others within the federal sphere. For example, the federal Criminal Code protects magistrates and peace officers from civil liability when carrying out their duties with respect to administration of the criminal law. This has the effect of aiding the enforcement of criminal law, but it also has the effect of taking away a civil right of a person imprisoned through some excess of jurisdiction. It is impossible to analyze fully the process by which a court would uphold the validity of such a provision. It can be argued that the court simply concludes that "criminal law" ought to include the protection of magistrates and peace officers. Or it can be said that the court considers the salient effect of the law to be the furtherance of criminal justice. Sometimes the courts express their conclusions in one form, sometimes in the other, but the results probably represent an interaction of the two concepts.

In examining the elements of a constitutional decision, then, it is necessary to keep in mind the two questions which the court must ask: (1) What is the effect, or what are the effects, of the legislation in question? and (2) Are the most significant effects among those which are permitted to the enacting legislature under the BNA Act?

9. Lederman, "Classification of Laws and the British North America Act," in Corry, Cronkite, and Whitmore, *Legal Essays in Honour of Arthur Moxon* (1953), 183, at 196.
10. *Ibid.*, at 196–97. See also *A.G. for Man.* v. *A.G. for Can.*, [1929] A.C. 260, at 266–68 (P.C. 1928). But see *Robertson et al.* v. *The Queen*, [1963] S.C.R. 651, at 657–58, 41 D.L.R. (2d) 485, at 494 where it was suggested that a statute may have a constitutionally permissible "purpose" even though its "effect" would be inconsistent with this "purpose." This seems to ignore the long-established rules against "colourable" legislation discussed *supra* at 39.

NON-FACTUAL ELEMENTS

To answer these questions the courts must resort to both factual and non-factual material. Non-factual material will be used primarily, though not exclusively, in answering the second question which involves the characterization of legislation in terms of the BNA Act. Non-factual material as referred to herein includes the bare words of the BNA Act and the impugned statute, together with the rules of statutory interpretation, precedent, and judicial creativity. We cannot begin to survey these elements in detail for they embrace almost the whole of substantive constitutional law which is outside the scope of this work. A brief look must suffice.

It is clear that the court must in each case start with an examination of the text of the constitution and of the statute in question.[11] In seeking the meaning of each they can make use of the common law rules of statutory interpretation.[12] These rules,[13] which are themselves artificial in concept and uncertain in application, may not yield a final result with respect to meaning. But they may solve the easiest problems and provide a starting point for the solution of others.

More important among the non-factual sources is the mass of precedent bearing on any constitutional decision. Precedent will be most influential in producing an answer to the second question referred to above: Are the salient effects of an impugned statute within the area permitted to the enacting legislature? The answer to this question will involve some express or implied conclusion as to the proper scope of a head of section 91 or 92, and as to the relative importance of various possible "effects" of the statute in question. The reports are of course full of pronouncements on the scope of the various heads of jurisdiction in sections 91 and 92. We have been told, for example, that "regulation of trade and commerce" includes regulation of interprovincial and international commerce,[14] but not intraprovincial commerce.[15] "Criminal law" includes the prohibition of acts combined with penal sanctions,[16] so long as the prohibition is primarily

---

11. This would include an examination of the statute in its legal context. That is, other statutes and judicial decisions related to it can be examined to assist in determining its meaning. See *Reference re Alberta Statutes*, [1938] S.C.R. 100, [1938] 2 D.L.R. 81; *P.A.T.A.* v. *A.G. for Can.*, [1931] A.C. 310 (P.C.); *Canadian Federation of Agriculture* v. *Quebec*, [1951] A.C. 179 (P.C.).
12. See MacDonald, "Constitutional Interpretation and Extrinsic Evidence" (1939), 17 *Can. B. Rev.* 77.
13. See Willis, "Statute Interpretation in a Nutshell" (1938), 16 *Can. B. Rev.* 1.
14. *Citizens' Insurance Company* v. *Parsons* (1881), 7 App. Cas. 96 (P.C.).
15. *In re Board of Commerce*, [1922] 1 A.C. 191 (P.C.).
16. *P.A.T.A.* v. *A.G. for Can.*, [1931] A.C. 310 (P.C.).

intended to protect the public as such and is not a guise for regulating local commerce.[17]

Canadian constitutional jurisprudence abounds with such propositions. They do not necessarily yield any obvious result in a given case, however, as it is not immediately apparent how they relate to a particular statute the validity of which is in question. Is the most important feature of a statute its effect on interprovincial trade, or its effect on property and civil rights in the province? Precedent does not often give the answer to such a question, though it may.[18] The answer is more likely to come from judicial intuition or a judicial policy decision, possibly (but not probably) aided by a resort to factual material as to effect. Precedent re-emerges as a potent force after the court has singled out the important and the unimportant features of the challenged legislation. The court will then resort to the well-recognized, judicially created, principles for the determination of constitutional validity. If the major effect of a federal statute pertains to "criminal law," and a minor effect pertains to matters which for other purposes would fall within "property and civil rights," the court will apply the so-called "trenching" doctrine and uphold the legislation. If the major effect of a provincial law is the regulation of taverns or highway traffic, and federal legislation also exists regulating these matters, the court may apply the "double-aspect" doctrine and uphold both, or if it finds a "conflict" may strike down the provincial law on the basis of the "paramountcy" doctrine. If federal legislation is found to pertain to a matter of inherent "concern of the Dominion as a whole," even though not referable to one of the enumerated heads of section 91, it may be upheld even though it may interfere with matters otherwise within the provincial sphere. These rules or doctrines are all judicial glosses on the actual terms of the BNA Act.[19] They may well have hindered as much as helped in the intelligent analysis of challenged legislation.[20] So strongly has precedent operated in

17. *Canadian Federation of Agriculture* v. *A.G. for Que.*, [1951] A.C. 179 (P.C. 1950).
18. The courts have shown an unnecessarily strong tendency at times to apply, or misapply, precedent in characterizing statutes. For example, all statutory efforts of Parliament to license insurance companies have been characterized as invasions of the provincial domain over property and civil rights. Precedent was the major justification given for this finding in a series of cases. See Smith, *The Commerce Power in Canada and the United States* (1963), at 77–91.
19. They have been amply expounded and analyzed elsewhere. See e.g. *A.G. for Can.* v. *A.G. for B.C.*, [1930] A.C. 111; LaBrie, *supra* note 6; Mundell, *supra* note 5; Laskin, *Canadian Constitutional Law* (3rd ed., 1966), at 85–144, 197–271. Perhaps the simplest and most lucid analysis is that of Dean Lederman, *supra* note 9, at 201–06.
20. See e.g. Laskin, "Peace, Order and Good Government Re-examined" (1947), 25 *Can. B. Rev.* 1054.

this area, however, that a court would find it difficult to ignore these rules in reaching a final conclusion as to constitutional validity.

Precedent will be far less influential in the process of answering the first question referred to above: What is the effect of the impugned statute? The effect of a particular statute is likely to be unique, unless it is basically similar to other legislation not only in form but also in the context within which it is expected to operate. Each new statute should raise a new question as to its effect. The rules of statutory interpretation or judicial experience with similar legislation may yield a satisfactory answer in some cases. A resort to factual material should be permittted elsewhere. The dead hand of precedent should not shut out factual illumination.

To a limited extent precedent has nevertheless precluded further inquiry as to statutory effect. With respect to one head of jurisdiction, at least, that of provincial power over "direct taxation within the province . . .," the courts have looked more to precedent than to practice in determining the effect of taxation measures. The Privy Council early adopted John Stuart Mill's definition of direct and indirect taxes: "A direct tax is one which is demanded from the very persons who it is intended or desired should pay it. Indirect taxes are those which are demanded from one person in the expectation and intention that he shall indemnify himself at the expense of another; such are the excise or customs."[21] Having accepted this as the basis of distinguishing a direct tax from an indirect tax, the courts have been unwilling to ascertain as a matter of fact whether the tax in question is or is not imposed in such a way as to permit a passing-on. They have declined to be guided by the opinions of economists on the actual effect of the tax.[22] Instead they have tended automatically to treat certain kinds of taxes as direct, other kinds as indirect. It appears to have been accepted as a matter of law that a tax on land is always a direct tax.[23] A tax on commodities is always an indirect tax, even if the possibilities of passing it on are slight.[24] Conversely, a consumption tax is a direct tax even though in a large area of commercial activity it is capable of being passed on.[25]

21. As approved in *Bank of Toronto* v. *Lambe* (1887), 12 App. Cas. 575, at 583 (P.C.).
22. *Ibid.*, at 581–82; *Cairns Construction Ltd.* v. *Government of Saskatchewan* (1958), 27 W.W.R. (n.s.) 297, 16 D.L.R. (2d) 465 (Sask. C.A.), appeal dismissed [1960] S.C.R. 619, 24 D.L.R. (2d) 1 without reference to this point.
23. *A.G. for B.C.* v. *Esquimalt & Nanaimo Ry.*, [1950] A.C. 87 (P.C. 1949); *C.P.R.* v. *A.G. for Sask.*, [1952] 2 S.C.R. 231, [1952] 4 D.L.R. 11.
24. *A.G. for B.C.* v. *McDonald Murphy Lumber Co.*, [1930] A.C. 357 (P.C.); *Lower Mainland Dairy Products Sales Adjustment Commmittee* v. *Crystal Dairy Ltd.*, [1933] A.C. 168 (P.C. 1932).
25. *Cairns Construction* case, *supra* note 22.

As Professor K. C. Davis has pointed out,[26] there is a certain judicial tendency to convert difficult questions of fact into presumptions of law. For example, because it would be difficult to ascertain whether each child coming before the courts had the mental capacity to commit a crime, it came to be presumed conclusively that a child under seven could not form the intent and that one over fourteen could. This recognized tendency probably provides an explanation for the courts substituting the presumed effect for the actual effect of taxing statutes. In defence of the courts it might also be argued that a statute should be upheld if it operates "approximately" within the powers of the enacting legislature and that peculiar circumstances in which it would transgress constitutional limitations ought not to invalidate the whole statute.[27] On the other hand, there is a strong argument for finding the statute to be "inapplicable" in such circumstances. This would equally save the statute without giving it an effect inconsistent with the constitution. It is suggested that the courts should re-examine their legal presumptions as to the effect of various forms of taxes. Equally they should be very cautious about substituting presumptions of law for findings of fact in other areas of constitutional adjudication.

These then are the principal uses of precedent – in establishing the scope of the heads of jurisdiction in sections 91 and 92, in assessing the constitutional consequences of a determination as to effect and to some extent in assigning "effect" to certain types of statutes. But this does not fully demonstrate the overwhelming force of stare decisis in Canadian constitutional law. Our courts, and the Privy Council in particular, have displayed an early enthusiasm to generalize and a subsequent reluctance to ignore.[28] While one may deprecate an excessive reliance on precedent in the elaboration of such a fundamental document, it is too much to expect that the Canadian constitution will readily escape its past. Precedent will probably remain the single most important factor in future adjudication.

The most imponderable of the non-factual elements in constitutional adjudication is the creative role of the judiciary. Judges may be primarily influenced by precedents. In many cases their deliberations may be aided by an examination of facts. But in the final analysis a large measure of value judgment will be required to reach a conclusion. The effects of legislation may be objectively demonstrable (the court permitting) but this will not yield an answer as to the validity. There remains the question,

26. Davis, 2 *Administrative Law Treatise* (1958), at 364.
27. For an explanation of this principle in Australian constitutional law see Lane, "Facts in Constitutional Law" (1963), 37 *Austl. L.J.* 108.
28. This was forcefully demonstrated by Professor (now Mr. Justice) Laskin, *supra* notes 7 and 20.

are the important effects within the scope permitted to this legislature? To answer this the judge must decide which in his view are the most important effects of the statute, and he must decide what as a matter of policy is the desirable extent of a particular head of jurisdiction.

The subjective element in such decisions can scarcely be denied. In assessing the relative importance of various effects of a law, for example, the Privy Council has held that the salient effect of one provincial law, which reduced the principal on farm mortgages in years of crop failure, was the regulation of "interest."[29] A few years later, the Supreme Court of Canada concluded that the most significant effect of another provincial law, which authorized a reduction of both principal and interest on unconscionable contracts, was the regulation of "property and civil rights."[30] Logic and precedent alone would not produce such inconsistent results. Another example may be seen in the growing judicial tendency to find distinct effects for provincial and federal statutes which, prima facie, appear to be duplicative or nearly identical.[31] This must reflect some inarticulate policy decision in favour of concurrent powers.

Again, in determining the proper scope of the various heads of jurisdiction the policy element will frequently appear. It was a policy decision which denied to "regulation of trade and commerce" the control of intra-provincial commerce, which withdrew from "peace, order, and good government" the capacity to "trench" on provincial heads, and which sought means to fence in the unruly beast, "criminal law." Similarly, policy considerations gave to "property and civil rights" a meaning broad enough to cover most commercial activity not otherwise specifically described in the BNA Act. Whether these were wise or unwise decisions it is unnecessary to say, but policy decisions they surely were.

This is by no means intended as a criticism of the use of policy considerations in constitutional decisions. Indeed, such considerations are irresistible. But they should be recognized as an element in the adjudicative process, and litigants should prepare themselves accordingly. Policy decisions should where possible be based on sound, relevant material of both a factual and a non-factual nature. The factual element will be discussed later. Non-factual material appropriate for submission would include arguments urging those constitutional objectives which the parties consider most desirable. With the policy alternatives thus analyzed for it the court

29. *A.G. for Sask.* v. *A.G. for Can.*, [1949] A.C. 110 (P.C. 1948).
30. *Barfried Enterprises Ltd.* v. *A.G. for Ont.*, [1963] S.C.R. 570, 42 D.L.R. (2d) 137.
31. For a discussion of these cases see Lederman, "The Concurrent Operation of Federal and Provincial Laws in Canada" (1963), 9 *McGill L. J.* 185.

could, in the light of the factual material and its own predilections, more readily reach a sound and consistent policy decision.

FACTUAL ELEMENTS

The foregoing have all been "internal" matters in the interpretation process – that is, internal to the BNA Act or to the statute, internal to the case law or to the court. All these elements would be brought to bear (perhaps with different emphasis) even in the absence of submission by a party. On the other hand, "factual elements" as herein conceived embrace all the "external" matters which may be introduced by the parties into the decisional process. The suggestion is frequently made that Canadian constitutional adjudication has suffered from a lack of the factual element. It is therefore hoped that the classification into factual and non-factual elements will be analytically useful, both in clarifying the role of facts in this process and in suggesting means by which appropriate facts may be introduced.

THE RELEVANT FACTS

It is important first to decide what the objectives of proof should be, assuming one can introduce appropriate evidence. It is necessary here to refer back to the two basic questions of constitutional adjudication as set out earlier: (1) What is the effect, or what are the effects of the legislation in question? (2) Are the most significant effects among those permitted to the enacting legislature under the BNA Act?

To the extent that the answer to these crucial questions involves an interpretation of that Act, facts will be of limited assistance. The courts have generally treated the BNA Act as a statute and in construing it have not looked beyond those matters permitted by the ordinary rules of statutory interpretation.[32] Though facts have been examined in a few cases, this has been for the purpose of ascertaining the meaning of words in a dictionary sense and not for the purpose of determining the broad objectives or purpose of the fundamental Act.[33] Indeed, any trend towards increased

32. MacDonald, "Judicial Interpretation of the Canadian Constitution" (1936), 1 *U. Toronto L.J.* 260; MacDonald, "Constitutional Interpretation and Extrinsic Evidence" (1939), 17 *Can.B.Rev.* 77.
33. For example in *Edwards* v. *A.G. for Can.*, [1930] A.C. 124 (P.C. 1929), where Lord Sankey gave his now famous description of the constitution as a "living tree," the resulting decision was based on factors examined in accordance with the conventional rules of statutory interpretation. In the *Eskimo Reference* [1939] S.C.R. 104, [1939] 2 D.L.R. 417, considerable evidence was examined to ascertain the common understanding of the word "Indians" in 1867. Again this is within the

use of facts in the interpretation of the BNA Act would now have to be viewed with caution. Available evidence of the *travaux préparatoires* leading up to its passage is very limited.[34] Also, evidence as to the situation prevailing at the time of Confederation or the intention of the framers in relation to that situation should now be considered with some hesitation. Conditions have so drastically changed since 1867 that the particular context in which the Act was passed may have little bearing on the context in which it is now expected to operate. The more crucial question now is: What would the framers have intended had conditions been in 1867 as they are today?[35] Even if the courts could now be induced to make use of external evidence as to the conditions of that time such evidence would be of limited value in answering this hypothetical question.

In ascertaining the scope of the jurisdictional heads of the BNA Act our constitutional tribunals have had a particular preference for following, not the words of the constitution itself, but their own previous interpretations of it. Thus precedent dominates this field and factual elements could be significant only in the peripheral areas. The role of the judiciary in the elaboration of the constitution should be to maintain a suitable balance of power between the dominion and the provinces. This is a dynamic, on-going process which should be dominated neither by the circumstances of 1867 nor by the judicial decisions since 1867. While there is need for judicial reform, a plea for an enlarged role for factual considerations in the interpretation of the BNA Act itself would be both futile and misplaced.

Facts do have an important role, however, in the constitutional assessment of an impugned statute. Facts can help to establish the effect of an impugned statute, and the relative significance of its various effects if it has more than one. "Effect" is used here in its broadest sense. A study of effect should embrace a study of the context in which the statute is passed and is likely to operate. Such a study will aid the court in finding whether in fact (and not merely in form) the statute is within the scope of its legislative author. It may also clarify for the court the policy issue which it must face. Suppose, for example, that in a period of beef surpluses Parliament enacted legislation establishing a comprehensive quota system for sale of beef cattle. Suppose that the system could have the effect of pre-

---

conventional rules of statutory interpretation which permit a reference to historical context to clarify the meaning of particular words. This is clearly distinguishable from an examination of history for direct evidence of the purpose of an enactment such as the BNA Act.
34. See Laskin, *supra* note 19, at 153–55.
35. *Labour Relations Board of Sask.* v. *John East Iron Works*, [1948] 2 W.W.R. 1055, at 1065, [1948] 4 D.L.R. 673, at 682 (P.C.).

venting sales made solely within a province, between a local producer and a local consumer. Appropriate evidence here might show that previous surpluses had endangered interprovincial and international markets and caused a serious national problem. It might also show the curative effect which the impugned federal statute would have. Such evidence would enable the court to see that the most significant effect of the legislation would be, not interference with local contracts (suggesting to them "property and civil rights"), but rather the protection of an important area of interprovincial and international commerce (suggesting to them "regulation of trade and commerce" and perhaps "peace, order, and good government"). This evidence would also point to the policy issue. That is, is it more important to permit the national protection of this commercial activity, or to preserve intact local control over local contracts?

The relevance of these kinds of facts has been recognized in a number of situations. With respect to the constitutional relevance of a statute's factual context, the "emergency" power cases afford a ready example. To justify federal legislation which is not referable to one of the enumerated heads of section 91, it is necessary to invoke the general power with respect to "peace, order, and good government." But for such legislation to be valid, where it interferes with matters within an enumerated head of provincial jurisdiction in section 92, it must deal with an emergency or, more broadly, a matter which is inherently of concern to the dominion as a whole. The courts have implicitly recognized that this raises an essentially factual issue. In most cases they have shown a great respect for the opinion of Parliament or the government with respect to the existence of such a state of affairs, but they have always reserved the right to find the contrary on proper evidence. And on occasion they have rejected the government's judgment that a state of affairs existed sufficient to justify the exercise of this power.[36] On other occasions they have received evidence to show that a new technological development is inherently of national concern,[37] or that lack of action by the provinces has created a need for federal action to protect the national interest,[38] thus further satisfying themselves of the correctness of Parliament's decision.

36. For a more extensive discussion of this subject and the relevant cases see *supra* at 141–44.
37. See e.g. *Re Regulation and Control of Radio Communication in Canada*, [1931] S.C.R. 541, [1931] 4 D.L.R. 865, *aff'd* [1932] A.C. 304 (P.C.), where an article by a radio engineer descriptive of radio communication was put before the court; and see *Johanesson* v. *West St. Paul*, [1952] 1 S.C.R. 292, [1951] 4 D.L.R. 609, where the court took account of an affidavit which indicated the national aspect of aeronautics.
38. *Munro* v. *National Capital Commission*, [1966] S.C.R. 663, 57 D.L.R. (2d) 753, *affirming* [1965] 2 Ex. C.R. 579.

Similarly, to justify the exercise of Parliament's power over "criminal law" it now appears necessary to show that some danger, to the public as such, is thereby prohibited. Normally the courts will be prepared to accept Parliament's assessment of the facts.[39] But where facts are introduced which clearly demonstrate that the effect of the legislation is not to prevent some public danger or evil, an alleged criminal law enactment may be set aside as colourable.[40]

The case of *Home Oil Distributors Ltd.* v. *Attorney General for British Columbia* well illustrates the kind of evidence of surrounding circumstances which may be helpful in assessing the effect of statutes. The British Columbia legislature had enacted legislation empowering a provincial board to fix prices of coal, fuel oil, and gasoline sold within the province. On its face this legislation may have appeared purely local in nature. But surrounding circumstances cast doubts on its validity. Information in a preceding royal commission report indicated that a problem had arisen in British Columbia because California oil producers were dumping fuel oil there to the great detriment of the competing coal industry, while selling gasoline in the province at exorbitant prices because of an absence of competition. It was therefore contended that the provincial price-fixing legislation as applied in such a situation would have the effect of regulating international trade, a matter for Parliament. The trial judge took these surrounding circumstances into account in holding the legislation invalid.[41] The Court of Appeal also considered them to be relevant in establishing effect, though it concluded that interference with interprovincial trade was not the primary effect of the legislation.[42] The Supreme Court of Canada on appeal[43] largely ignored the evidence of surrounding circumstances and upheld the legislation. Kerwin J. (Rinfret J. concurring) held such evidence to be properly before the court while Davis J. held it inadmissible. The other judges made no reference to it. While the judicial attitude on admissibility was thus somewhat ambivalent, it is submitted that such facts were relevant to a proper understanding of the effect of the provincial statute.

Interrelated with the factual background of legislation are the practical consequences which will flow from its enactment. The classic case on this point is the *Alberta Bank Tax Reference*[44] of 1938. The provincial statute

---

39. For a full discussion and the relevant cases see *supra* at 144–45.
40. *Canadian Federation of Agriculture* v. *A.G. for Que.*, [1951] A.C. 179 (P.C. 1950).
41. [1939] 1 W.W.R. 666 (B.C. Sup. Ct.).
42. [1939] 1 W.W.R. 49, [1939] 1 D.L.R. 573; [1939] 2 W.W.R. 468, [1939] 3 D.L.R. 397.
43. [1940] S.C.R. 444, [1940] 2 D.L.R. 609.
44. *A.G. for Alta.* v. *A.G. for Can.*, [1939] A.C. 117 (P.C. 1938).

in question imposed an annual tax on banks operating within the province at a rate specified therein, based on both the paid-up capital and the reserve fund of the banks. The question arose as to whether this was a genuine exercise of the provincial power of "direct taxation within the province" or whether it was really a means of regulating "banking," a federal matter. Both the Supreme Court of Canada and the Privy Council held it to be banking legislation. They were satisfied that the effect of such legislation, given the rates of taxation as specified, would be the destruction of banking. The accuracy of this conclusion need not now detain us, but the principle was clearly established that the practical effect of an enactment is a proper consideration in constitutional adjudication. This was demonstrated by the fact that in a much earlier decision, the Privy Council had upheld provincial taxation of banks where the tax would not have this destructive effect.[45]

In *Texada Mines Ltd.* v. *Attorney General for British Columbia*[46] another provincial tax was held ultra vires because of its prohibitive effect. Here the legislature of British Columbia had imposed an annual tax of up to ten per cent of the value of minerals in producing areas. A contemporaneous statute provided a large bounty for iron made from ore smelted within the province. As there was at the time no smelter in the province, this was obviously designed to encourage development of a domestic iron and steel industry. The appellant company, an iron ore producer, challenged the legislation on the grounds that it created an export tax. The company introduced evidence to show that mining costs were so high that the addition of the tax would cause iron mines to operate at a substantial loss. Only where the bounty was received would iron mining be economic. As in the *Alberta Bank Tax* case, the Supreme Court was satisfied by this evidence that the effect of the tax would be virtually to prohibit mining for export: thus the Court concluded that the nature of the measure was not the raising of revenue but the regulation of interprovincial trade.[47]

The fact that a statute is wrongfully administered also may prove its illegal effect. In *Attorney General for British Columbia* v. *McDonald Murphy Lumber Ltd.* there was a question as to the validity of a statute similar to that in the *Texada Mines* case. Here a tax was imposed by statute on all timber cut in the province, but a rebate of all but a trifle was provided where the timber was used or manufactured in the province. The opinion of the Privy Council that this was an export tax was reinforced by the fact that the government had not bothered to collect the small tax

45. *Bank of Toronto* v. *Lambe*, supra note 21.
46. [1960] S.C.R. 713, 24 D.L.R. (2d) 81.
47. See also *B.C. Power Corp.* v. *A.G. for B.C.*, (1963) 44 W.W.R. (N.S.) 65, 47 D.L.R. (2d) 633 (B.C. Sup. Ct.) where an expropriation measure was invalidated because the effect would be to destroy a dominion company.

remaining payable on timber used locally.[48] In spite of judicial warnings elsewhere[49] that the validity of a statute should be judged from its terms and not from the way it is administered, evidence of administration may indicate an unlawful effect. The responsibility of the courts is to keep each level of government within its proper bounds. A government which achieves a prohibited goal through discriminatory administration of legislation threatens the federal structure as much as the legislature which enacts patently invalid legislation. Assume that instead of expressly providing for a rebate of the timber tax, the British Columbia legislature had imposed a uniform tax on all timber produced. Suppose further that the government collected the tax only from those who exported, but failed to collect it from the others. The court should be free to step in here to prevent what, in its practical effect, is as great an interference with free interprovincial trade as was the statute in the *McDonald Murphy* case. In such a case the court should not declare the statute to be ultra vires, however. It should only find that it is invalidly applied to those from whom the tax is collected, if such persons can demonstrate that the effect of government policy is to make it an export tax as applied to them.

Related to the problem of invalid effect through wrongful administration is that of invalid effect in application to particular individuals. A general statute may be valid in normal application but have an invalid effect as applied to a particular individual. Here again evidence of the effect as related to the circumstances of this individual is relevant in the judicial supervision of the federal structure. For example, in determining which government can regulate an "undertaking," it is necessary to decide whether it is local or interprovincial in nature. Here it is relevant to consider evidence as to how the undertaking is organized[50] and as to the amount of out-of-province business carried on in relation to the amount of intraprovincial business.[51] Similarly, where evidence shows that a business is national in scope, federal legislation regulating it does not relate to purely intraprovincial trade.[52]

How does this accord with the view that a statute should be allowed to operate "approximately" so that its validity is not affected by the rare situation where it might possibly offend against constitutional limita-

---

48. [1930] A.C. 357, at 363 (P.C.).

49. See Culliton J. A. in the *Cairns Construction* case, *supra* note 22, 27 W.W.R., at 329, 16 D.L.R. (2d), at 492.

50. *A.G. for Ont.* v. *Winner*, [1954] A.C. 541, at 581–83 (P.C.).

51. *Re Tank Transport Ltd.*, [1960] O.R. 497, 25 D.L.R. (2d) 161 (Ont. H. Ct.), affirmed on appeal without written reasons [1963] 1 O.R. 272, 36 D.L.R. (2d) 636 (Ont. C.A.); *R.* v. *Cooksville Magistrate's Court, ex parte Liquid Cargo Lines Ltd.*, [1965] 1 O.R. 84, 46 D.L.R. 700 (Ont. H. Ct.).

52. *Reader's Digest Association (Canada) Ltd.* v. *A.G. for Can.* (1965), 59 D.L.R. (2d) 54 (Que. Q. B.).

tions?[53] It is necessary to consider various possible situations here. If the statute is general in nature, it should be presumed not to apply to those situations where it would over-reach the scope of the enacting legislature. The statute can be held inapplicable to a particular situation without having its validity affected.[54] If, pursuant to a general statute, an order is made specifically dealing with a situation beyond the legislature's permissible constitutional scope, that order can be set aside without affecting the validity of the statute.[55] But where the statute by its terms specifically embraces some situations which are not within the sphere of the enacting legislature then it must be held to be ultra vires. For example, in *Attorney General for Ontario* v. *Winner*[56] the challenged Motor Carrier Act defined "motor carrier" as "a person, firm or company that operates or causes to be operated in the province a public motor bus. . . ." This clearly caught within its net persons operating interprovincial and international bus services as well as local services, and made the statute ultra vires. Here the legislature precluded the court from making any presumptions in favour of validity. When Winner showed that as applied to him it interfered with an international carrier the Privy Council had to treat this as a necessary consequence of the Act as drafted. Not only the restrictive licence granted to Winner, but also the Act itself, had to be set aside.

It can thus be demonstrated that effect of an impugned statute is one of the most important factors in any determination as to its validity. A finding as to effect in relation to total context will enable the court to see how far the legislature has gone, and clarify for it the policy issue of how far the legislature should be permitted to go. The relevant facts in establishing effect are those showing the circumstances in which the act was passed and the practical consequences of the enactment in relation to those circumstances. This analysis has been elaborated at some length because there is a vast confusion in the case law and the literature with respect to questions of relevance, admissibility, and the objectives of proof.

Much of the confusion stems from an attempt to apply rules of statutory interpretation to constitutional adjudication. These rules were originally designed solely for the purpose of understanding the "meaning" of statutes in a non-federal state. In the main they proceed on the assumption that meaning can be derived from within the statute. Thus they emphasize the importance of the "literal" or "plain" meaning of the statute. If the meaning of a particular section is not apparent the statute may be examined as a whole, if necessary in conjunction with other statutes *in pari materia*.

53. See *supra* note 27 and accompanying text.
54. *Reference re Saskatchewan Minimum Wage Act*, [1948] S.C.R. 248, [1948] 3 D.L.R. 801; *McKay* v. *The Queen*, [1965] S.C.R. 798, 53 D.L.R. (2d) 532.
55. See *Re Tank Transport* case, *supra* note 51.
56. *Supra* note 50.

Indicia as to word usage at the time of enactment may also be considered. In case of ambiguity, the absurd result is to be avoided in favour of the less absurd (but absurdity is to be tested in relation to circumstances existing at the time of enactment). Only the "mischief" rule contemplates a significant examination of external facts – those preceding the enactment of the legislation. By this rule a court may, when the meaning of a statute is not otherwise apparent, look to the preceding state of facts to find the "mischief" which the legislation was intended to cure. In spite of this rule the courts have only rarely[57] ventured to look at the factual background of legislation to ascertain its meaning.[58]

It is at once essential to distinguish the process of statutory interpretation from that of constitutional adjudication. The former involves merely a pursuit of "meaning," a concern only for what the legislature intended to convey by the words it used. The consequences of the legislation are irrelevant so long as they are those which the legislature intended. The word "intention" is used here figuratively because of the difficulty of ascribing an intention in the human sense to an elected assembly. This has led to a preoccupation with the words of the statute because they are the expression of this imaginary "intention."

The process of constitutional adjudication is vastly different. Here the essential question is not intention of the legislature but effect of the statute. In the majority of cases the two may be identical. But in the crucial cases the court must see what the statute really does, not what its framers intended it to do. Does a provincial statute revising loan contracts have the principal effect of altering "interest?" Does a federal statute introducing unemployment insurance disrupt contractual relations between employer and employee? These are the important questions to ask if the court is to maintain the division of powers as contemplated by the constitution.

Confusion has also arisen between the rules of evidence in ordinary litigation and the rules of evidence in constitutional litigation. Ordinary litigation involves facts pertaining to the immediate parties, what Professor K. C. Davis would call "adjudicative facts." These must be strictly proven. The court would be remiss here in going outside the record to consider facts not properly introduced as evidence. In constitutional cases there may also be "adjudicative facts" to the extent that issues involve the status and circumstances of parties before the court. But when the court turns to the question of the validity of the statute challenged in the pro-

57. See e.g. *Eastman Photographic Materials* v. *Comptroller General of Patents*, [1898] A.C. 571 (H. of L.).
58. For discussions of the rules of statutory interpretation see Willis, *supra* note 13; 36 *Halsbury's Laws of England* (3rd ed., 1961), at 382–411, Maxwell, *The Interpretation of Statutes* (11th ed., 1962), at 16–50.

ceedings, it is performing a legislative function. That is, it is about to make a determination as to validity which may affect not only the parties before the court but the public at large. Moreover, the decision will proceed not merely from given findings of pre-existing fact and law, but may also involve questions of policy. To aid in deciding such questions the courts may have to resort to "legislative facts" – facts of a general nature concerning the economic and social context of legislation. To the extent that the courts are prepared to acknowledge this legislative aspect of their function, they should be prepared to modify the rules of proof.[59]

THE ADMISSIBILITY OF EVIDENCE

Having thus identified the facts which are relevant in constitutional adjudication, and the general considerations which ought to guide the courts, we can examine and criticize the rules respecting admissibility of particular forms of evidence.

(a) Statements by Members of the Legislature

In cases involving only statutory interpretation such evidence has been held to be inadmissible.[60] Those who support its use argue that the purpose of statutory interpretation is to find the intention of the legislature, and that statements by members of the legislature in relation to the statute are logically relevant to this inquiry. While there is a danger that they may not reflect the intention of the majority, or may be misleading or self-serving, it is contended that this creates a problem of weight rather than of admissibility.[61] Opponents of such evidence contend that statements of members may have little or no logical connection with the actual meaning of the statute. They see a danger in introducing such evidence because it may divert attention from what the statute actually says. Distinctions are drawn between Canadian and United States legislative practice. It is said that, in the latter, committee proceedings are less dominated by political partisanship and that committee reports are more cohesive and informative. Thus there is more justification for the admission of such evidence in the courts of the United States.[62]

59. See Davis, *supra* note 26, at 353–63.
60. E.g. *R.* v. *West Riding of Yorkshire County Council*, [1906] 2 K.B. 676, at 700, 716 (C.A.), *rev'd* [1907] A.C. 29 (H.ofL.) on other grounds; *Hollinshead* v. *Hazleton*, [1916] 1 A.C. 428, at 438 (H.ofL.); *Gosselin* v. *The King* (1903), 33 S.C.R. 255, 7 C.C.C. 139.
61. See e.g. Kilgour, "The Rule Against the Use of Legislative History: Canon of Construction or Counsel of Caution?" (1952), 30 *Can.B.Rev.* 769.
62. See e.g. Corry, "The Use of Legislative History in the Interpretation of Statutes" (1954), 32 *Can.B.Rev.* 624.

The rule of exclusion in cases of statutory interpretation seems firmly settled. This may be unnecessarily restrictive, as the statements of legislators would seem to have relevance in explaining the meaning of obscure legislation. The dangers of admitting such evidence are exaggerated. It would be a rare case where suitable evidence bearing on a particular point of interpretation could even be produced. When produced, its weight would be assessed by the court. In most cases it would probably be given very little weight. But there are situations where it might prove useful.[63]

Statements of legislators have been equally excluded in constitutional cases. The rule here seems to have been clarified only recently. As late as 1938 Lord Maugham L. C. said, in the *Alberta Bank Tax Reference*, that "the object or purpose of the Act, insofar as it does not plainly appear from its terms and its probable effect, is that of an incorporeal entity, namely, the Legislature, and, generally speaking, *the speeches of individuals would have little evidential weight*."[64] This implies that such evidence would be admissible. But Lord Maugham had assumed in this case that the "purpose" of the statute (apparently in terms of the intention of its enactors) was a relevant consideration. On this assumption, it might follow that statements of intention in the legislature would logically have some bearing on the assessment of the statute for constitutional purposes.

Since this time, the Supreme Court of Canada appears to have ruled against the admissibility of all such evidence in constitutional cases. In *Texada Mines Ltd.* v. *Attorney General for British Columbia*[65] those attacking the tax on iron production sought to characterize it as an export tax. When the matter reached the Supreme Court, Locke J., delivering the unanimous judgment of the court, commented on the trial judgment.

While that learned judge, in the course of his judgment, referred to certain statements purporting to have been made by the Premier of the Province and the Minister of Mines to the effect that the legislation was designed to discourage the export of iron ore so that eventually an integrated steel industry could be established in the province, he made it clear that he came to this conclusion without reference to this. That such statement had been made was not proven at the trial and had the evidence been tendered it would, no doubt, have been rejected as inadmissible.[66]

This was *obiter dicta* only, as no such evidence had been presented. Nevertheless it indicated that the court was unanimous in its view that the

63. See e.g. *Canadian Wheat Board* v. *Nolan et al.*, [1951] S.C.R. 81, [1951] 1 D.L.R. 466, *rev'd sub nom. A.G. for Can.* v. *Hallett & Carey Ltd.*, [1952] A.C. 427 (P.C.); relevant parliamentary debates were ignored: see criticism in Kilgour, *supra* note 61.
64. [1939] A.C. 117, at 130–31 (P.C. 1938): emphasis added.
65. *Supra* note 46.
66. [1960] S.C.R., at 720, 24 D.L.R. (2d), at 87.

statements of legislators should not be admitted in proceedings involving the constitutional validity of legislation.

This view was reaffirmed in ratio decidendi in *Attorney General for Canada* v. *Reader's Digest Association (Canada) Ltd.*[67] In 1956 the federal government introduced in Parliament certain amendments to the Excise Tax Act which would have imposed a tax on advertising placed in any periodical containing at least twenty-five per cent editorial material identical to that contained in a non-Canadian periodical. *Reader's Digest*, to which the tax would have applied, sought a declaration that the amendments were ultra vires. It contended that the real purpose of the legislation was to discriminate against publications such as its own and in favour of purely Canadian publications. This was said to make the legislation not taxation but an interference with property and civil rights. To support its argument as to the real purpose of the legislation, *Reader's Digest* sought to introduce evidence as to statements with respect to the amendments made by the minister of finance both inside and outside Parliament. The trial judge refused to admit such evidence. When the appeal on this point reached the Supreme Court this view was upheld. All of the judges held the evidence as to the minister's statements to be inadmissible, and seven of them expressly approved Mr. Justice Locke's dictum in the *Texada Mines* case.

It was argued by the *Reader's Digest* that while the statements of legislators might be inadmissible in cases involving statutory interpretation alone, this rule should not apply where the question is one of ultra vires. It was argued that such evidence should be admissible where it is contended that the legislation is colourable. Cartwright J. (Locke J. concurring) directly rejected this contention. "It was conceded and is clear on the authorities that the statement of the Minister in introducing the bill would be inadmissible in aid of the interpretation of the statute as finally passed into a law. I can discern no difference in principle to afford a sufficient reason for holding it to be admissible when, the words of the statute being plain, it is sought to show that Parliament was encroaching upon a field committed exclusively to the provincial legislature."[68]

While one may deprecate the automatic application here of a rule developed for other circumstances, the result seems quite sound. The Supreme Court might well have asked what relevancy the statements of

67. [1961] S.C.R. 775, 30 D.L.R. 296. Followed in *Saumur* v. *A.G. for Que.*, [1963] Que. Q.B. 116, at 123, 135, 37 D.L.R. (2d) 703, at 712, 719, *aff'd* [1964] S.C.R. 252, 45. D.L.R. (2d) 627 without reference to this point. Also followed in *B.C. Power Corp.* v. *A.G. for B.C.* (1963), 44 W.W.R. 65, at 172, 47 D.L.R. (2d) 633, at 733–34 (B.C. Sup. Ct.).
68. [1961] S.C.R., at 792, 30 D.L.R., at 311.

the minister could have in proving a constitutional or unconstitutional effect for this statute. Surely a bad motive could not invalidate a permissible statute, nor could a good motive validate an impermissible statute. Those attacking the statute should have confined themselves to evidence showing that its preponderant effect was discrimination as between publications. This should have formed the evidential basis for what was at best a questionable[69] constitutional argument.

The same might be said of any other attempt to introduce evidence of legislators' statements in order to uphold or attack constitutional validity. The essential factual issue here is that of effect, and to this such statements have no logical relevancy. They might on occasion constitute a sound opinion as to what the effect of the statute will be. But opinion evidence can be introduced by direct testimony or other means. This gives an opportunity for the other party to cross-examine or challenge it.

(b) Royal Commission or Committee Reports

It is not uncommon in Anglo-Canadian governmental practice for a serious problem to be met initially by the appointment of a royal commission. The commission, normally enjoying a considerable independence of government control, brings in a report which sets out its findings of fact and recommendations for solution. The latter may be brought to varying degrees of fruition by subsequent legislation. The question arises as to what extent such reports may be admissible in evidence to aid in analyzing the subsequent legislation.

Where the issue is solely one of statutory interpretation it has been held that a royal commission report is not admissible proof of "intention" per se. In *Assam Ry. & Trading Co.* v. *Commissioners of Inland Revenue*[70] the company contended that a royal commission report which preceded the taxation statute in question would show that the interpretation most favourable to them was intended. Writing the judgment for the House of Lords, Lord Wright said that the commissioners' report was not proper evidence of Parliament's intention "because it does not follow that their recommendations were accepted."[71] But where a court by the use of the mischief rule becomes involved in an examination of the problem which Parliament obviously hoped to overcome, a commission report may be examined. Lord Wright was careful to distinguish the *Assam* case from the type of situation which had arisen in *Eastman Photographic Materials*

69. When the trial later proceeded, the action was dismissed: (1965), 59 D.L.R. (2d) 54.
70. [1935] A.C. 445 (H.ofL.).
71. *Ibid.*, at 458.

v. *Comptroller-General of Patents*.[72] In the *Eastman* case the House of Lords had to decide what an "invented word" was within the meaning of the Patent Acts. By looking at a royal commission report the judges ascertained the basic problem and the purpose of the legislation in relation thereto. Hence they concluded that the trade name in dispute before the House adequately qualified as an "invented word." The distinction between the two cases would appear to be that in *Assam* the report was rejected as subjective evidence of the state of mind of Parliament, whereas in *Eastman* it was accepted as objective evidence of the state of affairs with respect to which the legislation was enacted. The recommendations of the report in the *Assam* case would have no necessary relationship to Parliament's intention because Parliament might or might not have intended to adopt them in its legislation. But the facts as found in the report in the *Eastman* case would have some logical relevance to ensuing legislation on the subject, whether the recommendations of the report were adopted or rejected.[73]

The *Eastman* case appeared to leave open a possibility for the use of royal commission reports in statutory interpretation. In cases involving constitutional adjudication some use has been made of these reports, but the Supreme Court has recently raised serious doubts about their admissibility.

The leading example of the use of such a report in a constitutional case is *Ladore* v. *Bennett*.[74] The City of Windsor and certain neighbouring Ontario municipalities were in such financial difficulties that between 1931 and 1934 they defaulted on various debenture obligations. In 1934 a provincial royal commission was appointed. Its report in 1935 gave its findings as to these financial difficulties and their causes. Subsequently the provincial legislature by statute amalgamated the municipalities, and authorized the Ontario Municipal Board to alter their debenture obligations if necessary. This the Board did in 1937, scaling down the interest payable by the municipalities. The debenture holders sought a declaration that the legislation was invalid because it dealt with "interest," a federal matter. Those supporting the legislation contended that it was legislation in relation to "municipal institutions," a provincial matter. In support of this they sought to introduce the royal commission report to show that the legislation dealt with a situation involving the very existence of municipal government in the Windsor area. The debenture

72. *Supra* note 57.
73. See also Lord Denning M.R., in *Letang* v. *Cooper*, [1965] 1 Q.B. 232, at 240–41 (C.A.).
74. [1939] A.C. 468 (P.C.).

holders objected to the admission of the report and the Ontario courts upheld them. On appeal of the judgment of the Ontario Court of Appeal to the Privy Council, the debenture holders withdrew this objection, and Lord Atkin in his judgment indicated that the Judicial Committee had examined the report. He noted its findings as to the serious financial position of the municipalities, that taxation was at the breaking point with total default threatened, that provisions for maintenance of basic services were inadequate, and that if adequate provisions were made it would destroy the credit of the area in both the public and private sector. He then added this rather enigmatic comment. "Their Lordships do not cite this report as evidence of the facts there found, but as indicating the materials which the Government of the Province had before them before promoting in the Legislature the statute now impugned. . . ."[75] It is not clear what relevance the state of mind of the provincial cabinet would have per se in determining the validity of an enactment of the provincial legislature. Moreover the statement is inconsistent with Lord Atkin's actual decision. Later in his judgment he accepted the conclusions of the report that local government had in fact become "ineffective or non-existent because of . . . financial difficulties . . ." and that provincial action with respect to the financial difficulties was necessary in order to save the institutions themselves. He therefore upheld the legislation as being in relation to municipal institutions.

It seems obvious here that the Judicial Committee actually did accept the facts as found in the report. The test suggested by Lord Atkin as to the state of mind of the provincial government has no place in Canadian constitutional jurisprudence. There is in Canada no criterion of "reasonability" of governmental or legislative action, in contrast to situations in the United States involving legislative restraints related to freedoms guaranteed under the Bill of Rights. In substance, what the Privy Council did here was to find, by reference to the royal commission report, a factual context which made it clear that the chief effect of the impugned legislation would be the salvation of imperilled municipal institutions.

The use of royal commission reports was also referred to in passing by the Privy Council in *Attorney General for British Columbia* v. *Attorney General for Canada*.[76] This case involved a question referred by the governor general in council to the Supreme Court of Canada with respect to the validity of the new section 498A of the Criminal Code which prohibited certain forms of price discrimination. The enactment had been preceded by the federal Royal Commission on Price Spreads. The order

75. *Ibid.*, at 477.
76. [1937] A.C. 368 (P.C.).

of reference stated that "the Minister observes that said section 498A was enacted for the purpose of giving effect to certain recommendations contained in the Report of the Royal Commission on Price Spreads. . . ."[77] The provinces for their part sought to argue that the royal commission had nothing to do with criminal law, but instead was concerned with trade practices which came within provincial jurisdiction. Hence this statement in the reference order was said to be proof that the legislation was colourable. The judgments in the Supreme Court of Canada made no reference to the report and upheld the Criminal Code amendment. The Privy Council made brief reference to the provincial argument on this point and added that:

it probably would not be contended that the statement of the Minister in the order of reference that the section was enacted to give effect to the recommendations of the Royal Commission bound the Provinces or must necessarily be treated as conclusive by the Board. But when the suggestion is made that the legislation was not in truth criminal legislation, but was in substance merely an encroachment on the Provincial field, the existence of the report appears to be a material circumstance.[78]

"Material" to what, the Privy Council does not say. The implication is that the existence of a report dealing with what was essentially a provincial problem could show that curative federal legislation was colourable. In this case the evidence did not seem sufficiently strong as the Privy Council had no difficulty in upholding the amendment as proper criminal law.

While the Supreme Court ignored the royal commission report in *Attorney General for British Columbia* v. *Attorney General for Canada*, it was split on the issue in the *Home Oil* case. Here the provincial price-fixing legislation in the fuel industry was attacked as an interference with international trade. It was contended that a reference to a preceding royal commission report would show the international character of the industry which the legislation was to regulate. The courts of British Columbia[79] considered the royal commission report, the Court of Appeal holding it admissible "insofar only as it finds facts which are relevant to the ascertainment of the said alleged purpose and the effect of the enactment."[80] On appeal, three of the six Supreme Court of Canada judges ignored the existence of the report. Kerwin J., with whom Rinfret J. concurred, held the report to be admissible to establish the nature of the problem which the legislature was seeking to remedy. He looked upon this as an application of the "mischief" rule of statutory interpretation. On the other hand, Davis J. held the report to be inadmissible except with the consent of all

77. See [1936] S.C.R. 363, at 364.
78. [1937] A.C., at 376.   79. *Supra* notes 41 and 42.
80. [1939] 1 W.W.R., at 51, [1939] 1 D.L.R., at 574.

parties. That is, he would consider the report only as an admission of facts by parties against whom it might operate. This implies that he considered the facts in the report to be logically relevant, but not admissible because of unreliability, in the absence of an admission of such facts by adverse parties.

It is still not possible to say with assurance how the Supreme Court will ultimately resolve this issue. Dicta in the *Reader's Digest* case reopened the question without settling it. In that case counsel for *Reader's Digest* had relied on a dictum of Lord Wright in the *Assam* case to the effect that royal commission reports are of less evidentiary value than statements of ministers in the proof of legislative intention. He further argued that, because royal commission reports had been considered in some constitutional cases a fortiori the statements of the minister of finance ought to be considered. The majority, (Kerwin C. J., Taschereau, Abbott, Judson, Fauteux JJ. concurring) rightly treated the issue of admissibility of royal commission reports as irrelevant and declined to consider it. Cartwright J. (Locke J. concurring), in extensive dicta did deal with the point. After reviewing the authorities he concluded that: "there is no decision which requires us to hold that a report of a Royal Commission made prior to the passing of a statute and relating to the subject-matter with which the statute deals, but not referred to in the statute, is admissible in evidence in an action seeking to impugn the validity of that statute. In my opinion the general rule is that if objected to it should be excluded."[81] Ritchie J. (Martland J. concurring), while refraining from any general conclusion on the admissibility of such reports, commented that when they had been referred to in constitutional cases it was for purposes other than direct proof of legislative intention.

In assessing the effect of the decisions it is necessary to keep two issues distinct – that of relevance and that of admissibility. It is submitted that the question of relevance has been clearly decided in favour of royal commission reports. On principle, evidence which shows the factual context in which legislation is to operate is surely relevant to effect. This seems to have been recognized in those cases such as *Ladore* v. *Bennett* in the Privy Council and *Home Oils* in the British Columbia courts where reports were referred to. Even Mr. Justice Cartwright, who displays a certain antipathy to such reports in his dicta in the *Reader's Digest* case, justifies *Ladore* v. *Bennett* this way. "It is scarcely necessary to say that the statement that the rules of evidence may, in civil cases, be relaxed by the consent of parties does not mean that the parties can empower the Court to found its

81. [1961] S.C.R., at 791, 30 D.L.R. (2d), at 311.

decision on matters which are not, as a matter of law, germane to the issue which it is called upon to decide; it means rather that proof of matters which are germane may be made in such manner as the parties agree and not necessarily in strict compliance with the technical rules as to admissibility."[82] This indicates that the problem is not one of relevance, but of admissibility. Consistently with this, a majority in the Appellate Division of the Alberta Supreme Court recently held that legislative committee reports which had preceded the legislation attacked before the court were relevant to assist the court in ascertaining the circumstances in which the statute was passed. In *Walter et al.* v. *Attorney General for Alberta*[83] the parties agreed that such reports could be put before the court in proceedings to determine the validity of legislation restricting communal property-holding. The majority of the court apparently felt the reports to be relevant to the question of whether the legislation was in relation to matters of property or in relation to matters of religious belief.

Where parties do not agree to the introduction of such reports, the question of admissibility still remains open. In *Ladore* v. *Bennett* the evidence was admitted by consent; in *Attorney General for British Columbia* v. *Attorney General for Canada* (re section 498A of the Criminal Code) the report was incorporated by reference in the order in council referring the matter to the court; and in the *Walter* case the legislative reports were admitted by agreement of the parties. *Home Oils* stands out as the only case where a report was admitted in ordinary litigation over the objections of opposing parties, and here we have a clear decision only in the British Columbia courts. The Supreme Court majority ignored the issue of admissibility.

It is submitted that when the opportunity arises the Supreme Court should give a clear decision in favour of the admissibility of such reports. Evidence which is logically relevant ought to be legally admissible unless it offends against public policy or is inherently unreliable. The findings of an independent royal commission, composed of responsible members and staffed with experts, ought not lightly to be dismissed as unreliable. In the narrow sense such evidence must perhaps be regarded as hearsay. But it is suggested that in the pursuit of "legislative facts"[84] the court ought not to be bound by the technical rules of evidence. It should either admit such facts by means of a further exception to the hearsay rule or else it should simply take judicial notice of them. This may also require some

82. [1961] S.C.R., at 789, 30 D.L.R. (2d), at 308–09.
83. [1966] 58 W.W.R. (n.s.) 385, 60 D.L.R. (2d) 253.
84. See *supra* note 59 and accompanying text.

modification of the rules of judicial notice, in that the facts in a royal commission report may not be of general knowledge. A relaxation of normal rules is equally justified here. While the argument for the admission or judicial notice of reports of legislative or other committees may be less compelling, it is submitted that they are also relevant and thus worthy of consideration. The weight to be given their findings will necessarily vary considerably having regard to the composition of each particular committee and the context in which it made its study.

(c) Direct Evidence

It seems clear that sworn evidence as to the effect of a statute, if it complies with the normal rules of evidence, is admissible. There are weighty dicta contemplating the use of such evidence. In the *Alberta Bank Tax Reference* Lord Maugham L. C., said that the court, to determine the effect of a statute, could consider matters of which it could take judicial notice "and other evidence in a case which calls for it."[85] In the *Reader's Digest* case Mr. Justice Cartwright (Locke J. concurring) rejected the evidence of intention in the form of the minister's statements. But he added: "In the case at bar, it will be open to the parties to lead evidence to show the circumstances to which the impugned sections are to be applied but it must be evidence in a form that is legally admissible and the statement of the Minister, alleged in the plaintiff's declaration to have been made, is not in my opinion legally admissible."[86] An example of the use of such evidence may be seen in *Johanesson* v. *West. St. Paul*[87] where an affidavit of one of the parties, setting out certain facts about aerial navigation and commercial flying, was considered by the Supreme Court. This assisted it in finding that the federal Aeronautics Act regulated a matter going beyond purely provincial concern and was intra vires. While at least one trial judge has held that such evidence ought not to be considered where the effect of the statute is "plain,"[88] this approach seems too narrow for constitutional cases. For reasons previously mentioned, the inquiry in constitutional adjudication must be broader because here the crucial test is effect, not meaning. The only place where such evidence may be excluded as irrelevant is where the matter in issue has become one of law and not of fact, as in the "direct taxation" cases.[89]

---

85. [1939] A.C., at 130.
86. [1961] S.C.R., at 792–93, 30 D.L.R. (2d), at 312.
87. *Supra* note 37. See also *Texada Mines* case, *supra* note 46.
88. *Tolton Mfg. Co.* v. *Advisory Committee*, [1940] O.R. 301, [1940] 3 D.L.R. 383 (Ont. H.Ct.). For a criticism see "Comment" (1940), 18 *Can. B. Rev.* 657.
89. See *supra* at 152.

(d) Admissions

It is open to the parties to admit any relevant facts even though these might not be otherwise capable of proof. This was in effect what happened in *Ladore* v. *Bennett* where the debenture holders withdrew their objection to the admission of the royal commission report. The Privy Council obviously regarded the facts therein as relevant and took account of them. Facts may readily be admitted through the pleadings, where the matter commences as an ordinary action.[90] In the appellate courts they may be introduced through the appeal book or "case" containing the evidence, the contents of which are subject to agreement by the parties. Introduction of such material through the "case" has been impliedly approved by the Supreme Court in *Reference re Waters and Water Powers*[91] and permitted in *Reference re Regulation and Control of Radio Communication.*[92]

(e) Judicial Notice

By the ordinary rules of evidence, a court can take judicial notice only of "notorious" facts or facts of public, general knowledge. While there appears to be a large area of discretion as to what facts the courts will judicially notice, they have frequently limited themselves to matters of which virtually everyone would be aware.[93] The judicial practice in this regard has not been equal to the task of constitutional adjudication, where "legislative facts" may be required.

However, at least one case suggests that the courts will not confine themselves to a narrow concept of judicial notice in constitutional cases. In the *Alberta Bank Taxation Reference* both the Supreme Court and the Privy Council[94] took judicial notice of the fact that the Alberta tax if similarly applied by every province would prohibit the carrying on of banking in Canada. This led each court to conclude that the tax was invalid. The only direct evidence which had been introduced merely indicated the amount of the increase in bank taxation in Alberta. Such evidence did not per se disclose that this rate of tax would be prohibitive of banking in Alberta or in Canada as a whole. The "facts" of which these highest tribunals took notice were scarcely "notorious" facts within the normal scope of judicial notice. Whatever one may think of this particular decision, it shows a desirable broadening of the concept of judicial notice

---

90. See e.g. *Walter* case, *supra* note 83.
91. [1929] S.C.R. 200, [1929] 2 D.L.R. 481.
92. [1931] S.C.R. 541, [1931] 4 D.L.R. 865, *aff'd* [1932] A.C. 304 (P.C.).
93. See *Phipson on Evidence* (10th ed., 1963), at para. 46–59; 15 *Halsbury's Laws of England* (3rd ed., 1956), at 333–42.
94. [1938] S.C.R., at 128, [1938] 2 D.L.R. at 81; [1939] A.C., at 131–32 (P.C. 1938).

in a constitutional case. The court exercised its discretion creatively in this instance to enable it to assess the effect of the statute.

The Exchequer Court of Canada in *National Capital Commission* v. *Munro*[95] took judicial notice of a wide range of facts, though the Supreme Court of Canada on appeal found it unnecessary in upholding the decision to rely on these facts or to comment on their use. In deciding that the creation of a "green belt" around Ottawa was a legitimate exercise of Parliament's power with respect to the "peace, order, and good government" of Canada, Mr. Justice Gibson of the Exchequer Court took note of the pattern of development of other national capitals. He referred to such material as a memorandum on the development of Washington, D.C., issued by the late President Kennedy, to support his conclusion that the proper planning of national capitals is a matter inherently of national concern. It is to be hoped that other courts in the future will take an imaginative approach to the use of judicial notice.

In the use of judicial notice the judges might themselves take the initiative in collecting certain "legislative facts" relevant to the effect of impugned legislation. Perhaps some reforms might be instituted to provide assistance in this pursuit. For example, the higher courts should be more adequately equipped with legally trained staff for the judges. Also, provision might be made, as in the High Court of Australia, whereby the court could appoint an expert to supply information on difficult points.[96]

The court may be greatly aided by the parties in the process of judicial notice. He who seeks to introduce facts in this way should proceed with caution. Care should be taken to give opposing parties the opportunity to examine facts so submitted, to question their validity, or to offer additional material to the court. Thus in an ordinary action the material of which the court is asked to take judicial notice should be submitted at the trial where there is a greater opportunity for reply. While matters suitable for judicial notice ordinarily need not be pleaded, some reform in the rules of court might be introduced whereby parties intending to submit such material would have to plead the facts of which the court will be expected to take judicial notice. (This need not be extended to matters of law or other matters of which the courts are now required by statute to take judicial notice.)

The failure to give an adequate opportunity to challenge facts may preclude their introduction through factums in appellate courts. In *Reference re Waters and Water Powers*[97] the Supreme Court of Canada was asked

---

95. [1965] 2 Ex. C. R. 579, *aff'd* [1966] S.C.R. 663, 57 D.L.R. (2d) 753.
96. High Court Rules, O.38, r.2, referred to in Lane, *supra* note 27.
97. *Supra* note 91.

to answer a series of questions concerning the proprietary and legislative powers of the dominion and the provinces with respect to rivers and lakes. This involved various issues including the intended meaning of the term "navigation and shipping" in section 91, and the scope of the third schedule of the BNA Act which transferred certain property rights to Canada. The current state of navigation, water-power development, etc. was also relevant in establishing the dimensions of the problems in this area. Counsel for the attorney general of Canada filed a factum with an appendix of over 900 pages. The first 600 pages contained statutes, statutory orders, and treaties: all public documents in the usual sense whose admissibility could not be seriously questioned. Nor could their presence in the factum constitute a surprise to the parties opposed. The remaining 300 pages included a variety of factual materials such as records with respect to the volume of navigation in certain bodies of water, historical data as to the state of navigation and of road transport at the time of Confederation, a report of the Canada-United States Joint Board of Engineers on the proposed St. Lawrence seaway project, maps, a report of the commissioner of public works of the province of Canada dated June 30, 1867, and statements of the revenues of the various canals for several years preceding the reference. Counsel for the province of Ontario objected to the inclusion of this material on the grounds, *inter alia*, that they were taken by surprise by the insertion of this appendix shortly before the hearing and that there were other facts which they would want to put before the court if this material were to be admitted. Several judges seemed to sympathize with these objections. For example, Duff J. commented during argument that: "it is one thing to say that a particular document is admissible, if presented in such a way that both sides have an opportunity to present anything bearing on the question; it is another thing to have it put in in an ex parte way." Chief Justice Anglin similarly regarded the issue. He said to Mr. Rowell, K.C., counsel for the dominion, "If you seek to make part of the record what you say is part of the history you are doing something which the other side say should not be done, doing it ex parte." While the court never rejected the additional material, the judges asked counsel to reach an agreement as to its inclusion in the factum. Ultimately counsel agreed to a deletion of virtually all of the last 300 pages of the appendix, and the admission of the remainder.[98] Thus while the court did not finally hold this material to be improperly included in the factum, it probably would have done so had counsel not reached an agreement. The basis of rejection would have been the lack of warning to the other side and the

98. Record of oral argument at 1–41, 1253.

latter's inability at this late stage properly to counter such facts submitted for judicial notice.

Such practices may also contravene the rules of court. In *Saumur* v. *City of Quebec*[99] the appellant filed a factum of some 900 pages which included great quantities of factual material, much of it of an historical nature. A majority of the judges concurred with Kerwin J. who held the successful appellant not to be entitled to the costs of his factum. The factum was found not to comply with rule 30 of the Supreme Court. This rule specifies that the factum shall be "a brief of the argument" and Kerwin J. apparently felt that Saumur's factum went far beyond this. While rule 30 also permits the inclusion of "a concise statement of the facts," presumably this refers to the facts as found in the evidence included in the appeal book (case).

A party seeking to introduce facts for judicial notice must avoid these obstacles. The facts must be introduced at a sufficiently early stage that the other party is not taken by surprise. Probably the factum is not a suitable vehicle for introduction unless the other party consents. In *Attorney General for Canada* v. *Attorney General for Ontario* (Employment Insurance Reference)[100] the dominion sought to uphold the validity of federal unemployment insurance. Counsel in his factum included material to show the national economic gravity of unemployment. Among this material were tables of unemployment by months from 1921 to 1935, a table of the annual total volume of business in Canada from 1919 to 1934, tables showing expenditures by the dominion under various relief acts and loans made to the provinces for relief purposes, and tables showing unemployment in other countries during the same period. There is no indication that the other parties or the courts objected to the introduction of this material. In the absence of objection it was admitted, though it apparently played little part in the decision finally reached. The courts were disposed to rely on a priori conceptions rather than economic reality. Nevertheless this and the *Alberta Bank Tax* case show that, given a proper technique of introduction, judicial notice is a suitable means of placing legislative facts before the court. They also show that judicial notice may be taken of facts which are something less than "notorious."[101]

99. [1953] 2 S.C.R. 299, [1953] 4 D.L.R. 641.
100. [1937] A.C. 355 (P.C.).
101. It is obvious that in the *Employment Insurance* case the precise economic data would not be of public general knowledge. Counsel sought to associate these with facts ordinarily capable of judicial notice by the following argument at page 13 of his factum. "It is submitted that the said Act was enacted by the Parliament of Canada having regard to the general economic conditions existing in Canada, the facts of which were matters of general public knowledge and, accordingly, within the sphere of judicial notice. Convenient summaries and tables of statistical and

It is appreciated that until the courts are prepared to assume a more vigorous rule in the pursuit of facts and the examination of statutory effect, parties may encounter difficulty in attempts to have such material judicially noticed. It is obvious that a large measure of discretion rests with the judiciary in deciding what facts are capable of judicial notice. Canadian constitutional litigation would greatly gain in vitality if closer attention were paid to the factual context of legislation. Some of our worst precedents have arisen in cases where no facts were presented, or where the facts as presented were ignored.[102] Judicial notice applied to factual material put in through factum, argument, royal commission reports, or other material supplied by the parties, or applied to material acquired through the initiative of the judges themselves, would facilitate informed decisions in constitutional cases.

THE USE OF FACTUAL MATERIAL IN CONSTITUTIONAL REFERENCES

It only remains to note the special problem of fact-introduction associated with constitutional references. Here there are no pleadings and no trial. There is no contest in the usual sense, though the courts usually assure argument on all sides of the issue by appointing counsel to speak for unrepresented interests.

In the vast majority of references no evidence is put before the court. The order of reference contains a bare question as to the validity of a particular statute. Counsel for various interests then present factums and oral argument related to the various non-factual elements which have been previously described. While the courts may bring to bear certain assumptions of fact, usually inarticulate, the factual context is virtually ignored. This reflects an assumption common among both bench and bar that factual considerations with respect to effect of legislation are irrelevant. Critics of the reference system contend that it has produced unsatisfactory decisions for this very reason.[103]

---

other information disclosing facts then available to the Parliament of Canada and in light of which it must be assumed Parliament acted, are included in the appendix to this factum."

102. See e.g. Davison, "The Constitutionality and Utility of Advisory Opinions" (1938), 2 *U. Toronto L.J.* 254.

103. See e.g. Davison, *ibid.*; LaBrie, "Canadian Constitutional Interpretation and Legislative Review" (1950), 8 *U. Toronto L.J.* 298; MacDonald, "The Privy Council and the Canadian Constitution" (1951), 29 *Can. B. Rev.* 1021. There will obviously be some references where it will be impossible to ascertain any relevant facts. Where the question asked is completely abstract – for example where it requires an opinion as to the scope of jurisdiction over some matter unrelated to particular legislation or particular physical phenomena – it will be difficult to put it in a factual context.

It is quite possible to overcome much of this defect without abandoning the whole reference system. Chief Justice Rinfret in the *Wartime Leasehold Regulations Reference*[104] suggested that because decisions in reference cases are opinions and not judgments, the opinion ought to be based solely on the material submitted in the order of reference. This view seems unduly restrictive. Even if one regards reference decisions as opinions only, there are very good reasons for ensuring that the courts have all relevant facts before them when they deliver such opinions. There is such a strong tradition of "following" these "opinions" in later cases that more realism in their original formulation is important. Otherwise the opinions may contain unwarranted conclusions. Alternatively they will be so abstract and qualified that they will be of little assitance to those who seek the views of the court. A good example of the latter situation may be seen in *Reference re the Farm Products Marketing Act*.[105] The order of reference to the Supreme Court of Canada raised questions as to the validity of Ontario legislation under which marketing schemes were established. The validity of certain regulations made by the Farm Products Marketing Board was also questioned. The scope of the judicial inquiry here was severely limited at the outset by the opening clause of the first question, which said "assuming that the said Act applies only in the case of intra-provincial transactions. . . . " This forced the court to assume that which should have been one of the most controverted matters in issue. In an effort to have this matter more adequately dealt with the court, after the original argument, ordered further argument on a question specified by it. The question was to the effect that, assuming the scheme to cover the marketing of all hogs, peaches, and designated vegetables delivered to a processor in the province, could it validly regulate the production, transportation, and sale of such of these products as would ordinarily be exported from the province?[106] While this order perhaps raised more precisely the most difficult issues, it did not apparently provide the court with any more facts as to the actual course of trade in these various commodities.

This was important because, aside from the narrowness of the original questions, practically no facts had been submitted to the court as to how the scheme actually operated. The joint factum of the Canadian Federation of Agriculture, the Ontario Hog Producers' Marketing Board, and the Ontario Hog Producers' Co-operative did introduce certain facts to show

104. [1950] S.C.R. 124, [1950] 2 D.L.R. 1. The other judges were silent on this point.
105. [1957] S.C.R. 198, 7 D.L.R. (2d) 257.
106. [1957] S.C.R., at 201.

that charges made by the marketing board were service fees and not taxes. But the total lack of any other facts evoked complaints from the counsel appointed by the court to argue against the validity of the legislation. He pointed out the difficulty of determining the validity of the legislation without evidence of its operation. "It is understood that the Board is in fact authorizing extra-provincial marketing, e.g. Counsel are advised that the Ontario Hog Producers Co-operative has established a sales office in Montreal and that several thousand hogs a week from Eastern Ontario are sold in the Province of Quebec through that marketing agency. This is a matter of evidence which, it is submitted, might have a bearing on the Court's decision."[107] He urged the court, apparently without success, to exercise its powers under rule 67 to receive further evidence upon questions of fact. The resulting decision, typically conferred by a series of separate opinions, was unedifying. Virtually every answer was preceded by some qualification or assumption which, it was admitted, might not be supportable by the actual facts. It would give little guidance to those who wished to know whether a scheme such as the one actually operating in Ontario was or was not within provincial jurisdiction.

Facts can readily be introduced in various ways. The order of reference itself may embrace factual material. The danger in this procedure is that the referring government may tend to include only such facts as will support its legislation. A notable exception to this was the *Margarine Reference*[108] where the federal order in council referring the question bore evidence which enabled the court to invalidate a section of a federal statute.

A more equitable and reliable technique is to permit all participants (interested parties and counsel specially appointed to speak for interests not otherwise represented) to introduce such evidence as they may wish. This can be done by agreement, through inclusion in the appeal book or case. Where the parties cannot agree on the material to be submitted a special problem arises because there is no trial at which evidence can be presented. This problem was solved in the *Reference Re Eskimos*[109] by the Supreme Court which in its order fixing the date for the hearing of the reference appointed the registrar of the Court to hear in advance such evidence as the parties wished to present. The order also provided "that all the evidence so adduced and submitted on behalf of each of the interested parties be included, *quantum valeat* and subject to all just exceptions,

107. Factum at 11–12.
108. *Canadian Federation of Agriculture* v. *A.G. for Que.*, [1951] A.C. 179 (P.C. 1950).
109. [1939] S.C.R. 104, [1939] 2 D.L.R. 417.

in the Case. . . ." At issue here was the meaning of the word "Indians" where it appears among the federal heads of jurisdiction in the BNA Act. Did the term include Eskimos so as to bring them under federal jurisdiction? Both the dominion and Quebec presented an impressive array of witnesses before the Registrar. Evidence was taken from anthropologists, archivists, and historians. Maps, dictionaries, reports both official and unofficial were all put in evidence. Each counsel apparently agreed to admit the evidence of the opposing party, subject to the right to controvert or supplement it. All of this material was put into the case, on the understanding that the court could decide as to its weight and relevancy. As a result the court appears to have reached a well-informed opinion as to the proper interpretation of the BNA Act on this point. While the issue in the reference did not touch directly on the validity of any dominion or provincial legislation, this technique of fact-introduction would be equally useful in ascertaining the effect of an impugned statute. This practice is already adequately provided for in the rules of court. It also enables each side to hear fully the evidence of the other side, to challenge it, and to meet it with other evidence. This surely overcomes the difficulties encountered in the *Waters and Water Powers Reference* and in the 1953 *Saumur* case. The fact that it has apparently not been employed in any reference other than *Re Eskimos* does not detract from its validity. No doubt comparable procedures would be useful in provincial appellate courts in reference cases. Where necessary, appropriate rules should be framed to permit the taking of evidence in this way.

In addition, appellate courts which are obliged to hear reference cases ought to be permitted to appoint experts to provide them with information.[110] Such information should be made available to all parties in advance in order that they may have an opportunity to refute it if they wish.

It is submitted that a vigorous use of such procedures by bench and bar would practically eliminate the largest single complaint against the constitutional reference system.

CONCLUSION

It may be well to repeat the two basic questions involved in judicial review of a statute: (1) What is the effect, or what are the effects of the legislation

---

110. The High Court of Australia has such a power. See *supra* note 96. The Supreme Court of Canada would have power to make a similar rule pursuant to the Supreme Court Act, R.S.C. 1952, c. 259, s.103(1) (f) which authorizes the making of rules "with respect to investigations of questions of fact involved in any . . . reference."

in question? and (2) Are the most significant effects those which are permitted to the enacting legislature under the BNA Act?

It has been demonstrated that many elements, both factual and non-factual, enter into the determination of these questions. Once these elements are identified their relative importance can be better assessed. It is submitted that the factual elements have yet to receive the attention they deserve, largely because of the confusion over the purpose of fact-introduction in constitutional cases. The importance of facts has been demonstrated and the means of introduction suggested. A more general recourse to facts, particularly those pertaining to legislative effect, would diminish the importance of other elements in the adjudicative process and yield a more realistic jurisprudence.

CHAPTER SEVEN

Constitutional References

HISTORY

One of the most distinctive features of Canadian judicial review is its frequent resort to the constitutional reference system. This frequency can be demonstrated by a survey of the leading cases (those reaching the Privy Council up to 1949, the Supreme Court of Canada thereafter) decided from 1867 to 1966. Of one hundred and ninety-seven cases involving the distribution of legislative power, sixty-eight had their origins in a constitutional reference while one hundred and twenty-nine involved concrete cases. Nor does the fact that a third of the leading decisions were given in such proceedings reveal the full significance of constitutional references. In terms of impact on the political, social, and economic affairs of the country the decisions in these cases have had an effect far beyond their numerical proportion. It is therefore essential in any study of judicial review of legislation in Canada to give some particular attention to this device. While it has been ably discussed by others,[1] an attempt will be made here to assess it in relation to some of the issues raised elsewhere in this work.

The statutory reference system can claim ancestry in English common law. There were some examples of both the Crown[2] and certain courts[3] referring difficult questions to the judges for an opinion. More closely related was the precedent set by the Judicial Committee Act of 1833, section 4 of which conferred on the Crown the power to refer to that body "any such other matters whatsoever as His Majesty shall think fit."[4]

1. Davison, "The Constitutionality and Utility of Advisory Opinions" (1938), 2 *U. Toronto L. J.* 254; Rubin, "The Nature, Use and Effect of Reference Cases in Canadian Constitutional Law" (1959), 6 *McGill L. J.* 168.
2. See e.g. Inderwick, *The King's Peace* (1895), at 174–75; Plucknett, *A Concise History of the Common Law* (5th ed., 1956), at 162.
3. Plucknett, *ibid.*, at 162, 213, 347. For examples of this procedure see *In re London and Westminster Bank* (1834), 2 Cl. & F. 191, 6 E.R. 1127; *M'Naghten's Case* (1843), 10 Cl. & F. 200, 8 E.R. 718; *Hollins v. Fowler* (1875), L.R. 7 H.L. 757.
4. 3 & 4 Wm. IV c. 41. Used in *Re Cape Breton* (1846), 5 Moo. P.C. 259, 13 E.R.

It was the provision in the Judicial Committee Act which apparently inspired the introduction of this system into Canada in 1875.[5] In that year the Supreme Court of Canada was created, and its founding statute conferred on it this power and duty. The Supreme and Exchequer Courts Act provided as follows: "52. It shall be lawful for the Governor in Council to refer to the Supreme Court for hearing or consideration, any matters whatsoever as he may think fit; and the Court shall thereupon hear and consider the same and certify their opinion thereon to the Governor in Council: Provided that any Judge or Judges of the said Court who may differ from the opinion of the majority may in like manner certify his or their opinion or opinions to the Governor in Council."[6] Section 53 also permitted the Senate or House of Commons to refer bills before it to the court for a report. These reference provisions proved to be inadequate and were not used extensively in the next fifteen years. Normally there was no argument presented to the Court in reference cases. The Court took the view that it should not give reasons for its answers, but should only state its conclusion as to the validity or invalidity of legislation. The result was particularly unsatisfactory in the *McCarthy Act Reference*[7] in 1885 where a federal statute regulating the liquor traffic was found by the Supreme Court to be ultra vires. That Court and the Judicial Committee on appeal both declined to give reasons for their conclusions. As a result it was extremely difficult for Parliament or the government to ascertain the probable limits of federal power insofar as future legislation might be contemplated.

Edward Blake, a member of the opposition but a former attorney general who had originally introduced the Supreme and Exchequer Courts Act, pointed out these and other defects in his own work in a speech to the House of Commons in 1890.

Our present powers, Sir, are wholly inadequate for the effectual execution of the project in hand. There is no certainty – there is in ordinary cases rather an improbability – of our being able to reach the Judicial Committee; and as to all the three possible appeals or references, the Judicial Committee of the Privy Council, the Supreme Court, and the Imperial law officers, the machinery is extremely defective. There is no provision for the representation of the

---

489 (P.C.); *Re Parliamentary Privilege Act, 1770*, [1958] A.C. 331 (P.C.). See also Tarring, *The Law Relating to the Colonies* (1913), at 162–63 for other cases pertaining to colonial laws and powers.
5. Acknowledged in *A.G. for Ont. v. A.G. for Can.*, [1912] A.C. 571, at 585 (P.C.).
6. 38 Vict., c. 11, s. 52 (1875) (Can.).
7. Decision reported *Sess. Papers* No. 85a, at 12–13 (1885) (Can.). Argument reported *ibid.*, at 42–244. For a dicussion of this case see Smith, *The Commerce Power in Canada and the United States* (1963), at 49–57.

different interests; there is no provision for the ascertainment of facts; there is no provision for the reasoned opinion of the tribunal.[8]

Noting that in the *McCarthy Act Reference* and one other case special provision had been made for the appearance of counsel to represent the various interests, he held that the results were still unsatisfactory because of the absence of a reasoned opinion. Consequently, Blake, by a resolution, sought an amendment to correct these defects, but only for limited purposes. He proposed an improved reference system to be used only with respect to questions of law and fact pertaining to the federal government's use of the power to disallow provincial legislation and its appellate power in educational matters. The government accepted Blake's resolution, and Sir John A. Macdonald assured him that a suitable amendment would be introduced at the next session.

As a result the Supreme and Exchequer Courts Act was amended in 1891, the reference section quoted above being replaced by more elaborate provisions. In spite of Blake's preference for a broadened reference system applicable only to matters of disallowance and education, the new section extended as well to questions of law or fact touching the constitutionality of any provincial or federal legislation, and to "any other matter with reference to which he [the governor in council] sees fit to exercise this power." The Court was obliged to certify its opinion "with the reasons therefor, which shall be given in a like manner as in the case of a judgment upon an appeal to the said court. . . ." Where provincial legislation was involved the appropriate attorney general was to be notified and permitted to be heard. The court could direct that other interested persons could be heard, and it could appoint counsel to represent interests otherwise unrepresented. The opinion of the court, though "advisory only," was to be treated for purposes of appeal to the Judicial Committee "as a final judgment of the said court between parties." The court was also empowered to make such rules as might "seem best for the investigation of questions of fact involved in any reference thereunder."[9] Thus Blake's criticisms of the former provisions were largely met. There was to be representation of different interests, a clear right of appeal to the Judicial Committee, and, most importantly, a reasoned decision. The court was enabled to make appropriate rules for fact-finding in reference cases.[10] In this way the

8. [1890] 2 Can. H.C., *Debates*, at 4089–90.
9. 54–55 Vict., c. 25, s. 4 (1891) (Can.).
10. It would not appear that the court has ever made such rules, though this power is still continued by section 103(1)(f) of the present Supreme Court Act, R.S.C. 1952, c. 259 (see Appendix B). The only special measure the court has taken with respect to reference cases was to order the registrar to receive further evidence under section 67 of the (present) Act. See *supra* at 179–80.

reference system was immeasurably strengthened – a vast improvement on the procedure after which it was originally patterned. Apart from some clarifications introduced in 1906[11] these provisions remain substantially unchanged in the present Supreme Court Act,[12] the reference to Judicial Committee appeals having been deleted in 1956.

The federal reference system, though it had achieved a technical acceptability by 1891, had yet to establish its constitutional legitimacy. Some of the provinces objected to federal references on two grounds. First, it was contended that any reference of provincial legislation to a federal court was an invasion of the provincial field of jurisdiction to which the legislation pertained. Further, it was contended that this was not a proper judicial function, and that Parliament in the exercise of its power under section 101 of the British North America Act to create a "general Court of Appeal for Canada" could not confer on the "court" a non-judicial function. These objections were finally put to rest in *Attorney General for Ontario* v. *Attorney General for Canada*.[13] The Privy Council upheld the federal reference system as incidental to the establishment of a Court of Appeal. It regarded the answering of such questions as a non-judicial function, but nevertheless a duty properly imposed on the Court by statute.[14]

The provinces had other objections to the federal reference system as well. The period from Confederation up to 1896 had been marked by a vigorous assertion of federal jurisdiction. One manifestation of this was the frequent disallowance of provincial legislation by the federal government. Another was the creation of the Supreme Court of Canada, including the conferral of power on the federal cabinet to refer questions of legislative validity to that tribunal. The provinces apparently regarded this reference system as a sinister device intended primarily to enable the federal authorities to attack provincial legislation in a federally created court before which the province had no automatic right to appear. Provincial statesmen reacted with demands for increased provincial autonomy or equality of rights. Their views found expression in the interprovincial conference of 1887 in Quebec where five of the seven provinces were represented. The conference passed a series of resolutions calling for constitutional changes. The second resolution, noting that it was just as important that Parliament not assume to exercise provincial powers as that the provinces not assume to exercise federal powers urged "that to prevent any such assumption,

11. 6 Edw. VII, c. 50, s. 2 (1906) (Can.).
12. R.S.C. 1952, c. 259, ss. 55, 103(1)(f). See Appendix B.
13. *Supra* note 5.
14. For a full discussion of these issues see *supra* at 90–92.

there should be equal facilities to the Federal and Provincial Governments for promptly obtaining a judicial determination respecting the validity of Statutes of both the Federal Parliament and Provincial Legislatures; that Constitutional provision should be made for obtaining such determination before, as well as after, a Statute has been acted upon; and that any decision should be subject to Appeal as in other cases, in order that the adjudication may be final."[15] Their faith in a reference system to which either level of government would have equal access was attested to by the third resolution. This proposed that private litigants should be able to challenge the validity of legislation (federal or provincial) only within two years after enactment. Thereafter it should be challengeable only at the instance of the federal or provincial government.[16] This presumably contemplated the use of a reference in any dispute as to validity after the initial two year period.

While no such constitutional changes were ever effected, the resolutions of 1887 appear to have brought about the introduction, through provincial legislation, of provincial reference systems. It is surely no coincidence that three of the five provinces represented at the interprovincial conference introduced virtually identical legislation on this subject in 1890.[17] Over the course of the next sixty-three years the other provinces[18] followed the lead taken by these autonomy-conscious statesmen at the end of the nineteenth century.

The scope of the provincial reference power was from the beginning stated quite broadly. Typical of the 1890 statutes was Manitoba's which provided that "(1) The Lieutenant Governor in Council may refer to the Court of Queen's Bench or a Judge thereof, for hearing or consideration any matter which he thinks fit to refer, and the court shall thereupon hear or consider the same." This was obviously copied from the Judicial Committee Act of 1833 and the Supreme Court Act of 1875. It stated the power in the broadest terms possible, allowing the provincial cabinet to refer all matters which it "thinks fit." This could include questions of the validity of federal as well as provincial laws. It would permit the referral of bills not yet enacted.[19] Issues of fact as well as of law could be raised.

15. *Official Proceedings of the Inter-Provincial Conference, Quebec, 1887* (1887), at 28.
16. *Ibid.*
17. Stats. Man. 1890, c. 16; Stats. N.S. 1890, c. 9; Stats. Ont. 1890, c. 13.
18. Stats. B.C. 1891, c. 5; Stats. Que. 1898, c. 11; Ordinances N.W.T. 1901, c. 11 (carried forward into the laws of Alberta and Saskatchewan when they were created out of the Northwest Territories); Stats. N.B. 1928, c. 47; Stats. P.E.I. 1941, c. 16, s. 10; Stats. Nfld. 1953, c. 3.
19. *Reference re Labour Relations Act*, s. 46A, (1962) 40 W.W.R. (n.s.) 354, 36 D.L.R. (2d) 560 (Man. C.A.).

Identical or almost identical terminology has been adopted by nine of the ten provinces and continued in current statutes.[20] Only New Brunswick expressed the reference power differently. When it introduced references in 1928 it followed the pattern of the Supreme Court Act as revised in 1891 and 1906. The net effect of its legislation[21] would appear to be the same, however. One minor variation among the existing provincial statutes is the court to which such questions are to be referred. All provinces now provide for a reference directly to the highest provincial appellate court. But, in addition, Manitoba and Ontario permit a reference to the superior trial court or judge thereof, though this alternative is rarely used.

The original provincial reference statutes of 1890 in other respects were an improvement over, not an imitation of, the existing federal legislation. They sought to cure most of the defects which, in the same year, Edward Blake had ascribed to the reference provision in the Supreme Court Act. It will be remembered that these defects included the lack of opportunity for the various interests to be represented and heard, the lack of expressed reasons for the conclusions reached by the court, and the uncertainty with respect to the right of appeal from such decisions. The provincial statutes required the giving of reasons. They allowed the court to permit various interests to be heard, and to appoint counsel at public expense to represent unrepresented interests. The opinion of the court was to be "deemed a judgment . . . and an appeal shall lie therefrom as in the case of a judgment in an action." In these provisions the early provincial statutes anticipated the changes made in the Supreme Court Act in 1891. These provisions still appear in almost identical terms in the current reference statutes of all provinces. Small exceptions may be seen in Quebec where an opinion given in a reference is not subject to appeal, and in British Columbia, New Brunswick, and Quebec where no provision is made for appointment of counsel at public expense to appear for interests not otherwise represented.

As a result of this legislation the provinces achieved essentially all they had sought in the resolution at the 1887 interprovincial conference. They had provided for themselves "equal facilities . . . for promptly obtaining a judicial determination respecting the validity of Statutes of both the Federal Parliament and Provincial Legislatures. . . ." They could not refer a matter directly to the Supreme Court of Canada but they could obtain a respected opinion from the highest provincial court. While the purported right of appeal from a reference decision of a provincial court

20. R.S.A. 1955, c. 55; R.S.B.C. 1960, c. 72; R.S.M. 1954, c. 44; Stats. Nfld. 1953, c. 3; R.S.N.S. 1954, c. 50; R.S.O. 1960, c. 64; R.S.P.E.I. 1951, c. 79, s. 39; R.S.Q. 1964, c. 10; R.S.S. 1965, c. 86. See Appendix C.
21. R.S.N.B. 1952, c. 120, s. 24A.

to the Supreme Court of Canada was initially held invalid by the latter,[22] an amendment[23] to the Supreme Court Act in 1922 specifically permitted such appeals to that body. Meanwhile the Privy Council had willingly entertained appeals brought directly from provincial courts in reference cases.[24] Though appeals to the Supreme Court were governed by the restrictions of the Supreme Court Act, the provinces themselves seemingly had jurisdiction to create a right of appeal from their courts to the Privy Council. Moreover the Privy Council could always exercise the prerogative right of granting leave to appeal where the right was not conferred by law.[25] Thus, by referring a question to its local court, a provincial government could expect an answer ultimately from the Privy Council or (more recently), from the Supreme Court of Canada.

From this brief historical review of the reference system two facts emerge which place it in an interesting perspective. First, it may be seen that at both the federal and the provincial level this device was looked upon as an integral part of the functioning of the constitution. After several years of experience with the reference power under the Supreme Court Act, unsatisfactory as it had been, both government and opposition in the House of Commons were agreed that it should be retained. The debates in 1890 and 1891 primarily reveal a concern that the system should be made to operate properly. There was a general assumption that this is an important device for ensuring that neither Parliament nor the legislatures exceed their constitutional powers. Similarly, the resolutions at the 1887 interprovincial conference show that the provinces placed great emphasis on this device, their concern being that they should be equally entitled to resort to it. They also apparently felt that the role of private litigants in judicial review of legislation should be drastically limited.

Secondly, it is clear that both Parliament and the legislatures intended that the procedure in reference cases should be as similar as possible to the procedure employed in ordinary litigation. Issues were to be fully argued by opposing counsel, and reasons were to be given by the court for its decision. The debates in Parliament and the revised section of the Supreme Court Act also reveal a hopeful expectation that the Supreme Court would contrive methods to acquire more effectively the factual background upon which the opinions would be given. While this particular

22. *Union Colliery Co.* v. *A.G. for B.C.* (1897) 27 S.C.R. 637. For a full discussion see *supra* at 92–93.
23. Stats. Can. 1922, c. 48, s. 1.
24. See e.g. *A.G. for Ont.* v. *A.G. for Can.*, [1894] A.C. 189 (P.C.); *A.G. for Ont.* v. *Hamilton Street Ry.*, [1903] A.C. 524 (P.C. 1893); *A.G. for Can.* v. *A.G. for Que.*, [1921] 1 A.C. 413 (P.C. 1920).
25. See *supra* at 11–12, 23–27.

hope remains largely unfulfilled, the over-all objective of "judicializing" the reference procedure has been achieved. The approach taken by both bench and bar in references is scarcely distinguishable from an ordinary appeal. This is obviously what the nineteenth-century legislators sought to ensure.

AN ASSESSMENT

ADVANTAGES

Constitutional references frequently permit judicial review where the ordinary processes of the law would not. The development of those processes was centred on the protection of private rights. If an individual was suffering actual damage to an interest which the law deemed worthy of protection he was permitted to bring his case before a court. On the other hand, the courts generally discouraged the person with a trifling complaint or the officious litigant seeking to right some public wrong. As a result the common law provided few methods for the individual to protect the public interest where his own private interest was not uniquely threatened as well. Thus the rules of standing now create situations where the private litigant is unable to enforce constitutional norms.[26] In such cases the use of a reference may make possible judicial review and the preservation of the proper division of legislative powers.

Two examples previously noted will illustrate this point. First, it is doubtful that an individual voter has standing to complain of the improper delay of elections or the improper distribution of constituencies.[27] Yet in the case of elections for Parliament and distribution of seats in the House of Commons the directives of the BNA Act are quite clear. The reference system may be used to advantage here in applying the constitutional rules to a disputed situation.[28] Secondly, a provincial or federal taxpayer is probably without standing to challenge the constitutionality of governmental expenditures made out of the consolidated revenue fund.[29] Suppose that a taxpayer wished to challenge the right of the Parliament of Canada to vote the sum of money required for the proposed cost-sharing of provincial medical-care insurance schemes. He might contend that this was beyond the scope of federal powers, but he could not do so in court. This again is a place where a constitutional reference might be employed to advantage. While it might well be judicially decided that the "spending

26. See *supra* at 96–125.
27. See *supra* at 114–17.
28. As was done in *A.G. for P.E.I.* v. *A.G. for Can.*, [1905] A.C. 37 (P.C. 1904).
29. See *supra* at 117–20.

power" is unlimited, this is an issue which has not been thoroughly canvassed by the Supreme Court as yet. If the spending power were ever held to be coterminous with legislative power, Canadian federalism would suffer a dramatic change – much to the satisfaction of the provincial autonomists, no doubt. On the other hand, if the Supreme Court confirmed that the spending power is an unlimited one, it might put to rest at least some of the chronic complaints about federal grants and subventions for matters outside of Parliament's regulatory power. Only by a reference can these questions be judicially answered: (1) is the spending power limited? and (2) if limited, does it extend to the particular situation contemplated by the reference?

As well as permitting initial judicial review where it would not otherwise be available, a reference may be used to obtain the opinion of a higher court where an appeal would not lie. If an important constitutional decision is taken in a lower court it may be desirable to have the propriety of that decision authoritatively reviewed. Thus in 1947 the Saskatchewan Court of Appeal unanimously upheld the conviction of a postmistress under the provincial Minimum Wage Act for paying an employee less than the minimum wage. In the circumstances an appeal did not lie to the Supreme Court. The federal cabinet referred this question to the Court: "Was the Saskatchewan Court of Appeal right in holding in its decision in *Williams* v. *Graham* that the Minimum Wage Act . . . was applicable to the employment of Leo Fleming in the Post Office at Maple Creek, Saskatchewan?" The order in council referring this question recited the facts and the decision of the provincial court. It then pointed out the importance of this issue to the federal government:

And whereas there are between 11,000 and 12,000 Post Offices and Sub Post Offices in Canada in which Postmasters are employed on terms similar to those applicable to Mrs. Graham;
And whereas the Minister of Justice is informed by the Postmaster General, that, if the laws of the various provinces relating to hours of employment and minimum wages are applicable to persons employed in the post offices by Postmasters, the cost of operation of the postal service in certain provinces will be increased or the service in such provinces will have to be reduced. . . .

If the matter had not been taken to the Supreme Court there would obviously have been much uncertainty. The post office system would have had to observe The Minimum Wage Act in Saskatchewan even though the federal government had grave doubts as to the correctness of the decision of the provincial Court of Appeal. In other provinces it might have ignored provincial laws, at the risk of the prosecution of its postmasters as in Saskatchewan. A decision of the highest Canadian judicial

CONSTITUTIONAL REFERENCES

authority on the applicability of such legislation to post offices was therefore of great importance. When the reference was heard by the Supreme
Court, it came to the conclusion that the Court of Appeal had been wrong,
and that the provincial legislation was inapplicable.[30]

It is improbable that this precise type of situation would arise again
with respect to the Supreme Court of Canada. In 1949 the Supreme Court
Act was amended to permit appeals without limitation in any matter where
either the provincial appellate court or the Supreme Court gives leave. In
a constitutional case, such as the *Minimum Wage Reference*, leave would
no doubt be forthcoming from either court. Yet the reference will still be
a good substitute for an appeal in some cases. In some provinces there may
be situations where an appeal to the highest court is not available, and a
reference may be used. Or the parties to the original litigation may not
wish to carry a case to the Court of Appeal or the Supreme Court and the
provincial or federal attorney general may be powerless to do so.[31] There
is also the possibility that the courts may refuse leave to appeal a case
which the government feels should be appealed. While the government's
power should not be used lightly in such circumstances, the court could be
forced by a reference to deal with the issue on which they had refused leave
to appeal.[32]

In cases where judicial review will be ultimately possible through private
litigation, a reference may nevertheless be desirable to hasten the process.
To facilitate public or private planning it may be very valuable to have a
judicial opinion in advance with respect to the legality of a particular
course of action. For example, the government may wish to have clarified
the constitutionality of a nation-wide unemployment insurance scheme[33]
or a marketing scheme[34] before establishing elaborate machinery for its
operation. Or businessmen may want to know whether a particular government has power to incorporate their company or confer on them certain
rights and privileges. A good example of the latter may be seen in the
recent disputes over ownership of offshore minerals. A conflict of opinion
developed between various coastal provinces and the dominion with
respect to regulatory and proprietary rights over these resources, and in
some cases both the provincial government and the federal government

30. *Reference re Saskatchewan Minimum Wage Act,* [1948] S.C.R. 248, [1948]
3 D.L.R. 801.
31. See *supra* at 113.
32. Cf. *Reference re Regina* v. *Coffin,* [1956] S.C.R. 186, 7 D.L.R. (2d) 568;
"Comment" (1956), 34 *Can.B.Rev.* 967; *Reference re Regina* v. *Truscott* (1967),
62 D.L.R. (2d) 545.
33. E.g. *A.G. for Can.* v. *A.G. for Ont.,* [1937] A.C. 355 (P.C.).
34. E.g. *A.G. for B.C.* v. *A.G. for Can.,* [1937] A.C. 377 (P.C.).

issued exploration licences for the same areas. As the prime minister pointed out in his opening statement to the Federal-Provincial Conference on July 19, 1965,[35] it was important that exploration not be delayed as this would harm Canada's competitive position. In the federal government's view "the question of legal ownership and legal right must be settled before it is possible to consider intelligently what kind of arrangement, with regard to exploitation, would be fair and equitable to all concerned." Thus in April 1965 the government had referred to the Supreme Court various questions concerning regulatory and proprietary rights over minerals offshore from British Columbia. It was hoped that in this way both the conduct of intergovernmental arrangements and the long-range programming of exploration by the companies would be facilitated. Apart from a political compromise of the issue, the only alternative would have been to await some chance litigation where these issues could be decided.[36]

There will also be situations where speedy determination is more of a necessity than a convenience. Emergency conditions such as war make it imperative that the government be assured at once of the validity of proposed action. For example, if it wishes to create a regulatory system to ensure the maintenance of vital supplies and the prevention of waste, it cannot afford the luxury of waiting for chance litigation to uphold or strike down the scheme.[37]

A reference may also provide relief where a private citizen would not find it convenient to take a constitutional case to the higher courts. A litigant may have grave doubts about the validity of a statute applied against him, but it is less expensive for him to drop his objections than to carry the case to an appeal. Yet such a statute applied similarly to dozens or hundreds of people may collectively cause great expense or injustice. In addition, various lower courts may hold conflicting views as to the validity of the law, some upholding it and others deeming it invalid. If no affected individual is prepared to undertake the expense and trouble of appeal, the enforcement of the statute will fall into chaos and the law itself into discredit. A reference to an appellate court may provide the authoritative decision required to restore order. If the statute is held invalid, numerous

35. At 29–33.
36. The decision in the reference is reported at (1968), 62 W.W.R. (n.s.) 21, 65 D.L.R. (2d) 353 (S.C. Can. 1967). For a discussion of the substantive issues see Head, "The Legal Clamour over Canadian Off-Shore Minerals" (1967), 5 *Alberta L.R.* 311; Head, "The Canadian Offshore Minerals Reference: the Application of International Law to a Federal Constitution" (1968), 18 *U. Toronto L.J.* 131.
37. See e.g. *Reference re Chemicals Regulations*, [1943] S.C.R. 1, [1943] 1 D.L.R. 248.

citizens will be relieved from compliance with legislation which it was not practical for them to contest individually.

With respect to issues which the courts usually regard as non-justiciable a reference might be used to permit judicial determination. There are obviously many non-justiciable issues where the decision ought not to be made by the judiciary, in any form of procedure, because a policy determination is required. For example, the court ought not to be asked which is the government of China, or whether capital punishment is desirable. But there are other areas, such as the propriety of parliamentary procedure, where pre-established norms are available for application. It is not certain that a court would review a federal statute on the basis that it was passed by a procedure not in accordance with the BNA Act.[38] Yet the directions of the Act in this regard are as clear as those of sections 91 and 92 which the courts constantly apply. Judicial timidity could be overcome with a reference, because the judges are obliged[39] to answer questions referred to them.

Finally, references provide a flexible means for each level of government to police the constitutional excesses of the other level of government. The federal government was given this power in another form through the disallowance procedure. But federal disallowance of provincial legislation on the sole grounds that it was ultra vires fell into disfavour and by 1935 was expressly abandoned.[40] Even where the power was exercised on this ground, it was common for the federal government first to refer the question of validity to the Supreme Court and be guided by its advice. The reference is now the principal means for the government of Canada to challenge the validity of provincial legislation. It may of course refer such legislation on its own initiative[41] or at the request of the province concerned.[42] Equally, the provinces may challenge the validity of federal legislation by referring it to a provincial court, in this way ensuring that it will ultimately reach the highest tribunals.[43] In Ontario the attorney

38. See *supra* at 140–41.
39. *A.G. for B.C.* v. *A.G. for Can.*, [1914] A.C. 153 at 161–62 (P.C. 1913).
40. Report of Hon. E. Lapointe, Minister of Justice, reproduced in LaForest, *Disallowance and Reservation of Provincial Legislation* (1955), at 77. In subsequent cases of disallowance additional grounds were asserted.
41. E.g. *A.G. for Ont.* v. *A.G. for Can.*, [1896] A.C. 348 (P.C. 1895); *A.G. for Sask.* v. *A.G. for Can.*, [1949] A.C. 110 (P.C. 1948).
42. E.g. *Reference re Farm Products Marketing Act*, [1957] S.C.R. 198, 7 D.L.R. (2d) 257.
43. E.g. *A.G. for Ont.* v. *Reciprocal Insurers*, [1924] A.C. 328 (P.C.); *A.G. for Ont.* v. *Canada Temperance Federation*, [1946] A.C. 193 (P.C.); *A.G. for Can.* v. *C.P.R. & C.N.R.*, [1958] S.C.R. 285, 12 D.L.R. (2d) 625.

general may, in the alternative, seek a declaration that an act of Parliament is invalid,[44] but presumably the reference procedure would be speedier.

The essential advantage of the reference system thus appears to be facilitation of judicial review. In some cases it makes the impossible possible, in others it speeds the process where time is of the essence. To those for whom enforced judicial activism poses no threat, the constitutional reference may appear as an unmixed benefit. But it is also essential to consider some of the problems which arise out of its use.

DISADVANTAGES

The most frequent and serious criticism of judicial review by reference is its abstractness. It is said that a court cannot properly decide on the validity of a legislative scheme unless it is conversant with the factual context in which the statute operates. There are also widespread suspicions that legislation is more likely to be held invalid on a reference than in an ordinary case, and that federal legislation has suffered more in this way than provincial legislation.[45]

A statistical analysis only partly supports these latter allegations. A study of leading constitutional cases from 1867 to 1966 (those reaching the highest tribunal available, either the Privy Council or the Supreme Court) shows that of thirty-seven references involving the validity of provincial statutes, legislation was held invalid in seventeen. This represents a mortality rate of almost forty-six per cent. In other proceedings involving the validity of provincial statutes, there was a finding of ultra vires in thirty-five out of ninety-two cases, or a mortality rate of over thirty-eight per cent. Thus the contrast is far from marked, and is probably unreliable because of the relatively small numbers involved and the existence of other factors.[46]

In references involving federal statutes in the same period, there was a finding of invalidity in ten out of thirty-one cases. The mortality rate of thirty-two per cent is actually much better than the average for provincial references. However, federal statutes did fare relatively much better in non-reference proceedings. Here there was a finding of invalidity in only five of thirty-seven cases, a rate of under fourteen per cent. Thus it can be seen that federal statutes have suffered less frequently in refer-

---

44. See *supra*, at 77–78.
45. See the various articles cited by Rubin, *supra* note 1, at 182–84.
46. It could be argued, for example, that statutes are referred to the courts only where there are serious doubts as to validity, whereas private litigants frequently raise insubstantial constitutional issues in the course of proceedings primarily involving other issues.

ences than have provincial statutes, though, as between references and other proceedings, the references have worked relatively more to the disadvantage of federal legislation.

Any such statistical analysis is necessarily crude and of limited value, because it overlooks all other relevant factors. Nevertheless, if the critics of the reference system were wholly correct, one would expect to see more starkly defined contrasts. It is quite possible that the differences noted are explicable on the basis of other factors.[47]

This is not to say that there have been no abstract reference decisions, or that they have not had a serious effect on the development of the Canadian constitution. One need only look at a few examples. In the *1916 Insurance Reference* the Supreme Court was asked for an opinion as to the validity of certain sections of the federal Insurance Act, 1910. This legislation required the federal registration of insurance companies before they could carry on business. It was broad enough to cover provincially incorporated companies carrying on business in Canada outside the province of incorporation. A majority of the Supreme Court confined itself to an exercise in semantics, holding that the federal power to regulate "trade and commerce" could not include "a trade." The insurance business was regarded as "a trade," hence not susceptible to federal control.[48] One of the dissenting judges, Davies J., took a more realistic approach. He took judicial notice of the national significance of the insurance business, the mobility of insured persons, and the possible national repercussions of the failure of a major company. This enabled him to find that the business of insurance was clearly a matter of national trade and commerce.[49] But the Privy Council on appeal sided with the majority below, Viscount Haldane at his dogmatic best holding that "it must now be taken that the authority to legislate for the regulation of trade and commerce does not extend to the regulation by a licensing system of a particular trade in which Canadians would otherwise be free to engage in the provinces."[50] Here was a reference involving the bare question "Are sections 40 and 70 of the Insurance Act, 1916, or any and what part or parts of the said sections, ultra vires of the Parliament of Canada?" No factual information was included with the reference, nor apparently was any otherwise presented to the court. Without consideration of the factual context in which the legislation would operate, the majority of the Supreme Court and the Privy Council set aside the legislation on a conceptual analysis of the

47. It may also be noted that most of the references of federal legislation were taken at a time when judicial trends generally were against federal power.
48. (1913), 48 S.C.R. 260, 15 D.L.R. 251.
49. For a discussion of the decision see Smith, *supra* note 7, at 80–84.
50. *A.G. for Can.* v. *A.G. for Alta*, [1916] 1 A.C. 588, at 596 (P.C.).

word "trade." The net result was to bar the Parliament of Canada from regulating businesses which were interprovincial in scope, where their operations could be analytically dismembered into a collection of "particular trades" carried on in particular provinces.

That the results might easily have been different in a concrete case with facts before the court may be seen by contrasting the decision with that of the Quebec Court of Queen's Bench (Appeal Side) in *Reader's Digest Association (Canada) Ltd.* v. *Attorney General of Canada*.[51] There a federal tax on advertising material published in the appellant's magazine was attacked in a declaratory action as, *inter alia*, a regulation of intraprovincial trade because approximately one quarter of the magazine's Canadian sales were in the province of Quebec where it was published. A majority of the court rejected this contention. Even though the measure might constitute regulation as well as taxation, it was held that as applied to the appellant it was not a regulation of a business confined to a single province. The court noted that the appellant sold the same magazine both inside and outside Quebec and that the advertising material was "national in scope." The business was regarded by Rinfret J. (Tremblay C.J.Q. and Taschereau J. concurring) as "one and indivisible." The *1916 Insurance Reference* was considered and held inapplicable. Nevertheless one might well suspect that had the courts in the *1916 Insurance Reference* had before them the kind of facts on the insurance business corresponding to those on the publishing business considered in the *Reader's Digest* case, the result in the 1916 decision might well have been the opposite. The *1916 Insurance Reference* was an abstract decision and it was one of many such reference decisions which had far-reaching and unfortunate consequences.

Three decisions from 1937 provide similar examples. *The Natural Products Marketing Act Reference*[52] concerned the validity of federal legislation purporting to authorize federal regulation of marketing of certain agricultural products. Marketing schemes were to be confined to commodities whose "principal market" was outside the province of growth. While it probably could have been demonstrated that the regulation of local sales was inextricably linked with the control of interprovincial and international marketing (clearly a federal matter), both the factums and the judgment ignore such factual considerations. The Judicial Committee proceeded on a series of abstract propositions, foremost of which was the prohibition against federal control of trade which is "ex-

51. (1965), 59 D.L.R. (2d) 54.
52. *A.G. for B.C.* v. *A.G. for Can.*, [1937] A.C. 377 (P.C.).

clusively local." In this it assumed a separability between local and non-local trade which the facts would probably have refuted.[53]

The second of these cases was the *Employment Insurance Reference*.[54] The federal statute in question would have established a system of compulsory insurance against unemployment, to be paid for in part by "contributions" required of both employers and employees. Counsel for the dominion did introduce through his factum some impressive economic data showing the grave and national character of the unemployment problem.[55] But the Privy Council ignored the factual context of the legislation, confining itself to more familiar and congenial conceptualism. The only important consequences of this legislation it could see were compulsory alteration of contracts of employment through forced insurance deductions, and the operation of an insurance business. This automatically made the federal legislation a usurpation of the sacred provincial "property and civil rights" jurisdiction. The fact that the effect on contracts and insurance was a mere incident of a scheme essentially directed to the relief of nation-wide hardship, the greater rationalization of federal-provincial financial relations, and the stabilization of the national economy, was completely ignored by the Judicial Committee.

The other reference in this trilogy pertained to federal legislative attempts in the fields of labour relations and treaty implementation. Canada had ratified certain conventions adopted by the International Labour Organization with respect to labour standards. Subsequently Parliament enacted three statutes, the Weekly Rest in Industrial Undertakings Act, the Minimum Wages Act, and the Limitation of Hours of Work Act. On the basis of earlier decisions it was clear that these statutes infringed on provincial jurisdiction over property and civil rights (i.e. contracts of employment) unless they could be justified under some overriding federal power. In the *Labour Conventions Reference*[56] the dominion contended, *inter alia*, that once a matter had become of international concern and the subject of a treaty, it ought to be considered within federal legislative jurisdiction over the "peace, order, and good government" of Canada. The arguments and the judgment all proceeded by a series of abstract precepts, with the Privy Council once again characterizing the legislation as an unwarranted interference with "property and civil rights."

53. See *R.* v. *Klassen* (1959), 29 W.W.R. (n.s.) 369, 20 D.L.R. (2d) 406 (Man. C.A.); Cf. *U.S.* v. *Darby* (1941), 312 U.S. 100; *Wickard* v. *Filburn* (1942), 317 U.S. 111.
54. *A.G. for Can.* v. *A.G. for Ont.*, [1937] A.C. 355 (P.C.).
55. Discussed fully *supra*, at 176.
56. *A.G. for Can.* v. *A.G. for Ont.*, [1937] A.C. 326 (P.C.).

Numerous other examples could be cited to support the claim that reference decisions are frequently abstract. These particular ones were selected because of their far-reaching consequences.

The *1916 Insurance Reference* was influential in a number of later cases where Parliament was denied the power to cope with nation-wide commercial problems because this was characterized as regulation of a particular trade within each province.[57]

The *Natural Products Marketing Act Reference* created a constitutional impasse in the regulation of agricultural marketing. It made clear that though the provinces could not regulate local trade in such a way as to interfere with interprovincial trade, neither could Parliament interfere with intraprovincial trade in the course of regulating interprovincial or international trade. As the normal flow of trade in agricultural products does not readily break down into these constitutionally distinct categories until almost the time of consumption, it is impossible to ascertain which government can regulate production quotas, inspection, or grading of a given item of produce.[58] A literal application of the Privy Council's edicts would at best have resulted in confusion and expensive duplication of effort. The situation has been partially relieved only through the inter-delegation of administrative authority.

The *Employment Insurance Reference* created an obstacle, partially legal and partially psychological, to any future proposals for federal social security measures. The effect with respect to unemployment insurance itself was overcome by a 1940 constitutional amendment[59] expressly conferring jurisdiction on Parliament. But when in 1950 consideration was being given to a possible federal contributory old-age pension scheme the deputy minister of justice advised that Parliament would be precluded from enacting such a measure by virtue of the 1937 Privy Council decision.[60] The government apparently accepted this view and obtained a constitutional amendment the next year.[61] However, it was not until a further fourteen years and another constitutional amendment[62] that Par-

57. *In re Board of Commerce Act*, [1922] 1 A.C. 191 (P.C. 1921); *A.G. for Ont. v. Reciprocal Insurers*, [1924] A.C. 328 (P.C.); *Toronto Electric Commissioners v. Snider*, [1925] A.C. 396 (P.C.).
58. See Corry, "Difficulties of Divided Jurisdiction," in *Report of the Royal Commission on Dominion-Provincial Relations, 1940*, Appendix 7, *passim*; Smith, *supra* note 7, at 139–43.
59. 3–4 Geo. VI, c. 36 (1940).
60. *Minutes, Joint Committee of the Senate and the House of Commons on Old Age Security* (Wednesday, May 31, 1950), at 1161–71.
61. 14–15 Geo. VI, c. 32 (1951).
62. British North America Act, 1964, 12–13 Eliz. II, c. 73.

liament actually introduced a contributory scheme.[63] Other federal social security measures such as hospitalization insurance and the proposed medical care insurance programme have proceeded on the assumption that the proper role of the government of Canada is cost-sharing. These insurance plans operate under provincial law with large subventions from the general revenues of the federal government.

The *Labour Conventions Reference*, denying Parliament the power to implement treaties properly entered into by the Crown in right of Canada, has been a continuing source of difficulty in the conduct of foreign affairs.[64] It has also given rise to exaggerated provincial ambitions. In the negotiation of the Columbia River Treaty and its Protocol, for example, the government of British Columbia could take the position that it would not proceed to implement the treaty unless it was revised to meet provincial demands. This posed problems in the conduct of negotiations with the United States – problems in an area for which the province had no political responsibility. More recently Quebec has contended that, because Ottawa cannot implement treaties involving matters within provincial jurisdiction, the provincial and not the federal government should negotiate and sign such treaties. It is thus still too early to assess the total impact of the *Labour Conventions Reference* on Canada's international posture.

This analysis of a few important cases adds weight to the charge that reference decisions have tended to be abstract. It also demonstrates the great and largely unfortunate effect which such decisions have had on Canadian constitutional development. Indeed one can argue that reference decisions are more likely to have a widespread effect because of the circumstances in which the reference technique is frequently used. Governments are most likely to refer to the courts legislation which is not only constitutionally questionable but also controversial because of its economic, political, or social importance. Thus references are particularly dangerous because the opinion subsequently rendered by the court will naturally have far-reaching implications. This might suggest to some that in future the reference device should be limited or abolished. It is submitted that this conclusion is unjustified.

First it must be acknowledged that, abstract though most reference decisions have been, much of the fault has lain with the courts. The

63. Canada Pension Plan, Stats. Can. 1965, c. 51.
64. See Szablowski, "Creation and Implementation of Treaties in Canada" (1956), 34 *Can. B. Rev.* 28, at 54–56; Lederman, "Legislative Power to Implement Treaty Obligations in Canada," in Aitchison, *The Political Process in Canada* (1963), at 171.

reasoning processes employed by them have often been similar in both reference and ordinary cases. They have laid stress on precedent and a priori reasoning rather than on facts and conscious policy-making. In some concrete cases where factual material might have been readily available, neither counsel nor court appear to have relied on it.[65] Thus, part of the Olympian detachment from facts seemingly stems from general judicial practice rather than from the particular procedure employed.

Secondly, there are situations where there is no need for a factual study of legislative effect. This arises where the issue is solely that of an interpretation of a section of the BNA Act where no legislation is involved. These cases will be rare, and the decisions therein may be of limited use. But occasionally they will be valuable, where the issue in question is sufficiently narrow. For example in *Edwards* v. *Attorney-General for Canada*[66] the question was whether the word "persons" in section 24 of the BNA Act included women, thus making the latter eligible for appointment to the Senate. The answer turned completely on the intention of the Act. The effect of each possible interpretation was readily apparent. A similar decision was necessary in the *Reference re Eskimos*[67] where the court had to decide whether the word "Indians" in section 91 (24) included Eskimos, thus bringing them under federal jurisdiction. The affirmative answer given by the Supreme Court was very helpful, because the extent of federal power over Indians was already well defined. It only remained to exercise the same powers with respect to Eskimos. While facts were considered in the rendering of the opinion, they were facts pertaining to the meaning of words as employed by the Imperial Parliament in 1867. There were no other facts which could have been considered, because there was no legislative scheme purporting to regulate Eskimos. Thus it may be seen that where an opinion may usefully be rendered as to the meaning of the BNA Act, even in the absence of a legislative scheme and facts showing legislative effect, a reference is legitimate. Though the decision may be abstract in one sense, it will be useful because of the context in which it is given.

Thirdly, and most importantly, the solution for bad decisions is reform, not abandonment, of the reference system. This will involve an increased alertness in the courts and the bar with respect to the relevance of the factual context. It will require the use of existing or new techniques, urged elsewhere herein,[68] for fact-introduction. It will require the careful fram-

---

65. See e.g. *Board of Commerce Act* case and the *Toronto Electric Commissioners* case, *supra* note 57.
66. [1930] A.C. 124 (P.C. 1929).
67. [1939] S.C.R. 104, [1939] 2 D.L.R. 417.
68. See *supra*, at 177–80.

ing of questions so that issues may be raised as precisely as possible. The courts should avoid answering questions not clearly included in the reference order.[69] Where the order of reference does not provide a precise question and a factual context, and no suitable evidence is introduced, the court should refuse to give an opinion.[70] If these principles were faithfully applied in reference cases, there would be far less complaint of abstractness.

Lesser criticisms of the reference system include that of possible interference with private rights. Judges have occasionally hesitated to answer a referred question because, though worded generally, it may precisely cover issues on which the rights of specific individuals may turn. It is thought unfair to render such decisions where individuals who may be seriously affected are not represented before the court. As previously noted, this criticism appears specious for the same may be said of almost any decision. A case between litigants A and B may involve issues similar to those at stake between C and D. An unfavourable decision in A v. B, for example, may have grave implications for C. But it has never been suggested that C should be a party in A. v. B. References are actually more flexible in this matter because the court is at liberty to permit almost anyone to participate in the argument.[71]

The real fault lies, not in the initial reference decision having possible implications for private individuals, but rather in the misplaced fidelity with which such decisions are subsequently followed. This is part of the broader complaint that reference decisions have generally been given undue precedent value. In other words, what were originally intended to be opinions only have been treated as judgments.

When the Supreme Court Act was amended in 1891 reference opinions were described as "advisory only." This was soon ignored and until recently the Privy Council and Supreme Court expressly followed the decisions in earlier federal references with undiscriminating zeal.[72] Not until 1957 (after the "advisory only" provision had actually been dropped from the Supreme Court Act) did the Supreme Court suggest the possibility that it would ignore earlier reference decisions, even those of the Judicial Committee. It then stated that it was not bound by a decision of the Judicial Committee rendered in a reference involving some of the same issues and parties now before it in a concrete case. It may be noted,

69. *Reference re Magistrate's Court Act*, [1965] S.C.R. 772, 55 D.L.R. (2d) 701.
70. For a full discussion of this point see *supra*, at 133–35.
71. *Ibid*.
72. See Rubin, "The Nature, Use and Effect of Reference Cases in Canadian Constitutional Law" (1959), 6 *McGill L.J.* 168, at 175–79.

however, that this was *obiter dicta*, for the Supreme Court accepted the opinion of the Privy Council.[73]

It is to be hoped that this judicial declaration of independence will not be forgotten by its authors. Uncritical following of reference decisions brings discredit on the whole reference system. The rendering of opinions on hypothetical questions or on issues affecting private rights would create few problems if they were not subsequently treated as conclusive. An opinion on an abstract question should be regarded as of limited value, valid only in relation to the assumptions and facts on which it was rendered. Moreover, it can hardly be considered to preclude further contestation by anyone, whether parties or non-parties to the reference, because it does not render the issue res judicata.[74] It may be argued further that the Supreme Court, as successor to the Privy Council and as the final appellate court, should no longer consider itself bound by any previous decisions (its own or the Privy Council's) in any type of proceeding. The Privy Council asserted such freedom, but rarely exercised it. The Supreme Court should do both.[75] Judicial creativity may present the only practical means of future constitutional reform.[76]

Should the provincial courts follow reference opinions? To opinions rendered in the Supreme Court and Privy Council, in federal references, it is submitted that the lower courts should show great respect and no more. It should be kept in mind that these opinions are not judgments, though they are certainly of great weight. Mr. Justice Locke in *C.P.R.* v. *Estevan*,[77] by holding that the Supreme Court was not bound by its own or the Privy Council's opinions, clearly implied that such opinions were not binding on any court.

The position might be distinguishable where a provincial court is faced with a previous decision of a higher court on a provincial reference. Most of the provincial reference statutes state that the opinion of the court "shall be deemed a judgment." In *Milk Board* v. *Hillside Dairy Ltd.*[78] the British Columbia Court of Appeal considered itself bound by an earlier decision of the Supreme Court of Canada in an appeal on a provincial reference. At issue in both cases was the validity of a particular British Columbia

73. *C.P.R.* v. *Town of Estevan*, [1957] S.C.R. 365, 7 D.L.R. (2d) 657. See also dicta in *Reference re Regina* v. *Coffin*, [1956] S.C.R. 186, at 187, 7 D.L.R. (2d) 568, at 570.
74. See *supra*, at 126–28. *Coffin* case, *supra* note 73.
75. See Laskin, "The Supreme Court of Canada: A Final Court of and for Canadians" (1951), 29 *Can. B. Rev.* 1038; Joanes, "Stare Decisis in the Supreme Court of Canada" (1958), 36 *Can. B. Rev.* 175, at 193–200.
76. The prospects for a workable amendment procedure have virtually disappeared.
77. [1957] S.C.R., at 368, 7 D.L.R. (2d), at 659–60.
78. (1963) 43 W.W.R. (n.s.) 131, 40 D.L.R. (2d) 731 (B.C.C.A.).

statute. Two of the judges in the Court of Appeal, writing for the majority, took the position that all reference decisions are binding. In this they ignored the *Estevan* case and relied on an earlier but emphatic Supreme Court decision[79] to this effect. While this authority would now be questionable, Mr. Justice Sheppard also stated a second ground for his decision: "[T]he opinion, although a reference, is by statute stated to be a judgment. . . . This court is therefore bound by that judgment and is restricted to matters not determined thereby. . . ."[80] With respect, this conclusion appears unnecessary. It is clear from the statute that the opinion is deemed to be a judgment for the purpose of appeal. The Supreme Court itself has held that the statute, by stating that an opinion shall be "deemed" a judgment, indicates that it is not a judgment.[81] And even if it is a judgment, it is obviously of a very special kind, limited in its effect. Consequently, provincial courts should be free to ignore their own or the higher courts' decisions in provincial references.

Combined with the abandonment of stare decisis with respect to reference opinions, there should be a more discriminating use of such opinions when invoked for persuasive purposes. In analyzing what a reference actually "decided," the opinion should be carefully examined in relation to the precise hypotheses put to the court and the facts, if any, before it. Such analysis may reveal that the opinion decided very little, in which case it ought not to be an embarrassment in subsequent cases.

In sum, it is suggested that the fault lies more in judicial practice than in the reference system. Judicial reform would remove the substance of this complaint.

CONCLUSION

The controversy over references is really an aspect of the larger controversy with respect to the role of the judiciary in a federal state. Judicial activists will generally approve of a system which overcomes obstacles to judicial review. Those who take a more restricted view of the role of the judiciary will see it as a hazardous procedure, burdening the courts with hypothetical questions and producing premature decisions with mischievous consequences.

On balance the case for the use of references seems more supportable. If one accepts the courts as the best arbiters of the federal structure, he should favour a system which facilitates judicial review. The common law which Canada inherited from England was deficient in public law

79. *A.G. for Can.* v. *Higbie*, [1945] S.C.R. 385, [1945] 3 D.L.R. 1.
80. 43 W.W.R. (n.s.) at 144–45, 40 D.L.R. (2d) at 746.
81. *Union Colliery Co.* case, *supra* note 22.

remedies suitable for a federal state. The private law rules of standing and justiciability would leave some constitutional norms unenforced, or would cause expense and delay in the resolution of constitutional issues. While this leaves with the executive branch a complete discretion as to when such issues are to be put before the courts, this should not cause serious concern. This is surely preferable to having the time, place, and scope of judicial review left entirely to the vagaries of private litigation. Historically the reference system was conceived of as a means of advising the executive branch of government. The rendering of such opinions was held to be non-judicial in nature, and opinions are now regaining their status as advice, not judgments. When regarded thus as a specialized and extraordinary function, the delivery of opinions need not be treated as a corruption of the strictly judicial processes of the courts. Yet, if "the law" is essentially a "prophec[y] of what the courts will do . . ."[82] there is no better basis for prophecy of what the courts will do in a concrete case than an opinion of the same court on the same subject in advance.

But there still remains ample need for reform in the use of constitutional references. In this area where the judges cannot decline jurisdiction, the cabinet must itself exercise self-restraint in referring questions. The questions must not be too abstract or too premature. The issues must be precisely defined by the government in the order of reference. Counsel for the interests represented in the hearing must be astute to present all relevant factual material. The judges must have regard to the facts, and must frame their answers no more broadly than the circumstances warrant. They must also examine critically earlier opinions and be prepared to disregard those which were based on insufficient information.

With some conscious effort, the reference system can be made a perfectly respectable method of judicial review. Criticisms[83] of "advisory opinions" as used in some states of the United States need not deter Canadians unduly. The Canadian constitution lacks the vague standards which are almost impossible of application save in concrete cases. Moreover Canadian procedures for hearing and argument are already generally superior to their American counterparts.[84] It is within the power of government, bench, and bar to eliminate other defects in the Canadian system and make it uniquely successful.

Even a perfected reference system must play a secondary role in judicial review, however. A decision based on complete facts is to be preferred to

82. See Holmes, "The Path of the Law" (1897), 10 *Harv. L. Rev.* 457, at 460–61.
83. See e.g. Frankfurter, "A Note on Advisory Opinions" (1924), 37 *Harv. L. Rev.* 1002; "Note" (1959), 72 *Harv. L. Rev.* 723, at 731–33.
84. For a discussion of procedures in the ten states using advisory opinions see "Note" (1956), 69 *Harv. L. Rev.* 1302.

one based on incomplete facts, and a binding authority is likely to be more reliable than an advisory opinion. Thus, if other circumstances are equal and judicial review through a concrete case is feasible, it should be preferred. Before launching a reference the government should be satisfied that its use will be advantageous for one of the reasons previously mentioned.[85] In this way the reference system will be recognized as a valuable supplement to, not a usurpation of, ordinary litigation in concrete cases.

85. See *supra*, at 189–94.

CHAPTER EIGHT

The Future of Judicial Review

Canadian judicial review is a graft on the trunk of an inherited common law system. Parliamentary supremacy was a fundamental principle of that system. But the basic assumption of judicial review is that legislative power is limited, as it must be in a federal state. To ensure the success of this grafting operation it is necessary to accommodate the vital forces of parliamentary supremacy to the restraints of federalism. This creative task – a task primarily for the courts – is by no means yet completed. It is of utmost importance that those engaged in the process should recognize the proper role of judicial review. This role has two aspects.

Narrowly stated, the role of judicial review is the maintenance of the federal system. The courts must ensure that each legislature stays within its own sphere and does not upset the division of powers contemplated by the British North America Act. All branches of government must co-operate with the courts in this endeavour.

The legislatures themselves must facilitate judicial review of their statutes. We have seen that both Parliament and the provincial legislatures have a large potential power to limit or regulate the courts of their own creation. Since the constitution has provided no guarantee of the judicial power, the legislatures must behave responsibly in this field. On the one hand, legislatures should refrain from attempts such as we have seen to bar judicial review. On the other hand, they should where necessary enact measures to improve its techniques. For example, they could remove some of the obstacles arising out of the judicial requirements of standing. To this end they could give a statutory right of action to a federal or provincial taxpayer, in this way giving him privileges equal to those of a municipal taxpayer or a company shareholder. He could then bring an action for a declaration where he feels that government expenditures are being made unlawfully, provided that other prerequisites for judicial review are met. Legislative reform of the reference system would also be desirable. Provision could be made for a trial-like hearing, before a court registrar or other officer, in order that factual material might more readily be introduced. This is particularly important in those provincial courts where the rules of court do not so provide. But a statutory right of hearing in the Supreme Court of Canada would also be valuable. The existing power to order such a hearing is rarely used. If a hearing could be had as a matter of right, the parties might more readily resort to fact-introduction by this means.

Parliament and the legislatures should also use the appropriate machinery of constitutional amendment to guarantee the existence and jurisdiction of the Supreme Court of Canada. At present both these matters are completely subject to alteration by Parliament alone. While it is unthinkable that any Parliament would destroy the effectiveness of the Court, it is not consistent with the Court's role as the ultimate arbiter of constitutional disputes that it should exist at the sufferance of one of the potential disputants. This will be discussed more fully later in this chapter.

The executive branch of government can also assist in making the courts effective as constitutional arbiters. Most importantly, provincial and federal cabinets should be more ready to resort to the courts for a decision as to the constitutionality of various forms of legislation. Without seeking a judicial opinion governments may take, or refrain from, action on the basis of false constitutional assumptions. For example, the *Employment Insurance Reference* of 1937 has no doubt cast an unnecessarily long shadow over various federal social security measures. What was at best a highly questionable decision was given the broadest possible interpretation by federal authorities. As a result it inhibited introduction of old age, survivors', and dependants' pension schemes. It undoubtedly has deterred Parliament from serious thought of federally operated hospitalization or medical care insurance programmes.[1] Moreover, unnecessary bickering continues between the federal and provincial authorities over certain areas of jurisdiction without any judicial resolution ever being sought. For example, some provinces have long complained of federal spending on education, cultural activities, health facilities, or highways. As long as such disputes remain unresolved further federal action is inhibited while provincial grievances continue to foment. A resort to the courts might clarify the legal position, so that attempts at a resolution of such conflicts could at least proceed on an intelligent basis. Otherwise the constitution will be lost sight of in the welter of federal-provincial negotiations constantly in process. Without a clarification of the constitutional position, many of these proceed on a basis of political accommodation: the respective bargaining strength of the parties is measured by popular support, not legal

1. See *supra*, at 197, 198–99.

right. In the process, the fundamental values embodied in the constitutional division of powers may be completely overlooked. A return to law is now required.

To get these issues out of politics and into court the respective governments could most readily resort to constitutional references. Other procedures also available have been described elsewhere in this work.[2] References should be used with discrimination, in situations where the issue is sufficiently precise to make a judicial opinion worthwhile. A completely abstract opinion is likely to be more of a hindrance than a help in the proper maintenance of the federal structure.

The courts themselves must provide the basic guarantee of judicial review, however. First, they must defend their right of review against legislative or executive attack. This may be difficult so long as legislatures have the constitutional power to create, abolish, or regulate the jurisdiction of the courts. Legislative power in this area must be respected up to a point. But the courts must circumvent attempts to prevent judicial review of statutes where, as Chief Justice Kerwin said, the legislature would otherwise "achieve the same results as if the legislation were valid."[3]

Secondly, the courts must relax some of their judicially created barriers to judicial review. In particular they can rationalize the rules of standing to overcome some of the arbitrary distinctions of the common law. They should treat standing in constitutional cases as a discretionary matter. As long as there is a sufficiently precise constitutional issue raised, the courts should be prepared to entertain the proceedings. If this really leads to inconvenience through an overburdening of the judicial system it will be time enough then to exercise the discretion against officious attacks on constitutionality. Similarly, "unnecessary" constitutional issues could be decided, provided that they are precise enough to warrant some opinion being given.

The courts are the most neutral agencies in a federal state for the enforcement of constitutional norms. In these various ways the legislative and executive branches, and the courts themselves, can ensure that the important issues of constitutional law are judicially determined.

Beyond this rather negative role of policing the federal system lies the broader role of constitutional development. In the process of keeping each legislative body within its own sphere, the courts should constantly re-examine the accepted definitions of legislative power. The need and the opportunity for dynamic constitutional interpretation are both apparent.

2. See *supra*, at 104–06, 113–14.
3. *B.C. Power Corp.* v. *B.C. Electric Co.*, [1962] S.C.R. 642, at 644–45, 34 D.L.R. (2d) 196, at 275–76. Discussed *supra*, in chapters two, three, four.

The need arises out of the fading prospects for a flexible constitutional amending procedure. While Canada has had to resort to the Parliament of the United Kingdom for all important constitutional amendments in the past, active consideration has been given in recent years to a Canadian procedure for amending the BNA Act. The procedure most likely to be adopted[4] will require the unanimous consent of Parliament and the ten provincial legislatures before there can be any redistribution of legislative power. It is unlikely that such a procedure will ever produce a constitutional amendment involving changes in provincial jurisdiction.[5] Even if a better formula is ultimately adopted, political factors will deter any significant constitutional change through formal amendments. It is axiomatic that the constitution, like all law, must adjust to changing conditions. Change by formal amendment being a practical impossibility, change by judicial redefinition becomes a necessity.

Is our existing judicial structure adequate for the tasks of enforcing and developing the constitution? As the keystone of this structure, the Supreme Court of Canada requires the closest scrutiny if one is to answer the question. It is fundamental to a vital ongoing federalism predicated on judicial review that its highest appellate court should enjoy the respect of most segments of the country. In Canada there is a growing concern that some provinces will be unwilling henceforth to have constitutional issues decided by the Supreme Court. One of the fundamental complaints is that the Court is a purely federal emanation, a creation of Parliament, which is subject to restriction or even abolition by that body. Appointments to the Court are completely in the hands of the federal cabinet. Though in these senses a purely "federal" institution, its jurisdiction is virtually unlimited, including constitutional disputes between the federal government and the provinces and appeals in matters purely of provincial law. Various suggestions have been made to change the constitution, method of appointment, and modus operandi of the Court.[6] While it is not necessary to canvass all these possibilities here, it is possible to suggest a fundamental approach for revision of the Supreme Court. It is essential that the Court should be given a constitutional rather than a purely statutory basis. Its size, method of appointment, and minimum jurisdiction should all be spelled out in the

4. Set out in the White Paper, *The Amendment of the Constitution of Canada* (1965), at 110–21.
5. See Alexander, "A Constitutional Strait Jacket for Canada" (1965), 43 *Can. B. Rev.* 262; Strayer, "Amendment of the Canadian Constitution: Why the Fulton-Favreau Formula?" (1965) 1 *Can. Legal Studies* 119.
6. See e.g. Morin, "A Constitutional Court for Canada" (1965), 43 *Can. B. Rev.* 545; Azard, "La Cour Suprême du Canada et l'application du droit civil de la Province de Québec" (1965), 43 *Can. B. Rev.* 553; Abel, "The Role of the Supreme Court in Private Law Cases" (1965), 4 *Alberta L. Rev.* 39.

constitution. In defining these requirements, care must be taken to ensure that they will commend themselves to most segments of the country and thus ensure a proper role for the Court in constitutional development.

The number of judges might well be reviewed to ensure that there are enough members to carry on the heavy work of the Court. The method of their appointment could be revised in order to formalize some system of extensive consultation. Whatever changes are made here, they must preserve the integrity of the Court as a judicial, not a representational, institution.

The constitutional guarantee of the Court's jurisdiction should be drafted with particular care, lest the extensive jurisdiction now enjoyed by the Court be narrowed by restraints such as are found in the judicial powers in the American and Australian constitutions. As a minimum, the Supreme Court should be guaranteed a jurisdiction to hear appeals with leave from the final decision (including a reference decision) of the highest court in any province. It should also be made clear that Parliament can confer additional powers on the Supreme Court, whether or not these are judicial in nature. Some may contend that the jurisdiction of the Court should be drastically reduced. It is submitted that the better approach would be to put the composition of the Court beyond dispute and then allow it the jurisdictional freedom to play a full role as a court of final appeal; at liberty to hear and determine questions in their entirety without artificial distinctions based, for example, on the type of law involved in the case.

The opportunity for judicial creativity exists for the taking. The Supreme Court of Canada, whether in its present or a revised form, is now freed from the alien strictures of the Privy Council and should assume the leadership here. Whether that Court pays lip service to the doctrine of stare decisis in constitutional matters is not very important. A court suitably disposed can distinguish earlier decisions where it becomes apparent that conditions have since changed or where a new approach is obviously required. The Supreme Court must avoid the dead hand of precedent in coping with new legislation enacted to deal with new situations. As a Canadian court, versed in Canadian affairs, its duty is clear. And no longer must it move with caution in anticipation of the Privy Council's

> ... old sing-song
> This time in Latin, muttering *stare decisis*.[7]

In this process of adaptation of the constitution, the courts must take more cognizance of the world of facts. In particular they must examine the

7. Scott, "Some Privy Counsel" (1950), 28 *Can.B.Rev.* 780.

factual context in which legislation is enacted, and its practical effect. This will reveal the social and economic dynamics of legislation, thus laying bare the essence of the constitutional problem. To achieve this end old judicial habits of thought must be abandoned, particularly in the field of admissibility of evidence. Judicial review of legislation must be recognized as a unique process. Confusion with the ordinary processes of statutory interpretation or private litigation must cease, to the end that all relevant facts may be placed before the court. The admission of material such as royal commission reports, and the more vigorous exercise of judicial notice are among the reforms required here. It is essential that the courts appreciate the nature of the process in which they are engaged and the relevant issues to be determined. If they can once do this, reforms in rules of evidence should easily follow.

Judicial reform will avail little if parties and their counsel do not take the initiative in fact-introduction. They too must grasp the nature of constitutional adjudication, and ensure that the relevant materials are placed before the court.

Judicial review of legislation can be a vital force for the preservation of Canadian federalism. It can maintain the fundamental divisions of power while redefining these divisions in terms of current developments. But judicial review must be vigorously and intelligently applied. This is the challenge for governments, legislatures, litigants, and, most importantly, the courts themselves.

APPENDIXES

Appendix A

A CONSOLIDATION OF THE
BRITISH NORTH AMERICA ACTS, 1867–1965

(This consolidation is printed with the permission of the Queen's Printer, Ottawa, and Mr. E. A. Driedger, Q.C., who prepared this consolidation. Some schedules included in the consolidation have not been reproduced here, and the original consolidation should be consulted where the full text is required for purposes of interpretation.)

THE BRITISH NORTH AMERICA ACT, 1867*

Consolidated with amendments, as of January 1, 1967

An Act for the Union of Canada, Nova Scotia, and New Brunswick, and the Government thereof; and for Purposes connected therewith.

29th March, 1867.

WHEREAS the Provinces of Canada, Nova Scotia and New Brunswick have expressed their Desire to be federally united into One Dominion under the Crown of the United Kingdom of Great Britain and Ireland, with a Constitution similar in Principle to that of the United Kingdom:

And whereas such a Union would conduce to the Welfare of the Provinces and promote the Interests of the British Empire:

And whereas on the Establishment of the Union by Authority of Parliament it is expedient, not only that the Constitution of the Legislative Authority in the Dominion be provided for, but also that the Nature of the Executive Government therein be declared:

And whereas it is expedient that Provision be made for the eventual Admission into the Union of other Parts of British America:[1]

I *Preliminary*

1 This Act may be cited as The British North America Act, 1867.   Short title

2 Repealed.[2]

● ●

*30 and 31 Victoria, c. 3.

1. The enacting clause was repealed by the *Statute Law Revision Act, 1893*, 56–57 Vict., c. 14 (U.K.). It read as follows:

Be it therefore enacted and declared by the Queen's Most Excellent Majesty, by and with the Advice and Consent of the Lords Spiritual and Temporal, and Commons, in this present Parliament assembled, and by the Authority of the same, as follows:

2. Section 2, repealed by the *Statute Law Revision Act, 1893*, 56–57 Vict., c.14 (U.K.), read as follows:

2. The Provisions of this Act referring to Her Majesty the Queen extend also to the Heirs and Successors of Her Majesty, Kings and Queens of the United Kingdom of Great Britain and Ireland.   *Application of Provisions referring to the Queen*

217

II *Union*

3 It shall be lawful for the Queen, by and with the Advice of Her Majesty's Most Honourable Privy Council, to declare by Proclamation that, on and after a Day therein appointed, not being more than Six Months after the passing of this Act, the Provinces of Canada, Nova Scotia, and New Brunswick shall form and be One Dominion under the Name of Canada; and on and after that Day those Three Provinces shall form and be One Dominion under that Name accordingly.[3]

Declaration of Union

4 Unless it is otherwise expressed or implied, the Name Canada shall be taken to mean Canada as constituted under this Act.[4]

Construction of subsequent Provisions of Act

5 Canada shall be divided into Four Provinces, named Ontario, Quebec, Nova Scotia, and New Brunswick.[5]

Four Provinces

6 The Parts of the Province of Canada (as it exists at the passing of this Act) which formerly constituted respectively the Provinces of Upper Canada and Lower Canada shall be deemed to be severed, and shall form Two separate Provinces. The Part which formerly constituted the Province of Upper Canada shall constitute the Province of Ontario; and the Part which formerly constituted the Province of Lower Canada shall constitute the Province of Quebec.

Provinces of Ontario and Quebec

● ●

3. The first day of July, 1867, was fixed by proclamation dated May 22, 1867.

4. Partially repealed by the *Statute Law Revision Act, 1893*, 56–57 Vict., c. 14 (U.K.). As originally enacted the section read as follows:
   4. The subsequent Provisions of this Act shall, unless it is otherwise expressed or implied, commence and have effect on and after the Union, that is to say, on and after the Day appointed for the Union taking effect in the Queen's Proclamation; and in the same Provisions, unless it is otherwise expressed or implied, the Name Canada shall be taken to mean Canada as constituted under this Act.

5. Canada now consists of ten provinces (Ontario, Quebec, Nova Scotia, New Brunswick, Manitoba, British Columbia, Prince Edward Island, Alberta, Saskatchewan and Newfoundland) and two territories (the Yukon Territory and the Northwest Territories).
   The first territories added to the Union were Rupert's Land and the North-Western Territory, (subsequently designated the Northwest Territories), which were admitted pursuant to section 146 of the *British North America Act, 1867* and the *Rupert's Land Act, 1868*, 31–32 Vict., c. 105 (U.K.), by Order in Council of June 23, 1870, effective July 15, 1870. Prior to the admission of these territories the Parliament of Canada enacted the *Act for the temporary Government of Rupert's Land and the North-Western Territory when united with Canada* (32–33 Vict., c. 3), and the *Manitoba Act* (33 Vict., c. 3), which provided for the formation of the Province of Manitoba.
   British Columbia was admitted into the Union pursuant to section 146 of the *British North America Act, 1867*, by Order in Council of May 16, 1871, effective July 20, 1871.

7   The Provinces of Nova Scotia and New Brunswick shall have the same Limits as at the passing of this Act. Provinces of Nova Scotia and New Brunswick

8   In the general Census of the Population of Canada which is hereby required to be taken in the Year One thousand eight hundred and seventy-one, and in every Tenth Year thereafter, the respective Populations of the Four Provinces shall be distinguished. Decennial Census

III   *Executive Power*

9   The Executive Government and Authority of and over Canada is hereby declared to continue and be vested in the Queen. Declaration of Executive Power in the Queen

10   The Provisions of this Act referring to the Governor General extend and apply to the Governor General of the Time being of Canada, or other the Chief Executive Officer or Administrator for the Time being carrying on the Government of Canada on behalf and in the Name of the Queen, by whatever Title he is designated. Application of Provisions referring to Governor General

11   There shall be a Council to aid and advise in the Government of Canada, to be styled the Queen's Privy Council for Canada; and the Persons who are to be Members of that Council shall be from Time to Time chosen and summoned by the Governor General Constitution of Privy Council for Canada

● ●

Prince Edward Island was admitted pursuant to section 146 of the *British North America Act, 1867*, by Order in Council of June 26, 1873, effective July 1, 1873.

On June 29, 1871, the United Kingdom Parliament enacted the *British North America Act, 1871* (34–35 Vict., c. 28) authorizing the creation of additional provinces out of territories not included in any province. Pursuant to this statute, the Parliament of Canada enacted *The Alberta Act*, (July 20, 1905, 4–5 Edw. VII, c. 3) and *The Saskatchewan Act*, (July 20, 1905, 4–5 Edw. VII, c. 42), providing for the creation of the provinces of Alberta and Saskatchewan respectively. Both these acts came into force on Sept. 1, 1905.

Meanwhile, all remaining British possessions and territories in North America and the islands adjacent thereto, except the colony of Newfoundland and its dependencies, were admitted into the Canadian Confederation by Order in Council dated July 31, 1880.

The Parliament of Canada added portions of the Northwest Territories to the adjoining provinces in 1912 by *The Ontario Boundaries Extension Act*, 2 Geo. V, c. 40, *The Quebec Boundaries Extension Act, 1912*, 2 Geo. V, c. 45, and *The Manitoba Boundaries Extension Act, 1912*, 2 Geo. V, c. 32, and further additions were made to Manitoba by *The Manitoba Boundaries Extension Act, 1930*, 20–21 Geo. V, c. 28.

The Yukon Territory was created out of the Northwest Territories in 1898 by *The Yukon Territory Act*, 61 Vict., c. 6, (Canada).

Newfoundland was added on March 31, 1949, by the *British North America Act, 1949*, (U.K.), 12–13 Geo. VI, c. 22, which ratified the Terms of Union between Canada and Newfoundland.

and sworn in as Privy Councillors, and Members thereof may be from Time to Time removed by the Governor General.

12 All Powers, Authorities, and Functions which under any Act of the Parliament of Great Britain, or of the Parliament of the United Kingdom of Great Britain and Ireland, or of the Legislature of Upper Canada, Lower Canada, Canada, Nova Scotia, or New Brunswick, are at the Union vested in or exerciseable by the respective Governors or Lieutenant Governors of those Provinces, with the Advice, or with the Advice and Consent, of the respective Executive Councils thereof, or in conjunction with those Councils, or with any Number of Members thereof, or by those Governors or Lieutenant Governors individually, shall, as far as the same continue in existence and capable of being exercised after the Union in relation to the Government of Canada, be vested in and exerciseable by the Governor General, with the Advice or with the Advice and Consent of or in conjunction with the Queen's Privy Council for Canada, or any Member thereof, or by the Governor General individually, as the Case requires, subject nevertheless (except with respect to such as exist under Acts of the Parliament of Great Britain or of the Parliament of the United Kingdom of Great Britain and Ireland) to be abolished or altered by the Parliament of Canada.[6]

All Powers under Acts to be exercised by Governor General with Advice of Privy Council, or alone

13 The Provisions of this Act referring to the Governor General in Council shall be construed as referring to the Governor General acting by and with the Advice of the Queen's Privy Council for Canada.

Application of Provisions referring to Governor General in Council

14 It shall be lawful for the Queen, if Her Majesty thinks fit, to authorize the Governor General from Time to Time to appoint any Person or any Persons jointly or severally to be his Deputy or Deputies within any Part or Parts of Canada, and in that Capacity to exercise during the Pleasure of the Governor General such of the Powers, Authorities, and Functions of the Governor General as the Governor General deems it necessary or expedient to assign to him or them, subject to any Limitations or Directions expressed or given by the Queen; but the Appointment of such a Deputy or Deputies shall not affect the Exercise by the Governor General himself of any Power, Authority or Function.

Power to Her Majesty to authorize Governor General to appoint Deputies

15 The Command-in-Chief of the Land and Naval Militia, and of all Naval and Military Forces, of and in Canada, is hereby declared to continue and be vested in the Queen.

Command of armed Forces to continue to be vested in the Queen

16 Until the Queen otherwise directs, the Seat of Government of Canada shall be Ottawa.

Seat of Government of Canada

● ●

6. See the notes to section 129, *infra*.

IV *Legislative Power*

17 There shall be One Parliament for Canada, consisting of the Queen, an Upper House styled the Senate, and the House of Commons.

Constitution of Parliament of Canada

18 The privileges, immunities, and powers to be held, enjoyed, and exercised by the Senate and by the House of Commons, and by the Members thereof respectively, shall be such as are from time to time defined by Act of the Parliament of Canada, but so that any Act of the Parliament of Canada defining such privileges, immunities, and powers shall not confer any privileges, immunities, or powers exceeding those at the passing of such Act held, enjoyed, and exercised by the Commons House of Parliament of the United Kingdom of Great Britain and Ireland, and by the Members thereof.[7]

Privileges, etc. of Houses

19 The Parliament of Canada shall be called together not later than Six Months after the Union.[8]

First Session of the Parliament of Canada

20 There shall be a Session of the Parliament of Canada once at least in every Year, so that Twelve Months shall not intervene between the last Sitting of the Parliament in one Session and its first Sitting in the next Session.[9]

Yearly Session of the Parliament of Canada

THE SENATE

21 The Senate shall, subject to the Provisions of this Act, consist of One Hundred and Two Members, who shall be styled Senators.[10]

Number of Senators

● ●

7. Repealed and re-enacted by the *Parliament of Canada Act, 1875,* 38–39 Vict., c. 38 (U.K.). The original section read as follows:
  18. The Privileges Immunities, and Powers to be held, enjoyed, and exercised by the Senate and by the House of Commons and by the Members thereof respectively shall be such as are from Time to Time defined by Act of the Parliament of Canada, but so that the same shall never exceed those at the passing of this Act held, enjoyed, and exercised by the Commons House of Parliament of the United Kingdom of Great Britain and Ireland and by the Members thereof.

8. Spent. The first session of the first Parliament began on November 6, 1867.

9. The term of the twelfth Parliament was extended by the *British North America Act, 1916,* 6–7 Geo. V, c. 19 (U.K.), which Act was repealed by the *Statute Law Revision Act, 1927,* 17–18 Geo. V, c. 42 (U.K.).

10. As amended by the *British North America Act, 1915,* 5–6 Geo. V, c. 45 (U.K.), and modified by the *British North America Act, 1949,* 12–13 Geo. VI, c. 22 (U.K.).
The original section read as follows:
  21. The Senate shall, subject to the Provisions of this Act, consist of Seventy-two Members, who shall be styled Senators.
  The *Manitoba Act* added two for Manitoba; the Order in Council admitting British Columbia added three; upon admission of Prince

22 In relation to the Constitution of the Senate Canada shall be deemed to consist of Four Divisions:— Representation of Provinces in Senate
1 Ontario;
2 Quebec;
3 The Maritime Provinces, Nova Scotia and New Brunswick, and Prince Edward Island;
4 The Western Provinces of Manitoba, British Columbia, Saskatchewan, and Alberta;
which Four Divisions shall (subject to the Provisions of this Act) be equally represented in the Senate as follows: Ontario by twenty-four senators; Quebec by twenty-four senators; the Maritime Provinces and Prince Edward Island by twenty-four senators, ten thereof representing Nova Scotia, ten thereof representing New Brunswick, and four thereof representing Prince Edward Island; the Western Provinces by twenty-four senators, six thereof representing Manitoba, six thereof representing British Columbia, six thereof representing Saskatchewan, and six thereof representing Alberta; Newfoundland shall be entitled to be represented in the Senate by six members.

In the Case of Quebec each of the Twenty-four Senators representing that Province shall be appointed for One of the Twenty-four Electoral Divisions of Lower Canada specified in Schedule A. to Chapter One of the Consolidated statutes of Canada.[11]

23 The Qualification of a Senator shall be as follows: Qualifications of Senator
1 He shall be of the full age of Thirty Years:
2 He shall be either a natural-born Subject of the Queen, or a Subject of the Queen naturalized by an Act of the Parliament of Great Britain, or of the Parliament of the United Kingdom of Great Britain and Ireland, or of the Legislature of One of the Provinces of Upper Canada, Lower Canada, Canada, Nova Scotia,

● ●

Edward Island four more were provided by section 147 of the *British North America Act, 1867*; *The Alberta Act* and *The Saskatchewan Act* each added four. The Senate was reconstituted at 96 by the *British North America Act, 1915*, and six more Senators were added upon union with Newfoundland.

11. As amended by the *British North America Act, 1915*, and the *British North America Act, 1949*, 12–13 Geo. vi, c. 22 (u.k.). The original section read as follows:

22. In relation to the Constitution of the Senate, Canada shall be deemed to consist of Three Divisions: Representation of Provinces in Senate
1. Ontario;
2. Quebec;
3. The Maritime Provinces, Nova Scotia and New Brunswick;
which Three Divisions shall (subject to the Provisions of this Act) be equally represented in the Senate as follows: Ontario by Twenty-four Senators; Quebec by Twenty-four Senators; and the Maritime Provinces by Twenty-four Senators, Twelve thereof representing Nova Scotia, and Twelve thereof representing New Brunswick.

In the Case of Quebec each of the Twenty-four Senators repesenting that Province shall be appointed for One of the Twenty-four Electoral Divisions of Lower Canada specified in Schedule A. to Chapter One of the Consolidated Statutes of Canada.

or New Brunswick, before the Union, or of the Parliament of
Canada, after the Union:

3   He shall be legally or equitably seised as of Freehold for his
own Use and Benefit of Lands or Tenements held in Free and
Common Socage, or seised or possessed for his own Use and Benefit of Lands or Tenements held in Franc-alleu or in Roture, within
the Province for which he is appointed, of the Value of Four
thousand Dollars, over and above all Rents, Dues, Debts, Charges,
Mortgages, and Incumbrances due or payable out of or charged
on or affecting the same:

4   His Real and Personal Property shall be together worth Four
thousand Dollars over and above his Debts and Liabilities:

5   He shall be resident in the Province for which he is appointed:

6   In the Case of Quebec he shall have his Real Property Qualification in the Electoral Division for which he is appointed, or
shall be resident in that Division.

24   The Governor General shall from Time to Time, in the Queen's *Summons of Senator*
Name, by Instrument under the Great Seal of Canada, summon
qualified Persons to the Senate; and, subject to the Provisions of
this Act, every Person so summoned shall become and be a Member of the Senate and a Senator.

25   Repealed.[12]

26   If at any Time on the Recommendation of the Governor General *Addition of Senators in certain cases*
the Queen thinks fit to direct that Four or Eight Members be added
to the Senate, the Governor General may by Summons to Four or
Eight qualified Persons (as the Case may be), representing equally
the Four Divisions of Canada, add to the Senate accordingly.[13]

27   In case of such Addition being at any Time made, the Governor *Reduction of Senate to normal Number*
General shall not summon any Person to the Senate, except upon
a further like Direction by the Queen on the like Recommendation,
to represent one of the Four Divisions until such Division is
represented by Twenty-four Senators and no more.[14]

• •

12. Repealed by the *Statute Law Revision Act, 1893,* 56–57 Vict., c. 14
(U.K.). The section read as follows:
25. Such Persons shall be first summoned to the Senate as the Queen by Warrant *Summons of*
under Her Majesty's Royal Sign Manual thinks fit to approve, and their Names shall *First Body*
be inserted in the Queen's Proclamation of Union. *of Senators*

13. As amended by the *British North America Act, 1915,* 5–6 Geo. V,
c. 45 (U.K.). The original section read as follows:
26. If at any Time on the Recommendation of the Governor General the Queen *Addition of*
thinks fit to direct that Three or Six Members be added to the Senate, the Governor *Senators in*
General may by Summons to Three or Six qualified Persons (as the Case may be), *certain cases*
representing equally the Three Divisions of Canada, add to the Senate accordingly.

14. As amended by the *British North America Act, 1915,* 5–6 Geo. V,
c. 45 (U.K.). The original section read as follows:
27. In case of such Addition being at any Time made the Governor General shall *Reduction of*
not summon any Person to the Senate, except on a further like Direction by the *Senate to*
Queen on the like Recommendation, until each of the Three Divisions of Canada is *normal*
represented by Twenty-four Senators and no more. *Number*

28 The Number of Senators shall not at any Time exceed One Hundred and ten.[15]

Maximum Number of Senators

29 (1) Subject to subsection (2), a Senator shall, subject to the provisions of this Act, hold his place in the Senate for life.

Tenure of Place in Senate

2 A Senator who is summoned to the Senate after the coming into force of this subsection shall, subject to this Act, hold his place in the Senate until he attains the age of seventy-five years.[15A]

Retirement upon attaining age of seventy-five years

30 A Senator may by Writing under his Hand addressed to the Governor General resign his Place in the Senate, and thereupon the same shall be vacant.

Resignation of Place in Senate

31 The Place of a Senator shall become vacant in any of the following Cases:

Disqualification of Senators

1 If for Two consecutive Sessions of the Parliament he fails to give his Attendance in the Senate:

2 If he takes an Oath or makes a Declaration or Acknowledgment of Allegiance, Obedience, or Adherence to a Foreign Power, or does an Act whereby he becomes a Subject or Citizen, or entitled to the Rights or Privileges of a Subject or Citizen, of a Foreign Power:

3 If he is adjudged Bankrupt or Insolvent, or applies for the Benefit of any Law relating to Insolvent Debtors, or becomes a public Defaulter:

4 If he is attainted of Treason or convicted of Felony or of any infamous Crime:

5 If he ceases to be qualified in respect of Property or of Residence; provided, that a Senator shall not be deemed to have ceased to be qualified in respect of Residence by reason only of his residing at the Seat of the Government of Canada while holding an Office under that Government requiring his Presence there.

32 When a Vacancy happens in the Senate by Resignation, Death, or otherwise, the Governor General shall by Summons to a fit and qualified Person fill the Vacancy.

Summons on Vacancy in Senate

33 If any Question arises respecting the Qualification of a Senator or a Vacancy in the Senate the same shall be heard and determined by the Senate.

Questions as to Qualifications and Vacancies in Senate

● ●

15. As amended by the *British North America Act, 1915*, 5–6 Geo. v, c. 45 (U.K.). The original section read as follows:

28. The Number of Senators shall not at any Time exceed Seventy-eight.

Maximum Number of Senators

15A. As enacted by the *British North America Act, 1965*, Statutes of Canada, 1965, c. 4 which came into force on the 1st of June, 1965. The original section read as follows:

29. A Senator shall, subject to the Provisions of this Act, hold his Place in the Senate for Life.

Tenure of Place in Senate

34 The Governor General may from Time to Time, by Instrument under the Great Seal of Canada, appoint a Senator to be Speaker of the Senate, and may remove him and appoint another in his Stead.[16]

35 Until the Parliament of Canada otherwise provides, the Presence of at least Fifteen Senators, including the Speaker, shall be necessary to constitute a Meeting of the Senate for the Exercise of its Powers.

36 Questions arising in the Senate shall be decided by a Majority of Voices, and the Speaker shall in all Cases have a Vote, and when the Voices are equal the Decision shall be deemed to be in the Negative.

THE HOUSE OF COMMONS

37 The House of Commons shall, subject to the Provisions of this Act, consist of Two Hundred and sixty-five Members of whom Eighty-five shall be elected for Ontario, Seventy-five for Quebec, Twelve for Nova Scotia, Ten for New Brunswick, Fourteen for Manitoba, Twenty-two for British Columbia, Four for Prince Edward Island, Seventeen for Alberta, Seventeen for Saskatchewan, Seven for Newfoundland, One for the Yukon Territory and One for the Northwest Territories.[17]

38 The Governor General shall from Time to Time, in the Queen's Name, by Instrument under the Great Seal of Canada, summon and call together the House of Commons.

39 A Senator shall not be capable of being elected or of sitting or voting as a Member of the House of Commons.

40 Until the Parliament of Canada otherwise provides, Ontario, Quebec, Nova Scotia, and New Brunswick shall, for the Purposes of the Election of Members to serve in the House of Commons, be divided into Electoral Districts as follows:
1 *Ontario.* Ontario shall be divided into the Counties, Ridings of

• •

16. Provision for exercising the functions of Speaker during his absence is made by the *Speaker of the Senate Act*, R.S.C. 1952, c. 255. Doubts as to the power of Parliament to enact such an Act were removed by the *Canadian Speaker (Appointment of Deputy) Act, 1895*, 59 Vict., c. 3 (U.K.).

17. As altered by the *Representation Act*, R.S.C. 1952, c. 334, as amended by s.c. 1962, c. 17. The original section read as follows:
37. The House of Commons shall, subject to the Provisions of this Act, consist of the One hundred and eighty-one Members, of whom Eighty-two shall be elected for Ontario, Sixty-five for Quebec, Nineteen for Nova Scotia, and Fifteen for New Brunswick.
See now the *Electoral Boundaries Readjustment Act*, Statutes of Canada, 1964–65, c. 31.

Counties, Cities, Parts of Cities, and Towns enumerated in the First Schedule to this Act, each whereof shall be an Electoral District, each such District as numbered in that Schedule being entitled to return One Member.

2 *Quebec.* Quebec shall be divided into Sixty-five Electoral Districts, composed of the Sixty-five Electoral Divisions into which Lower Canada is at the passing of this Act divided under Chapter Two of the Consolidated Statutes of Canada, Chapter Seventy-five of the Consolidated Statutes for Lower Canada, and the Act of the Province of Canada of the Twenty-third Year of the Queen, Chapter One, or any other Act amending the same in force at the Union, so that each such Electoral Division shall be for the Purposes of this Act an Electoral District entitled to return One Member.

3 *Nova Scotia.* Each of the Eighteen Counties of Nova Scotia shall be an Electoral District. The County of Halifax shall be entitled to return Two Members, and each of the other Counties One Member.

4 *New Brunswick.* Each of the Fourteen Counties into which New Brunswick is divided, including the City and County of St. John, shall be an Electoral District. The City of St. John shall also be a separate Electoral District. Each of those Fifteen Electoral Districts shall be entitled to return One Member.[18]

41 Until the Parliament of Canada otherwise provides, all Laws in force in the several Provinces at the Union relative to the following Matters or any of them, namely,—the Qualifications and Disqualifications of Persons to be elected or to sit or vote as Members of the House of Assembly or Legislative Assembly in the several Provinces, the Voters at Elections of such Members, the Oaths to be taken by Voters, the Returning Officers, their Powers and Duties, the Proceedings at Elections, the Periods during which Elections may be continued, the Trial of controverted Elections, and Proceedings incident thereto, the vacating of Seats of Members, and the Execution of new Writs in case of Seats vacated otherwise than by Dissolution,—shall respectively apply to Elections of Members to serve in the House of Commons for the same several Provinces. *Continuance of existing Election Laws until Parliament of Canada otherwise provides*

Provided that, until the Parliament of Canada otherwise provides, at any Election for a Member of the House of Commons for the District of Algoma, in addition to Persons qualified by the Law of the Province of Canada to vote, every Male British Subject, aged Twenty-one Years or upwards, being a Householder, shall have a Vote.[19]

● ●

18. Spent. The electoral districts are now set out in the *Representation Act*, R.S.C. 1952, c. 334, as amended. See also the *Electoral Boundaries Readjustment Act*, Statutes of Canada, 1964–65, c. 31.

19. Spent. Elections are now provided for by the *Canada Elections Act*,

42 Repealed.[20]

43 Repealed.[21]

44 The House of Commons on its first assembling after a General Election shall proceed with all practicable Speed to elect One of its Members to be Speaker. *As to Election of Speaker of House of Commons*

45 In case of a Vacancy happening in the Office of Speaker by Death, Resignation, or otherwise, the House of Commons shall with all practicable Speed proceed to elect another of its Members to be Speaker. *As to filling up Vacancy in Office of Speaker*

46 The Speaker shall preside at all Meetings of the House of Commons. *Speaker to preside*

47 Until the Parliament of Canada otherwise provides, in case of the Absence for any Reason of the Speaker from the Chair of the House of Commons for a Period of Forty-eight consecutive Hours, the House may elect another of its Members to act as Speaker, and the Member so elected shall during the Continuance of such Absence of the Speaker have and execute all the Powers, Privileges, and Duties of Speaker.[22] *Provision in case of Absence of Speaker*

48 The Presence of at least Twenty Members of the House of Commons shall be necessary to constitute a Meeting of the House for the Exercise of its Powers, and for that Purpose the Speaker shall be reckoned as a Member. *Quorum of House of Commons*

• •

s.c. 1960, c. 38; controverted elections by the *Dominion Controverted Elections Act*, R.S.C. 1952, c. 87; qualifications and disqualifications of members by the *House of Commons Act*, R.S.C. 1952, c. 143 and the *Senate and House of Commons Act*, R.S.C. 1952, c. 249.

20. Repealed by the *Statute Law Revision Act, 1893*, 56–57 Vict., c. 14 (U.K.). The section read as follows:

42. For the First Election of Members to serve in the House of Commons the Governor General shall cause Writs to be issued by such Person, in such Form, and addressed to such Returning Officers as he thinks fit. *Writs for First Election*

The Person issuing Writs under this Section shall have the like Powers as are possessed at the Union by the Officers charged with the issuing of Writs for the Election of Members to serve in the respective House of Assembly or Legislative Assembly of the Province of Canada, Nova Scotia, or New Brunswick; and the Returning Officers to whom Writs are directed under this Section shall have the like Powers as are possessed at the Union by the Officers charged with the returning of Writs for the Election of Members to serve in the same respective House of Assembly or Legislative Assembly.

21. Repealed by the *Statute Law Revision Act, 1893*, 56–57 Vict., c. 14 (U.K.). The section read as follows:

43. In case a Vacancy in the Representation in the House of Commons of any Electoral District happens before the Meeting of the Parliament, or after the Meeting of the Parliament before Provision is made by the Parliament in this Behalf, the Provisions of the last foregoing Section of this Act shall extend and apply to the issuing and returning of a Writ in respect of such vacant District. *As to Casual Vacancies*

22. Provision for exercising the functions of Speaker during his absence is now made by the *Speaker of the House of Commons Act*, R.S.C. 1952, c. 254.

49 Questions arising in the House of Commons shall be decided by a Majority of Voices other than that of the Speaker, and when the Voices are equal, but not otherwise, the Speaker shall have a Vote. *Voting in House of Commons*

50 Every House of Commons shall continue for Five Years from the Day of the Return of the Writs for choosing the House (subject to be sooner dissolved by the Governor General), and no longer. *Duration of House of Commons*

51 1 Subject as hereinafter provided, the number of members of the House of Commons shall be two hundred and sixty-three and the representation of the provinces therein shall forthwith upon the coming into force of this section and thereafter on the completion of each decennial census be readjusted by such authority, in such manner, and from such time as the Parliament of Canada from time to time provides, subject and according to the following rules: *Readjustment representation in Commons*

I There shall be assigned to each of the provinces a number of members computed by dividing the total population of the provinces by two hundred and sixty-one and by dividing the population of each province by the quotient so obtained, disregarding, except as hereinafter in this section provided, the remainder, if any, after the said process of division. *Rules*

II If the total number of members assigned to all the provinces pursuant to rule one is less than two hundred and sixty-one, additional members shall be assigned to the provinces (one to a province) having remainders in the computation under rule one commencing with the province having the largest remainder and continuing with the other provinces in the order of the magnitude of their respective remainders until the total number of members assigned is two hundred and sixty-one.

III Notwithstanding anything in this section, if upon completion of a computation under rules one and two, the number of members to be assigned to a province is less than the number of senators representing the said province, rules one and two shall cease to apply in respect of the said province, and there shall be assigned to the said province a number of members equal to the said number of senators.

IV In the event that rules one and two cease to apply in respect of a province then, for the purposes of computing the number of members to be assigned to the provinces in respect of which rules one and two continue to apply, the total population of the provinces shall be reduced by the number of the population of the province in respect of which rules one and two have ceased to apply and the number two hundred and sixty-one shall be reduced by the number of members assigned to such province pursuant to rule three.

V On any such readjustment the number of members for any province shall not be reduced by more than fifteen per cent below the representation to which such province was entitled under rules one to four of this subsection at the last preceding readjustment of the representation of that province, and there shall be no reduction in the representation of any province as a result of which that province would have a smaller number of members than any other province that according to the results of the then last decennial census did not have a larger population; but for the purposes of any subsequent readjustment of representation under this section any increase in the number of members of the House of Commons resulting from the application of this rule shall not be included in the divisor mentioned in rules one to four of this subsection.

VI Such readjustment shall not take effect until the termination of the then existing Parliament.

2 The Yukon Territory as constituted by chapter forty-one of the statutes of Canada, 1901, shall be entitled to one member, and such other part of Canada not comprised within a province as may from time to time be defined by the Parliament of Canada shall be entitled to one member.[23]

Yukon Territory and other part not comprised within a province

• •

23. As enacted by the *British North America Act, 1952*, R.S.C. 1952, c. 304, which came into force on June 18, 1952. The section, as originally enacted, read as follows:

51. On the Completion of the Census in the Year One Thousand eight hundred and seventy-one, and of each subsequent decennial Census, the Representation of the Four Provinces shall be re-adjusted by such Authority, in such Manner, and from such Time, as the Parliament of Canada from Time to Time provides, subject and according to the following Rules:

Decennial Re-adjustment of Representation

1 Quebec shall have the fixed Number of Sixty-five Members.
2 There shall be assigned to each of the other Provinces such a Number of Members as will bear the same Proportion to the Number of its Population (ascertained at such Census) as the Number Sixty-five bears to the Number of the Population of Quebec (so ascertained):
3 In the Computation of the Number of Members for a Province a fractional Part not exceeding One Half of the whole Number requisite for entitling the Province to a Member shall be disregarded; but a fractional Part exceeding One Half of that Number shall be equivalent to the whole Number:
4 On any such Re-adjustment the Number of Members for a Province shall not be reduced unless the Proportion which the Number of the Population of the Province bore to the Number of the aggregate Population of Canada at the then last preceding Re-adjustment of the Number of Members for the Province is ascertained at the then latest Census to be diminished by One Twentieth Part or upwards:
5 Such Re-adjustment shall not take effect until the Termination of the then existing Parliament.

The section was amended by the *Statute Law Revision Act, 1893*, 56–57 Vict., c. 14 (U.K.) by repealing the words from "of the census" to "seventy-one and" and the word "subsequent".

By the *British North America Act, 1943*, 6–7 Geo. VI, c. 30 (U.K.) redistribution of seats following the 1941 census was postponed until the first session of Parliament after the war. The section was re-enacted by the *British North America Act, 1946*, 9–10 Geo. VI, c. 63 (U.K.) to read as follows:

51. (1) The number of members of the House of Commons shall be two hundred and fifty-five and the representation of the provinces therein shall forthwith upon the coming into force of this section and thereafter on the completion of each decennial census be readjusted by such authority, in such manner, and from such time as the Parliament of Canada from time to time provides, subject and according to the following rules:—

1 Subject as hereinafter provided, there shall be assigned to each of the provinces a number of members computed by dividing the total population of the provinces by two hundred and fifty-four and by dividing the population of each province by the quotient so obtained, disregarding, except as hereinafter in this section provided, the remainder, if any, after the said process of division.
2 If the total number of members assigned to all the provinces pursuant to rule one is less than two hundred and fifty-four, additional members shall be assigned to the provinces (one to a province) having remainders in the computation under rule one commencing with the province having the largest remainder and continuing

51A Notwithstanding anything in this Act a province shall always be entitled to a number of members in the House of Commons not less than the number of senators representing such province.[24]

Constitution of House of Commons

52 The Number of Members of the House of Commons may be from Time to Time increased by the Parliament of Canada, provided the proportionate Representation of the Provinces prescribed by this Act is not thereby disturbed.

Increase of Number of House of Commons

MONEY VOTES; ROYAL ASSENT

53 Bills for appropriating any Part of the Public Revenue, or for imposing any Tax or Impost, shall originate in the House of Commons.

Appropriation and Tax Bills

54 It shall not be lawful for the House of Commons to adopt or pass any Vote, Resolution, Address, or Bill for the Appropriation of any Part of the Public Revenue, or of any Tax or Impost, to any Purpose that has not been first recommended to that House by Message of the Governor General in the Session in which such Vote, Resolution, Address, or Bill is proposed.

Recommendation of Money Votes

55 Where a Bill passed by the Houses of the Parliament is presented to the Governor General for the Queen's Assent, he shall declare, according to his Discretion, but subject to the Provisions of this Act and to Her Majesty's Instructions, either that he assents thereto in the Queen's Name, or that he withholds the Queen's Assent, or that he reserves the Bill for the Signification of the Queen's Pleasure.

Royal Assent to Bills, etc.

56 Where the Governor General assents to a Bill in the Queen's Name, he shall by the first convenient Opportunity send an authentic Copy of the Act to one of Her Majesty's Principal Secretaries of State, and if the Queen in Council within Two Years after Receipt

Disallowance by Order in Council of Act assented to by Governor General

• •

with the other provinces in the order of the magnitude of their respective remainders until the total number of members assigned is two hundred and fifty-four.

3 Notwithstanding anything in this section, if upon completion of a computation under rules one and two, the number of members to be assigned to a province is less than the number of senators representing the said province, rules one and two shall cease to apply in respect of the said province, and there shall be assigned to the said province a number of members equal to the said number of senators.

4 In the event that rules one and two cease to apply in respect of a province then, for the purpose of computing the number of members to be assigned to the provinces in respect of which rules one and two continue to apply, the total population of the provinces shall be reduced by the number of the population of the province in respect of which rules one and two have ceased to apply and the number two hundred and fifty-four shall be reduced by the number of members assigned to such province pursuant to rule three.

5 Such readjustment shall not take effect until the termination of the then existing Parliament.

(2) The Yukon Territory as constituted by Chapter forty-one of the Statutes of Canada, 1901, together with any Part of Canada not comprised within a province which may from time to time be included therein by the Parliament of Canada for the purposes of representation in Parliament, shall be entitled to one member.

24. As enacted by the *British North America Act, 1915*, 5–6 Geo. V, c. 45 (U.K.).

thereof by the Secretary of State thinks fit to disallow the Act, such Disallowance (with a Certificate of the Secretary of State of the Day on which the Act was received by him) being signified by the Governor General, by Speech or Message to each of the Houses of the Parliament or by Proclamation, shall annul the Act from and after the Day of such Signification.

57 A Bill reserved for the Signification of the Queen's Pleasure shall not have any Force unless and until, within Two Years from the Day on which it was presented to the Governor General for the Queen's Assent, the Governor General signifies, by Speech or Message to each of the Houses of the Parliament or by Proclamation, that it has received the Assent of the Queen in Council.

Signification of Queen's Pleasure on Bill reserved

An Entry of every such Speech, Message, or Proclamation shall be made in the Journal of each House, and a Duplicate thereof duly attested shall be delivered to the proper Officer to be kept among the Records of Canada.

v *Provincial Constitutions*

EXECUTIVE POWER

58 For each Province there shall be an Officer, styled the Lieutenant Governor, appointed by the Governor General in Council by Instrument under the Great Seal of Canada.

Appointment of Lieutenant Governors of Provinces

59 A Lieutenant Governor shall hold Office during the Pleasure of the Governor General; but any Lieutenant Governor appointed after the Commencement of the First Session of the Parliament of Canada shall not be removeable within Five Years from his Appointment, except for Cause assigned, which shall be communicated to him in Writing within One Month after the Order for his Removal is made, and shall be communicated by Message to the Senate and to the House of Commons within One Week thereafter if the Parliament is then sitting, and if not then within One Week after the Commencement of the next Session of the Parliament.

Tenure of Office of Lieutenant Governor

60 The Salaries of the Lieutenant Governors shall be fixed and provided by the Parliament of Canada.[25]

Salaries of Lieutenant Governors

61 Every Lieutenant Governor shall, before assuming the Duties of his Office, make and subscribe before the Governor General or some Person authorized by him Oaths of Allegiance and Office similar to those taken by the Governor General.

Oaths, etc., of Lieutenant Governor

● ●

25. Provided for by the *Salaries Act*, R.S.C. 1952, c. 243 as amended by S.C. 1963, c. 41.

62   The Provisions of this Act referring to the Lieutenant Governor extend and apply to the Lieutenant Governor for the Time being of each Province, or other the Chief Executive Officer or Administrator for the Time being carrying on the Government of the Province, by whatever Title he is designated. Application of provisions referring to Lieutenant Governor

63   The Executive Council of Ontario and of Quebec shall be composed of such Persons as the Lieutenant Governor from Time to Time thinks fit, and in the first instance of the following Officers, namely,—the Attorney General, the Secretary and Registrar of the Province, the Treasurer of the Province, the Commissioner of Crown Lands, and the Commissioner of Agriculture and Public Works, with in Quebec the Speaker of the Legislative Council and the Solicitor General.[26] Appointment of Executive Officers for Ontario and Quebec

64   The Constitution of the Executive Authority in each of the Provinces of Nova Scotia and New Brunswick shall, subject to the Provisions of this Act, continue as it exists at the Union until altered under the Authority of this Act.[26A] Executive Government of Nova Scotia and New Brunswick

65   All Powers, Authorities, and Functions which under any Act of the Parliament of Great Britain, or of the Parliament of the United Kingdom of Great Britain and Ireland, or of the Legislature of Upper Canada, Lower Canada, or Canada, were or are before or at the Union vested in or exerciseable by the respective Governors or Lieutenant Governors of those Provinces, with the Advice or with the Advice and Consent of the respective Executive Councils thereof, or in conjunction with those Councils, or with any Number of Members thereof, or by those Governors or Lieutenant Governors individually, shall, as far as the same are capable of being exercised after the Union in relation to the Government of Ontario and Quebec respectively, be vested in and shall or may be exercised by the Lieutenant Governor of Ontario and Quebec respectively, with the Advice or with the Advice and Consent of or in conjunction with the respective Executive Councils, or any Members thereof, or by the Lieutenant Governor individually, as the Case requires, subject nevertheless (except with respect to such as exist under Acts of the Parliament of Great Britain, or of the Parliament of the United Kingdom of Great Britain and Ireland,) to be Powers to be exercised by Lieutenant Governor of Ontario or Quebec with Advice, or alone

• •

26. Now provided for in Ontario by the *Executive Council Act*, R.S.O. 1960, c. 127, and in Quebec by the *Executive Power Act*, R.S.Q. 1964, c. 9.

26A. A similar provision was included in each of the instruments admitting British Columbia, Prince Edward Island, and Newfoundland. The Executive Authorities for Manitoba, Alberta and Saskatchewan were established by the statutes creating those provinces. See the footnotes to section 5, *supra*.

abolished or altered by the respective Legislatures of Ontario and Quebec.[27]

66 The Provisions of this Act referring to the Lieutenant Governor in Council shall be construed as referring to the Lieutenant Governor of the Province acting by and with the Advice of the Executive Council thereof.

Application of Provisions referring to Lieutenant Governor in Council

67 The Governor General in Council may from Time to Time appoint an Administrator to execute the Office and Functions of Lieutenant Governor during his Absence, Illness, or other Inability.

Administration in Absence, etc., of Lieutenant Governor

68 Unless and until the Executive Government of any Province otherwise directs with respect to that Province, the Seats of Government of the Provinces shall be as follows, namely,—of Ontario, the City of Toronto; of Quebec, the City of Quebec; of Nova Scotia, the City of Halifax; and of New Brunswick, the City of Fredericton.

Seats of Provincial Governments

LEGISLATIVE POWER

1 ONTARIO

69 There shall be a Legislature for Ontario consisting of the Lieutenant Governor and of One House, styled the Legislative Assembly of Ontario.

Legislature for Ontario

70 The Legislative Assembly of Ontario shall be composed of Eighty-two Members, to be elected to represent the Eighty-two Electoral Districts set forth in the First Schedule to this Act.[28]

Electoral districts

2 QUEBEC

71 There shall be a Legislature for Quebec consisting of the Lieutenant Governor and of Two Houses, styled the Legislative Council of Quebec and the Legislative Assembly of Quebec.

Legislature for Quebec

72 The Legislative Council of Quebec shall be composed of Twenty-four Members, to be appointed by the Lieutenant Governor, in the Queen's Name, by Instrument under the Great Seal of Quebec, One being appointed to represent each of the Twenty-four Electoral Divisions of Lower Canada in this Act referred to, and each

Constitution of Legislative Council

27. See the notes to section 129, *infra*.

28. Spent. Now covered by the *Representation Act*, R.S.O. 1960, c. 353, as amended by S.O. 1962–63, c. 125, which provides that the Assembly shall consist of 108 members, representing the electoral districts set forth in the Schedule to that Act.

holding Office for the Term of his Life, unless the Legislature of Quebec otherwise provides under the Provisions of this Act.[29]

73 The Qualifications of the Legislative Councillors of Quebec shall be the same as those of the Senators for Quebec.[30]

Qualification of Legislative Councillors

74 The Place of a Legislative Councillor of Quebec shall become vacant in the Cases, *mutatis mutandis*, in which the Place of Senator becomes vacant.

Resignation, Disqualification, etc.

75 When Vacancy happens in the Legislative Council of Quebec by Resignation, Death, or otherwise, the Lieutenant Governor, in the Queen's Name, by Instrument under the Great Seal of Quebec, shall appoint a fit and qualified Person to fill the Vacancy.

Vacancies

76 If any Question arises respecting the Qualification of a Legislative Councillor of Quebec, or a Vacancy in the Legislative Council of Quebec, the same shall be heard and determined by the Legislative Council.

Questions as to Vacancies, etc.

77 The Lieutenant Governor may from Time to Time, by Instrument under the Great Seal of Quebec, appoint a Member of the Legislative Council of Quebec to be Speaker thereof, and may remove him and appoint another in his Stead.[31]

Speaker of Legislative Council

78 Until the Legislature of Quebec otherwise provides, the Presence of at least Ten Members of the Legislative Council, including the Speaker, shall be necessary to constitute a Meeting for the Exercise of its Powers.

Quorum of Legislative Council

79 Questions arising in the Legislative Council of Quebec shall be decided by a Majority of Voices, and the Speaker shall in all Cases have a Vote, and when the Voices are equal the Decision shall be deemed to be in the Negative.

Voting in Legislative Council

80 The Legislative Assembly of Quebec shall be composed of Sixty-five Members, to be elected to represent the Sixty-five Electoral Divisions or Districts of Lower Canada in this Act referred to, subject to Alteration thereof by the Legislature of Quebec: Provided that it shall not be lawful to present to the Lieutenant Governor of Quebec for Assent any Bill for altering the Limits of any of the Electoral Divisions or Districts mentioned in the Second

Constitution of Legislative Assembly of Quebec

● ●

29. Spent. Now covered by the *Legislature Act*, R.S.Q. 1964, c. 6 as amended by S.Q. 1965, c. 11; the membership remains at twenty-four, representing the divisions set forth in the *Territorial Division Act*, R.S.Q. 1964, c. 5, as amended by S.Q. 1965, c. 12.

30. Altered by the *Legislature Act*, R.S.Q. 1964, c. 6, s. 7, which provides that it shall be sufficient for any member to be domiciled, and to possess his property qualifications, within the Province of Quebec.

31. Spent. Now covered by the *Legislature Act*, R.S.Q. 1964, c. 6.

Schedule to this Act, unless the Second and Third Readings of such Bill have been passed in the Legislative Assembly with the Concurrence of the Majority of the Members representing all those Electoral Divisions or Districts, and the Assent shall not be given to such Bill unless an Address has been presented by the Legislative Assembly to the Lieutenant Governor stating that it has been so passed.[32]

3 ONTARIO AND QUEBEC

81 Repealed.[33]

82 The Lieutenant Governor of Ontario and of Quebec shall from Time to Time, in the Queen's Name, by Instrument under the Great Seal of the Province, summon and call together the Legislative Assembly of the Province.

Summoning of Legislative Assemblies

83 Until the Legislature of Ontario or of Quebec otherwise provides, a Person accepting or holding in Ontario or in Quebec any Office, Commission, or Employment, permanent or temporary, at the Nomination of the Lieutenant Governor, to which an annual Salary, or any Fee, Allowance, Emolument, or Profit of any Kind or Amount whatever from the Province is attached, shall not be eligible as a Member of the Legislative Assembly of the respective Province, nor shall he sit or vote as such; but nothing in this Section shall make ineligible any Person being a Member of the Executive Council of the respective Province, or holding any of the following Offices, that is to say, the Offices of Attorney General, Secretary and Registrar of the Province, Treasurer of the Province, Commissioner of Crown Lands, and Commissioner of Agriculture and Public Works, and in Quebec Solicitor General, or shall disqualify him to sit or vote in the House for which he is elected, provided he is elected while holding such Office.[34]

Restriction on election of Holders of offices

84 Until the Legislatures of Ontario and Quebec respectively otherwise provide, all Laws which at the Union are in force in those Provinces respectively, relative to the following Matters, or any of

Continuance of existing Election Laws

● ●

32. Altered by the *Legislature Act*, R.S.Q. 1964, c. 6 as amended by S.Q. 1965, c. 11 and the *Territorial Division Act*, R.S.Q. 1964, c. 5 as amended by S.Q. 1965, c. 10; there are now 108 members representing the districts set out in the *Territorial Division Act*.

33. Repealed by the *Statute Law Revision Act, 1893*, 56–57 Vict., c. 14 (U.K.). The section read as follows:

81. The Legislatures of Ontario and Quebec respectively shall be called together not later than Six Months after the Union.

First Session of Legislatures

34. Probably spent. The subject-matter of this section is now covered in Ontario by the *Legislative Assembly Act*, R.S.O. 1960, c. 208, and in Quebec by the *Legislature Act*, R.S.Q. 1964, c. 6.

them, namely,—the Qualifications and Disqualifications of Persons to be elected or to sit or vote as Members of the Assembly of Canada, the Qualifications or Disqualifications of Voters, the Oaths to be taken by Voters, the Returning Officers, their Powers and Duties, the Proceedings at Elections, the Periods during which such Elections may be continued, and the Trial of controverted Elections and the Proceedings incident thereto, the vacating of the Seats of Members and the issuing and execution of new Writs in case of Seats vacated otherwise than by Dissolution,—shall respectively apply to Elections of Members to serve in the respective Legislative Assemblies of Ontario and Quebec.

Provided that, until the Legislature of Ontario otherwise provides, at any Election for a Member of the Legislative Assembly of Ontario for the District of Algoma, in addition to Persons qualified by the Law of the Province of Canada to vote, every male British Subject, aged Twenty-one Years or upwards, being a Householder, shall have a vote.[35]

85 Every Legislative Assembly of Ontario and every Legislative Assembly of Quebec shall continue for Four Years from the Day of the Return of the Writs for choosing the same (subject nevertheless to either the Legislative Assembly of Ontario or the Legislative Assembly of Quebec being sooner dissolved by the Lieutenant Governor of the Province), and no longer.[36] *Duration of Legislative Assemblies*

86 There shall be a Session of the Legislature of Ontario and of that of Quebec once at least in every Year, so that Twelve Months shall not intervene between the last Sitting of the Legislature in each Province in one Session and its first Sitting in the next Session. *Yearly Session of Legislature*

87 The following Provisions of this Act respecting the House of Commons of Canada shall extend and apply to the Legislative Assemblies of Ontario and Quebec, that is to say,—the Provisions relating to the Election of a Speaker originally and on Vacancies, the Duties of the Speaker, the Absence of the Speaker, the Quorum, and the Mode of voting, as if those Provisions were here re-enacted and made applicable in Terms to each such Legislative Assembly. *Speaker, Quorum, etc.*

• •

35. Probably spent. The subject-matter of this section is now covered in Ontario by the *Election Act*, R.S.O. 1960, c. 118, the *Controverted Elections Act*, R.S.O. 1960, c. 65 and the *Legislative Assembly Act*, R.S.O. 1960, c. 208, in Quebec by the *Elections Act*, R.S.Q. 1964, c. 7, the *Provincial Controverted Elections Act*, R.S.Q. 1964, c. 8 and the *Legislature Act*, R.S.Q. 1964, c. 6.

36. The maximum duration of the Legislative Assembly for Ontario and Quebec has been changed to five years by the *Legislative Assembly Act*, R.S.O. 1960, c. 208, and the *Legislature Act*, R.S.Q. 1964, c. 6 respectively.

4 NOVA SCOTIA AND NEW BRUNSWICK

88 The Constitution of the Legislature of each of the Provinces of Nova Scotia and New Brunswick shall, subject to the Provisions of this Act, continue as it exists at the Union until altered under the Authority of this Act.[37]

89 Repealed.[38]

6 THE FOUR PROVINCES

90 The following Provisions of this Act respecting the Parliament of Canada, namely,—the Provisions relating to Appropriation and Tax Bills, the Recommendation of Money Votes, the Assent to Bills, the Disallowance of Acts, and the Signification of Pleasure on Bills reserved,—shall extend and apply to the Legislatures of the several Provinces as if those Provisions were here re-enacted and made applicable in Terms to the respective Provinces and the Legislatures thereof, with the Substitution of the Lieutenant Governor of the Province for the Governor General, of the Governor General for the Queen and for a Secretary of State, of One Year for Two Years, and of the Province for Canada.

VI *Distribution of Legislative Powers*

POWERS OF THE PARLIAMENT

91 It shall be lawful for the Queen, by and with the Advice and Consent of the Senate and House of Commons, to make Laws for the Peace, Order, and good Government of Canada, in relation to all Matters not coming within the Classes of Subjects by this Act

• •

37. Partially repealed by the *Statute Law Revision Act, 1893,* 56–57 Vict., c. 14 (U.K.) which deleted the following concluding words of the original enactment:

and the House of Assembly of New Brunswick existing at the passing of this Act shall, unless sooner dissolved, continue for the Period for which it was elected.

A similar provision was included in each of the instruments admitting British Columbia, Prince Edward Island, and Newfoundland. The Legislatures of Manitoba, Alberta and Saskatchewan were established by the statutes creating those provinces. See the footnotes to section 5, *supra.*

38. Repealed by the *Statute Law Revision Act, 1893,* 56–57 Vict., c. 14 (U.K.). The section read as follows:

5 *Ontario, Quebec, and Nova Scotia.* 89. Each of the Lieutenant Governors of Ontario, Quebec and Nova Scotia shall cause Writs to be issued for the First Election of Members of the Legislative Assembly thereof in such Form and by such Person as he thinks fit, and at such Time and addressed to such Returning Officer as the Governor General directs, and so that the First Election of Member of Assembly for any Electoral District or any Subdivision thereof shall be held at the same Time and at the same Places as the Election for a Member to serve in the House of Commons of Canada for that Electoral District.

Marginal notes:
- Constitutions of Legislatures of Nova Scotia and New Brunswick
- Application to Legislatures of Provisions respecting Money Votes, etc.
- Legislative Authority of Parliament of Canada
- First Elections

assigned exclusively to the Legislatures of the Provinces; and for greater Certainty, but not so as to restrict the Generality of the foregoing Terms of this Section, it is hereby declared that (notwithstanding anything in this Act) the exclusive Legislative Authority of the Parliament of Canada extends to all Matters coming within the Classes of Subjects next herein-after enumerated; that is to say,—

1   The amendment from time to time of the Constitution of Canada, except as regards matters coming within the classes of subjects by this Act assigned exclusively to the Legislatures of the provinces, or as regards right or privileges by this or any other Constitutional Act granted or secured to the Legislature or the Government of a province, or to any class of persons with respect to schools or as regards the use of the English or the French language or as regards the requirements that there shall be a session of the Parliament of Canada at least once each year, and that no House of Commons shall continue for more than five years from the day of the return of the Writs for choosing the House: provided, however, that a House of Commons may in time of real or apprehended war, invasion or insurrection be continued by the Parliament of Canada if such continuation is not opposed by the votes of more than one-third of the members of such House.[39]

1a The Public Debt and Property.[40]

2   The Regulation of Trade and Commerce.

2a Unemployment insurance.[41]

3   The raising of Money by any Mode or System of Taxation.

4   The borrowing of Money on the Public Credit.

5   Postal Service.

6   The Census and Statistics.

7   Militia, Military and Naval Service, and Defence.

8   The fixing of and providing for the Salaries and Allowances of Civil and other Offices of the Government of Canada.

9   Beacons, Buoys, Lighthouses, and Sable Island.

10 Navigation and Shipping.

11 Quarantine and the Establishment and Maintenance of Marine Hospitals.

12   Sea Coast and Inland Fisheries.

13 Ferries between a Province and any British or Foreign Country or between Two Provinces.

14 Currency and Coinage.

15 Banking, Incorporation of Banks, and the Issue of Paper Money.

● ●

39. Added by the *British North America (No. 2) Act, 1949*, 13 Geo. VI, c. 81 (U.K.).

40. Re-numbered by the *British North America (No. 2) Act, 1949*.

41. Added by the *British North America Act, 1940*, 3–4 Geo. VI, c. 36 (U.K.).

16 Savings Banks.
17 Weights and Measures.
18 Bills of Exchange and Promissory Notes.
19 Interest.
20 Legal Tender.
21 Bankruptcy and Insolvency.
22 Patents of Invention and Discovery.
23 Copyrights.
24 Indians, and Lands reserved for the Indians.
25 Naturalization and Aliens.
26 Marriage and Divorce.
27 The Criminal Law, except the Constitution of Courts of Criminal Jurisdiction, but including the Procedure in Criminal Matters.
28 The Establishment, Maintenance, and Management of Penitentiaries.
29 Such Classes of Subjects as are expressly excepted in the Enumeration of the Classes of Subjects by this Act assigned exclusively to the Legislatures of the Provinces.

And any Matter coming within any of the Classes of Subjects enumerated in this Section shall not be deemed to come within the Class of Matters of a local or private Nature comprised in the Enumeration of the Classes of Subjects by this Act assigned exclusively to the Legislatures of the Provinces.[42]

• •

42. Legislative authority has been conferred on Parliament by other Acts as follows:

1. The *British North America Act, 1871*, 34–35 Vict., c. 28 (U.K.).

2. The Parliament of Canada may from time to time establish new Provinces in any territories forming for the time being part of the Dominion of Canada, but not included in any Province thereof, and may, at the time of such establishment, make provision for the constitution and administration of any such Province, and for the passing of laws for the peace, order, and good government of such Province, and for its representation in the said Parliament. — Parliament of Canada may establish new Provinces and provide for the constitution etc., thereof

3. The Parliament of Canada may from time to time, with the consent of the Legislature of any Province of the said Dominion, increase, diminish, or otherwise alter the limits of such Province, upon such terms and conditions as may be agreed to by the said Legislature, and may, with the like consent, make provision respecting the effect and operation of any such increase or diminution or alteration of territory in relation to any Province affected thereby. — Alteration of limits of Provinces

4. The Parliament of Canada may from time to time make provision for the administration, peace, order, and good government of any territory not for the time being included in any Province. — Parliament of Canada may legislate for any territory not included in a Province

5. The following Acts passed by the said Parliament of Canada, and instituted respectively,—"An Act for the temporary government of Rupert's Land and the North Western Territory when united with Canada"; and "An Act to amend and continue the Act thirty-two and thirty-three Victoria, chapter three, and to establish and provide for the government of "the Province of Manitoba," shall be and be deemed to have been valid and effectual for all purposes whatsoever from the date at which they respectively received the assent, in the Queen's name, of the Governor General of the said Dominion of Canada." — Confirmation of Acts of Canada, 32 & 33 Vict. (Canadian) cap. 3; 33 Vict., (Canadian) cap 3

6. Except as provided by the third section of this Act, it shall not be competent for the Parliament of Canada to alter the provisions of the last-mentioned Act of the said — Limitation of powers of

APPENDIXES

EXCLUSIVE POWERS OF PROVINCIAL LEGISLATURES

92 In each Province the Legislature may exclusively make Laws in relation to Matters coming within the Classes of Subject next herein-after enumerated; that is to say,— Subjects of exclusive Provincial Legislation

1 The Amendment from Time to Time, notwithstanding anything in this Act, of the Constitution of the Province, except as regards the Office of Lieutenant Governor.

2 Direct Taxation within the Province in order to the raising of a Revenue for Provincial Purposes.

3 The borrowing of Money on the sole Credit of the Province.

4 The Establishment and Tenure of Provincial Offices and the Appointment and Payment of Provincial Officers.

5 The Management and Sale of the Public Lands belonging to the Province and of the Timber and Wood thereon.

6 The Establishment, Maintenance, and Management of Public and Reformatory Prisons in and for the Province.

7 The Establishment, Maintenance, and Management of Hospitals, Asylums, Charities, and Eleemosynary Institutions in and for the Province, other than Marine Hospitals.

8 Municipal Institutions in the Province.

9 Shop, Saloon, Tavern, Auctioneer, and other Licences in order to the raising of a Revenue for Provincial, Local, or Municipal Purposes.

10 Local Works and Undertakings other than such as are of the following Classes: (*a*) Lines of Steam or other Ships, Railways, Canals, Telegraphs, and other Works and Undertakings connecting the Province with any other or others of the Provinces, or extending beyond the Limits of the Province; (*b*) Lines of Steam Ships between the Province and any British or Foreign Country;

• •

Parliament in so far as it relates to the Province of Manitoba, or of any other Act hereafter establishing new Provinces in the said Dominion, subject always to the right of the Legislature of the Province of Manitoba to alter from time to time the provisions of any law respecting the qualification of electors and members of the Legislative Assembly, and to make laws respecting elections in the said Province. Parliament of Canada to legislate for an established Province

The *Rupert's Land Act, 1868*, 31–32 Vict., c. 105 (U.K.) (repealed by the *Statute Law Revision Act, 1893*, 56–57 Vict., c. 14 (U.K.)) had previously conferred similar authority in relation to Rupert's Land and the North-Western Territory upon admission of those areas.

2. The *British North America Act, 1886*, 49–50 Vict., c. 35, (U.K.).

1. The Parliament of Canada may from time to time make provision for the representation in the Senate and House of Commons of Canada, or in either of them, of any territories which for the time being form part of the Dominion of Canada, but are not included in any province thereof. Provision by Parliament of Canada for representation of territories

3. The *Statute of Westminster, 1931*, 22 Geo. v. c. 4, (U.K.).

3. It is hereby declared and enacted that the Parliament of a Dominion has full power to make laws having extra-territorial operation. Power of Parliament of a Dominion to legislate extra-territorially

(c) Such Works as, although wholly situate within the Province, are before or after their Execution declared by the Parliament of Canada to be for the general Advantage of Canada or for the Advantage of Two or more of the Provinces.

11 The Incorporation of Companies with Provincial Objects.

12 The Solemnization of Marriage in the Province.

13 Property and Civil Rights in the Province.

14 The Administration of Justice in the Province, including the Constitution, Maintenance, and Organization of Provincial Courts, both of Civil and of Criminal Jurisdiction, and including Procedure in Civil Matters in those Courts.

15 The Imposition of Punishment by Fine, Penalty, or Imprisonment for enforcing any Law of the Province made in relation to any Matter coming within any of the Classes of Subjects enumerated in this Section.

16 Generally all Matters of a merely local or private Nature in the Province.

EDUCATION

93 In and for each Province the Legislature may exclusively make Laws in relation to Education, subject and according to the following Provisions:— *Legislation respecting Education*

1 Nothing in any such Law shall prejudicially affect any Right or Privilege with respect to Denominational Schools which any Class of Persons have by Law in the Province at the Union:

2 All the Powers, Privileges, and Duties at the Union by Law conferred and imposed in Upper Canada on the Separate Schools and School Trustees of the Queen's Roman Catholic Subjects shall be and the same are hereby extended to the Dissentient Schools of the Queen's Protestant and Roman Catholic Subjects in Quebec:

3 Where in any Province a System of Separate or Dissentient Schools exists by Law at the Union or is thereafter established by the Legislature of the Province, an Appeal shall lie to the Governor General in Council from any Act or Decision of any Provincial Authority affecting any Right or Privilege of the Protestant or Roman Catholic Minority of the Queen's Subjects in relation to Education:

4 In case any such Provincial Law as from Time to Time seems to the Governor General in Council requisite for the due Execution of the Provisions of this Section is not made, or in case any Decision of the Governor General in Council on any Appeal under this Section is not duly executed by the proper Provincial Authority in that Behalf, then and in every such Case, and as far only as the Circumstances of each Case require, the Parliament of Canada may make remedial Laws for the due Execution of the Provisions of

this Section and of any Decision of the Governor General in Council under this Section.[43]

94 Notwithstanding anything in this Act, the Parliament of Canada may make Provision for the Uniformity of all or any of the Laws relative to Property and Civil Rights in Ontario, Nova Scotia, and New Brunswick, and of the Procedure of all or any of the Courts in Those Three Provinces, and from and after the passing of any Act in that Behalf the Power of the Parliament of Canada to make Laws in relation to any Matter comprised in any such Act shall, notwithstanding anything in this Act, be unrestricted; but any Act of the Parliament of Canada making Provision for such Uniformity shall not have effect in any Province unless and until it is adopted and enacted as Law by the Legislature thereof.

Legislation for Uniformity of Laws in Three Provinces

● ●

43. Altered for Manitoba by section 22 of the *Manitoba Act*, 33 Vict., c. 3 (Canada), (confirmed by the *British North America Act, 1871*), which reads as follows:

22. In and for the Province, the said Legislature may exclusively make Laws in relation to Education, subject and according to the following provisions:—
1 Nothing in any such Law shall prejudicially affect any right or privilege with respect to Denominational Schools which any class of persons have by Law or practice in the Province at the Union:
2 An appeal shall lie to the Governor General in Council from any Act or decision of the Legislature of the Province, or of any Provincial Authority, affecting any right or privilege, of the Protestant or Roman Catholic minority of the Queen's subjects in relation to Education:
3 In case any such Provincial Law, as from time to time seems to the Governor General in Council requisite for the due execution of the provisions of this section, is not made, or in case any decision of the Governor General in Council on any appeal under this section is not duly executed by the proper Provincial Authority in that behalf, then, and in every such case, and as far only as the circumstances of each case require, the Parliament of Canada may make remedial Laws for the due execution of the provisions of this section, and of any decision of the Governor General in Council under this section.

Legislation touching schools subject to certain provisions

Power reserved to Parliament

Altered for Alberta by section 17 of *The Alberta Act*, 4–5 Edw. VII, c. 3 which reads as follows:

17. Section 93 of The British North America Act, 1867, shall apply to the said province, with the substitution for paragraph (1) of the said section 93 of the following paragraph:—
1. Nothing in any such law shall prejudicially affect any right or privilege with respect to separate schools which any class of persons have at the date of the passing of this Act, under the terms of chapters 29 and 30 of the Ordinances of the Northwest Territories, passed in the year 1901, or with respect to religious instruction in any public or separate school as provided for in the said ordinances.
2. In the appropriation by the Legislature or distribution by the Government of the province of any moneys for the support of schools organized and carried on in accordance with the said chapter 29 or any Act passed in amendment thereof, or in substitution therefor, there shall be no discrimination against schools of any class described in the said chapter 29.
3. Where the expression "by law" is employed in paragraph 3 of the said section 93, it shall be held to mean the law as set out in the said chapters 29 and 30, and where the expression "at the Union" is employed, in the said paragraph 3, it shall be held to mean the date at which this Act comes into force."

Education

Altered for Saskatchewan by section 17 of *The Saskatchewan Act*, 4–5 Edw. VII, c. 42, which reads as follows:

17. Section 93 of the British North America Act, 1867, shall apply to the said province with the substitution for paragraph (1) of the said section 93 of the following paragraph:—

Education

APPENDIXES

OLD AGE PENSIONS

94A The Parliament of Canada may make laws in relation to old age pensions and supplementary benefits, including survivors' and disability benefits irrespective of age, but no such law shall affect the operation of any law present or future of a provincial legislature in relation to any such matter.[44]

Legislation respecting old age pensions and supplementary benefits

AGRICULTURE AND IMMIGRATION

95 In each Province the Legislature may make Laws in relation to Agriculture in the Province, and to Immigration into the Province; and it is hereby declared that the Parliament of Canada may from Time to Time make Laws in relation to Agriculture in all or any of the Provinces, and to Immigration into all or any of the Provinces; and any Law of the Legislature of a Province relative to Agriculture or to Immigration shall have effect in and for the Province as long and as far only as it is not repugnant to any Act of the Parliament of Canada.

Concurrent Powers of Legislation respecting Agriculture, etc.

● ●

1. Nothing in any such law shall prejudicially affect any right or privilege with respect to separate schools which any class of persons have at the date of the passing of this Act, under the terms of chapters 29 and 30 of the Ordinances of the Northwest Territories, passed in the year 1901, or with respect to religious instruction in any public or separate school as provided for in the said ordinances.

2. In the appropriation by the Legislatue or distribution by the Government of the province of any moneys for the support of schools organized and carried on in accordance with the said chapter 29, or any Act passed in amendment thereof or in substitution therefor, there shall be no discrimination against schools of any class described in the said chapter 29.

3. Where the expression "by law" is employed in paragraph (3) of the said section 93, it shall be held to mean the law as set out in the said chapters 29 and 30; and where the expression "at the Union" is employed in the said paragraph (3), it shall be held to mean the date at which this Act comes into force.

Altered by Term 17 of the Terms of Union of Newfoundland with Canada (confirmed by the *British North America Act, 1949*, 12–13 Geo. VI, c. 22 (U.K.)), which reads as follows:

17. In lieu of section ninety-three of the British North America Act, 1867, the following term shall apply in respect of the Province of Newfoundland:

In and for the Province of Newfoundland the Legislature shall have exclusive authority to make laws in relation to education, but the Legislature will not have authority to make laws prejudicially affecting any right or privilege with respect to denominational schools, common (amalgamated) schools, or denominational colleges, that any class or classes of persons have by law in Newfoundland at the date of Union, and out of public funds of the Province of Newfoundland, provided for education,

(a) all such schools shall receive their share of such funds in accordance with scales determined on a non-discriminatory basis from time to time by the Legislature for all schools then being conducted under authority of the Legislature; and

(b) all such colleges shall receive their share of any grant from time to time voted for all colleges then being conducted under authority of the Legislature, such grant being distributed on a non-discriminatory basis.

44. Added by the *British North America Act, 1964*, 12–13, Eliz. II, c. 73 (U.K.). Originally enacted by the *British North America Act, 1951*, 14–15 Geo. VI, c. 32 (U.K.), as follows:

"94A. It is hereby declared that the Parliament of Canada may from time to time make laws in relation to old age pensions in Canada, but no law made by the Parliament of Canada in relation to old age pensions shall affect the operation of any law present or future of a Provincial Legislature in relation to old age pensions."

243

VIII *Judicature*

96 The Governor General shall appoint the Judges of the Superior, District, and County Courts in each Province, except those of the Courts of Probate in Nova Scotia and New Brunswick. — Appointment of Judges

97 Until the laws relative to Property and Civil Rights in Ontario, Nova Scotia, and New Brunswick, and the Procedure of the Courts in those Provinces, are made uniform, the Judges of the Courts of those Provinces appointed by the Governor General shall be selected from the respective Bars of those Provinces. — Selection of Judges in Ontario, etc.

98 The Judges of the Courts of Quebec shall be selected from the Bar of that Province. — Selection of Judges in Quebec

1 Subject to subsection two of this section, the Judges of the Superior Courts shall hold office during good behaviour, but shall be removable by the Governor General on Address of the Senate and House of Commons. — Tenure of office of Judges

2 A Judge of a Superior Court, whether appointed before or after the coming into force of this section, shall cease to hold office upon attaining the age of seventy-five years, or upon the coming into force of this section if at that time he has already attained that age.[44A] — Termination at age 75

100 The Salaries, Allowances, and Pensions of the Judges of the Superior, District, and County Courts (except the Courts of Probate in Nova Scotia and New Brunswick), and of the Admiralty Courts in Cases where the Judges thereof are for the Time being paid by Salary, shall be fixed and provided by the Parliament of Canada.[45] — Salaries etc., of Judges

101 The Parliament of Canada may, notwithstanding anything in this Act, from Time to Time provide for the Constitution, Maintenance, and Organization of a General Court of Appeal for Canada, and for the Establishment of any additional Courts for the better Administration of the Laws of Canada.[46] — General Court of Appeal, etc.

● ●

44A. Repealed and re-enacted by the *British North America Act, 1960,* 9 Eliz. II, c. 2 (U.K.), which came into force on the 1st day of March, 1961. The original section read as follows:

99. The Judges of the Superior Courts shall hold Office during good Behaviour, but shall be removable by the Governor General on Address of the Senate and House of Commons. — Tenure of office of Judges of Superior Courts

45. Now provided for in the *Judges Act,* R.S.C. 1952, c. 159, as amended by S.C. 1963, c. 8, 1964–65, c. 36 and 1966–67, c. 76.

46. See the *Supreme Court Act,* R.S.C. 1952, c. 259, and the *Exchequer Court Act,* R.S.C. 1952, c. 98.

APPENDIXES

VIII Revenues; Debts; Assets; Taxation

102 All Duties and Revenues over which the respective Legislatures of Canada, Nova Scotia, and New Brunswick before and at the Union had and have Power of Appropriation, except such Portions thereof as are by this Act reserved to the respective Legislatures of the Provinces, or are raised by them in accordance with the special Powers conferred on them by this Act, shall form One Consolidated Revenue Fund, to be appropriated for the Public Service of Canada in the Manner and subject to the Charges in this Act provided. *Creation of Consolidated Revenue Fund*

103 The Consolidated Revenue Fund of Canada shall be permanently charged with the Costs, Charges, and Expenses incident to the Collection, Management, and Receipt thereof, and the same shall form the First Charge thereon, subject to be reviewed and audited in such Manner as shall be ordered by the Governor General in Council until the Parliament otherwise provides. *Expenses of Collection, etc.*

104 The annual Interest of the Public Debts of the several Provinces of Canada, Nova Scotia, and New Brunswick at the Union shall form the Second Charge on the Consolidated Revenue Fund of Canada. *Interest of Provincial Public Debts*

105 Unless altered by the Parliament of Canada, the Salary of the Governor General shall be Ten thousand Pounds Sterling Money of the United Kingdom of Great Britain and Ireland, payable out of the Consolidated Revenue Fund of Canada, and the same shall form the Third Charge thereon.[47] *Salary of Governor General*

106 Subject to the several Payments by this Act charged on the Consolidated Revenue Fund of Canada, the same shall be appropriated by the Parliament of Canada for the Public Service. *Appropriation from Time to Time*

107 All Stocks, Cash, Banker's Balances, and Securities for Money belonging to each Province at the Time of the Union, except as in this Act mentioned, shall be the Property of Canada, and shall be taken in Reduction of the Amount of the respective Debts of the Provinces at the Union. *Transfer of Stocks, etc.*

108 The Public Works and Property of each Province, enumerated in the Third Schedule to this Act, shall be the Property of Canada. *Transfer of Property in Schedule*

109 All Lands, Mines, Minerals, and Royalties belonging to the several Provinces of Canada, Nova Scotia, and New Brunswick at the Union, and all Sums then due or payable for such Lands, Mines, Minerals, or Royalties, shall belong to the several Provinces of Ontario, Quebec, Nova Scotia, and New Brunswick in which the *Property in Lands, Mines, etc.*

●●

47. Now covered by the *Governor General's Act*, R.S.C. 1952, c. 139.

245

same are situate or arise, subject to any Trusts existing in respect thereof, and to any Interest other than that of the Province in the same.[48]

110 All Assets connected with such Portions of the Public Debt of each Province as are assumed by that Province shall belong to that Province.

Assets connected with Provincial Debts

111 Canada shall be liable for the Debts and Liabilities of each Province existing at the Union.

Canada to be liable for Provincial Debts

112 Ontario and Quebec conjointly shall be liable to Canada for the Amount (if any) by which the Debt of the Province of Canada exceeds at the Union Sixty-two million five hundred thousand Dollars, and shall be charged with Interest at the Rate of Five per Centum per Annum thereon.

Debts of Ontario and Quebec

113 The Assets enumerated in the Fourth Schedule to this Act belonging at the Union to the Province of Canada shall be the Property of Ontario and Quebec conjointly.

Assets of Ontario and Quebec

114 Nova Scotia shall be liable to Canada for the Amount (if any) by which its Public Debt exceeds at the Union Eight million Dollars, and shall be charged with Interest at the Rate of Five per Centum per Annum thereon.[49]

Debt of Nova Scotia

115 New Brunswick shall be liable to Canada for the Amount (if any) by which its Public Debt exceeds at the Union Seven million Dollars, and shall be charged with Interest at the Rate of Five per Centum per Annum thereon.

Debt of New Brunswick

116 In case the Public Debts of Nova Scotia and New Brunswick do not at the Union amount to Eight million and Seven million Dollars respectively, they shall respectively receive by half-yearly Payments in advance from the Government of Canada Interest at Five per Centum per Annum on the Difference between the actual Amounts of their respective Debts and such stipulated Amounts.

Payment of interest to Nova Scotia and New Brunswick

117 The several Provinces shall retain all their respective Public Property not otherwise disposed of in this Act, subject to the Right of Canada to assume any Lands or Public Property required for Fortifications or for the Defence of the Country.

Provincial Public Property

● ●

48. The four western provinces were placed in the same position as the original provinces by the *British North America Act, 1930*, 21 Geo. v, c. 26 (U.K.).

49. The obligations imposed by this section, sections 115 and 116, and similar obligations under the instruments creating or admitting other provinces, have been carried into legislation of the Parliament of Canada and are now to be found in the *Provincial Subsidies Act*, R.S.C. 1952, c. 221.

118 Repealed.[50]

119 New Brunswick shall receive by half-yearly Payments in advance from Canada for the Period of Ten Years from the Union an additional Allowance of Sixty-three thousand Dollars per Annum; but as long as the Public Debt of that Province remains under Seven million Dollars, a Deduction equal to the Interest at Five per

Further Grant to New Brunswick

● ●

50. Repealed by the *Statute Law Revision Act, 1950*, 14 Geo. VI, c. 6 (U.K.). As originally enacted, the section read as follows:

118. The following Sums shall be paid yearly by Canada to the several Provinces for the Support of their Governments and Legislatures:

Grants to Provinces

	Dollars
Ontario	Eighty thousand.
Quebec	Seventy thousand.
Nova Scotia	Sixty thousand.
New Brunswick	Fifty thousand.

Two hundred and sixty thousand;

and an annual Grant in aid of each Province shall be made, equal to Eighty Cents per Head of the Population as ascertained by the Census of One thousand eight hundred and sixty-one, and in the Case of Nova Scotia and New Brunswick, by each subsequent Decennial Census until the Population of each of those two Provinces amounts to Four hundred thousand Souls, at which Rate such Grant shall thereafter remain. Such Grants shall be in full Settlement of all future Demands on Canada, and shall be paid half-yearly in advance to each Province; but the Government of Canada shall deduct from such Grants, as against any Province, all Sums chargeable as Interest on the Public Debt of that Province in excess of the several Amounts stipulated in this Act.

The section was made obsolete by the *British North America Act, 1907*, 7 Edw. VII, c. 11 (U.K.) which provided:

1. (1) The following grants shall be made yearly by Canada to every province, which at the commencement of this Act is a province of the Dominion, for its local purposes and the support of its Government and Legislature:—

Payments to be made by Canada to provinces

(*a*) A fixed grant—
where the population of the province is under one hundred and fifty thousand, of one hundred thousand dollars;
where the population of the province is one hundred and fifty thousand, but does not exceed two hundred thousand, of one hundred and fifty thousand dollars;
where the population of the province is two hundred thousand, but does not exceed four hundred thousand, of one hundred and eighty thousand dollars;
where the population of the province is four hundred thousand, but does not exceed eight hundred thousand, of one hundred and ninety thousand dollars;
where the population of the province is eight hundred thousand, but does not exceed one million five hundred thousand, of two hundred and twenty thousand dollars;
where the population of the province exceeds one million five hundred thousand, of two hundred and forty thousand dollars; and
(*b*) Subject to the special provisions of this Act as to the provinces of British Columbia and Prince Edward Island, a grant at the rate of eighty cents per head of the population of the province up to the number of two million five hundred thousand, and at the rate of sixty cents per head of so much of the population as exceeds that number.
(2) An additional grant of one hundred thousand dollars shall be made yearly to the province of British Columbia for a period of ten years from the commencement of this Act.
(3) The population of a province shall be ascertained from time to time in the case of the provinces of Manitoba, Saskatchewan, and Alberta respectively by the last quinquennial census or statutory estimate of population made under the Acts establishing those provinces or any other Act of the Parliament of Canada making provision for the purpose, and in the case of any other province by the last decennial census for the time being.
(4) The grants payable under this Act shall be paid half-yearly in advance to each province.
(5) The grants payable under this Act shall be substituted for the grants or subsidies (in this Act referred to as existing grants) payable for the like purposes at the commencement of this Act to the several provinces of the Dominion under the provisions of section one hundred and eighteen of the British North America Act 1867, or of any Order in Council establishing a province, or of any Act of the Parliament of Canada containing directions for the payment of any such grant or subsidy, and those provisions shall cease to have effect.
(6) The Government of Canada shall have the same power of deducting sums charged against a province on account of the interest on public debt in the case of the

30–31 Vict., c. 3

Centum per Annum on such Deficiency shall be made from that Allowance of Sixty-three thousand Dollars.[51]

120   All Payments to be made under this Act, or in discharge of Liabilities created under any Act of the Provinces of Canada, Nova Scotia, and New Brunswick respectively, and assumed by Canada, shall, until the Parliament of Canada otherwise directs, be made in such Form and Manner as may from Time to Time be ordered by the Governor General in Council.   *Form of Payments*

121   All Articles of the Growth, Produce, or Manufacture of any one of the Provinces shall, from and after the Union, be admitted free into each of the other Provinces.   *Canadian Manufactures, etc.*

122   The Customs and Excise Laws of each Province shall, subject to the Provisions of this Act, continue in force until altered by the Parliament of Canada.[52]   *Continuance of Customs and Excise Laws*

123   Where Customs Duties are, at the Union, leviable on any Goods, Wares, or Merchandises in any Two Provinces, those Goods, Wares, and Merchandises may, from and after the Union, be imported from one of those Provinces into the other of them on Proof of Payment of the Customs Duty leviable thereon in the Province of Exportation, and on Payment of such further Amount (if any) of Customs Duty as is leviable thereon in the Province of Importation.[53]   *Exportation and Importation as between Two Provinces*

124   Nothing in this Act shall affect the Right of New Brunswick to levy the Lumber Dues provided in Chapter Fifteen of Title Three of the Revised Statutes of New Brunswick, or in any Act amending   *Lumber Dues in New Brunswick*

● ●

grant payable under this Act to the province as they have in the case of the existing grant.

(7) Nothing in this Act shall affect the obligation of the Government of Canada to pay to any province any grant which is payable to that province, other than the existing grant for which the grant under this Act is substituted.

(8) In the case of the provinces of British Columbia and Prince Edward Island, the amount paid on account of the grant payable per head of the population to the provinces under this Act shall not at any time be less than the amount of the corresponding grant payable at the commencement of this Act, and if it is found on any decennial census that the population of the province has decreased since the last decennial census, the amount paid on account of the grant shall not be decreased below the amount then payable, notwithstanding the decrease of the population.

See the *Provincial Subsidies Act*, R.S.C. 1952, c. 221, *The Maritime Provinces Additional Subsidies Act*, 1942–43, c. 14, and the Terms of Union of Newfoundland with Canada, appended to the *British North America Act, 1949*, and also to *An Act to approve the Terms of Union of Newfoundland with Canada*, chapter 1 of the statutes of Canada, 1949.

51. Spent.

52. Spent. Now covered by the *Customs Act*, R.S.C. 1952, c. 58, the *Customs Tariff*, R.S.C. 1952, c. 60, the *Excise Act*, R.S.C. 1952, c. 99 and the *Excise Tax Act*, R.S.C. 1952, c. 100.

53. Spent.

that Act before or after the Union, and not increasing the Amount of such Dues; but the Lumber of any of the Provinces other than New Brunswick shall not be subject to such Dues.[54]

125 No Lands or Property belonging to Canada or any Province shall be liable to Taxation.

Exemption of Public Lands, etc.

126 Such Portions of the Duties and Revenues over which the respective Legislatures of Canada, Nova Scotia, and New Brunswick had before the Union Power of Appropriation as are by this Act reserved to the respective Governments or Legislatures of the Provinces, and all Duties and Revenues raised by them in accordance with the special Powers conferred upon them by this Act, shall in each Province form One Consolidated Revenue Fund to be appropriated for the Public Service of the Province.

Provincial Consolidated Revenue Fund

IX   Miscellaneous Provisions

GENERAL

127 Repealed.[55]

128 Every Member of the Senate or House of Commons of Canada shall before taking his Seat therein take and subscribe before the Governor General or some Person authorized by him, and every Member of a Legislative Council or Legislative Assembly of any Province shall before taking this Seat therein take and subscribe before the Lieutenant Governor of the Province or some Person authorized by him, the Oath of Allegiance contained in the Fifth Schedule to this Act; and every Member of the Senate of Canada and every Member of the Legislative Council of Quebec shall also, before taking his Seat therein, take and subscribe before the Governor General, or some Person authorized by him, the Declaration contained in the same Schedule.

Oath of Allegiance, etc.

129 Except as otherwise provided by this Act, all Laws in force in Canada, Nova Scotia, or New Brunswick at the Union, and all

Continuance of existing Laws, Courts, Officers, etc.

●●

54. These dues were repealed in 1873 by 36 Vict., c. 16 (N.B.). And see *An Act respecting the Export Duties imposed on Lumber*, etc., (1873) 36 Vict., c. 41 (Canada), and section 2 of the *Provincial Subsidies Act*, R.S.C. 1952, c. 221.

55. Repealed by the *Statute Law Revision Act, 1893*, 56–57 Vict., c. 14 (U.K.). The section read as follows:

127. If any Person being at the passing of this Act a Member of the Legislative Council of Canada, Nova Scotia, or New Brunswick to whom a Place in the Senate is offered, does not within Thirty Days thereafter, by Writing under his Hand addressed to the Governor General of the Province of Canada or to the Lieutenant Governor of Nova Scotia or New Brunswick (as the Case may be), accept the same, he shall be deemed to have declined the same; and any Person who, being at the passing of this Act a Member of the Legislative Council of Nova Scotia or New Brunswick, accepts a Place in the Senate, shall thereby vacate his Seat in such Legislative Council.

As to Legislative Councillors of Provinces becoming senators

Courts of Civil and Criminal Jurisdiction, and all legal Commissions, Powers, and Authorities, and all Officers, Judicial, Administrative, and Ministerial, existing therein at the Union, shall continue in Ontario, Quebec, Nova Scotia, and New Brunswick respectively, as if the Union had not been made; subject nevertheless (except with respect to such as are enacted by or exist under Acts of the Parliament of Great Britain or of the Parliament of the United Kingdom of Great Britain and Ireland,) to be repealed, abolished, or altered by the Parliament of Canada, or by the Legislature of the respective Province, according to the Authority of the Parliament or of that Legislature under this Act.[56]

130 Until the Parliament of Canada otherwise provides, all Officers of the several Provinces having Duties to discharge in relation to Matters other than those coming within the Classes of Subjects by this Act assigned exclusively to the Legislatures of the Provinces shall be Officers of Canada, and shall continue to discharge the Duties of their respective Offices under the same Liabilities, responsibilities, and Penalties as if the Union had not been made.[57] *Transfer of Officers to Canada*

131 Until the Parliament of Canada otherwise provides, the Governor General in Council may from Time to Time appoint such Officers as the Governor General in Council deems necessary or proper for the effectual Execution of this Act. *Appointment of new Officers*

132 The Parliament and Government of Canada shall have all Powers necessary or proper for performing the Obligations of Canada or of any Province thereof, as Part of the British Empire, towards Foreign Countries, arising under Treaties between the Empire and such Foreign Countries. *Treaty Obligations*

133 Either the English or the French Language may be used by any Person in the Debates of the Houses of the Parliament of Canada and of the Houses of the Legislature of Quebec; and both those Languages shall be used in the respective Records and Journals of those Houses; and either of those Languages may be used by any Person or in any Pleading or Process in or issuing from any Court of Canada established under this Act, and in or from all or any of the Courts of Quebec. *Use of English and French Languages*

The Acts of the Parliament of Canada and of the Legislature of Quebec shall be printed and published in both those Languages.

• •

56. The restriction against altering or repealing laws enacted by or existing under statutes of the United Kingdom was removed by the *Statute of Westminster, 1931*, 22 Geo. v, c. 4 (U.K.).

57. Spent.

APPENDIXES

ONTARIO AND QUEBEC

134 Until the Legislature of Ontario or of Quebec otherwise provides, the Lieutenant Governors of Ontario and Quebec may each appoint under the Great Seal of the Province the following Officers, to hold Office during Pleasure, that is to say,—the Attorney General, the Secretary and Registrar of the Province, the Treasurer of the Province, the Commissioner of Crown Lands, and the Commissioner of Agriculture and Public Works, and in the Case of Quebec the Solicitor General, and may, by Order of the Lieutenant Governor in Council, from Time to Time prescribe the Duties of those Officers, and of the several Departments over which they shall preside or to which they shall belong, and of the Officers and Clerks thereof, and may also appoint other and additional Officers to hold Office during Pleasure, and may from Time to Time prescribe the Duties of those Officers, and of the several Departments over which they shall preside or to which they shall belong, and of the Officers and Clerks thereof.[58]

Appointment of Executive Officers for Ontario and Quebec

135 Until the Legislature of Ontario or Quebec otherwise provides, all Rights, Powers, Duties, Functions, Responsibilities, or Authorities at the passing of this Act vested in or imposed on the Attorney General, Solicitor General, Secretary and Registrar of the Province of Canada, Minister of Finance, Commissioner of Crown Lands, Commissioner of Public Works, and Minister of Agriculture and Receiver General, by any Law, Statute, or Ordinance of Upper Canada, Lower Canada, or Canada, and not repugnant to this Act, shall be vested in or imposed on any Officer to be appointed by the Lieutenant Governor for the Discharge of the same or any of them; and the Commissioner of Agriculture and Public Works shall perform the Duties and Functions of the Office of Minister of Agriculture at the passing of this Act imposed by the Law of the Province of Canada, as well as those of the Commissioner of Public Works.[59]

Powers, Duties, etc. of Executive Officers

136 Until altered by the Lieutenant Governor in Council, the Great Seals of Ontario and Quebec respectively shall be the same, or of the same Design, as those used in the Provinces of Upper Canada and Lower Canada respectively before their Union as the Province of Canada.

Great Seals

137 The words "and from thence to the End of the then next ensuing Session of the Legislature," or Words to the same Effect, used in

Construction of temporary Acts

●●

58. Spent. Now covered in Ontario by the *Executive Council Act*, R.S.O. 1960, c. 127 and in Quebec by the *Executive Power Act*, R.S.Q. 1964, c. 9 as amended by 1965, c. 16.

59. Probably spent.

any temporary Act of the Province of Canada not expired before the Union, shall be construed to extend and apply to the next Session of the Parliament of Canada if the Subject Matter of the Act is within the Powers of the same as defined by this Act, or to the next Sessions of the Legislatures of Ontario and Quebec respectively if the Subject Matter of the Act is within the Powers of the same as defined by this Act.

138 From and after the Union the Use of the Words "Upper Canada" instead of "Ontario," or "Lower Canada" instead of "Quebec," in any Deed, Writ, Process, Pleading, Document, Matter, or Thing, shall not invalidate the same.

As to Errors in Names

139 Any Proclamation under the Great Seal of the Province of Canada issued before the Union to take effect at a Time which is subsequent to the Union, whether relating to that Province, or to Upper Canada, or to Lower Canada, and the several Matters and Things therein proclaimed, shall be and continue of like Force and Effect as if the Union had not been made.[60]

As to issue of Proclamations before Union, to commence after Union

140 Any Proclamation which is authorized by any Act of the Legislature of the Province of Canada to be issued under the Great Seal of the Province of Canada, whether relating to that Province, or to Upper Canada, or to Lower Canada, and which is not issued before the Union, may be issued by the Lieutenant Governor of Ontario or of Quebec, as its Subject Matter requires, under the Great Seal thereof; and from and after the Issue of such Proclamation the same and the several Matters and Things therein proclaimed shall be and continue of the like Force and Effect in Ontario or Quebec as if the Union had not been made.[61]

As to issue of Proclamations after Union

141 The Penitentiary of the Province of Canada shall, until the Parliament of Canada otherwise provides, be and continue the Penitentiary of Ontario and of Quebec.[62]

Penitentiary

142 The Division and Adjustment of the Debts, Credits, Liabilities, Properties, and Assets of Upper Canada and Lower Canada shall be referred to the Arbitrament of Three Arbitrators, One chosen by the Government of Ontario, One by the Government of Quebec, and One by the Government of Canada; and the Selection of the Arbitrators shall not be made until the Parliament of Canada and the Legislatures of Ontario and Quebec have met; and the Arbitrator chosen by the Government of Canada shall not be a Resident either in Ontario or in Quebec.[63]

Arbitration respecting Debts, etc.

●●●

60. Probably spent.

61. Probably spent.

62. Spent. Penitentiaries are now provided for by the *Penitentiary Act*, s.c. 1960–61, c. 53.

63. Spent. See pages (xi) and (xii) of the Public Accounts, 1902–03.

143 The Governor General in Council may from Time to Time order that such and so many of the Records, Books, and Documents of the Province of Canada as he thinks fit shall be appropriated and delivered either to Ontario or to Quebec, and the same shall thenceforth be the Property of that Province; and any Copy thereof or Extract therefrom, duly certified by the Officer having charge of the Original thereof, shall be admitted as Evidence.[64]

<small>Division of Records</small>

144 The Lieutenant Governor of Quebec may from Time to Time, by Proclamation under the Great Seal of the Province, to take effect from a Day to be appointed therein, constitute Townships in those Parts of the Province of Quebec in which Townships are not then already constituted, and fix the Metes and Bounds thereof.

<small>Constitution of Townships in Quebec</small>

145 Repealed.[65]

XI Admission of Other Colonies

146 It shall be lawful for the Queen, by and with the Advice of Her Majesty's Most Honourable Privy Council, on Addresses from the Houses of the Parliament of Canada, and from the Houses of the respective Legislatures of the Colonies or Provinces of Newfoundland, Prince Edward Island, and British Columbia, to admit those Colonies or Provinces, or any of them, into the Union, and on Address from the Houses of the Parliament of Canada to admit Rupert's Land and the North-western Territory, or either of them, into the Union, on such Terms and Conditions in each Case as are in the Addresses expressed and as the Queen thinks fit to approve, subject to the Provisions of this Act; and the Provisions of any Order in Council in that Behalf shall have effect as if they had been enacted by the Parliament of the United Kingdom of Great Britain and Ireland.[66]

<small>Power to admit Newfoundland, etc., into the Union</small>

• •

64. Probably spent. Two orders were made under this section on the 24th of January, 1868.

65. Repealed by the *Statute Law Revision Act, 1893*, 56–57 Vict., c. 14, (U.K.). The section reads as follows:

X *Intercolonial Railway*
145. Inasmuch as the Provinces of Canada, Nova Scotia, and New Brunswick have joined in a Declaration that the Construction of the International Railway is essential to the Consolidation of the Union of British North America, and to the Assent thereto of Nova Scotia and New Brunswick, and have consequently agreed that Provision should be made for its immediate Construction by the Government of Canada: Therefore, in order to give effect to that Agreement, it shall be the Duty of the Government and Parliament of Canada to provide for the Commencement, within Six Months after the Union, of a Railway connecting the River St. Lawrence with the City of Halifax in Nova Scotia, and for the Construction thereof without Intermission, and the Completion thereof with all practicable Speed.

<small>Duty of Government and Parliament of Canada to make Railway herein described</small>

66. All territories mentioned in this section are now part of Canada. See the notes to section 5, *supra*.

147 In case of the Admission of Newfoundland and Prince Edward Island, or either of them, each shall be entitled to a Representation in the Senate of Canada of Four Members, and (notwithstanding anything in this Act) in case of the Admission of Newfoundland the normal Number of Senators shall be Seventy-six and their maximum Number shall be Eighty-two; but Prince Edward Island when admitted shall be deemed to be comprised in the Third of the Three Divisions into which Canada is, in relation of the Constitution of the Senate, divided by this Act, and accordingly, after the Admission of Prince Edward Island, whether Newfoundland is admitted or not, the Representation of Nova Scotia and New Brunswick in the Senate shall, as Vacancies occur, be reduced from Twelve to Ten Members respectively, and the Representation of each of those Provinces shall not be increased at any Time beyond Ten, except under the Provisions of this Act for the Appointment of Three or Six additional Senators under the Direction of the Queen.[67]

As to Representation of Newfoundland and Prince Edward Island in Senate

SCHEDULES

THE THIRD SCHEDULE

Provincial Public Works and Property to be the Property of Canada

1 Canals, with Lands and Water Power connected therewith.
2 Public Harbours.
3 Lighthouses and Piers, and Sable Island.
4 Steamboats, Dredges, and public Vessels.
5 Rivers and Lake Improvements.
6 Railways and Railway Stocks, Mortgages, and other Debts due by Railway Companies.
7 Military Roads.
8 Custom Houses, Post Offices, and all other Public Buildings, except such as the Government of Canada appropriate for the Use of the Provincial Legislature and Governments.
9 Property transferred by the Imperial Government, and known as Ordnance Property.
10 Armouries, Drill Sheds, Military Clothing, and Munitions of War, and Lands set apart for general Public Purposes.

● ●

67. Spent. See the notes to sections 21, 22, 26, 27 and 28, *supra*.

THE FOURTH SCHEDULE

Assets to be the Property of Ontario and Quebec conjointly
Upper Canada Building Fund.
Lunatic Asylums.
Normal School.
Court Houses,
  in
Aylmer, } Lower Canada
Montreal,
Kamouraska.
Law Society, Upper Canada.
Montreal Turnpike Trust.
University Permanent Fund.
Royal Institution.
Consolidated Municipal Loan Fund, Upper Canada.
Consolidated Municipal Loan Fund, Lower Canada.
Agricultural Society, Upper Canada.
Lower Canada Legislative Grant.
Quebec Fire Loan.
Temiscouata Advance Account.
Quebec Turnpike Trust.
Education—East.
Building and Jury Fund, Lower Canada.
Municipalities Fund.
Lower Canada Superior Education Income Fund.

Appendix B

EXTRACTS FROM THE SUPREME COURT ACT

(These extracts are taken from the *Supreme Court Act*, R.S.C. 1952, c. 259 as amended, and are printed here with the permission of the Queen's Printer, Ottawa. The original Act and amendments should be consulted where the full text is required for purposes of interpretation.)

THE SUPREME COURT ACT,*

ss. 55, 56, 103.

References by Governor in Council

55   1   Important questions of law or fact touching (*a*) the interpreta- Governor
tion of the *British North America Acts*; (*b*) the constitutionality may refer
or interpretation of any Dominion or provincial legislation; (*c*) questions for
the appellate jurisdiction as to educational matters, by the *British* opinion
North America Act, 1867, or by any other Act or law vested in the
Governor in Council; (*d*) the powers of the Parliament of Canada,
or of the legislatures of the provinces, or of the respective governments thereof, whether or not the particular power in question has
been or is proposed to be exercised; or (*e*) any other matter,
whether or not in the opinion of the Court *ejusdem generis* with
the foregoing enumerations, with reference to which the Governor
in Council sees fit to submit any such question; may be referred
by the Governor in Council to the Supreme Court for hearing and
consideration; and any question touching any of the matters aforesaid, so referred by the Governor in Council, shall be conclusively
deemed to be an important question.

2   Where a reference is made to the Court under subsection (1) Opinion of
it is the duty of the Court to hear and consider it, and to answer Court
each question so referred; and the Court shall certify to the
Governor in Council, for his information, its opinion upon each
such question, with the reasons for each such answer; and such
opinion shall be pronounced in like manner as in the case of a
judgment upon an appeal to the Court; and any judge who differs
from the opinion of the majority shall in like manner certify his
opinion and his reasons.

3   Where the question relates to the constitutional validity of any Notice to
Act that has heretofore been or is hereafter passed by the legisla- be given to
ture of any province, or of any provision in any such Act, or in interested
case, for any reason, the government of any province has any
special interest in any such question, the attorney general of such
province shall be notified of the hearing, in order that he may be
heard if he thinks fit.

4   The Court has power to direct that any person interested, or, Notice to
where there is a class of persons interested, any one or more per- interested
persons

• •

*R.S.C., 1952, c. 259 as amended by Stats. Can. 1956, c. 48.

sons as representatives of such class, shall be notified of the hearing upon any reference under this section, and such persons are entitled to be heard thereon.

5 The Court may, in its discretion, request any counsel to argue the case as to any interest that is affected and as to which counsel does not appear, and the reasonable expenses thereby occasioned may be paid by the Minister of Finance out of any moneys appropriated by Parliament for expenses of litigation. R.S., c. 35, s. 55; 1956, c. 48, s. 7. *[Appointment of counsel by Court]*

References by Senate or House of Commons

56 The Court, or any two of the judges thereof, shall examine and report upon any private bill or petition for a private bill presented to the Senate or House of Commons, and referred to the Court under any rules or orders made by the Senate or House of Commons. R.S., c. 35, s. 56. *[Report upon any private bill or petition]*

103 1 The judges of the Supreme Court, or any five of them, may, from time to time, make general rules and orders (*a*) for regulating the procedure of and in the Supreme Court, and the bringing of cases before it from courts appealed from or otherwise, and for the effectual execution and working of this Act, and the attainment of the intention and objects thereof; (*b*) for allowing appeals *in forma pauperis* by leave, notwithstanding the provisions of this or any other Act requiring the giving of security for costs, and for allowing a respondent leave to defend *in forma pauperis*; (*c*) for empowering the Registrar to do any such thing and transact any such business as is specified in the rules or orders, and to exercise any authority and jurisdiction in respect of the same as is now or may be hereafter done, transacted or exercised by a judge of the Court sitting in chambers in virtue of any statute or custom or by the practice of the Court; (*d*) for fixing the fees and costs to be taxed and allowed to, and received and taken by, and the rights and duties of the officers of the Court; (*e*) for awarding and regulating costs in such Court in favour of and against the Crown, as well as the subject; and (*f*) with respect to matters coming within the jurisdiction of the Court, in regard to references to the Court by the Governor in Council, and in particular with respect to investigations of questions of fact involved in any such reference.

2 Such rules and orders may extend to any matter of procedure or otherwise not provided for by this Act, but for which it is found necessary to provide, in order to ensure the proper working of this Act and the better attainment of the objects thereof.

3 All such rules as are not inconsistent with the express provisions of this Act have force and effect as if herein enacted.

4 Copies of all such rules and orders shall be laid before both Houses of Parliament at the session next after the making thereof. R.S., c. 35, s. 104; 1949 (2nd Sess.), c. 37, s. 6; 1951, c. 61, s. 2; 1956, c. 48, s. 18.

Appendix C

THE CONSTITUTIONAL QUESTIONS ACT

(This Act is printed here with the permission of the Queen's Printer, Regina.)

THE CONSTITUTIONAL QUESTIONS ACT*

An Act respecting the Decision of Constitutional and other Provincial Questions

Her Majesty, by and with the advice and consent of the Legislative Assembly of Saskatchewan, enacts as follows:

1 This Act may be cited as *The Constitutional Questions Act.* Short title

2 The Lieutenant Governor in Council may refer to the Court of Appeal for hearing and consideration any matter that he thinks fit, and the court shall thereupon hear and consider the matter. R.S.S. 1953, c. 78, s. 2. Reference to Court of Appeal

3 The court shall certify to the Lieutenant Governor in Council its opinion on the matter referred, with the reasons therefor, which shall be given in the same manner as in the case of a judgment in an ordinary action; and a judge who differs from the opinion of the majority may in the same manner certify his opinion and his reasons. R.S.S. 1953, c. 78, s. 3. Court to certify opinion

4 Where the matter relates to the constitutional validity of an Act that has heretofore been or is hereafter passed by the Legislature or of any Ordinance passed by the Legislative Assembly of the North-West Territories or of some provision in any such Act or Ordinance, the Attorney General of Canada shall be notified of the hearing in order that he may be heard if he sees fit. R.S.S. 1953, c. 78, s. 4. Notice to Attorney General of Canada

5 The court may direct that any person interested, or, where there is a class of persons interested, any one or more persons as representatives of that class, shall be notified of the hearing, and those persons shall be entitled to be heard. R.S.S. 1953, c. 78, s. 5. Notice to persons interested

6 Where any interest affected is not represented by counsel the court may request counsel to argue the case in that interest, and reasonable expenses thereof shall be paid out of the consolidated fund. R.S.S. 1953, c. 78, s. 6. Appointment of counsel for unrepresented interests

7 The opinion of the court shall be deemed a judgment of the court and an appeal shall lie therefrom as in the case of a judgment in an action. R.S.S. 1953, c. 78, s. 7. Appeal

● ●

*R.S.S., 1965, c. 86.

8 1   Where in a court in Saskatchewan the constitutional validity of an Act or enactment of the Parliament of Canada or of the Legis- lature or the validity of an order in council is brought in question, the Act, enactment or order in council shall not be adjudged to be invalid until after notice has been given to the Attorney General of Canada or the Attorney General of Saskatchewan, as the case may be.

[marginal note: Notice to Attorneys General of Canada and Saskatchewan before Act declared invalid]

2   The notice shall state what Act or part of an Act or what order in council or part thereof is in question, and the day on which the question is to be argued, and shall give such other particulars as are necessary to show the constitutional point proposed to be argued.

3   The notice shall be served six days before the day named for the argument.

4   The Attorney General of Canada and the Attorney General of Saskatchewan shall be entitled, as of right, to be heard, either in person or by counsel, notwithstanding that the Crown is not a party to the action or proceeding in which the question arises. R.S.S. 1953, c. 78, s. 8.

9 1   Where pursuant to an agreement with the Government of Canada entered into under *The Taxation Agreement Act, 1952, The Taxation Agreement Act*, chapter 58 of *The Revised Statutes of Saskatchewan, 1953, The Tax Rental Agreement Act, 1957*, or *The Income Tax Act*, chapter 62 of these Revised Statutes, or an agreement of a like nature and having like purposes, a matter is to be referred to the Court of Appeal, it shall be referred to the court and the form and terms of the reference shall be such as may be agreed upon by the parties to the agreement or if they cannot agree the form and terms shall be determined by the Chief Justice of Saskatchewan upon the application of either party.

[marginal note: Reference pursuant to taxation agreement]

2   The Attorney General of Canada and the Attorney General of any other province that after the first day of January, 1952, entered or hereafter enters into an agreement with the Government of Canada of a like nature and having like purposes to an agreement mentioned in subsection (1) may appear before the court and be heard as a party in respect of any matter referred under this Act pursuant to that agreement. R.S.S. 1953, c. 78, s. 9.

Table of Cases

Index

Supreme Court of Canada Rules
evidence, power to receive further, 179
hearing, participation in, 112n
leave to appear in appeal, 112n
notice to attorney general, 42–43

Tarnopolsky, W. S., 140n
Taschereau, C. J., 102, 103, 132
Taschereau, Henri, A., 22
taxation: *see* BNA Act, ss. 91(3), 92(2) and (9)
trade and plantations committee of Privy Council, 11, 13
Travaux préparatoires, 156
Treaty of Union with Scotland, 30

United States Constitution
Bill of Rights, generally, 137–38
generally, 5
Macdonald, J. A., refers to, 15–16
references to specific provisions
Article III, 35, 36, 93–94, 210
Article VI, 35
Amendment XIV, 116

Watson, Lord, 32, 121
Weekly Rest in Industrial Undertakings Act, 1935 (Can.), 197
Westminster, Statute of, 1931, 7, 26, 27
Wilson, J., 108
Wright, Lord, 166, 170

www.ingramcontent.com/pod-product-compliance
Lightning Source LLC
Chambersburg PA
CBHW020248030426
42336CB00010B/666